A HISTORY

OF THE

GRANDPARENTS

I NEVER HAD

A HISTORY

GRANDPARENTS

Translated by JANE KUNTZ

STANFORD STUDIES IN JEWISH HISTORY AND CULTURE
Edited by David Biale and Sarah Abrevaya Stein

OF THE

I NEVER HAD

IVAN JABLONKA

STANFORD UNIVERSITY PRESS
Stanford, California

Stanford University Press
Stanford, California

A History of the Grandparents I Never Had was originally published in French under the title
Histoire des grands-parents que je n'ai pas eus: Une enquête © Editions du Seuil, 2012.

Collection La Librairie du XXIe siècle, sous la direction de Maurice Olender.

This work, published as part of a program providing publication assistance, received financial support
from the French Ministry of Foreign Affairs, the Cultural Services of the French Embassy in the
United States and FACE (French American Cultural Exchange).

FRENCH
VOICES

Printed in the United States of America on acid-free, archival-quality paper.

Library of Congress Cataloging-in-Publication Data

Names: Jablonka, Ivan, 1973– author.
Title: A history of the grandparents I never had / Ivan Jablonka ; translated
  by Jane Kuntz.
Other titles: Histoire des grands-parents que je n'ai pas eus. English |
  Stanford studies in Jewish history and culture.
Description: Stanford, California : Stanford University Press, 2016. |
  Series: Stanford studies in Jewish history and culture | "Originally
  published in French under the title Histoire des grand-parents que je n'ai
  pas eus." | Includes bibliographical references.
Identifiers: LCCN 2015040900 | ISBN 978-0-8047-9544-9 (cloth : alk. paper)
Subjects: LCSH: Jablonka, Matès. | Jablonka, Idesa. | Jablonka, Ivan,
  1973—Family. | Jews, Polish—France—Biography. | Holocaust, Jewish
  (1939–1945)—France.
Classification: LCC DS135.F89 J3313 2016 | DDC 940.53/180922—dc23

LC record available at http://lccn.loc.gov/2015040900

ISBN 978-0-8047-9938-6 (electronic)

Designed by Bruce Lundquist
Typeset at Stanford University Press in 11/15 Adobe Garamond

The souls of fathers who, for so many ages, had suffered and
died in silence, descended into their sons, and spoke.
JULES MICHELET
History of the French Revolution [trans. Charles Cocks]

Writing is the memory of their death and the assertion of my life.
GEORGES PEREC
W, or the Memory of Childhood [trans. David Bellos]

CONTENTS

FOREWORD

David Biale and Sarah Abrevaya Stein

As the Holocaust fades further into history, it seems to loom larger and larger in memory. Seventy years after the end of the war, a second and third generation born after those traumatic events continues to wrestle with their meaning. Indeed, it is striking how that struggle becomes ever more intense just as the firsthand witnesses pass from the scene and their testimony can only be recovered second-hand or through dusty documents.

Within the growing literature of memory, that produced in France occupies a special place. There are many reasons for this. France was the primary destination of refuge for German, Austrian and Polish Jews, even before the war, more than doubling the French Jewish population from 150,000 to 340,000. During the Holocaust itself, the Vichy regime was one of the most eager to collaborate with the Nazis, passing anti-Jewish legislation as early as the fall of 1940 and before the Germans even demanded it. The police and the railroad authorities—to name but two French authorities—participated fully in the roundup and deportation of the Jews to their deaths. And, yet, the fact that over 75,000 Jews—and not more—were deported to the death camps, while some 264,000 survived, says much about the willingness of ordinary French men and women to hide and protect those whom their own government was hunting. And many of these were foreign Jews, whom Vichy targeted first.

The French record is therefore complex, even contradictory. And given the relatively high rate of survival, the French Jewish community, still today, has deep and extensive connections to that past as well as an increasing culture of commemoration. Indeed, no casual tourist in Paris—or elsewhere in France—can fail to notice the plaques on schools, memorializing the Jewish pupils brutally deported from the neighborhood, or on ordinary houses where others were sheltered and thereby saved.

The culture of Holocaust memory therefore owes a great deal to French creativity. One thinks of that iconic memoir, Elie Wiesel's *Night*; André Schwarz-Bart's pioneering novel, *The Last of the Just*; Jean-François Steiner's angry polemic, *Treblinka*; and Claude Lanzmann's masterpiece, *Shoah*. To this list, we can now add Ivan Jablonka's *A History of the Grandparents I Never Had*. We have here a project of recovery, not only by a grandson who never knew his grandparents (as the title tells us), but also by the historian's father, who was barely three years old when his mother and father were seized by the French police, interned in Drancy and shipped to Auschwitz in March 1943.

Unlike the other works just mentioned, however, Jablonka's book, written in luminescent prose, is the meticulous product of a historian who combines oral interviews with survivors and their descendants with archival and other printed evidence—all with the ambition of filling a historical void. In Jablonka's words: "To do history is to lend an ear to the pulse of silence, to attempt to replace an anguish so intense as to suffice unto itself, with the sweet, sorrowful respect the human condition inspires in us. This is my work." As he strains against silence, Jablonka refuses to indulge his imagination, even where he has gaps in his story. Near the end, he relaxes this firm historical rule when he tries to reconstruct his grandfather Matès's months in Auschwitz, since the evidence suggests the possibility that he may have been assigned to the Sonderkommando that worked in the crematoria. Because his death was not witnessed or recorded, Jablonka entertains several possibilities, but all within the realm of the plausible.

As a history of the Holocaust, *A History of the Grandparents I Never Had* has certain virtues that are missing from more synoptic accounts. This is the story of two people—not six million—and not only of their tragic fate but also of their dreams and struggles. It has the virtue of a micro-history in that we come to identify with these two passionate young people—Matès and Idesa—whom Jablonka has brought to life (one is tempted to say: "resurrected"). At the same time, through their particular stories, we also engage a panorama of twentieth-century Jewish history, for Jablonka refuses to let the Holocaust serve as the inevitable telos of his story: just as his two protagonists could not know their fate, so we must attend to their hopes and dreams before the iron cage closed.

Jablonka reconstructs in vivid detail the shtetl of Parczew, southeast of Warsaw, during the interwar period. It was highly symptomatic of the time that Shloyme Jablonka, the fervently orthodox keeper of the ritual bathhouse, should have had five children all of whom embraced Communism. The winds of secularism and revolution thus blew through this small Jewish community, carrying along many of its children with them. Why they should have abandoned tradition so decisively and taken up the red flag remains hard to fathom, but the break was dramatic and irreversible. Both Matès and Idesa were prepared to undergo imprisonment at the hands of the Polish government for their beliefs, as fervently held as was the religiosity of their forebears.

Like tens of thousands of other Polish Jews, oppressed by rising anti-semitism, political persecution and economic misery, Matès and Idesa flee for France. But the land of "liberty, equality, fraternity" is not as welcoming as it had been in the past to refugees and migrants. We are struck by the desperation of foreign Jews in the late 1930s, many of them—especially the Germans and Poles—divested of their citizenship but rejected by France. How eerily familiar it sounds today, as similarly desperate Africans and Middle Easterners attempt to crash the borders of Europe. To be stateless in the 1930s, as Hannah Arendt, herself a stateless Jew in France, reminds us, prefigured what has become so much of the human condition. If for no other reason, this part of the book should be required reading for those seeking to gain some perspective on the crisis of migration today.

Another little known story is the role of foreign Jews in the French army after the beginning of the Second World War. Despite the cruelties of the French state, which had rejected them and tried, with varying degrees of success, to deport them, many rushed to enlist, motivated in part by hopes of regularizing their status and in part by the fervent desire to defeat fascism. Absent any direct account by Matès of his experiences in the war, especially after the German invasion of May 1940, Jablonka skillfully reconstructs what Matès must have gone through by use of both military histories and memoiristic accounts by others.

The final chapters of the book concern the German occupation and the looming threat of a much more ominous deportation. Here, too, lacking any direct account by Matès or Idesa, except for a few fragments, Jablonka painstakingly traces those who lived in the same hiding place in Paris and solicits information from them and their relatives. Stunningly, the small passageway where his grandparents hid with their children is but a few steps from where Ivan Jablonka's own children attended preschool, a sign of how intimate are these sites of memory.

The war years are a tale of darkness and light: the darkness of Auschwitz and the light of rescue. The sheer goodness manifested by so many people in saving Suzanne and Marcel, Jablonka's aunt and father, cannot compensate for the loss, but it somehow comes close to evening the ledger: the Polish Christian who told the gendarmes who had come to take Matès and Idesa that the children were his; Annette and Constant—she Idesa's cousin and he a French non-Jewish anarchist—who served as the children's guardians; and the elderly couple named Courtoux, who sheltered the children for a year and a half in the Brittany countryside. And these in addition to underground organizations like the Rue Amelot Committee, all of whose members risked their lives so that others, especially children, might live.

Ivan Jablonka tells this story in passionate yet reserved style, appropriate to the historian, even when writing about his own family. He interjects himself sparingly into the tale, but to good effect, so that we can appreciate the challenge of reconstructing two lives seemingly swept away by history. In meeting that challenge, he has not only given new life to the dead of his family but also made them our family.

PREFACE

I have set out, as a historian, in search of the grandparents I never had. Because their lives were over long before mine began, Matès and Idesa Jablonka are at once close relatives and perfect strangers. They were faceless victims of the great twentieth-century tragedies: Stalinism, World War II, and the annihilation of European Jewry.

I have no grandparents on my father's side, and that's how it has always been. There are Constant and Annette, of course, my father's guardians, but it's not the same thing. There are also my maternal grandparents, who managed to survive the war with yellow stars pinned to their chests. In June 1981, when I was going on 8 years old, I wrote a letter to say how much I loved them. My writing was awkward and unpolished, full of spelling mistakes and dotted with little hearts at the end of each sentence. At the bottom of the stationery was a baby elephant wearing a black beret, skipping through a jungle of giant flowers. Here is what I wrote:

> You can be sure that when you are dead, I'll be thinking of you sadly for the rest of my life. Even when life is over for me too, my own children will know about you. And even their children will know about you when I am in my grave. For me, you'll be my gods, my beloved gods who will watch over me and nobody else. I will be thinking: my gods are my shield, whether I am in heaven or hell.

What was I told—or not told—that would have inspired me to pen such a testament at the age of seven and a half? Was it my historian's calling or a child's resigned response to the crushing duty of remembrance, as one link in the chain of departed souls, to keep our heritage alive? For I can now see more clearly that these childish promises were addressed not so much to my maternal grandparents as to the ones who had been forever absent. My father's parents were dead, had always been dead. They were my guardian gods, they would bless and keep me, even after I had joined them in that other place. It can be reassuring to anchor oneself in primal scenes and foundational traumas, but in my case, there was never any moment of revelation: no one ever sat me down to tell me the "terrible truth." Their murder had always been familiar: there are family truths just like there are family secrets.

The little boy grew up, and did not grow up. I am 38 today, married with children of my own. I am the temporal projection of these souls long gone, but I wonder whether I have the strength to carry them forward. Could I not nourish their lives with mine, rather than endlessly dying their death? But what did Matès and Idesa Jablonka leave behind, except their two orphaned children, a handful of letters and a passport? It would be sheer madness to attempt to recover the lives of two strangers, with so little to go on! Even still alive, they were already invisible; history pounded them into dust.

These ashes of an era are not enclosed in some family mausoleum; they are suspended in the air, wafting on the breeze, moistened by sea mists, powdering our rooftops, stinging our eyes and assuming the guise of a flower petal, a comet or a dragonfly, anything light and fleeting. These anonymous souls belong not to me but to us all. Before they are erased forever, I felt it urgent to recover their traces, the footprints they left on life, the involuntary evidence of their time on earth.

Hence my research began, conceived at once as a family biography, an act of justice and an extension of my work as a historian. It is a birthing, the opposite of a murder investigation, and it led me quite naturally to their birthplace.

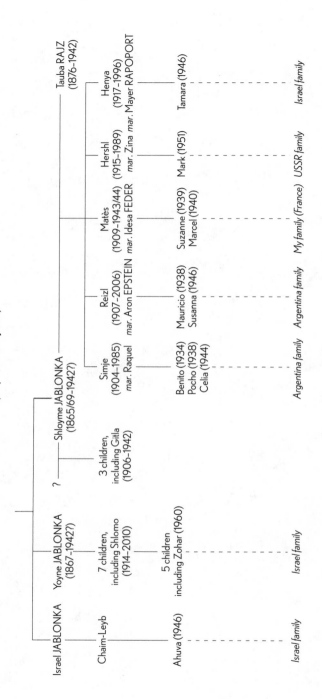

JABLONKA FAMILY
(simplified family tree)

FIGURE 1. Jablonka Family (simplified family tree, ©PAO Seuil)

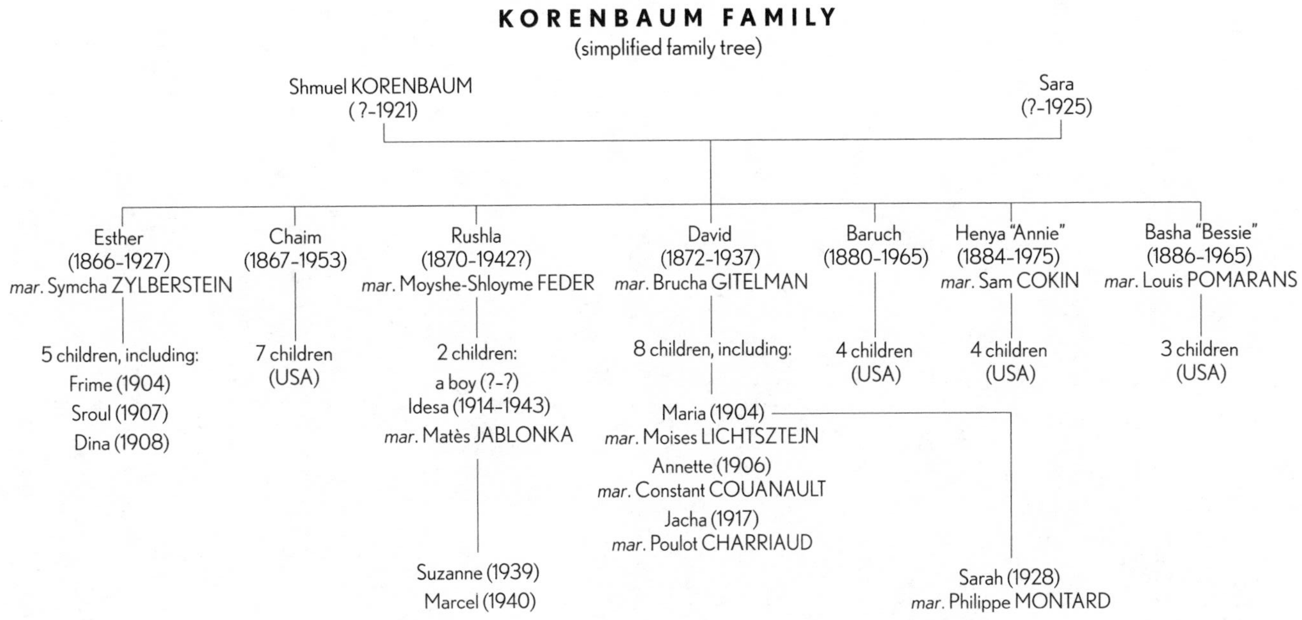

KORENBAUM FAMILY
(simplified family tree)

FIGURE 2. Korenbaum Family (simplified family tree, © PAO Seuil)

1

JOHN

LITTLE-APPLE-TREE

IN HIS VILLAGE

People sometimes ask about the origin of my name, their name. The question is somewhat disingenuous, for the name could hardly sound more Polish, where it means "little apple tree." Ivan Jablonka, John Little-Apple-Tree, or just plain *Jean Pommier*, in French, the commonest of names. I am less sensitive to the comic overtones of the name, once translated, than to its protective mundaneness. There is another name, however, that fills me with pride, a legendary name this time, one that defies translation: Parczew, the Jewish town where they were born 100 years ago. When pronounced *parshef* in Polish, this name has a singular effect on me. It sounds more exotic than our family name, our little apple tree, a trivial shrub growing in the backyard. Parczew, with its end-of-the-alphabet consonants, its bighearted sounds, its final *w* that rises like smoke from a campfire, with hints of clay—that's where we come from. My father was born in Paris during the war, and I have never lived anywhere else, but we seem to be linked affectively, viscerally, to this little Polish backwater that takes forever to find on a map, somewhere between Lublin and Brest-Litovsk, out near the borders with Belarus and Ukraine.

On his trip to Parczew in 2003, my father had his picture taken in front of a sign at the entrance to the town, off to the right at the edge of a field. His hand rests on the sign, while he smiles into the camera, looking a bit ill at ease. How I want to go there too, rest my hand on that sign and smile. For me, Parczew gives off a fragrance, a musicality, but also suggests a color: green. It is an almost fluorescent, yellowish green, like the dazzling color of a prairie by Chagall, a native of Vitebsk, in Belarus. Parczew makes my lips pucker, like a tart apple, but also suggests a more intense shade of green, grassier, a fiddler balancing on a roof, a pair of oxen pulling a cart, or a goat flying off on a garnet cloud.

Jews in the West today are making an increasing number of pilgrimages to the shtetls of their forebears.[1] They return home with photos, impressions and emotions to share. On my parents' trip to Parczew, they attempted to revive memories, as my father would approach passersby in a mixture of Russian and Polish: "Hello, my name is Marcel Jablonka, my parents were born here." This got him nowhere. They even hired a guide, an elderly lady who walked them through the town, conferring with friends and acquaintances, knocking on doors in search of answers, but to no avail. Disheartened, they returned to France. My father would have to live his life knowing almost nothing about his own parents, apart from a few random fragments provided by Annette, his guardian, a cousin of his mother's, and by Reizl, his Argentinian aunt, the one we call *Tía*, "aunt" in Spanish. This ignorance was a source of great anguish, for as a boy, he had felt no need to ask his parents' cousins, friends and former neighbors to tell him what they remembered. And whenever anyone did try to do so, he would say he wasn't interested. He had no parents, that's all. Further discussion would only make his suffering worse. Now, he wishes he knew more, regrets his youthful refusal to find out. "I was an idiot," he says, furious with himself. But what can he do now? Everyone is dead and gone.

I go to see Colette, a family friend whose parents came from Parczew. She made the trip in the summer of 1978, shortly before the election of Pope John Paul II. It turns out that my parents' visit was a stroll in the park compared to hers, which proved dismal and disturbing. It was pouring rain. After making their way along the muddy lanes, Colette and her mother arrived at the home of an ancient couple whose address they had been given. One low-ceilinged room, two tiny beds with crocheted coverlets, embroidery on the wall and a gargantuan meal on the table. Not only did the hosts distinctly remember Colette's grandfather, a tripe butcher by trade, but they had nothing but fine memories of him! At four in the afternoon, it was almost dark. Intent upon finding her old house, Colette's mother set out, but what with the destruction caused by war, the waning light, the drenching rain and her forty-year absence, the search came to nothing. At one point, she thought she recognized her in-laws' house, and the brick building that looked like the Polish school she attended as a girl. In the end, overcome with emotion, she began to wander aimlessly through the boggy streets, holding back her tears, soaked to the skin, speaking Polish to her daughter and French to the locals, utterly confused. On the verge of collapse, they made their way back to the car, which was parked in a water-logged square. Suddenly, a drunk emerged out of nowhere and started banging on the hood of the car: he needed a match to light his cigarette.

Now, it's my turn. In Warsaw, I meet up with Audrey, who is working on a dissertation on anti-Jewish violence since the war and who has agreed to serve as my interpreter and guide. We drive for two hours along a highway clogged with truck traffic. After Lublin, the road takes us through forests as it cuts through the countryside. Soon, warehouses, machine shops, garages and a smattering of homes signal an industrial zone. Then, houses turn into neighborhoods and suddenly, we've arrived. Parczew, my shtetl. But Parczew bears little resemblance either to Chagall's images or to the muddy mess Colette and her mother encountered 30 years earlier. The newly blacktopped road is full of nice Fiats and Volkswagens, and the freshly painted homes give the town an Austrian flavor, so that one hardly notices here and there the collapsing hovels amidst thickets of weeds.

Audrey pulls in next to a public park, where we meet up with Bernadetta, a French teacher in Włodawa, with whom I have exchanged a few emails. In the car, she briefs us on what she has scheduled: first a visit to where the old Jewish cemetery once stood, then on to what was formerly the synagogue and finally a get-together with Marek Golecki, the son of Parczew's sole "Righteous," that is, a Gentile who risked his life to save Jews during the war. She then passes on some copies of general information on the town's history, some newspaper clippings and an ethnographic narrative intended for the younger generations, in which an elderly Polish woman recalls the Jews of Parczew.

We are now looking out onto the Jewish cemetery: it has become the public park. Planted with beeches and birches that shade the grassy areas, it is crisscrossed with paths where we see couples, joggers and mothers pushing strollers. I wander along in the spring sunshine, taking it all in, with my heart dancing. I have accomplished what I set out to do: I am treading lightly on the land of my ancestors. In one corner of the park, standing in front of two tombstones, Audrey and Bernadetta chat as they wait for me to finish my walk. The first stone—tilted slightly, made of pale grey marble—bears an inscription by the mayor of Parczew in honor of the "Polish soldiers taken prisoner during the war," killed by the Germans in 1940. The second stone—horizontal, made of dark grey marble, with a Star of David—bears a bilingual epitaph in Hebrew and Polish written by a Belgian Jew: "Here are buried 280 Jewish soldiers of the Polish army, shot and killed in February 1940 by Hitler's assassins. Among the victims lies my father, Abraham Salomonowicz, born in 1898." Faded dahlias grace the tombstone.

We get back in the car and head to the synagogue, built in the late nineteenth century to replace the old wooden synagogue which has since been destroyed. On the freshly painted golden-yellow building, one story high with windows in the shape of stone tablets, there is a sign that reads "Second-hand clothing imported from England," and a smaller sign next to it announcing a 50%-off sale. Bernadetta, walking ahead of me, says in her delightfully old-fashioned French: "Please don't take offense."

She's right, of course. Even though the rare documents I have gathered regarding my grandparents all mention "Parczew" (whether spelled Parezew, or Parczen or Poutchef), I know full well that I have no claim to this place; I am nothing more than a tourist. We climb some stairs and end up in a vast space where the mostly female clientele is sorting through hundreds of dresses, skirts, pants, shirts, T-shirts and coats that hang from rows of rails that fill the room. The walls are depressingly grey, and fluorescent lights dangle from the ceiling, giving an overall impression of shabbiness. Still, the cracked linoleum is waxed and gleaming; it is a kind of polished indigence. As soon as my camera flash goes off, men behind the cash register turn and glare at me: I'm not sure if I look like a Jew, a Westerner or both, but I'm not from around here, that's for certain. Some of their items, hanging from some piping, are visible in the picture I secretly snap as we scurry back down the stairs: a mauve dress with rhinestones around the collar, a wedding dress, a beige negligée studded with flowers, a nightgown in an orange and blue pattern.

We continue our visit of Parczew. Next to the synagogue, and in the same golden yellow, is the former Jewish study house, now proudly displaying a sign reading *Dom Weselny*, which means "reception hall." Built in the early 1920s to replace the first study house, now a distillery, it was turned into a movie theater after the war, before becoming today's reception hall.[2] I vaguely recall a photo in which my father stands somewhat stiffly on the steps outside a movie house, its decrepit yellowish exterior covered in graffiti. It must have been cleaned up and repainted before becoming the locale it is today, an all-purpose hall for weddings, banquets and other festivities.

Our tour finally takes us to see Marek Golecki. With close-cropped white hair, a moustache and the paunch of a fifty-year-old, Marek lives on Kościelna, or Church Street, in a three-story cement brick house that he built himself. He is the last "Jew" of Parczew. Not a real Jew, of course, since the 5,000 or so Jews who were living in and around the town were murdered during the war, and the few survivors—who had emerged from the surrounding forests where they had found refuge from the harsh winters and famines, the German search operations and the partisan racketeering—ended up leaving the town after the pogrom of 5 February 1946. But because of his father, who had been declared "Righteous among the Nations" for his role in saving Jews, Marek is not exactly popular in the town. He serves us refreshments and tells us about how, in the 1970s, his barn was destroyed in what looked like an arson attack. When he went to the town council to demand some form of compensation, the mayor told him to go ask his "Jewish friends" for help.[3] I fear that my gift of a bottle of port that I brought from France will cause him further harm—I'm another "Jewish friend"—but Marek doesn't care what people say, and in any case, he is not being treated as a pariah, as we are able to observe during our walk with him around the town, where he stops to talk auto repair and garden hoses with his neighbors.

The next day, we go to the town hall. Audrey explains the purpose of our visit to the office head who, looking a bit puzzled, goes out and returns a few minutes later with three thick volumes: the rabbinical records. Amidst this thicket of pen strokes, I get ready to discover the name of my grandmother, Idesa, but the office manager replies that there is no entry, because the year of her birth, 1914, was a somewhat troubled time. Her marriage certificate, on the other hand, two decades later, is definitely there in the records, which refer to "Idesa Korenbaum . . . daughter of Rushla Korenbaum, unmarried."[4] Family names have a way of revealing certain truths: my grandmother was an illegitimate child. Once back in France, I'll have the opportunity to verify, through my father's birth certificate, that Idesa's exact name was Korenbaum-*vel*-Feder, the Polish word *vel* in this context meaning "also known as." She was indeed illegitimate, but not abandoned, since she also bore the name of her father, Mr. Feder. As a child, Idesa lived with her mother, Rushla Korenbaum, a brother I know nothing about, and perhaps their father. In Yiddish, Feder means "feather," and Korenbaum, "bark tree" (as opposed to tree bark), which makes no sense. Family names have a poetry of their own.

What were things like on my grandfather's side, in Matès Jablonka's family? Here, the office manager pulls out some ordinary-looking birth certificates, but I feel I'm being entrusted with secret information, never before revealed, possibly scandalous. The Jablonka siblings include, in descending order, Simje (born in 1904), Reizl (1907), Matès (1909), Hershl (1915) and Henya (1917), three boys and two girls, all born under the Czarist empire.[5] Nothing there that I don't already know, apart from a tragedy that my father was unaware of: in 1913, a younger brother, Shmuel, died at the age of two.

Their parents—my great-grandparents—were named Shloyme and Tauba. Not only were they not married, but their children were acknowledged only belatedly. Hershl, born in 1915, was not declared at the records office until the late 1920s, supposedly "because a world war was breaking out." Likewise, Henya's birth certificate was not drawn up until 1935, a delay of eighteen years ascribed, this time, to "family reasons." One senses here a rather negligent patriarch getting his complicated house in order late in life by officially recording the last of his children. On my grandparents' marriage certificate, Tauba, over sixty years of age by then, is finally recorded by her married name, Jablonka. And all is right with the world! But since the children of Shloyme Jablonka and Tauba bore their father's name from birth, it goes without saying that their line of descent was a matter of public knowledge, as was the case for my grandmother.

So, there were five Jablonka siblings, not counting the baby who died at age two. Simje and Reizl, the two eldest, future émigrés to Argentina; Matès, my grandfather, the brother admired by all; and then the last two, Hershl and Henya, future émigrés to the Soviet Union. But this spread of births, from 1904 to 1917, actually starts even earlier: by cross-checking documents available online at the Yad Vashem site, I discover that old Shloyme had two sons and a daughter from a previous wife, all of whom were murdered with their families in 1942. The information was provided by Hershl and Henya themselves, though they were a bit unsure of the dates and of the spelling of their half-sister's and half-brothers' first names. From Buenos Aires, Simje's son confirms the existence of these earlier children, and adds that the half-sister, Gitla, had been disabled ever since she fell off a table as a baby.

The complexity of piecing together these unstable families of varying legitimacy calls to mind a dialogue between some poor wretch and the writer I. L. Peretz in the late nineteenth century, while the latter was collecting data about the Russian Jewish population at the request of a philanthropist. Here is Peretz carrying out his survey:

"'How many children?'

At this point, the man had to think. He then began counting on his fingers. With his first wife, the ones that were his: one, two, three; hers, one, two; with his second wife . . . But all this counting has started to annoy him!

'Nu, let's just say six.'

'I'm afraid "just say" isn't good enough. I need to know more precisely than that. . . .'

So he begins counting on his fingers again, to arrive at a grand total this time—God be praised—that amounts to three more than his last count a moment earlier.

'Nine children. May God bless them all with a solid constitution and long-lasting health.'"[6]

Nine is also the total number of children arrived at by the venerable Shloyme Jablonka, a good father, if not an especially good husband. The *Yizkor Bukh* of Parczew, the "book of remembrance" published by the survivors of World War II, a volume of local history in Hebrew and Yiddish meant to bring the lost shtetl back to life,[7] devotes exactly one line to the man: Shloyme was in charge of the Parczew baths. It goes without saying that such a modest occupation would have earned him barely enough to meet his family's needs. At the Jablonkas', no one ever went hungry, but the house was small and sparsely furnished. In bad weather, everyone tried to stay indoors, for the rain and snow brought in on everyone's shoes would have turned the earthen floor into a muddy mess in no time. But since they had to go out for bread, to use the outhouse, to get water and wood and to attend religious services, the only clean place in the whole house at the end of the day was underneath the dining table, which is where the children would play. When Tauba was ill, their half-sister Gitla would come to help out, so that the children all loved her like a mother and relations between the two women grew tense. One or the other would bring dinner to the Friday evening table, after the head of the household had poured the wine and recited prayers, while the children looked on in wonderment.

Matès, my grandfather, was five years old at the outbreak of World War I. After the first setbacks suffered by the Russians, the Germans invaded Parczew in 1915, and photos of the period—some are available in a database at sztetl.org—show a parade of tarpaulin-covered carts and soldiers on horseback or on foot, with guns slung over their backs and spiked helmets and backpacks, crossing through the town; the elder locals look on with worried expressions while the street urchins laugh. Compared to the war that was to follow, this occupation was almost kindly, though it did give rise to some troublesome incidents. The *Yizkor Bukh* refers to looted shops, famine, a cholera epidemic, work camps and inflation. "Russian currency was used to make paper; 500-ruble notes could be found lying in the street. Children played at collecting small change. Each child would have a cloth sack full of coins as they scoured the streets for more."[8]

But there was also such hope! For the German invaders promised equality for the Jews, spoke of cultural autonomy and even authorized a few initiatives (a library opened in Parczew during that time), while the Russians, who suspected Jews of spying for the Germans, were deporting them to camps on the Dnieper.[9] Children learned to live with war. "Young people were starting to be affected by the same war hysteria as adults," explains the *Yizkor Bukh*. "Two sides formed. On every Shabbat, the children would stage pitched battles. One side was led by the brother of Rabbi Mordechai Saperstein . . . ; Israel Straiger Rosenberg (who lives in the United States now) led the other. The girls also took part in the fighting as 'nurses.' Using stones as weaponry, with the river as their dividing line, both sides produced casualties."[10] But when they weren't playing these war games, the children would swim in the Piwonia in the summer, and skate on it in winter. On Sunday mornings, they would go down to wash their pitchers and utensils. And life would continue, with costumes on Purim, archery and banners on *Lag Ba-Omer*, to commemorate the Jews' revolt against the Romans, and so on.

The Germans occupied Parczew until 1918, when Bolshevik Russia called for peace and relinquished its Polish territories. One hundred and twenty-three years after being carved up by Russia, Austria and Prussia, and a half-century after the crushing of its national insurrection, Poland was reborn as a state. Pilsudski, the socialist leader and war hero, became head of the fledgling republic. Born Russian, my grandparents became Polish, and that is how I present them today.

Matès attended the *kheyder*, the religious school. I have no definitive evidence for this, but I don't see how it could have been otherwise. It was certainly the case for his older brother Simje and his younger brother Hershl. (Hershl's son tells how the teacher, the *melamed*, would rap the naughty students' knuckles with an iron ruler and that, as a further punishment, they would have to stand holding a bar against their backs.) Colette's father also attended. According to the *Yizkor Bukh*, boys went to the *kheyder* as early as three years old. The *melamed*'s assistant would arrive at the parents' home and leave with the young schoolboy perched on his shoulders. At first, the boy would cry his eyes out, but the mothers were relieved to have one fewer child underfoot.[11]

Six or seven *melamdim* are singled out for honors in the *Yizkor Bukh*: Eije, with his white beard, whose teachings were reserved for only the most talented; Brawerman, who was called the Slavutycher, for his home village of Slavutych, and his wife who taught girls other things besides prayers; and the Bauman sisters, who specialized in foreign languages, but who could also teach knitting and embroidery. There was also Velvel the Lame, a legendary jokester, whose calligraphy was superb and whose voice was so pure that whenever he sang with his daughters at home, passersby would stop at the window to listen. Sosha Zuckermann, whose pupils affectionately called her Aunt Sosha, would often grab them by their braids to make them sit and read through their prayers. Since she asked for no fee, her lessons were open to even the indigent, and thanks to her, a third of the young girls of Parczew knew how to read. Who knows whether one of these teachers might have taught little Matès to read the Bible, recite the weekly Torah portion, comment on texts or interpret the world with the help of famous episodes like Adam and Eve, Cain and Abel, Sodom and Gomorrah, King David, the Tower of Babel, the revolt of the Maccabees, the Ten Commandments? In all likelihood, Matès celebrated his bar mitzvah when he was thirteen, which would have been 1922. And with so many instructors in the town, why would my grandmother Idesa not also have been introduced to the holy texts, in addition to knitting? Official documents say she was a seamstress.

In 1920, when Idesa was just turning six, an elementary school system based on the French model was adopted, and a "Polish" public school was inaugurated in Parczew. Reizl, Matès's older sister, attended this school until she was fourteen. According to her children, who reminisce with me about her on their sun-drenched patio in Buenos Aires, this was where she acquired her taste for schooling and study, but she also had to put up with insults and anti-Semitic taunts (numerous documents attest to strong anti-Semitism in Parczew during the interwar period: provocation from the *Endeks*,[12] attempts at forced conversion, an anti-Jewish riot in 1932, etc.). Colette's mother, born in 1914 like my grandmother, took Yiddish lessons at home but also attended the Polish school, the very school she will think she recognizes, decades later, in the pouring rain, as she experiences a moment of panic when she plunges back into anti-Semitic, alcoholic Poland. In the early 1920s, she learned German as a foreign language. I am struck by this detail: fifteen years later, during a police interrogation, Idesa would declare that she spoke Yiddish as her native language, as well as Polish, the official language, but also German.

In the shtetls, Jews spoke Yiddish. At school, the young girls were either introduced to Polish or else built on the rudiments of the language that they had picked up in the street with their *goy* playmates. In the ethnographic account of the Jews of Parczew that Bernadetta gave me, the author, an old Polish woman, writes: "Most of them never learned to speak Polish correctly. Jewish children went to Polish schools, but I knew from a teacher there that, in their preparatory classes, they had to start from scratch." And she hastens to add, as if to show that they weren't trying to force Jewish children to assimilate: "Even at school, there were teachers of Jewish religion. Polish teachers used to accompany the children to synagogue."[13] So, which was it: anti-Semitism or tolerance? Polonization or respect for Jewish difference? One didn't exclude the other. In the aftermath of World War I, and under pressure from the West, Poland ratified the Minority Treaty, which granted Jews religious minority status, a further argument for stigmatizing the Jewish girls at school or in the street. And what about the boys? Neither Matès nor his brothers were allowed to attend Polish public school, because according to old Shloyme, it was out of the question for a boy to study without wearing a *kippah*.

At my request, Bernard, my Yiddish translator, deduces my grandparents' level of education based on three extant letters written in their hand. After all, archaeologists are able to reconstruct an entire world out of a few fragments of a column. Idesa's Yiddish is colorful and colloquial, more German-inflected than that of Matès. She writes by ear, the way words sound to her. In a letter to Simje and Reizl, who had moved to Buenos Aires in the 1930s, to say hello to her brother-in-law and sister-in-law, she uses the dialect form *a griss* instead of *a gruss*. She also spells out her Hebrew phonetically, like Yiddish, and this failure to distinguish between the two proves her low literacy, a bit like someone with only oral

English spelling "daughter" as "dauder." She even closes her letters with "*dein Idès*," even though her name in Hebrew, Judith or Yehudith, should be transcribed as *Yidess*. Matès, on the other hand, has better Yiddish, untainted by outside influences, but sometimes his fine penmanship can't seem to keep up with his thought process, and he often skips auxiliary verbs. He must have read quite a lot of books and newspapers, unlike his fellow yeshiva students who spent all their time in Bible study and could barely string together a sentence in Yiddish. One vagueness in his spelling involves whether to write *e* or *i*, a sign that he probably never edited or published anything, for then such mistakes would have been rectified and eliminated. Thus, sometimes he writes *Yidess*, and at other times *Yidiss*. At the bottom of official documents, he signs awkwardly "Matès Jablonka," or "Matys Jablonka," or rather "Jabłonka" with the barred *l*, which in Polish is pronounced "Yabwonka." However, although Matès wrote better Yiddish than Idesa, I assume she spoke better Polish than he did, since she attended the local Polish school.

The Jablonkas lived at 33 Szeroka Street, or "Broad" Street. As happens among siblings everywhere, there were fights, alliances and apocryphal anecdotes. Reizl, it is said, was protective of Hershl because he was little, and Matès would defend him against Simje's outbursts. But the story is just as often told the other way around. One day, when Mama Tauba made an apple pie and found that she didn't have enough fruit, she placed what she had in the center and put it in the oven to bake. As soon as it was out, Hershl grabbed the dish, removed all the fruit with a knife and devoured it all himself. Once the crime was discovered, the little glutton got the beating of his life from Matès. As adolescents, Hershl and Henya were very close. The two youngsters loved to walk in the nearby woods and to swim in the Piwonia. (By then, Simje and Reizl were already adults and would soon be leaving for Buenos Aires.) A photo shows the three youngest side by side, a year or two before their incarceration. On the right, Hershl, looking a bit dazed and glassy-eyed, is wearing a cap a couple of sizes too big. Matès is on the left, the mentor of the threesome. His cap is pulled down firmly over his forehead, his chest thrust out proudly, and a massive black coat shows off his athletic build (in fact, he is only five foot four). He seems to take up half the photo. His gaze is distant, hard-edged; it grabs your attention and holds it, but his raised eyebrows give him a look of surprise ("It's unbelievable how much your father looks like him!" exclaimed my wife when she first saw this photo). Wedged between the two brothers, Henya, cute as a button in her little beret, is gazing off wistfully into the distance. She looks about twelve or thirteen; the picture must have been taken in the late 1920s.

The years passed, and Henya was growing up. She would complain, her daughter tells me during our visit to the ruins of Caesarea in Israel, that her older sister Reizl got all the new clothes, and that all she got were hand-me-downs. Henya wanted her own coat, one that no one had worn before her. The issue was raised at a family gathering, and the request was granted. They went to the tailor's, negotiated a price, picked out fabric, had measurements taken. Right around that time, Reizl announced that she was leaving to join Simje in Argentina. So, guess who got the new coat, in the end? This episode gives the impression of Reizl as domineering, overbearing. Yet, here is what she confesses to her own daughter on her deathbed, in a *geriatrico* somewhere in the suburbs of Buenos Aires. There was a boy in Parczew that she was head-over-heels in love with. Old Shloyme consented to his daughter's wish to marry, and went to seek out the boy's father. They discussed and came to an agreement. But scarcely had the boy obtained the dowry than he bolted and was never heard from again. Reizl moved to the next village over to hide her chagrin and shame. According to her daughter, her decision to leave for Argentina, in 1936, had everything to do with this incident. "I have never loved any man so much," sighed *Tía* Reizl before breathing her last.

On our walk with Marek, he points things out: here is Nowa Street (New Street, formerly Jews Street) and the walls of the ghetto during the war; over there, the place where the butcher shop used to be, the leather-workers union hall, the saddlers' shops. Marek is too young to have seen any of these in their heyday. All I can see, as he points this way and that, are facades, wrought-iron balconies, vegetable gardens behind hedges and half-abandoned flowerbeds. Next, Marek leads us from Church Street to turn right on Embankment Street, then onto New Street. From there, we go up November 11 Street a ways, and then take a tour of the Grand Square, the *Rynek*, which then opens onto Frog Street, then Broad Street, right near the river—a circuit I am conscientiously following on the little map I have downloaded from the internet. This is what one might call central Parczew, the core of the shtetl, 100% Jewish before the war. But there weren't only Jews in the shtetl: in 1787, there were 680 Jews, in 1865, 2,400, in 1921 around 4,000 and by 1939, 5,100, or what amounts to about half the population in each era.[14] According to the commercial records for 1929, businesses were flourishing: fifty-five grocery stores, thirty-nine cobblers, sixteen notions shops, two sweets shops, not to mention countless bakers, butchers, hosieries and sales outlets for tea, tobacco and alcohol, almost all run by Jews. For instance, the Wajsman family owned and ran the four beauty parlors in town.[15] Broad Street, which I have just entered, is bent and angled, about 100 yards long, with little detached dwellings on one side and on the other, an auto shop, a warehouse and a hardware store. On the doorframes, not a single little hole or slanted notch that might conjure the memory of a *mezuzah*. All of a sudden, it occurs to Marek that we should meet an elderly lady who knew the Jews back then and maybe even, with a little luck, my grandparents. She lives on the other side of town, in a grim apartment building. We climb the four floors up, my heart pounding in anticipation. A neighbor opens the door: so sorry, the lady has just been taken to the hospital.

So, Parczew is one of those provincial towns, one of thousands throughout the world, with its little main street and mini-mart, its shops full of hideous gift items and last year's fashions, its government buildings, dish antennae, its local gossips, its schoolchildren coming home from class, lugging their backpacks, its signs on the outskirts indicating the next town over, 10 or 20 miles away, identical in every way to this one. This is the land where my little apple tree took root. But 33 Broad Street is less than inspiring.

There is one street in particular that the *Yizkor Bukh* mentions often: Żabia Street (Frog Street, since the river is nearby). This is how it looked in the 1920s: although extremely narrow, it was bursting with life. The community's most important buildings were found there: the old wooden synagogue where people would crowd for morning prayer, the Hassidic Ger Oratory, bastion of ultra-orthodox believers, the yeshiva for Russian students funded by a charity, the offices of various Zionist organizations and of the *Profesioneler Fareyn*, or Professional Union, whose workers would disturb the prayers of the devout with their sewing machines, their brawls, their love songs and worker slogans. Rich and poor lived side by side, with crumbling, dimly lit hovels, their tiny windows barely above street level, sitting next to the homes of the well-to-do, and adjacent to shops one would enter down a steep little stairway to be waited on by a wigged yenta. Unlike the other streets of Parczew, Frog Street was paved with asphalt, except in front of holy places, where one came and went on wooden sidewalks.

On Tuesdays, market day, crowds would pour into the street, thronging the stalls, taverns, synagogue and oratories, and gather around carts full of foods of all sorts. Polish peasants in from the surrounding countryside would mingle with the old Jews in their caftans, with the Hassidim in their collarless shirts, with loiterers looking for deals, with craftsmen and porters, everybody ferreting about, haggling and purchasing—eggs, chickens, meat, fish, grains, wood, linen, fabrics and furs, jewelry, leather goods, baskets and glass—after which one would go have a shoe resoled or knock back a glass of vodka along with some herring and pickles. Competition was fierce among merchants, who would scream and shout in a colorful Yiddish. Should Tuesday fall on a Jewish holiday, there would be no market, for the peasants all knew that no one would be open for business.[16]

Marek, Audrey and I make a tour of the *Rynek*, a quiet square where the elderly come to sit on benches beneath the cool, shady chestnut trees. On the other side of the street are lines of shops—a toy store, a hairdresser—painted in pastel colors, pink and sky blue, mauve and beige, burnt sienna. On 23 July 1942, the Parczew ghetto was pillaged, and 4,000 people were rounded up into this square and deported to Treblinka.[17] In her ethnographic text intended for future generations, the elderly Polish woman describes the scene:

> The square was full of people sitting on the ground. Anyone who stood up was shot. Around noon, the death march began. With their guns and dogs, the Germans escorted this column of old people, mothers with children, the ailing and feeble. Still today, I can see my school friend holding her mother's hand, bleeding from her leg where she had been shot. Next to her, a dead child. A young Jewish woman, in shock at the sight, tried to run off into a field, and was shot dead. They were all taken to the train station and loaded into boxcars.[18]

After a second *Aktion* in October 1942, 2,500 people (Parczew natives or refugees from the surrounding region) were deported to Treblinka. A few hundred people managed to escape into the woods nearby, with the last of the Jews being sent to a work camp in Miendzyrzec Podlaski, 30 miles to the north.[19]

These old Poles sitting on their benches in the *Rynek*, in the shade of the chestnut trees, staring into space with their toothless grins, were perhaps present at these scenes, or may have participated in the 1946 pogrom when they were in high school.[20] But they are now only shadows of their former selves, and in that sense, they are somehow my ancestors' counterparts, fleeting silhouettes wandering through the halls of time, ethereal thread-like figures that glimmer in the mists, like those uncles, the *barbe* and other legendary figures from the Jewish Piedmont region that Primo Levi honors in the first chapter of his *Periodic Table*.

I know nothing about Moyshe Feder, my grandmother's father, except that he gave his name to his illegitimate daughter (Idesa Korenbaum, "also known as" Feder) and that he had two other daughters by his legal wife. The Korenbaums were from Maloryta, a shtetl in the Russian empire, today's Belarus, some 100 miles from Parczew and Brest-Litovsk. Rushla Korenbaum, my grandmother's mother, had six siblings, among whom were Chaim, who became a peddler in Rhode Island, and David, a woodsman who rode his sleigh from one Russian nobleman's estate to the next, keeping an eye on how fast the fir trees were growing and singling out the finest specimens for the lumberjack's ax.

I have no way of knowing whether the Jablonkas were among the first Jews to settle in Parczew in 1541. I can go back only as far as the nineteenth century. My grandfather's mother was named Tauba, "the dove." Born in 1876. No profession. Suffered from thyroid and kidney ailments. They thought about taking her to Warsaw to see a specialist, but the cost of the trip and the operation was beyond their means. Her late-in-life husband, the father of my grandfather, was named Shloyme. Some sources say he was born in 1865, others say 1868. In the Parczew rabbinical records, he is sometimes listed as a "laborer," sometimes as a *laznik*, a Polish word designating a servant employed at the king's baths. I asked Simje's and Reizl's children, my father's Argentinian cousins, what they knew about their grandfather from Parczew. The answer came in an email: Shloyme was a very pious man; we have no pictures of him because his religious convictions did not allow for photographs, in obedience to the commandment that forbids graven images. And he was in charge of the *mikvah*, the ritual baths.

One day, when Bernard is translating a chapter of the Parczew *Yizkor Bukh* for me, I am overjoyed to discover that my grandfather is mentioned: "Shloyme Jablonka is the *beder*" (which means the "bathhouse guardian").[21]

"At last, I'm certain of something," I tell Bernard. "My great-grand-father was in charge of the *mikvah*."

"No," exclaims Bernard, looking up from the book, upset. "You're con-fusing *mikvah* and *bod*."

The *mikvah* is a basin into which one is fully immersed, a kind of cistern with steps leading all the way down to the bottom. It needs to be fed from a naturally flowing water source, such as a river, the sea, a spring or direct rainfall. The *mikvah* must hold a minimum of forty *seah* of water, or approximately 88 gallons. Men go on Saturday morn-ings, and on the eve of Yom Kippur. At the end of menstruation, women are required by religious law to cleanse themselves there, while an elderly woman checks to see whether the entire body has been immersed and that all parts of the body are cleansed, even the most intimate folds. Naturally, schedules for men and women are separate: women go after nightfall, for otherwise, the details of their private lives would be known to all.

The *bod*, or public bath, on the other hand, serves no other purpose than bodily hygiene, with no ritual aspect at all. It is the shtetl sauna: a wooden building, plank floor, and a wood-burning furnace to heat the bricks. Water is then poured over the hot bricks to produce steam, causing bathers to sweat and body lice to burst. "It's nice and warm," says Bernard, in a purring voice. Men sit around naked and trade gossip while, under the supervision of the *beder*, a young apprentice stimulates their circula-tion by whipping the men's backs with a broom made of birch switches. And they finish their session by rinsing off with buckets of cold water.

So my Argentinian relatives say that Shloyme was the guardian of the *mikvah*, while the "book of remembrance" says he was the *beder*.

For weeks I puzzle over these alternatives, as if my great-grandfather's soul were at stake: ritual bath or public bath? The imperative of immersion or the pleasures of the sauna? On my trip to Buenos Aires in the sweltering heat of December 2010, I probe the memories of Simje's and Reizl's children to try to settle it one way or the other. Reizl's son refers to his mother's ambivalence: whenever he asked what her father did for a living, she would dodge the question or answer evasively. One day he sat down next to her and asked pointedly: "So tell me, mama, he wasn't a thief or something, was he?" And she exclaimed: "A *ganef*? Goodness, whatever made you think such a thing?" But the fact remains that Reizl was somehow ashamed of her father. I ask Simje's and Reizl's children whether it was indeed a *mikvah* where he worked, as they had written in their email. "Yes, the ritual bath. You know, the steam bath." An answer that leaves me as puzzled as ever. As it happens, the two baths are often in close proximity to one another, and there is a simple reason for that: one never goes unwashed to the *mikvah*. In a town as small as Parczew, they probably shared the same building.

Old Shloyme was very religious, explains Simje's son, solemn and soft-spoken as he leans against the ornate buffet in the living room. "He didn't talk much," adds Simje's daughter as she drinks her yerba mate through a silver straw while I take notes on my laptop. "But he was *cariñoso*, affectionate. He expressed his love in acts, not words." Apparently, he had a cat that would dart through his legs as he tried to leave the house for the synagogue in the morning. His children were his only wealth. He would tell them stories, teach them to play chess, slip them a little something to eat during the Yom Kippur fast. Simje, the eldest, inherited his *tefillin* (small leather boxes containing tiny scrolls with verses from the Torah, attached to the head and arm by thin leather straps) but also his talent for chess. He used to lose on purpose to encourage his own children to have the confidence to play. He would say: "When I lose, I win, because it's my children who are winning." Simje died of cancer in Buenos Aires in 1985, so I was never able to meet him, nor his sister, *Tía* Reizl.

One family story tells of the time the baths were closed down for sanitary reasons. Matès somehow managed to circumvent the closure, but the story is short on details: did he break through a wall to get in? No one knows for sure. The police arrived and made note of the violation, threatening to arrest Shloyme, but Matès intervened and claimed responsibility. "I'm the one who did it. Take me to jail, not him." The good son, protector of his own, stood up to the police. That's how I see my grandfather, and Reizl always says he was the bravest of the five siblings. As it happens, neither father nor son had anything to worry about, at least not in this case. The story would appear to be authentic, for my grandfather's court record, dating back to 1933–1934, contains a letter in which a spiteful neighbor warns Shloyme that if he doesn't pay a certain amount, the bathhouse will be closed down.

"That's so typical," says Bernard triumphantly, with a knowing smile.

Jewish establishments were frequently shut down over hygiene issues. In post-World War I Poland, national minorities were subjected to petty annoyances of all sorts: Jewish schools were declared unsafe, places of worship too cramped, *mikvah* steps too slippery, and so on. As often happens with Bernard, this subject sends him off on a tangent. At the entrance to the synagogues, there was always a big barrel of water where the faithful were supposed to wash each hand three times. But the dirty water splashed back into the barrel and onto the ground, creating a mess, so that people preferred to enter the synagogue directly, skirting the mud puddles. In Lithuania in the late nineteenth century, goats would defecate in the middle of the street and root around in garbage piles. Bernard's anecdotes suggest that perhaps the Parczew police had every reason to crack down. But an episode from the *Yizkor Bukh* soon confirms his earlier intuition: after World War I, the building that housed the study house and the *mikvah* was confiscated and the new Polish state set up government offices, a police station, a courtroom, etc. The study house was turned into a distillery, which made use of the water that once fed the bathhouse, none of which prevented the Jews from going back there in secret to pray.[22] It would appear, in conclusion, that old Shloyme was a victim of state-sponsored anti-Semitism (not to mention the neighbor, who would appear to have been a blackmailer).

When he wasn't tending to the bathhouse and his children, Shloyme would have been studying. An extract from the *Yizkor Bukh* says this:

> The town had a great reputation throughout the province and beyond for its Talmudic students, its men of knowledge and its Kabbalah scholars, among whom was *Reb* Mendel Rubinstein, son of Velvel, *Reb* Israel Jablonka the watchmaker, *Reb* Benjamin-Bria Beytel, who made gaiters,

Reb Moyshe-Ber the professor, *Reb* Godel Rabinovitch and bathhouse guardian *Reb* Shloyme Jablonka, a name of some renown. At Israel Jablonka's home, there was a considerable library with thousands of volumes. He received a copy of every book published in Poland.[23]

With the title *Reb*, or "Master," attached to his name, Shloyme Jablonka seems to have been a person of some standing in the community, his piety and erudition making up somehow for his indigence, especially since his association with the sauna-*mikvah*, despite its defects, ushered him into the realm of the sacred. This was not uncommon: the assistants to Rabbi Epstein (who handled Henya's illegitimacy issue in 1935), the members of the *Chevra Kadisha* who were in charge of mortuary rites, the man who performed ritual slaughter, the cantor at the synagogue and the *shulklaper* whose job it was to wake people for prayer by tapping on their shutters all had a certain status. I picture Shloyme as one of those old men in Rembrandt paintings, surrounded by a halo of light. But maybe he was partially deaf and foul-smelling.

Today, the Kabbalah fascinates many, and not just celebrities like Madonna. I am amused to think that an international rock star would be impressed by these wise men gravely hunched over their illegible scrawls in the backroom of some synagogue or in a cottage where candlelight filters through the warped wooden siding. In the shtetl, these initiates are known as "the people of *khen*" or "the men of concealed wisdom" who strive to uncover the secrets of the universe. During a service, Jewish men wind their *tefillin* straps seven times around their arms. Why seven? For Kabbalah believers, each time around represents a virtue bequeathed from God and embodied by one of the seven patriarchs of Israel: Abraham's goodness, Isaac's submissiveness, Moses's everlastingness, Aaron's respect for all creatures, David's peace, etc. One is admitted into study of the Zohar, the foundational work of the Kabbalah, only after the age of forty, and only if one already knows by heart the Torah, the Gemara, and the Nevi'im, or Book of Prophets. Steeped in symbol and metaphor, these mystics are tireless interpreters of the Zohar, digging ever deeper into the strata of meaning, ever further from common understanding, to reach the very foundation of the spiritual universe.[24]

So, what is left? Shloyme combed his beard, Shloyme put on his fur hat before leaving for the synagogue, Shloyme studied at his table while everyone else was asleep, Shloyme deepened his knowledge of God, and in the end, the great night of mystery carried him off forever; for there remains not so much as a signature at the bottom of some official document from this man who preferred to declare himself illiterate rather than to write in any language other than Hebrew. This poor and pious man, father of nine, twice married, keeper of the waters, exegete of holy texts, who shunned worldly riches and cameras, exists as a conjecture in my head, while his ragged but still supple leather *tefillin* lie in a drawer in Buenos Aires.

Nothing is known about his last days. In the family, some claim he died of typhus at a ripe old age right before the war, while others say he was gassed at Treblinka along with the entire Parczew Jewish community. And I read in the *Yizkor Bukh* that a certain Shloyme Jablonka, in the midst of a Nazi *Aktion*, after hiding a neighbor and her children in his cellar, went out to the main square seeking news, and never returned.[25] The story itself is credible, but there is no way of knowing whether it was him since so many share the same names. As for Tauba, she was deported to Włodawa and then murdered in a neighboring camp, perhaps Sobibor. We know this thanks to *Tía* Reizl, who in turn learned it from Yozef Stern, a neighbor in Parczew who went into exile in Canada after the war. For it was not until 1945, when postal communication resumed, that Simje and Reizl learned of their parents' deaths.

Israel Jablonka, the watchmaker, also a Kabbalah follower, is Shloyme's brother (or perhaps half-brother), "the man of a thousand books" whose library was a treasure trove. He was disabled after losing a leg during a pogrom, it is thought, and had to walk with crutches. The children were very fond of their uncle. Whenever he came to the house, Simje and Matès would dress up in their sisters' dresses and pretend to dote on him, then he would go hobbling away, pretending to be horrified. That was their game. He loved to attend the shows put on by traveling theater troupes that came through Parczew. One day, he is said to have declared, rubbing his stomach: "My dear, we may not be eating anything today, but we're going to the theater!"

Among Shloyme's other brothers, the only one I can positively identify is Yoyne, Jona in Polish, the self-made man of the family, owner of a fabric business and a bakery at the corner of Frog and Church Streets. In the 1929 business directory, the name J. Jablonka is also mentioned under "kitchenware." Early in the war, Yoyne sat on the Parczew *Judenrat* along with other local notables. As an instrument of the Germans, this council carried out the Nazis' orders by collecting "fines," supplying the Wehrmacht, cleaning out confiscated homes and implementing repressive measures, such as the compulsory wearing of a white armband bearing the Star of David and rounding up people for forced labor. In February 1940, it was this *Judenrat* that was in charge of feeding Jewish war prisoners in transit to the Biała Podlaska camp, further north, and of burying the 280 corpses abandoned along the way (burial would take two days, since the frozen ground had to be broken up with axes).[26]

In June of the same year, according to the *Yizkor Bukh*, Yoyne Jablonka received a message from the Lublin voivodeship ordering him to make all scrap iron in the region available to the authorities. The laborers he recruited to do the work would have passes that allowed them to stay out beyond the evening curfew and excused them from other forced labor. They could be on the road until 9 p.m., whether on foot or by cart, a considerable privilege that allowed them to glean a little food. One night, Zonenshayn, one of the fortunate scrap collectors, was dragged out of bed by baton-wielding agents and herded into an athletic field behind the church, where dozens of men had already been packed together. In the early morning, the SS made them line up and do calisthenics, as women and children massing outside the fence looked on. At this point, the *Judenrat* arrived at the scene, headed by Yoyne. He met with the SS, who proceeded to announce: "All scrap collectors step out of line." A few men came forward, and they were allowed to go free. The director of the Polonka sawmill was able to save his workers in the same way. Everyone else was marched off to the train station and loaded onto boxcars bound for a work camp. Women rushed forward to give the men packages of food, but the Germans pushed them back with their rifle butts. "The cries of children and weeping of women were indescribable," wrote Zonenshayn in the *Yizkor Bukh*. (I wonder whether this scene replayed incessantly in his mind as he gazed out at the container ships docked in the port of Haifa, where he began his new life.) As a go-between with the

Germans, one cog in the death machine that would crush him in the end, Yoyne Jablonka belonged to that "grey area" where victims, in the hope of saving other lives as well as their own, cooperated with the executioners. May he rest in peace! All his children were murdered during the war, with the single exception of his son Shlomo, who managed an eleventh-hour escape to Palestine.

There are other elders whom I would like to symbolically include on my family tree, as the knottiest of roots: Feygue Chtchoupak's grand-father, a fishmonger, always ready to help poor girls with their dowries and to distribute herring on Shabbat to his penniless neighbors; Ra-khmiel the saddler, whom the porters venerated, since he would open his house to them, where they could warm themselves at his fireplace and tell stories to the children who would gather around him before falling asleep on their bed of hay, murmuring *Shema Yisrael*;[27] the "pious apostate" of Parczew who lived well into his nineties, with a flowing beard and a touch of madness, immortalized in a photograph showing him smoking on the Sabbath (with the blessing of the rabbis, since he claimed it soothed his asthma).[28] The souls of these Jewish elders, I be-lieve, have migrated into the man who brought this civilization alive for me, Bernard, my Yiddish translator, with his trimmed beard, cropped white hair, eyes glowing like embers—a math teacher in another life, today a lecturer at a Paris university and pillar of the Boulogne syna-gogue. My fondness for him stems not only from his patient translation, hour after hour, week after week, of the less-than-scintillating text of the Parczew *Yizkor Bukh*; he also embodies what I think of as Jewish wisdom, garrulousness, erudition and mischievousness. Not to men-tion that the only time I was to see his eyes well up with tears occurred not when Zonenshayn recalled the last days he spent with his five-year-old daughter before being sent to the gas chamber, nor when Feygue Chtchoupak's youngest daughter was wandering in the woods in the midst of winter, nor when Rachel Gottesdiner would recall her lovely, lively schoolmates murdered in the prime of life—rather, it was upon learning that Israel Jablonka, the watchmaker with a taste for the Kab-balah, received hundreds of books from all over Poland: "Even in a little backwater like Parczew, there was such a love of scholarship!"

All these vignettes fit nicely into the shtetl setting with its picturesque old synagogue, the wooden sidewalks, the lopsided houses with
their worm-eaten beams, the charitable societies, bakers, tailors, tinkers,
the cemetery where ancestral tombs date back to the sixteenth century.
Parczew and its scholars, Parczew and its pure-hearted Hassidim, good
folk, simple and warm, always ready to share whatever little they had.
Peals of laughter, Sabbath strolls in the Yashinke forest. Listen to this Yiddish song that brings to life the cottages, the rivers, the pine trees: "My
shtetl, my little home, where I dreamt such lovely dreams!" But I do not
wish to paint too idyllic a portrait of Parczew. Nostalgia and song lyrics
conceal a darker side, the backwardness and conservatism, the yoke of
religious taboos and absurd superstitions, life in a tiny, stultifying society where gossip, mutual surveillance and mediocrity were accepted as
the will of the Almighty. "Religious prohibitions were strictly obeyed,"
writes the elderly Polish woman in her ethnographic account, "and even
educated Jews, such as doctors and dentists, had to abide by them out of
respect for their fellow Jews."[29]

"Did you hear that *Reb* Berl didn't attend prayers this afternoon?"

"Oy, what are you talking about?"

"It's true, he stayed home and napped instead!"

On the evening of Sabbath, you aren't allowed to light a candle until it is
pitch dark out; otherwise, everyone will know and this will cause a scandal.

"Look over at Yenta's. Don't light the candle until she does."

A crowd gathers in front of the synagogue:

"There's been a pogrom in Pinsk."

"Let us fast and pray."

Some father to his son, all suited up in black:

"Don't run! Don't whistle! Don't read Tolstoy! Movies and plays are a
bitul zman, a waste of time."

Look at Parczew with its crumbling houses, mud-clogged streets, and
eagle-eyed gossips. See the shtetl where I. L. Peretz turned up in the late
nineteenth century, among the roosters and the cattle, the fur-hatted
bigots and hunchbacks, children splashing around in mud puddles with
the geese, the bedridden sick and ailing with no one to attend to them,
schoolchildren riveted to their Talmud, young women in wigs, all these

"tired, ashen faces," all these men "sapped of their virility, wandering about in a stupor like zombies."[30] A suitable antidote to Sholem Asch's romantic vision![31] Things began to change in the early twentieth century. In his Yiddish-language play *Chained in the Synagogue Vestibule*, in which a boy is pilloried for loving a girl above his station, Peretz portrays people's exasperation with religion: kosher meat is hugely overpriced, the rabbi is in league with the well-to-do and excommunicates actors who dare to perform on the Sabbath.[32] Religious zealots are like the "pious cat" whose foul breath kills the canary: they smother everyone.[33] Shloyme Jablonka, with his *mikvah*-steam bath where patrons comment on the latest news, would seem to have been slightly more tolerant than the average. He deplored modern life, but when his daughters left the hairdresser with short bobs, he feigned indifference. He let them attend the Polish public school, but restricted his sons' horizons to the study of the holy books. So, this is the atmosphere in which my grandparents grew up: religious closed-mindedness on the one hand, anti-Semitism on the other. By the time they were twenty, life there had become unbearable. The urge to revolt began to take hold, a desire to overthrow the old order. Communism would be their salvation.

Marek drives us through the Parczew forest. Trees fly by for miles and miles, in a bit of a blur. When city-dwellers like myself imagine a walk in the woods, we see butterflies, a carpet of hyacinths, walking paths and gaily chirping birds. But the forest of Parczew is not alive. Its green is dark, almost black. The silent pines, whose foliage filters out most of the sunlight, their thin rays sharp as stalactites, saturate the space, dissolving any point of reference. Ponds and clearings are surrounded by thickets. At the foot of the trunks, there is a chill, something oppressive in the air. You hear a stirring in the branches above, and you look up to see a slice of sky; it is then you realize that you are a captive of the forest, and that its trees alone can breathe. But I am perhaps somewhat obsessed by the manhunts that took place during the winter of 1943, the barking of German shepherds, the panic, the blown-up bunkers, the sudden sight of corpses at a bend in the road. A hiding place was discovered, and everyone scattered into the forest. Feygue Chtchoupak made a run for it with her daughter Myriam, her only one remaining. They hadn't eaten in two days but had to flee, without looking back. Barking in the distance, the killers were on their trail: run, run faster. They were getting closer, they would catch up any minute now. Feygue ordered her daughter to stop and lie down. She pulled up tufts of grass and covered her motionless daughter, then lay down next to her. The killers soon arrived with their dogs. Don't move. Don't breathe. Eyes closed against the hard ground. They came but kept going, and went right by. A miracle.[34]

Marek leads us to the foot of the official monument, a graded succession of concrete steles, three meters high, with a brick stairway, set against a gigantic cross: "To the Memory of the Polish and Soviet Partisans, 1942–1944." The wind is picking up, the trees begin to sway and it starts to rain. A few drops at first, then a full storm pounds the entire region. Beyond the forest are pastures, sawmills, tar works, ponds and fields of unripe wheat, waterwheels and windmills, and still more forests that I imagine from a bird's eye view. I take in the panorama of the Podlachia plain, one of the country's most fertile. In the nineteenth century, the forest of Parczew was a haven for bandits, but it also provided some sustenance to the poor, who would obtain permits to gather berries and mushrooms that they would sell to the rich. These raspberries and mushrooms would save lives during the war.

At twilight, we arrive at an inn located on a stud farm in Makoszka, on the edge of the forest. In this nineteenth-century-style manor house, as we glide along the red tiled floor from one room to the next, our pace slowing as we gaze, we feel enveloped by the velvet draperies, the shine of the wooden beams against the lusterless wrought-iron pokers and chandeliers. Over there, a decorative saddle on a trestle, next to some miniature Tartar horses; over here, a porcelain tea service exhibited on a pedestal table. Elsewhere, deer antlers, pheasant plumage, ornately sculpted rifles, bandoliers and decorative cartridge pouches. A semicircular staircase leads up to our rooms, each with its heavy oak door. For dinner, our hostess serves us a snack-style supper of dark bread, assorted raw vegetables, jam and sweet tea, which we eat all by ourselves at one end of an immense table that stretches all the way to a fireplace the size of a mine entrance. We finish just before seven, and begin our evening's activities. In the downstairs living room, Audrey translates the documents that Bernadetta has given me, while I read a chapter of her dissertation by the fire. The rain has not let up, soaking the ground around the paddock and stalls, while the horses are kept dry inside. The forest gives off a strong scent of humus. The place couldn't be cozier.

Matès was a leatherworker, or to be exact, a saddler, *rimer* in Yiddish, *rymarz* in Polish. During the 1970s, Hershl, who had become "the uncle from Baku," just as Reizl's name had given way to "*la Tía*," came to visit my father: "Your father," he told him, "made harnesses for horses." Official documents confirmed this. So it was that Matès made not only harnesses, but halters, straps and reins, in addition to items no one even recognizes anymore, which I enjoy enumerating here: cruppers, stirrup leathers, girth straps, bridles, martingales, blinkers and nosebands. This is a litany of early adolescence in the mid-1920s, for boys started work early in those days. After the *kheyder*, Colette's father became an apprentice at twelve. Matès began around the same age, most certainly with a Parczew saddler. Apprentices had to learn the basics first: a supple wrist and an eye for good leather, cleanliness in the workshop and proper storage of tools. It is a craft of astounding complexity. "The apprentice," says a manual from the 1920s, "must first learn to properly thread his needles, to use clamps, position his awl and drive it straight in without twisting, before passing the needles through."[35] Next, he learns to cut, stitch, stuff and oil, as well as to polish the brass buckles, all of which involves hours of painstaking work to attain perfection. And while at his workbench, with patient concentration, Matès would reproduce a secularized version of his father's daily rites at morning prayer: winding the leather strap seven times counterclockwise around his upper arm, placing a second one on his forehead, right at the hairline, adjusting the little boxes containing bits from the Torah, and ending with straps wound around his arm and hand. Maybe he would check daily that the water in the *mikvah* was pure and still, that the plug was secure, and that rainwater that flowed directly into the basin through the gutters contained no impurities.

Matès had a real trade, but the oversupply of saddlers in Parczew, the economic crisis and general anti-Semitic sentiment made it hard to get a start in life. Under a 1927 law, craftsmen were issued their certification only after training at a vocational school. Since enrollment was costly, apprenticeships were available only with certain masters and the final exam was conducted in Polish, the law had the effect of eliminating Jewish candidates.[36] By that date, Matès had turned eighteen and had been working in leather for a number of years, but as a simple laborer. How do I know this? I found no document or testimony that would suggest he had his own shop, while there is evidence that he regularly attended meetings of the local leatherworkers union and Communist youth groups. I conclude that he must have worked for someone else (C. Engelman, U. Engelman, D. Goldberg, A. Pilczer, J. Sokolowski or S. Solarz, according to the directory of professions for 1929), unless he was out of work altogether. Whatever the case, he was at the bottom of the social ladder, just above the destitute. It seems unfair, for it is quite clear to me that a self-employed saddler would have been getting lots of work. Everyone got around in horse-drawn carts, peasants used draft animals to plow, and all those bridles and harnesses would eventually wear out and need replacement: between manufacture and customer service, one could earn a living. Thus, a Parczew saddler could have been as prosperous as a provincial French garage mechanic today—so long as the villagers didn't set up a picket to prevent Christians from entering.

All testimony concurs that Idesa was a beauty. We have a grand total of six photographs of her, which is already quite a trove: a full-length portrait of a skinny teenager in a pleated skirt and pumps, frozen before the camera like Pierrot in the glare of the studio's artificial light, her hand affectionately placed on the shoulder of her mother, Rushla Korenbaum; another picture of her in front of a tree and some undergrowth, accompanied by an unidentified, slightly older man; a few ID photos where she is wearing tops and jackets with pointy collars that must have been the fashion then. In one group shot of some Parczew youths, she glows in the fullness of her seventeen years—the picture would have been taken in the early 1930s. Her eyes shine with the same darkness and depth as her hair. In the hollow of her neck, around her eyebrows, in her dimples, in the curl of her full mouth, shadows bring out the velvety whiteness of her complexion. The dark braids that tumble down either side of her face brush her plump cheeks, while her silk scarf highlights the first hints of her womanly charms as she barely emerges from adolescence. Her beauty far outshines that of the other girls, who are all fussy and affected, or overweight, or nearsighted, their hair stiff with spray, or their noses too big for their faces. The half-wit next to her knows it, too, his gaze brazenly fixed on her.

According to *Tía* Reizl, who concedes it without the slightest jealousy, Idesa was the most beautiful girl in Parczew. It was like in the fairytales: my grandfather fell madly in love with her. But Idesa was already going out with someone else, and worse than that, Matès didn't quite measure up. He was rather short, with reddish-blond hair and freckles that caused him great shame. One day, he sought out a healer who said she could erase them with a special cream. The operation proved an utter failure and, heartsick, he went back home, where the whole family made fun of him. But Matès had many fine qualities. Here is the portrait that Henya's daughter draws of him some eighty years later, based on what she has gleaned from her mother's memories: Matès was a *mamzer*, that is, a clever type, one who always finds the way out of a sticky situation. Everyone praised his heart and helpfulness, his readiness to lend a hand, carry heavy loads, or move furniture. No amount of work was too daunting. In a word, a mensch, quick-witted and big-hearted, but tough at the same time, not to be provoked. That's what the sabras are like today, concludes Henya's daughter on her fragrant terrace in Hadera, north of Tel Aviv: "A cactus fruit, sweet inside, but bristling with spines."

Transformed by love, undaunted by obstacles, Matès would repeat to anyone listening: "I'll get that girl! I swear that someday she'll be my wife."

I link this account to *Tía* Reizl's, which my father brought back from a trip to Argentina. Energetic, cheerful, determined, enterprising—these were Matès's best features. "He would sing, and everywhere he went, other folks would start singing along." He was different from the others, his brothers in particular, who were feebler, more easily discouraged. Across the street from the family home, there was a shop, run by Idesa's brother, that sold kerosene (today it is a mechanic's shop). At noon, Idesa would bring him his lunch, and Matès would gaze at her out the window as she passed. He would call on his mother to witness: "Do you like her?" Later on, he managed to court Idesa without arousing any suspicions with his future mother-in-law: "Matès is such a trustworthy guy that, when he comes over to the house, I leave them alone." So, this is the beginning of their love story, as remembered—or fantasized—by *Tía* Reizl, who herself experienced such bitter disappointment. I would have so loved to sit down with her and ask more questions, methodically and tenderly, to learn even more. But Reizl died in 2006, a year before I started my research. I never did meet her. In photographs taken near the end of her life, she looks like a little old lady with a suntan, smiling, still having something up her sleeve, exuding goodness in her flowered dress that accentuates her pudginess. I have trouble making the connection in my head between *Tía*, the doting granny in faraway Buenos Aires, and Reizl, the stocky young girl in the back row of the photograph of Parczew kids and the emigrant who boarded the ship in 1936 with the overcoat intended for her younger sister. Such is time and its diffractions. We have ID photos of Matès and Idesa, but by virtue of this same diffracted vision, I have trouble conjuring their image as a couple, as life partners, because there exists not a single picture of them together.

In the morning, the sun shines brightly on the Makoszka forest. A bee is buzzing between the windowpane and the lace curtains. With the covers pulled up to my chin, snug and warm, I think back to yesterday's wanderings, after our walk in the forest with Marek. It is four in the afternoon, we have skipped lunch and are beginning to feel hungry. Parczew has no restaurants, and even the shops are starting to close for the day. We finally end up in a tavern, a kind of basement labyrinth, a corridor dimly lit with the occasional fluorescent tube. The place is a haunt for idlers, young men playing pool, couples snuggling in corners, far from the pinball machines whose buttons and score displays blink in the darkness. It isn't quite a low-life pub—not smoky enough, no drug traffickers or petty criminals—nor could it pass for a nightclub, without the earsplitting thump of a techno beat. It isn't like anything else, in fact, but no other place could better capture what I am feeling at this moment: sticky and rueful, from the skin to the marrow.

Audrey orders pizzas. We stare at each other, at a loss for words. Something oppressive makes me want to flee this town, with its synagogue–flea market, its cemetery-park, its Jews Street renamed New Street, its tidy little *Rynek*, its soulless inhabitants. But I am not the first, and far from the most sorely aggrieved. In 1968, Baruch Niski, exiled in the So-viet Union, was able to visit his native shtetl, where he felt like a com-plete stranger.

> Here, in this square with the red flowers, this used to be the big market-place. And that movie theater, that was once the study house where the rabbi lived. You see those stables over there? That's where the Orthodox Church once stood. And over there was the public bathhouse. You see that pile of coal there? That was Itzhak Fischer's house. . . . Children gather around us and stare, as if we were zoo animals. A little girl asks her mother if we're Jews, and if so, why did people chase us out and kill us, since we look like such nice folks. I am sitting in the park, formerly the cemetery. Trees rise pensively, each an orphan of some upheaval. I am alone, orphaned as well. Everything around me is steeped in sad-ness. The trees seem to recite the Kaddish, and whisper, "Why have you come? Why?"[37]

I have never seen a Jewish cemetery. To be sure, I have been to the Bagneux cemetery in Paris, I have visited the graves of Argentinian, Israeli and American Jews, I have walked the Prague cemetery, which merges in my mind with Chagall's 1917 painting, where the chaotic jumble of tomb-stones seems to come alive, as if the dead were pushing away the slabs with a knee or an elbow. But what does a shtetl graveyard look like? There is evidence that Poland's last Jewish cemeteries are fast disappearing, choked with weeds and other vegetation; that's when they haven't been turned into junkyards or shooting ranges. In Parczew's public park, there are only two headstones remaining, a light grey one and another dark grey, in re-membrance of the 280 Jewish soldiers among the routed Polish army who were executed while being transferred. What about the Jews of Parczew? There must have been thousands of graves, the Zonenshayn family, the Wajsman family, the Fiszman family, the Chtchoupak family, the Feders, the Jablonkas, rich and poor, tradesmen, fishmongers, seventeenth-century rabbis, and little Shmuel who died at age two. Apart from the lawns and trees, there is nothing left. In the Parczew town archives, maintained at Radzyń Podlaski, where we go two days later, we unearth a census taken among males a few years after the war, probably for use by the military.

Everyone listed is marked as *rzymsko-katolicki*, which meant that there were only Catholics living in Parczew by then. Another document turns up in this archive: the street-by-street list of postwar occupants of what were once Jewish houses. Hundreds of names appear, all Catholics.[38] There is no denying it: the Jews of Parczew never existed.

I'm going over all this in my mind as I watch the waiter rushing back and forth with his tray full of beer mugs. In Western Europe, they like to trumpet the fact that the Allies defeated Hitler, laid low the hideous beast, etc. And yet, one need only set foot in a village like Parczew to realize how brilliantly the Nazis won the war against the Jews. Genocide, that demiurgic drive in reverse, gave rise to an ethnically pure Poland in the wake of the war. But Polish society's own anti-Semitism was also at work. In 1939, Poland was home to 3.5 million Jews, some 10% of the population. After the war, the 250,000 survivors gradually left the country, an exodus accelerated by anti-Jewish riots in Rzeszów (June 1945); pogroms in Krakow (two deaths in August 1945), Parczew (three deaths in February 1946) and Kielce (forty-two deaths in July 1946); and 118 murders carried out in the region of Lublin.[39] Today, there are scarcely 12,000 Jews in the whole country. A documentary on the shtetl of Brańsk, near the border with Belarus, shows the region's last synagogue, no longer in use and falling into ruin, as a flock of sheep wanders out the door. In Brańsk proper, the road leading past the church is paved with Jewish tombstones. Others have been refashioned to serve as millstones. In the 1990s, a philo-Semite—another "lackey of the Jews"—managed to bring back 175 stones to the old cemetery, which was then called a lapidarium. But once this same man became deputy mayor, he refrained from saying anything about Jews (60% of the population prior to the war) at the town's 500th anniversary celebration.[40] The town archives show that requests for restitution on behalf of the heirs in America and Israel all met with flat refusals in the late 1940s. The heirs were told that the houses had been destroyed, that their effects had been sold, etc.[41]

But what if the Poles were also suffering as a result of this genocide? As she is telling me about her trip to Parczew, Colette proposes this idea that stuns me at first: "I realized what a great vacuum had been created by the destruction of Polish Jewry, as if Parczew had lost its soul. Between Poles and Jews, there had been a fierce love-hate relationship." As if to back her up, the old Polish woman recalls in her ethnographic text that "every Pole had his Sroul or his Moyshe." What now, after Sroul and Moyshe have disappeared? As we stand on the threshold of the synagogue-turned-consignment store, Bernadetta, the French teacher serving as our guide, implies that this transformation might seem surprising, but that it is also understandable. Communist and post-Communist Poland took a pragmatic approach toward property in default of heirs, and put the buildings to use. But is it really proper for a former place of worship to end up as a sheep pen or a used clothing store, a saloon, as was the case in Chelm, or a firehouse, a warehouse or a movie theater?[42]

The Jews of Parczew did leave traces, such as the rabbinical registry. In a 120-page brochure issued by the town hall that covers four centuries of local history, four pages are devoted to the Jews: in 1541, "the mayor of Parczew allowed Jews to settle on the outskirts of the town," and in 1996, "a resident of Parczew, Mr. Ludwik Golecki, received the medal of the Righteous among Nations, awarded by the Yad Vashem Institute in Tel Aviv." And since the return of democracy, hasn't Poland witnessed a renewal of interest in all things Jewish?[43] A 1996 law restores places of worship and cemeteries to their original communities. In Zamość, a seventeenth-century synagogue has been beautifully restored. Kazimierz, the old Jewish quarter of Krakow, has traded in its drunks and prostitutes for more upscale night spots. Cities are organizing festivals of Yiddish culture and inaugurating memorial monuments. Research seminars abound at universities and klezmer music has become trendy. One artist even covered the walls of the city with the slogan "Jew, I miss you."

I'm not sure what to think. Those who advocate for Jewish-Polish friendship have certainly got it right, for things are indeed changing. But how can I care about their tourist-friendly Judaism, all this folk dancing on mass graves? What if I were to return to our synagogue and drive out the merchants from the temple? Or dare to spoil a wedding celebrated in the former Jewish study house? What if I went to court to start the procedure for reclaiming our property, our house at 33 Broad Street? The waiter arrives with our pizzas, here in this underworld dug out beneath *judenrein* Parczew, and I have before me the material embodiment of how I have been feeling for the past several hours: on one of the piz-zas, the cook has drawn a spiral of ketchup, a sticky swirl that starts at the outer edge and circles around the ham, cheese and blackened mush-rooms. I sit a long time transfixed by this bloody, worm-like coil, unable to take my first bite.

2

PROFESSIONAL

REVOLUTIONARIES

Parczew, a Saturday in 1914. The young Jews came out in large numbers to hold an outdoor meeting to confer about how they might get the great Yiddish-language writer Sholem Aleichem to come to town at some point on his tour of Poland. Despite their political differences—the children of the well-to-do leaned toward Zionism, while their working-class peers tended toward socialism—it was decided unanimously, after a number of impassioned speeches, that two of their cohort would travel to Lublin to respectfully extend an invitation to their idol. To defray the travel expenses, all participants chipped in a ruble each. A few weeks later, when the news arrived that Sholem Aleichem had declined their invitation for health reasons (his burial in New York, in 1916, would be attended by a crowd 100,000 strong), the young people of Parczew broke out in vehement protest. Once calm had returned, the children of the bourgeoisie recovered their 1 ruble each, but the "cobbler's quarter" decided to devote their money to the purchase of books, thereby creating the early stages of the trilingual library, in Yiddish, Hebrew and Polish, which would come together a few months later at the home of Motel Polusetski, a bookbinder, one of the emissaries who had been sent to Lublin.[1]

After World War I, people's thirst for knowledge was channeled into political activism. Released from captivity in 1918, Israel-Issar Goldwasser, one of the first Parczew Communists, established evening classes for learning Yiddish and breathed new life into the theater scene with inventive staging and more contemporary repertoire.[2] The local athletic clubs Hapoel ("worker" in Hebrew) and Maccabee (the Jews who resisted the Seleucids in the second century BCE) organized soccer games, dances, shows and lectures. Gone was the sickly Jew bent over his Talmud, incapable of lifting a hammer or swimming across the Piwonia. The time had come for a new man! Parczew was honored by lecturers of all stripes, orators from all over. Reading groups formed, and the library expanded into an association. You could go there to read, sing, recite poetry or devour the Warsaw newspapers. Discussions touched on all topics: religion, atheism, poetry, theater, revolution, Palestine, Yiddish and Hebrew, bank credit, foreign policy, self-defense militias.[3] It was time for a fresh start.

Jewish political parties sprang up everywhere. The Bund, which headed up dozens of organizations, youth movements, labor unions, sports clubs and publications, defended the proletariat by merging Yiddish culture and class struggle. There was also the loose Zionist network, broken into parties and currents that reached beyond their common founding goal of an autonomous Jewish nation. They covered the whole spectrum of political membership: general Zionists who defended the rights of Jews in Poland itself, religious workers of the *Poale Mizrahi*, socialists from the right-leaning *Poale Zion*, Marxists from the left-leaning *Poale Zion* who were influential among the intelligentsia, young pioneers and right-wing Zionists, or "revisionists," who advocated emigration to Palestine. Even the orthodox had their own party, *Agudat Israel*, the keeper of tradition, aligned with Pilsudski in exchange for greater religious autonomy.[4] They were the dominant force among Parczew Jewry: they controlled the *Kehilla*, the local organizational structure, and in the 1929 municipal elections, they won nine seats out of twenty-one.[5] "Everyone believed in something, and in his own way, aspired to a better world," writes Faiwel Schrager, then a Zionist socialist, born into a family of eight children deep in the province of Grodno.[6]

As for my own grandparents, they were Communists, and struggled to build a classless society, freed from the bonds of exploitation, misery, oppression, religion, anti-Semitism, war and nationalism, including Zionism. A new will would rise out of the ruins of the old order, and people would cease to suffer or cause suffering to others. This was not some pipe dream, but an absolute imperative, a historical certainty. All the siblings—Simje, Reizl, Matès, Hershl and Henya—were Communists. That much my father already knew at the time I was starting my research, and he even asserted that his parents had been sentenced to five years in prison for painting anti-government slogans on the town walls. My goal, as I fly to Poland in May 2009, two years after having made contact with a number of archives, is to verify on the ground the various things I have been told, to compare my grandfather's path with that of my grandmother and to understand the reasons for their political commitment and subsequent incarceration. Before heading off to Parczew, Audrey and I make an important discovery at the State Archive of Lublin: we find the nearly complete series of "sociopolitical" reports by the Lublin voivodeship during the interwar period, which provide accounts of the activities of Jews, minorities, Communists and all those liable to threaten the young state. The collection includes dozens of confidential police reports on the "subversive trade union movement" in the district of Włodawa, where Parczew is located.[7] I am deeply curious when I see Matès Jablonka's 1934 trial mentioned.

One of the great triumphs of the Bolshevik Revolution in Russia was Poland's recovered independence. The Polish Communist Party (KPP) was born in 1918 through the merging of the left wing of the Polish Socialist Party, which promoted Polish independence, and the social-democratic party of Rosa Luxemburg, with its more revolutionary, internationalist orientation. The following year, the KPP joined the Komintern.[8] In Parczew, news of the October Revolution filtered through, thanks to "workers coming from Warsaw, 'educated young ladies' and young people who were well versed in Russian literature."[9] A core of activists took shape around Israel-Issar Goldwasser, the theater director. In 1919, in a new development of the Russo-Polish conflict, Bolshevik tanks rolled into Parczew. Believing that the hour of revolution had finally arrived, Rabbi Epstein's daughter created the Revkom, a revolutionary committee in charge of greeting the Red Army, and exhorted her peers to take possession of the pharmacy and other shops.[10] The same held true in Warsaw: as the Red Army drew closer, the Communists called for work stoppages to make it easier for the revolutionary soldiers and to prevent the Polish propertied classes, backed by France, to extinguish the flame of hope coming from the East. The Soviet advance was stopped in its tracks by the "miracle of the Vistula" in August 1920, which saved Polish independence. In the end, Pilsudski succeeded in pushing the border 125 miles further east, annexing a part of Ukraine and Belarus at the expense of the Soviets.[11]

In Parczew as in the rest of the country, the KPP recruited throughout the 1920s. After Rabbi Epstein's daughter's setback, the movement restructured itself in 1922 around newly created trade union cells among leather and textile workers. That same year, the tanners went out on strike for the first time, followed by the distillery workers.[12] This shtetl Communism might come as a surprise: unlike Lodz, the big industrial town, Parczew did not have a single factory and there was no mass accumulation of capital. But wherever there was exploitation and oppression, there were Communists. This is just as true outside big urban centers in the Polish region of Włodawa as it is among the sharecroppers in France's Limousin region. In the interwar period, Polish Jews were subjected to expropriation, fiscal discrimination, exclusion from public markets, racial quotas at the university and abusive hiring and firing policies in the civil service and other areas of the economy. In 1932, Dr. Thon, rabbi and president of a Jewish caucus in the parliament, speaks of "the utter despair among Jewish youth, who feel they have no future ahead, since Jews have been eliminated from all areas of economic activity."[13] These young people, coming from the working class or the disenfranchised lower middle class, rooted in a secular Yiddish-speaking world, joined the KPP in droves. Local authorities were well aware of this, as indicated in a 1927 report: "In towns, particularly Parczew and Włodawa, the KPP movement is very much underground, recruiting in young Jewish worker circles, but never managing to penetrate the older Jewish age group, nor craftsmen or small merchants."[14] In 1933, when Poland was being hit hard by the world economic crisis, the KPP and its satellite organizations reached a total of more than 30,000 members, not an insignificant number considering how harshly these groups were being repressed. In Parczew, they numbered somewhere between 100 and 200.[15]

Let us imagine ourselves in this shtetl, meeting up with a young tailor, a young saddler and their friends. Abram Fiszman and Malka Milechsberg, Colette's parents, became Communists in the late 1920s, when they were in their mid-teens. At my grandfather's trial, it would be stated that the Parczew police had been monitoring the accused since 1929: at that point, he was twenty, and Idesa was fifteen. From this, I conclude that they became militants at about the same time as Colette's parents, who were in fact friends of theirs. By then, Matès had long since completed his professional training and was earning a living, more or less, while rounding out his leatherworker activity by writing political tracts for the cause. The young man rose quickly in the local Party apparatus. At the time of his trial, he was referred to as a "dynamic, active militant" who was a member of "the local cell of the Polish Communist Party, where he holds the position of technician"[16] (a *technik* is in charge of the publishing and peddling of Party tracts and brochures, and is a member of the editorial board). He was also a local official for the Communist Youth organization, or KZMP, to which Idesa also belonged. Perhaps this is where they fell in love, even before the kerosene shop sightings.

Until this point, everything might seem ordinary: young, underpaid workers devoted heart and soul to the Party. But to truly grasp the reality of the situation, we have to cast aside the French stereotypes of the typical Communist: the farmworkers of "red" southern France, the car assembly plant workers of Billancourt, fellow activists selling the leftist paper *L'Humanité* at a marketplace. For although it is obvious that Communism was both a way of life and an act of faith for millions of people, it is also important to understand that Matès and Idesa were taking enormous risks. In the 1930s, Polish Communists could spend years in prison, right at the age when others of their cohort would be arm in arm with their fiancées, saving for their future life together. By joining the Party, they were agreeing not only to sacrifice their personal lives to the revolution, but to radically break with everyone and every-thing, to perform the supreme, unforgivable transgression: the militant KPP member is the man clenching a knife between his teeth, the thief in the night, the enemy of the nation, henchman of the Russians who for so long had kept Poland in a state of servitude and who, after their defeat by Pilsudski's armies in 1921, were waiting for their moment of revenge. It stands to reason, then, that Communists would be hated by one and all, and that their internationalist outlook would be seen as utter betrayal. And what if, to make matters worse, they were also Jewish, if the Red Devil also had a hooked nose? What resulted was *żydo-komuna*, or the "Judeo-Communist Plot," the hydra spewed from the bowels of the earth that had to be ruthlessly eradicated.

Since the Party was illegal, its partisans were constantly being hunted down, which meant they became very skilled at clandestine operations. It is hard for us in the 2010s—unless we have keen memories of the Resistance in World War II—to imagine the life of self-discipline and conspiracy that these twenty-year-olds chose: speak to no one, use pseudonyms and coded language, be rigorously punctual, ensure you're not being followed, and always remain absolutely sober. To prevent informers from infiltrating the network, cells were reduced to just a few members and operated indepen-dently of each other, with each militant reporting to only one contact in the hierarchy. They would gather in the woods, in cemeteries, in sports clubs or in people's homes, and this siege mentality meant that they all grew up very fast.[17] An anecdote about Simje, told by his daughter while we were on our way, despite the sweltering heat and traffic jams, to the cemetery of the *Asociación Mutual Israelita Argentina*, where he is buried: at one of the underground meetings held at the home on Broad Street, Simje's girlfriend was tasked with keeping watch out in front of the house. The police arrived through the back door and took everyone away. This entire time, the girlfriend stood in front of the house, arms crossed. Forty years later, *Tío* Simje still laughed about it, playfully teasing the woman who would become his wife, Raquel.

As the person in charge of propaganda materials, a *technik* by defini-tion had to be fairly well educated. My grandparents held this position one after the other, but there is no one left to tell me whether Idesa had read Bukharin's *The ABCs of Communism*, or August Bebel's *Women and Socialism*, or whether Matès was a passionate reader of Leonid Andreyev's *The Seven Who Were Hanged*, written after the failed 1905 revolution, and which tells the story of the last night on earth of a group of "terrorists." I would have had to resort to fiction had I not discovered some absolutely exceptional documents in the Warsaw Archives: my grandfather's court and prison records, a 729-page bundle that recorded the militant's every deed until 1937, when he was released from prison.[18] During a house search on Broad Street in 1933, the police seized papers annotated in his handwriting, in which he had detailed the success of the Soviet Union's Five-Year Plan. These notes amount to a recording of his voice:

> In 1929, there were 29,000 tractors, and by 1932, that number had grown to 146,000. Fifteen years of cultural work in the Soviets: in Czarist Russia, there was an 85% illiteracy rate; by 1926, the rate had dropped to 45%. Today, it hovers between 10 and 15%. . . . Compared to 1928, machine production increased by a factor of four. Compared to the prewar period, ten. . . . The Five-Year-Plan allowed for the opening of 200,000 kolkhozes [collective farms] and 5,000 sovkhozes [state-run farms]. Between them, they plant 75% of the farmland.[19]

Matès was not alone in his enthusiasm. French Communists were stunned at Stalin's accomplishments. The Italian author of a 1934 book on the collectivization of the Soviet countryside, using similar statistics, hails "the admirable drive and heroism" with which the Soviet population had fulfilled its mission.[20] While the USSR was writing new chapters to its success story, capitalist countries, exhausted by a world war that had left 9 million dead, sank still deeper into their stock market crash. Elsewhere, Matès made observations about recent developments in the class struggle in Europe and the United States:

> A hunger march in London.
> America. Miners striking in New York. A veterans march. . . .
> Germany. Work stoppages in the chemical industries.
> Spain. Soldiers out on strike.

Vienna. The unemployed on a hunger march.

Czechoslovakia. Peasants are fighting.

Poland. Strikes. Fights.

What do all these struggles teach us? We are at a point of decisive confrontation, a world war.

These words are worth far more than their face value, for they show
us, beyond the slogans intended to mobilize the masses, the individual
thoughts of a self-taught revolutionary, as he collected and assimilated data
that would prove his position unassailable. This is the conscience, and the
confidence, of an insurgent trying to heal the world from within his shtetl,
just as Israel Jablonka had opened his mind to the whole range of book
knowledge. Matès saw the prophecy of Marx and Engels on the verge of
fulfillment. Compared to these strikes and marches converging toward an
imminent final onslaught, the conflagration out of which would emerge
the classless society, what possible value could there be in Polish nationalism or Jewish identity? In March 1933, a police report noted that, for the
region of Włodawa, "it is possible to discern a certain enthusiasm among
Communists for Hitler's rise to power. They figure that, come spring, he
will provoke a war between Germany and Poland, which will effectively set
off a revolution in both countries."[21] The insurmountable contradictions
within imperialism would stoke popular anger, resulting in a revolution
throughout Europe that would break out in a matter of months, not years.

There is also some anecdotal evidence that sheds light on my grandfather's personality. Colette's parents were apparently great admirers of his,
to the point where he was something of an idol for them. ("I'm not exaggerating," she says, noticing my doubtful look.) Matès was quite charismatic, an excellent orator, and a hard-core Marxist. Tía Reizl echoes the
same view, speaking of her brother in glowing terms and with boundless
respect. In the late 1990s, in conversation with my own father, she insisted
that Matès was the key figure among the siblings, the male equivalent to
half-sister Gitla: when he spoke, people listened, thought hard about what
he said and inevitably approved of it. In the eyes of all, he embodied incor-
ruptibility, as a leader whose hard-line doctrinal positions were balanced
by personal fortitude and human warmth.

I have no reason to doubt the sincerity of all this praise. But Matès is also the only sibling who did not survive. Before the war, in fact, his older brother and sister addressed him very differently. Writing to the family from Buenos Aires in 1933, here is what Simje had to say: "Matès, I've already told you to drop that stupid 'technician' job of yours that's bound to get you into trouble. The police are going to drag you to court and put you in prison, you'll see. It can't go on much longer. Isn't there anyone besides you in the [illegible] to do the job? Take my advice and stop what you're doing, do you understand what I mean?" In another letter, this time sent from Chelm, where Reizl was getting over her failed love affair, she wrote, bitingly: "What are Henya and Hershl up to? . . . And you, Matès, how are you doing? Are you still working for all humanity, still preparing for a better tomorrow?"

These letters, translated from Yiddish into Polish in April 1934, at the time of the trial, are also included in my grandfather's sizable court record. Why in the world were the investigators interested in this family correspondence where siblings talk about the weather and complain at length that they aren't getting enough mail in return? Because it proved that even the brother and sister of the accused believed he had gone too far. On my trip to Buenos Aires, I present these letters to the children of Simje and Reizl, my father's cousins. Does this mean, I ask them, that their parents renounced Communism once they got to Argentina or Chelm? "Not at all," replies Benito, Simje's eldest. "In Argentina, the whole family is Communist, without exception. We used to get into fights, though, when it came to the 'reds' and the 'super-reds.'" In the late 1950s, when Benito was detained by the police for his opposition to the military government, his father refused to visit him in prison. Here again, Simje felt his son had gone too far. He could have merely read his Marx and Gramsci, paid his Party dues, attended meetings and carried his card. *Tía* Reizl considered herself a pure Communist, but in the 1950s, when other family members were getting rich, she prodded her husband, a furniture worker, to start his own business, like Simje had. The venture failed after a few years: they were destined to be proletarians after all, grassroots militants, not bosses. Further on still, Hershl, the little brother, who had come for a visit, filled the house with his complaints and ceaseless whining: Baku is dreadful, the shops are all empty, etc. It was Reizl's turn to make a scene: the Soviet Union is a wonderful place to live, where everyone is free and happy, and anyone who says differently is a liar! These 1934 letters, full of warnings and sarcasm when it came to the notion of "a better tomorrow," show the stark difference between the Communism of Simje and Reizl, laborers among the Party faithful, and that of Matès, the professional revolutionary whose trajectory was soon to hit the wall of the prison cell.

Thus, my grandfather was both the family firebrand and the leader of Parczew's Jewish Communist microcosm: this is the redheaded agitator in whom Idesa, the KZMP militant, the Broad Street kerosene seller's sister, was starting to take an interest. All my witnesses had heard their parents talking after the war about Matès's love for this dark-eyed beauty. "Madly in love," "together forever," etc. And yet, at the time, Abram and Malka Fiszman, Colette's parents, knew nothing of their relationship, although they were all close friends. The sweethearts' 1937 wedding took them unawares. Surprising—but after all, why not? Colette's parents were also carrying on a secret relationship at the time. One of their contemporaries had this to say: "We didn't live our own lives, we lived for the Party. . . . I was married to the Party, and my personal life was on hold."[22] In light of this testimony, it might seem astounding that two militants were able to fall in love at all. But in actual fact, several couples formed in the shadow of the Party. After all, heroism and romance often go hand in hand, and shared defiance, shoulder to shoulder in the face of overwhelming odds, causes hearts to beat in unison.

Their lives consisted of attending secret meetings, distributing tracts, scrawling slogans on banners and then the celebrations of their heroes: the anniversary of the deaths of the "three L's," Rosa Luxemburg, Karl Liebknecht, and Lenin, 16–21 January; of the Paris Commune uprising, 18 March; International Youth Day, 3 September; and of course, the October Revolution, 7 November. Each of these was a way to celebrate proletarian unity beyond all borders, in the grand tradition of Luxemburg and Trotsky.[23] The First of May, International Workers' Day, was a separate case, since it was a legal holiday celebrated by the Bund and the Polish Socialist Party as well. A police report, headed "Jewish labor unions," relates the sequence of events in Parczew on 1 May 1933. Starting around 9:30 a.m., some fifty members of the garment union and the leatherworkers union marched, in one direction, down 11 November Street, Warsaw Street and Marshal Pilsudski Street, and on the way back, up Church Street to the local union headquarters. Marchers held up their banners and chanted their anthems: "Hammer," "May Day" and "Carpenter's Daughter." No public disturbance occurred. In both unions, the report concluded, Communist influence was estimated at 10%.[24]

As I said, this account came under the heading of "Jewish labor unions": Is the commandment "Workers of the World, Unite!" etched into the tablets of Moses? It is true that Trotsky's name was Bronstein and that Zinoviev was born Apfelbaum. At the KZMP, the Communist Youth organization, half the members were Jews. Here is what Warsaw resident Moshe Garbarz had to say: "In the eyes of the police, 'Jew' meant 'revolutionary'; as a matter of fact, in my neighborhood, it was close to the truth."[25] Max Dinkes, originally from Przemysl in Galicia, stated: "In our city, I've never known a non-Jewish Communist."[26] Just as the Bolsheviks in Russia defended the Jews and denounced pogroms, so too did the KPP fight against anti-Semitism, considered a reactionary ideology meant to divide the proletariat. The Bund used the same language, but addressed to Jews. The KPP, for its part, was a multiethnic party open to both Catholics and Jews, to Belarusians as well as to Ukrainians (the proletariat is said to have no country). Due to the prevailing anti-Semitism in other Polish organizations, young justice-loving workers seeking emancipation from their Jewish identity had no choice but to join the Party, where they were rapidly assimilated. For them, Communism represented the sole expression of freedom. Thus, if many Communists were Jewish—and not the other way around, since only 0.2% of Jews opted for Communism in the interwar period—it's because they no longer felt Jewish.[27]

In the early stages of my research, I saw my grandparents' commitment to the cause as something perfectly natural, requiring no explanation. But in fact, it implied a break not only with the law, but with their family values. In the nineteenth century, mortals were damned to hellfire for giving themselves over to demonic powers. In the 1920s, they met the same fate for becoming godless revolutionaries. Take the case of Israel-Issar

Goldwasser and Nakhman Yozef Shuh, two former yeshiva students: after the Great War, they returned to Parczew as atheists, spreading their Marxist ideas at the study house and filling the library with impure books, to the great displeasure of the Talmudist Mendel Rubinstein, whose anger is recorded in the *Yizkor Bukh*: "They are poisoning the minds of young pious Hassidic girls, and to add insult to injury, they're talking about modernizing the *kheyder*." How dare they target the children! What had those poor lambs ever done? *Reb* Mendel got the word out to all of Parczew, and the next day, the Sabbath, before opening the Holy Ark to read the week's passage, the rabbi denounced in the strongest terms any parent who would send his child to this modern *kheyder*.[28]

Let us now take a closer look inside the families. What sort of reproach did Rabbi Epstein heap upon his beloved daughter after she founded the Revkom and called for the expropriation of the local pharmacist? I can hear him lamenting, like another rabbi, the father of Tsirele in Isaac Bashevis Singer's *Scum*: "She has a passion for all things modern, she goes to political meetings, reads newspapers and books, filling her head with who knows what kind of ideas. She won't go to the *mikvah* anymore. She is even claiming that men and women are equals!"[29] And how many evenings did he spend ranting and raving in the town's well-appointed drawing rooms, at the Erlichs', the Futermans', the Weissmans', at the home of Shapiro, who wielded the knife for ritual sacrifice, all of whose children were Party members? Those miscreants, still wet behind the ears, and now they claim to have discovered the laws of history? Wretched rebellion! They question whether Moses performed miracles on Mount Sinai, but they yammer away, quoting Marx and Darwin. *Yiddishkeyt* is dead and buried!

The scene is set, the warring parties in place: Marx versus Moses, the hammer and sickle versus the synagogue, tears and curses on both sides. Let us now visit the Jablonka household on Broad Street. Matès had been going bareheaded for several years, and refused to go to the synagogue with his father. One holy day, at a ceremony where young people are supposed to carry the Torah, it is rumored that he threatened to throw the scroll to the ground. Old Shloyme had been told, perhaps by his wife— or was it the police—that his children were Communists, that they believed the religion of their elders to be a form of alienation, a by-product of Czarist barbarity, and that rabbis were tools of bourgeois oppression. The venerable old man approached. His heart was heavy with both anger and sorrow, a deep, intimate sadness, for he felt that his education had somehow failed, that he had missed something along the way, through no fault of his own. Matès lowered his gaze as the patriarch drew nearer, but his blood was boiling.

This scene should sound familiar. You can find it in Alan Crosland's admirable *The Jazz Singer* (1927), film history's first talkie, which tells the story of a young jazz musician's revolt against his father, a cantor at the synagogue. To get an idea of the clash between Matès and old Shloyme, you need only substitute "Communism" for "jazz."

"How dare you bring Communism into my home?"

"You belong to yesterday's world! Tradition is fine, but times have changed. I'm going to live my life my way!"

There is a deeper truth to this fictitious dialogue: the "good-bye to God" referred to by Joseph Minc, who was born into a practicing Jewish family in Brest-Litovsk but joined the Party in 1924, at the age of sixteen.[30] Matès really did want to be Communist, and not Jewish. In prison, as one of the wardens explained at his trial, he wouldn't allow his fellow inmates to pray. In Buenos Aires, in the 1950s, Simje took up collections and organized meetings for the *Direkte Hilf,* The Jewish Committee for the Relief of War Victims, but he would not for all the world set foot in a synagogue. Even though the sons spoke Yiddish as did their fathers, they wanted to break free from the ghetto—as did their enemies the Zionists as well, by the way—and to embody a new generation: proud, free and toughened by the hard knocks of earlier times, they would be the sentinels of a world in the making.

But how easy is it to make a clean slate? At my request, Benito depicts his grandfather for me, the venerable Shloyme, whose *tefillin* he has inherited: "He was an ascetic, he made do with what he had. All five of his children were Communists, as were all their spouses. They were all ascetic too, in their own way. They talked about nothing but culture." Austerity and culture make for an interesting line of descent. One young Polish Jewish woman testifies: "I was the only girl in the family, and the only one to go over to Communism, despite my father's dire warnings that I was angering God, and that something terrible was going to happen to Jews as a result." And yet, "my father loved me. . . . He was proud to recognize in his daughter his own resoluteness."[31] I came across similar scenarios in the *Yizkor Bukh* itself: during the 1920s, in the wink of an eye, the young people of Parczew moved "from the prayer room to the Party, where they worked with such devotion and passion that even their elders had to look on with respect."[32]

Here they were, the new believers, the great faithful, the chosen people of the twentieth century! Their May Day celebrations would replace ancestral biblical holy days. Their ironclad discipline would replace the constraints of religion's rules and taboos. They, too, were studious and doctrinaire, uncompromising and orthodox. Their shadowy operations were Kabbalah-like in their mystery. Their faith surpassed even that of their fathers, their messianic zeal as strong as the one they had renounced; but this backhanded homage could manifest itself only through conflict. Like the prophets of old, they heralded universal harmony, but their prophesized redemption would save not only the children of Israel, but all of humanity, and in this world, not the next. Communism was the death and reincarnation of Judaism, the liberating heresy of these "non-Jewish Jews," as Isaac Deutscher says, of a whole line of revolutionaries, from Jesus to Trotsky by way of Spinoza, who cast off the shackles of religion to embrace universal truth, knowingly becoming pariahs persecuted by the very people they came to save.[33] Which brings me to this hypothesis, more plausible than the earlier one: Shloyme, the pious bathhouse guardian, did not repudiate his children. Not only did he accept their choices, but he shared in their ordeals. Matès's court file indicates that during his 1934 trial, his sixty-six-year-old father, "after being informed that he did not have to give evidence, said that he did wish to take the stand, and that the father remained present in the courtroom throughout the entire hearing." Was there even any conflict? The father was orthodox, like all those of his generation, and the son was Communist, like all the young people. It was nothing but a generation gap, nothing to get upset about.

But things were getting worse: during all of 1932 and into 1933, outsiders started calling upon the good folk of Parczew to join the revolution, hanging banners from the town's utility wires, playing cat and mouse with the police who would end their reports with the powerless but vaguely threatening statement: "Investigation ongoing."

On 21 January 1932, on the road between Parczew and Radzyń Podlaski, red cloth banners were deployed reading "Long Live the Revolutionary Struggle! Long Live the Celebration of the three L's: Lenin, Liebknecht, Luxemburg!"

On 30 May 1932, three new banners appeared: "Long Live the Red Army! Long Live the USSR! Long Live the Soviet Polish Republic!" They were signed by the Recruiting Committee of the Parczew KZMP.[34]

During the night of 15 to 16 May 1933, hanging from telephone wires on Church Street, a banner read: "Down with War against the USSR! Down with White Terror! Down with the Fascist Dictatorship of the Wretched Pilsudski!" This was also signed by the Parczew KZMP.

On the night of 30 August 1933, scrawled across a vendor's stall: "Long Live International Communist Youth Day!"

On the night of 19 December 1933, on Synagogue Street, hanging from the electricity wires: "Down with the Horrible Prystor Plan to Reduce Unemployment! Long Live the International Communist Revolution!" These were again signed by the KZMP, and again, there was an "investigation ongoing."[35]

These slogans, which could be read throughout the entire region—sometimes red on white background, other times white on red, usually in Polish, though sometimes in Ruthenian—reflected the Communist vision of the world: on one side, the "fascist" government of Pilsudski that starved the people and spread a reign of terror; and on the other, the freedom fighters who strove to forge a new Soviet republic, a way of reconciling the proletarian internationalism of Luxemburg and Trotsky with Stalin's policy of "socialism in one country." And yet, in May 1926, the KPP had supported Pilsudski's coup d'état, which was supposed to usher in the bourgeois stage of the revolution. It subsequently made up for its "May Error" by working with increasing zeal. In the early 1930s, right when Matès and Idesa were joining the movement, Poland was in the midst of a deep recession, as the government tabled social reforms, favored landowners, curtailed civil liberties and imprisoned opponents, while at the same time the Christian Democrats and the *Endeks* were stepping up their anti-Semitic propaganda. The treaty that protected minorities was rescinded.[36] Pilsudski remained quite popular despite the economic crisis, particularly among Jews, whom he had promised to protect.

It wasn't long before the police reacted, and in the summer of 1932, five young people aged fifteen to twenty-three were arrested. The detainees ended up informing on each other, and the report shows that it was Icek Sznajder who had hung the two banners signed by the KZMP. He denied everything, but the police investigators found red paint all over his clothes and hands, implicating him in the crime. The same inquiry revealed that the Parczew KZMP counted some 120 members, that its leader was a twenty-five-year-old saddler, that it had infiltrated the leatherworkers union, and that it answered to the Party's regional committee in Siedlce, where an underground printing operation churned out tracts, posters and newspapers.[37] As for the KPP itself, it was led by a twenty-eight-year-old peddler, Mayer Rapoport (Henya's future husband), and a thirty-nine-year-old merchant, Jojna Feder (an unknown brother of my grandmother's?).[38]

Radzyń Podlaski is a town not much larger than Parczew and just as inconsequential. Audrey parks in front of the castle. We have an appointment with the director of the archives, thanks to whom we have a promising lead: the proceedings of the Parczew police court, which is to say, of the most local court, in charge of petty cases such as slander or drunken brawls. We walk down into a basement area where the brick walls are covered in maps of Russia, and the furniture consists of a few Formica tables. It is four in the afternoon and the reading room is about to close. It's my last day in Poland; we're due back in Warsaw that evening, and will catch our flight the next morning. Audrey and I madly fill out the forms we need in order to consult the record books for 1931 and 1936: user name, date, research area, collection title, series, and article number. Ten minutes later, the clerk returns with boxes that he drops onto the table with a thud. We dig feverishly through the bundles, but time is running out and the archivist is already starting to look at his watch. A register with a black-and-white-marbled cover, *Repertorjum Kg. Sądu Grodzkiego w Parczewie*, 1933–1944. Table of contents. The J column. There are five references for Jablonka, four for 1933 alone. I go straight to that year, but the register is unwieldy and my trembling hands make it hard to handle. Here we are: page 57, case no. 538, recorded on 18 August 1933. Eighteen detainees, Matès Jablonka, Kuna Niski, Dawid Szklaz and others, article 251 of the Code of Criminal Law, the court has ruled that. . . . Audrey has scarcely enough time to read me the header before we're told we have to leave, closing time, and we've already been granted a fifteen-minute grace. The photocopies will arrive in Paris some time later.[39] The following paragraphs result from that source, cross-checked against confidential police reports on the "subversive trade union movement" in the region of Włodawa and against my grandfather's court file at the central Warsaw State Archives.

On 18 August 1933, Matès was arrested along with seventeen companions that he had allegedly trained for "a terrorist act against the members of a Zionist organization." It is unclear to me exactly what they were plotting, but their offense falls under article 251 of the Code of Criminal Law, which punishes any act of coercing someone else "through unlawful violence or threats."[40] One of the papers seized at his home lists Matès's grievances against Zionism: in 1932, near Jerusalem, Ben-Gurion had Arab laborers removed from work sites with the help of law enforcement and the British police; there were no Arab trades represented in the Histadrut, the central Jewish trade union; thousands of emigrants, taken in by the "preachers" who travelled the length and breadth of Poland peddling false hopes about the "land of good fortune," found nothing but squalor and misery and had to accept any work they could find to feed their families. Zionism, Matès goes on to say in those papers, "claims to be the answer to all the Jewish questions," where in fact it is nothing but a diversion based on an anachronism:[41] a Jewish state, the product of petit-bourgeois nationalism, would bring back the very exploitation and oppression that they were striving to eliminate. The real solution, altogether more realistic than Zionist fantasies, is revolution: universality versus Jewish alienation.

The Zionists were leading the Jewish proletariat astray, which explains why the Communists aimed their "terrorist acts" against them in particular. These attacks were commonplace in Parczew, as elsewhere. The *Yizkor Bukh* tells how Zionists and Communists would come to blows at weddings over where the auction money from the wedding cake would go: to the purchase of land in Palestine or to political prisoners? In the end, a compromise would usually be reached, a fifty-fifty split, but other quarrels were not always settled so amicably. In 1930, during the *Lag Ba-Omer* festivities, Zionists were assaulted by a gang of "trade unionists" wielding clubs and bottles of sand, a group that Matès, Hershl, Henya and others may well have already joined by then.[42]

The Parczew court sentenced Matès to six months in jail and a twenty-zloty fine, but his co-detainees were less severely punished: honor where honor is due! On 6 October 1933, Matès once again came before the judge, this time for "damage to another's property": was it a poster plastered to a shop front? The arrests were at times heated, as when Matès was charged with "insulting a civil servant" and sentenced to two months in jail.[43] Did he stand up to the police, as he had when the family bathhouse was shut down?

Thanks to the lengthy appeals process, Matès was still free. Trials, sentences, rumors about a godless, unpatriotic Communist, warnings from family members, from Simje in Buenos Aires and Reizl in Chelm: nothing seemed to work. Matès had his sights set on the "brighter tomorrow." And he proved particularly persuasive in that belief. A police report informs us that "on 18 November [1933] at 5 p.m., in Parczew, November 11th Street, Matès Jablonka, living at 33 Broad Street, member of the KZMP local committee, organized a Communist demonstration. Around forty young Jews took part. During the event, Matès Jablonka spoke to the crowd in Jewish; what he said remains to be determined. He also chanted the following slogans: 'Down with the government! Down with special tribunals! Down with the police! Long live Communism!'"[44]

This movement from "Jewish," or Yiddish, which the undercover police officer could not understand, to Polish, cited verbatim in the report, provides an important piece of information: although the speaker was bilingual, he harangued the crowd mainly in Yiddish. Lenin was convinced that Jews did not constitute a nationality, and since the KPP was a centralized organization in which individuals enjoyed no personal autonomy, the Polish Communist movement necessarily used Polish as its vehicle. But the Jewish street represented such potential as a revolutionary recruiting ground that in certain cases, it was deemed acceptable to wage propaganda campaigns in Yiddish.[45] Only a slight bending of the rules. This allowed the KPP to operate in Jewish circles, and this grassroots action was undertaken by local committees coordinated by a central Jewish bureau. In 1931, for instance, the Central Committee was so concerned by the Party's weak showing among the Jewish lower middle class and the impoverished masses that the central Jewish bureau received the order to step up its efforts by denouncing the closure of Jewish schools, condemning recent pogroms and so forth.[46] As a Communist, Matès was hostile to Jewish national aspirations, but he remained faithful to his mother tongue and empathized with the crowds he was addressing.

Behind the report's bureaucratic rhetoric, we can sense forty angry youths, including perhaps Idesa, Hershl, Henya, Mayer Rapoport, Icek Sznajder, Abram Fiszman and Malka Milechsberg, a modest assembly that the orator was able to arouse. What did he say exactly? The words themselves are lost to us. Perhaps he said something about the twilight of capitalist civilization, or about German speculators with their gang leader Hitler preparing for war. Perhaps he mentioned that labor strikes were breaking out all over Europe and America; that the Soviet Union was the only country in the world not experiencing economic instability or unemployment; that there were no more national divisions, no more anti-Semitism, no more profiteering; that no one went hungry and that illiteracy was disappearing; that the Five-Year Plan resulted in 20% annual growth, while production of coal, electricity, petroleum, steel, tractors, locomotives and grain were all increasing by leaps and bounds. He closed, one imagines, by declaring that the Soviet Union was a stronghold that we needed not only to defend, but to join, whatever the cost. He may have added that their comrades were dying of cold in the fort at Brisk, but that the fascist Pilsudski could never suppress revolution. The assembled crowd probably refrained from applauding, out of discretion, but they nodded in approval, eyes bright with excitement. The young leader then drove in the nail that sealed his fate, as the archive proves: "Down with the government! Down with special tribunals! Long live Communism!"

The report concludes thus: "On 20 November [1933], Matès Jablonka was arrested by the Parczew police, and on 21 November, was brought before the Parczew municipal court which, as a preventive measure, placed him under police surveillance requiring that he appear weekly at the local police station.[47]

Another page was added to Matès's police record when he was arrested for hanging banners during the night of 19 December 1933. The night prowler had been unmasked! Local detectives had finally gotten their hands on the elusive offender who had been creeping through the streets after dark to hang banners from the electrical wires. Several times over the course of 1933, Matès had accomplished this dangerous but thrilling mission. What was he feeling, late on some moonless night, as he aimed at the black wires strung across Synagogue Street in all its grimness, the same street I walk down now, heavyhearted, with Marek and Audrey? Did it feel like a prank played on the stuffy, reactionary bourgeoisie? On that subject, here is Louis Gronowski, born in 1904 near Włocławek, who entered the *kheyder* at six and the Young Communists at seventeen: "Among our group, there were some who were very good at getting red flags thrown over the electric wires, and took mischievous pleasure in watching the firemen on their ladders the next day trying to remove them."[48] Or was it a matter of pride, as with Moshe Zalcman, whose nocturnal task it was to distribute brochures and tracts to soldiers in their barracks on the eve of May Day celebrations? "Honored as I am to have been chosen for this mission, I am equally frightened by what it might entail. Every shadow looks like a policeman ready to pounce. But how relieved and happy I am once I have accomplished my duty!"[49]

Here is what Matès's banners looked like: a piece of red fabric, about 30" x 33", stretched across a wooden rod to which were attached wire hooks; the banner would unfurl once it hooked onto the electrical or telephone wires, with little terra cotta weights to keep it vertical.[50] The whole process of putting these together was relatively complex, and although one person could manage it, the work left behind definite traces. Thanks to a police investigation, we know that over the days preceding the operation of 19 December 1933, Matès had some terra cotta weights made and purchased ten *groszys'* worth of wire from a shopkeeper. After the banner was discovered on Synagogue Street, the merchant told the police that a "little Jew," a twenty-five-year-old redhead, had come to her shop and bought some wire, but she refused to say who he was[51] ("the boys from Matès Jablonka's organization threatened to kill her" said one witness at the trial). The police, who were now watching Matès like a hawk, conducted a search of the house on Broad

Street. There, they found six pages covered with notes about the success of the Five-Year Plan and Zionist misdeeds, an issue of the Yiddish workers' magazine *Trybune* dated October 1933, letters from Simje and Reizl begging their brother to cease his "technician" role, and most especially, two pieces of incontrovertible evidence: wooden rods like those used for making the banners, and in the oven, bits of terra cotta speckled with red paint.[52]

Matès was released, but not for long. On 27 February 1934, he was arrested along with Abram Fiszman, Colette's father, and six other militants, in another incident involving "damage to property."[53] A month later, Hershl, aged nineteen, and Henya, seventeen, the two youngest Jablonka siblings, were also swept up. On the afternoon of 4 April 1934, they interrupted a rally supporting the Balfour Declaration (the famous letter declaring Great Britain's agreement to create a "national Jewish homeland" in Palestine) by distributing anti-Zionist tracts from within the assembled crowd.[54] I laugh at the thought of Henya, wearing her charming little beret, causing a scene as she accuses the "Jewish imperialists" of colluding with the British to appropriate land that belongs to neither. But it was no laughing matter. For not only would these troublemakers pay dearly for their feat, not only would these internal struggles undermine a community already destabilized by economic hardship and mounting anti-Semitism, but the incident was also emblematic of the Communists' isolation, caught between the "bourgeois nationalist" Zionists, the Bundist "social traitors," and the "fascist" Pilsudski regime.

After his arrest on 27 February 1934, and because the appeals court had begun upholding a number of his previous convictions, Matès remained in prison, first in Parczew, then in Lublin, starting in April. I imagine that the *Rynek*—and perhaps the bathhouse, unless it had been shut down—were all abuzz with the news: "Have you heard that Shloyme's children are all behind bars?" "Their mother will die of a broken heart!" "*Oy vey*, everyone's going to start saying that all Jews are Bolsheviks again!" In the summer of 1934, Reizl, back from Chelm, went to visit Matès in prison, as did Gitla. In October, his lawyer, Karol Winawer, met him to discuss the upcoming trial, scheduled for 3 December 1934.[55]

The Winawer family boasted an illustrious line of freethinking politicians, journalists, writers, scientists and doctors. Former assistant to

Teodor Duracz, who defended Communists at the political trials during the interwar period—and was thus said to be in the pay of the Russians—Karol Winawer had his law practice in Warsaw, at 6 Szczygla Street. Working with the League of Human Rights (whose Polish branch was dissolved in 1937), he defended freedom of speech, fought against special tribunals and demanded amnesty for political prisoners. When it came to disclosing the inanity of police records, or disqualifying the testimony of informers, Winawer was second to none. His successor with Duracz described him in these terms: "Tall, youthful, very seductive, strong-nosed and greying a bit at the temples, always clean-shaven, with smiling eyes and a terrific sense of humor, he was one of the most pleasant people you could know, and perhaps the best political attorney I have ever met." In 1934, the year he defended Matès, Winawer pleaded at the Lutzk trial, in western Ukraine, on behalf of some Communist militants who had been imprisoned and mistreated for the previous three years.[56]

My grandfather's last trial took place on 3 December 1934 before the Lublin regional tribunal. He was accused of joining the KPP with the purpose of overthrowing the regime by violent means. Regrettably, I know nothing of what Matès must have been feeling at the time. To fill that gap, I'll refer to *Memoirs of a Jewish Revolutionary* by Hersh Mendel, born into the squalor of Jewish Warsaw and arrested in 1912 by the Okhrana, the Czar's secret police. Twenty years a Bundist, he awaited the trial with anxious excitement, "for this was, after all, my first appearance before the public. For the first time, I would have to speak. A confession, of course, was out of the question; going to trial demanded that I bear myself with honor, as was befitting a young revolutionary." In his cell, Hersh Mendel thought about people on the outside, and wondered whether they realized that men and women voluntarily gave up their freedom so that they, and the whole world, might be free. In preparation for the trial, he managed to shave, using a fastener from his jacket. When the big day arrived, he was well turned out, in a shirt and tie.[57]

A few random documents from my grandfather's court record make it possible to reconstruct a vague version of the hearing. Old Shloyme was present, with elderly and ailing Tauba at his side, along with Reizl and Gitla (Hershl and Henya, already in prison themselves, would be tried the following day, while Simje had already left for Argentina). The police described Matès as a "notorious Communist activist," a KPP member as well as a *technik* for the KZMP. He was accused of haranguing a group of forty young people and hanging a banner on Synagogue Street. Matès stubbornly denied the charges: the wooden rod found at his home was nothing but some old stick, he had no idea where the notes and the magazine also found there had come from, and so forth. As for his codefendant, Kuna Niski, he affirmed that he "didn't even know what the Communist Party is." The judges took into account the age of the defendants, but noted that Matès had proved "very politically active" and that he had indoctrinated young people into taking the path of violence. Thus, according to the fearsome articles 93 to 97 of the Code of Criminal Law, which punished "crimes against the state" that threatened Poland's independence or aimed to overthrow its institutions, Matès was sentenced to five years in prison and suspension of his civil rights (a sentence that would be upheld on appeal in February 1935). As for Kuna Niski, he was acquitted for lack of evidence.[58] The following day, by virtue of the same articles, Hershl and Henya were sentenced to a year in prison. They would be released after four months, in April 1935.

After the arrest of Matès and the others, one might have thought that the Parczew KZMP was left without leadership. But by spring 1934, my grandmother had stepped in to replace her sweetheart as the local cell's "technician." The charges that were made against her less than a year later allow us to piece together her activities until then.[59] In early 1935, a Party comrade brought her seventy posters calling for the "strengthening of revolutionary ranks" and the "fight against the fascist, reactionary, retrograde government." Among the lot, some also called upon the *Zukunft* Bundists and young peasant organizations to come together in a united front against Pilsudski. Zealous *technik* that she was, Idesa took it upon herself to spread the propaganda material through which the KZMP was echoing the left's new unification strategy, as defined by Bukharin and Stalin in 1934, after the Nazi victory in Germany. The socialists, Bundists and peasants, formerly castigated as "social traitors," were now the strongest allies against fascism (unlike in Spain and France, the Popular Front strategy ultimately failed in Poland, the Socialist Party and the Bund fearing infiltration by the Communists and demanding that the latter break with Moscow).[60]

On 13 January 1935, Idesa entrusted Hershl-Mendel Szlakow with two posters, while another two went to Szapsel Rojzman; they were to go paste them up after nightfall. The indictment continues with the testimony of a policeman: "On 14 January 1935, in the Parczew district of Włodawa, the policeman Niziolka was walking along the *Rynek* when he noticed something on the wall of Hippolyte Wasik's shop: a Communist poster bearing the KZMP header, addressing the young peasantry of the Siedlce region and surroundings. . . . As he kept walking down November 11th Street, the same policeman Niziolka noticed another identical poster on the walls of the fire station." Thanks to testimony by an informer (Colette's parents feared these "provocateurs," false militants who infiltrated the organization in order to give it away), the police steered its investigation toward Idesa. During a house search, all the posters were seized, as well as some tracts and brochures. The police also came across something in the shop: "two handcrafted notebooks made out of heavy green paper, machine-stitched and numbered 17 to 31 and 47 to 60. On each page was a round stamp and something written in ink at the bottom of the page." What were these notebooks all about? It remains a mystery. Idesa was immediately taken into custody.

On 18 June 1935, the itinerant Lublin regional tribunal, holding session in Parczew, opened the trial of Idesa, twenty-one years old, daughter of Moyshe Feder and Rushla Korenbaum. The tribunal was composed of three magistrates. Witnesses, including Niziolka, appeared one by one at the bar. The policeman Masiukiewicz praised the accused in spite of himself when he declared that the defendant, a KZMP *technik*, was one of the most prominent militants in Parczew. The young woman retorted that she had never belonged to any political movement and that she had no idea where the posters could have come from. One of the judges countered:

> The statement by the defendant Idesa Feder in which she claims that the posters somehow entered her house without her knowledge does not correspond to the evidence in the case. The fact that everyone has access to the hallway, as asserted by the witnesses Wertman, Bawnik and Rushla Feder, in no way invalidates the previous conclusions, since it is hard to conceive that a fellow Party member would have dropped off such

documents unbeknownst to the occupant, a known militant Communist under constant police surveillance.

Found guilty of a "crime against the state," in accordance with articles 93 to 97 of the Code of Criminal Law, Idesa was sentenced to five years in prison and fined 320 zlotys. However, because of her young age and clean prior record, the court agreed to lighten the sentence.[61]

Matès and Idesa, Hershl and Henya, as well as Icek Sznajder, who was sentenced to six years in February 1933, and Abram Fiszman, sentenced to thirteen months, were to join the approximately 17,000 political prisoners incarcerated in Poland at that time. Lives destroyed for hanging banners and storing posters. Granting free rein to my empathy, I will say that they were all victims of the young, authoritarian, antisocial republic; of the Code of Criminal Law tailored to destroy the opposition; of the special tribunals denounced by the KZMP banners as veritable emblems of repression and abuse of power. I will add to that list Pilsudski's unfortunate drift toward authoritarianism, Pilsudski himself having been a revolutionary sentenced to five years of hard labor in his youth, a socialist leader and the father of Polish independence, but much too comfortable in his dictator's uniform bristling with medals. In January 1934, rather than forming an alliance with the Soviet Union, he signed a nonaggression pact with Hitler's Germany. In June, he opened the Bereza Kartuska camp in order to intern Communists and Ukrainian nationalists. But from a different angle, one might also say that these jail sentences were the most effective way of containing those young hotheads who yearned to have pluralist Poland absorbed by Stalin's USSR.

The prison years, then. Idesa would be spending her twenty-second birthday in jail, one week after France's *Front Populaire* celebrated its victory.

Polish jails were places of suffering. Inherent in the sentence itself were the absence of freedom, poor living conditions and lack of privacy, but there was also suffering inflicted for a purpose. To psychologically break the inmates, the authorities constantly moved them from one prison to another, as far as possible from their families. As *Tía* Reizl told my father at the *geriatrico*, where she was peacefully finishing out her days, Matès was first incarcerated in Lublin before being transferred to the other side of the country, which meant she was unable to pay him one last visit—and it would have been the final one—before leaving for Argentina. Matès's file shows that he did time in four different locales: from Parczew, he was transferred to Lublin, then to Wronki, some 400 miles from Parczew, and finally to Sieradz, 217 miles from Parczew.

His file also contains a petition he sent from Sieradz, on 18 August 1936, to the head prosecutor at the Poznan appeals court:

> Over the two months I have spent in this prison, I have observed a steady worsening of the food served. At lunch and dinner, I usually get nothing but a liter of watered-down soup. On other days, I don't even get that much, since the meal consists of a half-liter of watery soup and about a fourth of a liter of plain potatoes. The bread, often underbaked and full of sand, causes all sorts of stomach problems. Last month, for two entire weeks, we got nothing but herring, and for a six-week stretch, they stopped giving us our Sunday portion of meat, which we used to get every other week. I get water on an irregular basis, no more than three or four times a week, and even then, in very small quantities, one to one and a half liters for [illegible] people. This deterioration of the prisoners' diet has recently caused me to suffer dizzy spells. Three months ago, an official decision came down calling for wire screens at the visiting station. Given that a trip by family members involves considerable expense and needless hardship, matters are only made worse by installing barriers between me and my family members, making their trip hardly worth all the time and effort.[62]

Is Matès exaggerating here to attract the prosecutor's attention, or did he endure even more hardships than either his petition or his court record make known? In their memoirs, all Polish political prisoners speak of violence, whether at the time of arrest or once behind bars. In the mid-1920s, Hersh Mendel, in charge of the KPP central Jewish bureau and member of the Revolutionary Military Committee, was jailed in Grodno. The food was awful: the rice and barley were swarming with maggots and the bread, under its charred crust, was still raw dough. Prisoners from Bialystok gave accounts of how prison guards would force them to rape their female fellow prisoners who were tied up naked on the ground. Hersh Mendel confirmed as much: "These very same women comrades, in fact, soon arrived as well and were in the depths of depression."[63] In June 1933, Gitla Leszcz, a young Jewish Communist, was arrested in Dębowa-Kłoda, not far from Parczew, after the police discovered tracts hidden in a bale of hay next to her house.

> The officers who came for me made me walk the whole way from Dębowa to Pinsk, and at every police station where we stopped, I was beaten and insulted. I arrived at Kowel completely exhausted and with bleeding feet, since I had walked the whole distance barefoot. The real tortures, however, started at the Kowel prison: they pulled out some of my fingernails, and the scars are still visible today. They put live coals on my legs. This torture went on for three days and three nights. They beat me on the back with a board, so that there would be no marks, until I began bleeding from my nose, mouth and ears.[64]

There is every reason to believe that Idesa met the same fate.

All this torture had but one purpose: to break the inmates' spirit, to maintain them in a state of utter dependence and wretchedness. Within this context, Matès's petition gives evidence of a certain feistiness. Another sign of resistance comes to us through a prison guard's complaint: during his detention in Parczew, Matès was constantly praising the Soviet system and defiantly organizing hunger strikes (all the while forbidding his fellow Jewish inmates to pray).[65] On 20 March 1934, he had his mattress taken away, as punishment for "constant insubordination." In Lublin, a few days after the verdict, the prosecutor granted his request for an audience with his younger sister Henya, who was being held in the same prison. At Sieradz, his conduct was seen as "appalling" throughout his entire incarceration: inmate Jablonka "showed solidarity with other Communists."[66]

Inside, political prisoners extracted from administrators the right to organize into a *komuna*, a group granted certain privileges: work exemptions, longer walks, visiting rights, permission to receive packages. Henya suffered from hunger, her daughter told me, as we walked among the graves at the cemetery where she is buried in the little town of Hadera, north of Tel Aviv. In a photograph taken in November 1936, a few months after her release, she looks gaunt, her hair cut like a boy's, a ghostly figure. When she was jailed again in 1939, she didn't even have a change of clothes. Her mother, Tauba, "the dove," managed to get some to her. The girls in the *komuna* demanded that she share them, but in violation of discipline, Henya refused, pointing out how much her mother must have sacrificed. But everywhere else, solidarity ruled. Many inmates had little formal education, so those with more schooling behind them helped the others. Together, they read the classics, learned about Darwinian theory and Marxist-Leninist economics, explored the French and Russian revolutions, perfected their Polish and dreamed of the socialist society to come. At this rate, Abram Fiszman learned more than he had in ten years on the outside. (Colette is convinced that Matès was with him at that point.)

Knowing that any Communist was liable to end up in prison at some point, most considered the incarceration as a necessary risk, an important stage or even a test, a career move, in a way. The convicted became the chosen ones. Prison did not break them, but instead hardened them and made them all the more determined, if that were possible. Transferred to Wilno, Hersh Mendel lectured his fellow inmates on Marxist doctrine, brought out a monthly publication in Belarusian and Yiddish, and marked the anniversary of the October Revolution with garlands and portraits of Lenin. As their hunger strike dragged on, the police took them to the hospital to be force-fed through a tube directly into the stomach. "Those who refused to open their mouths had their teeth knocked out with the nozzle."[67] With its study groups and thirst for knowledge, the *komuna* had something of the yeshiva about it, even though, alongside all those Jews, there were Belarusians and Ukrainians struggling against Polish occupation. Fraternity and mutual support prevailed over any anti-Semitism.

Thanks to an amnesty law, Matès was able to leave Sieradz on 8 December 1936, after two and a half years of detention. He was given three days to get home, some 220 miles away: his release papers specified that "he is to declare his presence at the Włodawa police station by 11 December 1936 at the latest."[68] As for Idesa, she was released in early 1937 "due to a mental illness contracted while in prison."[69] Today, we would call it a nervous breakdown. In light of the testimony I have presented, one can only imagine what she must have endured.

I wish the story could have stopped there: my grandparents were victims of a dictatorship, suffering unspeakable hardship for the sake of their lofty ideals, their love of humanity. The self-sacrifice and generosity that landed them in prison are indeed admirable. Even the apparently more moderate Simje and Reizl did not give up on their dreams when they immigrated to Argentina, land of opportunity: like them, their children would be Communists, opponents of dictatorship. Mauricio, Reizl's son, a stocky seventy-two-year-old with a fine, white moustache, joins us with his wife on their sunlit terrace to drink some yerba mate. I switch on my laptop and begin our interview. Mauricio was arrested in October 1974, under the government legally in power, the same night as hundreds of militant Communists and Peronists throughout the country. State of emergency declared. Parana Prison; Gualeguaychú high-security prison. No visits, no letters, no books. The Videla dictatorship. Repression, torture, summary executions. Transfer to the Resistancia federal prison, flown handcuffed to the floor of a military plane, at the mercy of the soldiers who, it is well known, would often eject their prisoners into the void.

One day, Reizl decided to go to Gualeguaychú, where she was told that visits were not authorized. Reizl replied that she would wait, determined that she was going to see her son—the same Reizl who, forty years earlier, had gone to see Matès at the Lublin prison; Reizl, who, had her son been one of the unfortunate prisoners thrown from a plane, would have become one of the Mothers of the Plaza de Mayo. In the end, they granted her ten minutes with her son. I ask Mauricio whether he ever began to have doubts, alone in prison, far from family and the world. No, never: we were sure of our ideas, we knew that Communism was the best possible option, and we never budged on that. A revolutionary does not doubt, is never afraid. Many people have made this choice. We don't think of ourselves as heroes. We take action, that's all.

Benito, Simje's son, takes me for a walk in Buenos Aires. We visit the Recoleta cemetery, burial place of Evita Peron, champion of the poor. "All the country's reactionaries are buried here," sighs Benito, dismissing with a sweep of his hand all the little shrines. Even if *Tío* Simje didn't devote his life to revolution the way Matès had, at least he taught his children to be good Communists, told them all about the October Revolution, the International Brigades, the Red Army, and Sputnik. Benito feels he has always been a Communist, that he was "born Communist." He joined the

Communist Youth at age fifteen and was jailed three times—four months in 1956 for criticizing the military government, one month in 1958 for subversive activities and four months in 1969 for anti-government propaganda. He even went to Moscow for schooling in Marxist-Leninist theory.

On his way back from his visits to the USSR, Benito would often make a stopover in Paris. One day in the late 1980s, he dropped by our place, completely dejected. "The professors say that Communism is over," he explained. "We South American students end up defending Communism against our teachers. No one in the Central Committee believes in anything anymore. They say that Communist ideals are better fulfilled in capitalist countries, that the Soviet Union has lost the scientific and technological battle."

Benito asked my father if all that was true. My father nodded. Benito remained silent. He had devoted his entire life to Communism, his energy, leisure time, weekends, for forty years. Could it be that he had been wrong all along? My father was a militant throughout the 1950s and long after the 1968 invasion of Czechoslovakia. I think it lasted all the way up to Mitterrand's election. "The Party was my family, my religion."

Here we are now, Benito, his sister and I, sitting at an outdoor table in one of Recoleta's choicest cafes, in the shade of the giant *ombú* tree. Benito asks me about France, about President Sarkozy: "When are people finally going to have their revolution?" I tell him that my book is about the heroes of the twentieth century, those who gave their lives to change humanity and society. Benito wonders who is going to make revolution today, destroy "reactionary capitalism," *cambiar la vida*, to change life for the better. I put my hand on his shoulder, but he protests: "We can't live without utopia! Everyone needs to hope!" Would my grandfather have also said, in his waning years, that "the idea is good but the implementation was bad"? Would he have constantly been talking "revolution," dizzy with the power of the word?

In 1950s Poland, politically inexperienced young people made up 80% of the Party faithful, but the old guard of the KPP and the KZMP constituted the hard core.[70] Jakub Berman, head of the Communist Youth in 1925, would become a member of the Politburo, where he was in charge of culture, propaganda and security, by the time he was twenty-four.[71] Adam Rayski, a Communist from the age of seventeen, secretary of the Bialystok

Komsomol and French resistance fighter within the MOI during World War II, returned to Poland and became president of the Committee on Press Publications. At the helm of this colossal structure that incorporated all the country's newspapers, photo agencies and printers, he embodied Poland's "freedom of the press" under Stalin.[72]

Poland's Communist Jews suffered bitter disappointments, but it was anti-Semitism that finally did them in. In the early 1950s, under President Bierut, anti-Jewish purges took place within the Party, the army and the civil service, and files were kept on Jews who had assumed Polish names. Jakub Berman was expelled from the Party as a "leader in the period of error and deviationist tendencies." The years 1967 to 1968 were marked by Władysław Gomułka's "fifth column" speech, part of a larger campaign against the "Zionists," that included further purges in all sectors and the dismantling of Jewish newspapers, schools, publishing houses and co-operatives, resulting in some 25,000 Jews leaving the country. Longtime Communist Jews were suddenly being vilified, ostracized, hounded out of their jobs and out of the Party, forced into exile. They were accused of betraying their country, as in the 1930s, but this time around, their comrades were in power. Thus, so late in life, these old Jews had to pack up and move, some to Israel, joining the "Zionist reactionaries," others to Western Europe among the "capitalist class enemies." These departures mark the end of a generation, the last chapter of the epic story that started in the Parczew shtetl, district of Włodawa, voivodeship of Lublin, whose protagonists were Matès Jablonka and Idesa Korenbaum-Feder, Hershl and Henya Jablonka, Mayer Rapoport, Icek Sznajder, with his paint-spattered coat lining, Abram Fiszman, father of Colette and Szapsel Rojzman, who on the night of 13 to 14 January 1935, ran the risk of a long prison sentence for his efforts to convince young peasants to join the united front.

My grandparents were both heroes and victims. Matès, with his 1936 petition to the Poznan appeals court, embodied the unbreakable spirit and dignity of man in the face of oppression. But should I be translating Colette's description—"your grandfather was a hard-core Marxist"—into the terms of Hannah Arendt, who spoke of fanatically inflexible militants, both gullible and cynical, brainwashed to the point of losing any trace of humanity or judgment?[73] Arthur Koestler is equally harsh in his *Darkness at Noon*: for Stalin's torturers as well as the old Bolsheviks they tormented, life was not supposed to be a "metaphysical brothel for emotions." Sympathy, friendship, love, nostalgia, repentance, all of that was mysticism, bourgeois rubbish. Have I the right to say that the Parczew revolutionaries paved the way for Bierut's Stalinist-style dictatorship?

I will not claim that right. There is no continuity between the hopes of 1933 and the repression of 1953. These modern-day Prometheans were seeking to break with the status quo and unleash the blessing of freedom in all its forms. It would be entirely too smug of us to assert, with ironclad certainty and the benefit of a century's hindsight, that the horrors to come had already been germinating, like the worm in the apple. And it would be an illusion to think that their aspirations were an illusion. Much more than a petty Party boss or some gutless ideologue, Matès was a son, a brother, a comrade, a boy in love, a man outraged by injustice. But what continues to haunt me is that, unbeknownst to him, his freedom and his voice were being poisoned by totalitarianism.

3

A MORE

"CIVILIZED"

ANTI-SEMITISM

The idea of doing a study of my grandparents goes back to 2007. The project took shape quickly: I would be writing the story of their history, or rather, a history book of their story, based on archival material, interviews, book sources, to which I would add contextual background and sociological perspectives. All of this would allow me *to get to know them*. As a narrative of their lives and a record of my investigation, it would bring them to light, not to life. More than their tragic end, it is their journey I was interested in, and our inconsolable grief would have no other expression than the desire to know. Thus began my feverish immersion into the archival holdings of France, Poland and elsewhere, in which I have striven to cast the broadest net possible, for a biography must provide for comparison among individuals: like the study of snow, it must reveal the driving force of an avalanche and the irreducible delicacy of a single snowflake. The firsthand witnesses are almost all dead, but what about the next generation? Has my grandparents' memory been channeled through the children of their siblings, through cousins, friends and neighbors?

For weeks on end, I go to my parents' to interview my father. He shows me photos and letters, which he carefully removes from their plastic sleeves, kept in a file. I drill him with questions, and he tells me whatever he can, which is practically nothing: the siblings, the bathhouse shut down by the police, beautiful Idesa, lovesick Matès and his five years in prison, the exile to France in the late 1930s. Here, we cross into the most familiar territory of our family history. My father was born in Paris in 1940, as was his sister the previous year. Was I not also born in Paris, as were my brother and cousin? We are all "French of Polish origin." We pore over the three letters in Yiddish written in the hand of Matès and Idesa, addressed to Simje and Reizl in Argentina. My father reads through the notes he jotted down many years before as he sat listening to *Tía* Reizl tell her stories. One particular line had escaped him. "Matès in Paris for YKUF convention."

I immediately get excited about this YKUF, which looks to me like a kind of Ellis Island, the gate through which waves of immigrants poured in. In fact, YKUF stands for *Yidishèr kultur-farband*, or Union for Yiddish Culture, a leftist Jewish organization that branched out after the war all the way to Latin America. After a quick web search, I find out that the YKUF was created at the World Congress for the Defense of Jewish Culture, held in Paris, from 17 to 21 September 1937, amidst the brotherly atmosphere of the *Front Populaire*. Hoping to lay my hands on the Congress's proceedings, I go over to the Medem Center, a Yiddish cultural association located behind Place de la République in Paris, on the first floor of a Haussmann-era building. The apartment is out of a bygone time, with black-and-white portraits of promoters of the Yiddish language, information bulletins thumbtacked to cork boards, and posters for concerts and conferences that took place years ago. I am shown into the library, all the way at the back of the apartment, at the end of a hallway leading to an office—where Bernard will later translate the Parczew *Yizkor Bukh* for me—and to a room where some elderly folks sitting around a U-shaped table watch as I pass, wondering no doubt what in the world I am doing there. That day, Erez is on duty, a young scholar fluent in Yiddish, Hebrew and German. He brings me the proceedings and leaves me to make sense of them on my own.

Photographs show an attentive audience, the podium, various speakers posing in front of a portrait of three elders. (Later, I will learn that they are the fathers of Yiddish literature: I. L. Peretz, the mustachioed Jewish goy torn between tradition and modernity; Mendele Moykher-Sforim, the portrayer of Jewish indigence; and Sholem Aleichem, who made fun of the lowly shtetl people but made us love them in spite of their failures, who brought out the universality of their misfortune.) After scouring every photo in search of Matès, I sit idle, waiting for help. My grandparents' language is utterly foreign to me. Erez takes pity on me, offering his assistance.

The World Congress for the Defense of Jewish Culture opened in Paris on 17 September 1937, at Wagram Hall, before a crowd of some 4,000 attendees. With Nazism rapidly on the rise, and Jews being physically assaulted in Germany and Eastern Europe, anti-fascism and the defense of Yiddish went hand in hand. This was the message delivered by attorney Chaim Sloves, Congress Secretary and the very soul of this "Jewish Cultural Front," in his opening address. Behind the podium sat the greatest minds of Yiddishland, intellectuals, writers, literary critics, the poet Shulstein, the journalist Wolf Wieviorka, all come to express their love for a language that some would call a mere dialect. The following day, a Saturday (the organizers were clearly not religious), they celebrated the vitality of Yiddish culture; on Sunday, panels debated the subject of Yiddish theater, of science in Yiddish, of Yiddish schools and Jewish art.[1] The event was a total success: 104 delegations from twenty-three countries the world over were in attendance, from Uruguay to Estonia, from Brazil and South Africa to Denmark and Czechoslovakia, and of course, the United States and Poland, whose delegation alone represented eighty-two institutions. But the only true friend was absent. Playwright and poet H. Leivick came to the podium and gravely deplored this empty seat: "Sitting here are the representatives of our tragic existence. Only one chair remains unoccupied, the one where the delegate of the Soviet Union's new Jewish culture should be sitting today. He is not here, he did not come."[2]

What the hundreds of Communist Jews in the audience could not have imagined was that, at the very moment that H. Leivick was delivering his speech, the Stalinist terror campaign was raging at full tilt, with its sweeping purges, arrests and executions by the tens of thousands. Nor did they know that this terror was anti-Semitic in nature, leading to the closure of Jewish schools in the USSR, the disappearance of Yiddish newspapers in Moscow, Kharkov and Minsk, and to the execution of numerous Jewish intellectuals and militants. The Jewish section of the Bolshevik Party, the *Yevsektia*, had been dissolved a few years earlier, its leaders dispatched as "Trotskyists" or "Bundists." The autonomous region of Birobidzhan in Siberia, reputedly a Jewish paradise, turned out to have been a sinister deception. How can I be sure that Matès was there that day to hear H. Leivick speak? Why would he have been attending the event that founded the YKUF, when he could have been building a new society where Jews would at last have their place? Why France and not the Soviet Union?

And, first of all, why did Matès leave Poland? By that, I mean: why in 1937, not before or after? The obvious answer is that life had become unlivable. After World War I, under pressure from President Wilson and the Allies, Poland had granted rights to national minorities, to Jews but also to Germans, Ukrainians and Belarusians. While the Polish parties were outraged by this diktat, many Jews were enticed by the possibility of being acknowledged as a full-fledged nationality as opposed to a foreign body to be expelled. In December 1918, the Zionists organized a National Congress of Polish Jews, where discussions touched on Jewish autonomy as well as civil and cultural rights.[3] These aspirations were unacceptable not only to the anti-Semites of the National Democracy party, the *Endeks*, but also to other parties that favored a nation-state on the French model. Throughout the entire Second Republic, the government, the various parties and the Catholic Church were accusing Jews of undermining national sovereignty by creating a state within the state, even though the Jews, unlike other minorities, never challenged Poland's territorial integrity and, with the exception of the Communists, remained devoted to their homeland. This exclusionary nationalism, which leaves no room for anyone who is not "ethnically Polish," only served to exacerbate traditional anti-Semitism, whether of religious or economic origin.[4]

The plight of the Jews worsened after Pilsudski's death in May 1935. The country's new strongman was Marshal Rydz-Śmigły, one of the architects of the "miracle on the Vistula," inspector general of the army, seconded by Foreign Minister Józef Beck and a coterie of colonels. Rydz-Śmigły, dubbed "The Little Polish Führer" due to the personality cult surrounding him, managed to acquire roughly 390 square miles and 230,000 inhabitants from Czechoslovakia, recently carved up by Hitler. The Camp of National Unity (OZN), a close ally of the regime, overtly advocated the "polonization" of socioeconomic life, or more to the point, the exclusion of Jews and minorities.[5] Increasingly susceptible to the *Endeks'* nationalist and anti-Semitic propaganda, the regime led Poland down the slippery slope to fascism, belatedly vindicating the KZMP banners.

This turn of events, in combination with the economic crisis, served to fan the fires of anti-Semitism: boycotts, looting, bloody skirmishes at universities, killings. During the second half of 1936, there were 197 assaults, 39 murders, over 1,200 wounded and 2,067 cases of smashed storefronts. Pogroms broke out in Odrzywol (November 1935), Czyzew (December 1935), Przytyk (March 1936), Minsk Mazowiecki (June 1936), Brest-Litovsk (May 1937) and Częstochowa (June 1937).[6] The press lashed out against the Jewish victims, and the murderers used their court trials to propagate their ideas. The government distanced itself from these acts of violence, in favor of a more "civilized" anti-Semitism: altering the electoral system to prevent Jews from running for office, imposing limitations on ritual slaughter, enforcing *numerus clausus* quotas in universities, de-Judaizing industries and trades by means of discriminatory taxes, etc. In August 1936, Poland asked the League of Nations for colonies where it could send all its Jews. Colonel Beck pressured France and Great Britain to make their colonies available as a "dumping ground" for this unwanted population. That fall, Blum (the French Prime Minister) and his foreign minister broached the subject with Beck, causing much jubilation in Warsaw, but France was planning to resettle only a few dozen families among the refugees already present on French soil.[7] Meanwhile, the *Endeks*, propelled by the young pro-Nazi generation, were calling for the expulsion of all Jews from Poland, where the

OZN launched a poster campaign throughout the country with signs reading "Don't Buy from Jews" and "A Poland without Jews Is a Free Poland."[8]

Nothing provides a better reflection of these twilight years than the photographs of Roman Vishniac. From 1936 to 1938, sensing that Nazism was beginning to cast its shadow across Europe, this Russian Jew living in exile in Berlin travelled the length and breadth of Eastern Europe to capture images of tinkers, water carriers, bagel vendors, students studying by lamplight, homeless old men wandering the streets, children wide-eyed with hunger. Of his 16,000 negatives, only 2,000 have survived, the rest having been confiscated by the authorities.

Warsaw, 1937. An old man, whose beard fails to mask his sunken cheeks, sits in a sort of makeshift cart. Here is Vishniac's note: "This man lost his legs in a Russian pogrom thirty years before. . . . Every day, before searching for work, [his son, a porter] brought his father out to the street and gave him bread and water for the day."

Uzhgorod, Ukraine, 1937. A four-year-old girl gazes out at us through a steamy window. She has to stay indoors all winter, for there is no money to buy her shoes.

Warsaw, 1937. An elderly Jewish couple in the street, deep in conversation. The man has his hand on his heart, the woman is holding her cheek. The man has just been fired from his job. "The owner had been well satisfied with him for twenty years, but that morning, three men came to the office to check whether any Jews were employed there. He was immediately dismissed, with no compensation and no hope of another job."[9]

Now let us make our way to the other end of Yiddishland, to Parczew. Matès and Idesa have just been released from prison. He has gone home to his parents' on Broad Street, and she has gone back to her mother's, the house whose vestibule had served as a cache for the seventy posters. What happened while they were gone? Nothing special, life as it had always been. The Peretz library served as a makeshift theater, the Zionists organized dances and concerts. The local Hapoel was used to stage a hit performance of *A Mother's Heart*, before an audience of 200 people. Yes, but what was really going on? In fact, the struggle never relented. In April 1935, the KZMP raised a banner on Synagogue Street that read "Long Live the First of May!" and "Down with the War against the USSR!" and "Down with the Fascist and Bloody Pilsudski Regime!" and "Free the Political Prisoners!" On 1 May 1936, the Workers Athletic Association called for a defense of peace against the Third Reich, which had its eye on Upper Silesia, and against Italy, on its way to conquering Ethiopia.[10]

And what about the goyim? Their hatred never abated. Assaults, bomb attacks, killings and pogroms throughout the country. The Przytyk pogrom in March 1936 aroused great concern.

Here is an excerpt from a confidential report dated 2 July 1936 on the activity of ethnic minorities in the district of Włodawa: the Jews were continuing to participate in national festivities (Constitution Day on 3 May, the anniversary of Pilsudski's death on 12 May), but less enthusiastically than in previous years, since they were no longer allowed to wear uniforms or decorations. "However, in certain places, such as Parczew, Jewish organizations did not take part at all, for fear of deepening the already existing hostility and ill will that the Polish population displayed toward them."[11]

Another excerpt, this one from a report dated 2 July 1936, also on the activity of ethnic minorities in the district of Włodawa:

> On 30 June, in towns and villages with a high concentration of Jews, in Włodawa, Parczew, Ostrow, Siedlce, Wisznice and Slavutych, in protest against anti-Jewish acts [in Przytyk], Jewish merchants, craftsmen and laborers took part in a "protest strike" by closing their shops and stopping work for two hours, between noon and 2 p.m. The orthodox Jews represented the strike as a protest against anti-Jewish persecution perpetrated by irresponsible locals, but for the Zionists and the others, it was a protest against what they felt to be a far too "diplomatic" ruling after the events of Przytyk. Particularly in evidence was the unanimous solidarity among the Jews, beyond any political differences, and this included the Communists. The Catholic, Polish and Ruthenian population reacted quite negatively to this strike action, which meant that, in places where boycotting Jews had never been an issue, such as Włodawa, certain Christians rallied their people to react to the Jewish strike by refusing to patronize Jewish businesses. This negative reaction on the part of the Christians resulted from the closure of Jewish shops, which represent up to 95% of businesses in the towns mentioned, bringing all commercial

activity to a complete halt for a period of two hours. More so than all the propaganda generated by the [nationalist party] *Stronnictwo Narodowe*, this event reminded the peasant and worker population, who came into the towns but were unable to make their purchases, that businesses were being run almost exclusively by Jews. It was generally agreed among the Christian population that it was up to the government to take strenuous measures against this kind of agitation. It is worth noting that shops closed everywhere except in Parczew, where it happened to be market day. Jewish merchants, for fear that such a strike would provide an excuse for further anti-Jewish violence, kept their shops open between noon and two, but behind closed doors. There was no public disorder.[12]

I am dumbfounded to learn all this, thanks to Audrey, whom I ask to repeat the whole passage to make sure I have not misunderstood: in 1936, with the country going after its eternal scapegoats, Parczew was cited by name as the most anti-Semitic of the whole region, the place where Jews didn't even dare go on strike or appear at official ceremonies. As early as 20 August 1932, four militants from the Greater Poland Party, among them a student from Lwów Polytechnic, home for summer vacation, touched off anti-Semitic violence in Parczew.[13] In the same vein, the *Yizkor Bukh* tells of the kidnapping and attempted forced conversion of a young Jewish girl, which was foiled by Gedalia, the Hebrew teacher, with the help of a few brawny boys.[14] All of this foreshadows the postwar pogrom of 1946 and the synagogue-turned-secondhand shop in the 2000s, and provides further evidence for the argument that Polish Jews in the interwar period were teetering on the "edge of destruction."[15]

After Matès and Idesa's return, new protests took place, this time against the Brest-Litovsk pogrom. On 24 May 1937, Parczew's Jewish merchants shuttered their shops between noon and 2. In Slavutych, a strike broke out, followed by a collection to help the victims of the pogrom. Throughout the region, Jews were starting to stay away from official ceremonies. On 19 November, there were further protests in Parczew, initiated by the head of the Jewish community, Rakhmiel Sherter (the future president of the *Judenrat*): grocery stores all opened an hour late, at 8:10 instead of 7:00.[16] Communists were no longer the only agitators.

The situation of Jews living in big cities and shtetls was worsened by the economic crisis, boycotting campaigns and state-sponsored anti-Semitism. During the 1930s, 40% of the Jews of Lodz were out of work. The law requiring shops to close on Sunday meant that Jewish merchants had to close two days in a row. As of 1932, all artisans had to be accredited by a commission, often anti-Semitic, which conducted its exam in Polish.[17] Did Matès go back to making harnesses and bridles? One thing is certain: his time in prison did not deter him from continuing the struggle. In Paris, where he was seeking refugee status, he would tell the League of Human Rights that, "wanted by the security police in April 1937, he fled in order to avoid an even harsher sentence."[18] His situation was not exceptional. For the brother of Moshe Garbarz, a Communist militant in Warsaw in the late 1920s, who was thrown into prison a first time for writing slogans on a wall, "the need to emigrate was growing urgent. He landed in prison a second time. . . . Now he had a police record. If he were caught one more time taking part in any left-wing action, it would be years before his release, and in a sorry state at that."[19] The police cracked down particularly hard on Communists, especially Jews.

This is why Matès went into exile: the anti-Semitism, both official and otherwise, the economic crisis, the dim prospects, and, finally, the real triggering element, repression by the state.

Lastly, though I have no way of knowing for sure, there is one other element that may have tipped the scales: Stalin's destruction of the KPP. In 1937, the Polish Communist leaders were invited to the USSR, where they were murdered in anonymous purges that effectively eliminated the founding members of the Party, heroes of the October Revolution, friends of Rosa Luxemburg, members of the Komintern executive committee, as well as the heads of Poland's detachment to the International Brigades along with several thousand militants. In 1938, the Komintern declared that the KPP was in fact a cover organization for the Polish secret service, a den of nationalists corrupted by fascism. As of mid-1938, official publications refrained from even mentioning it, as if it had never existed. Historians still debate the reasons for this crime: Stalin's resentment of the leaders who dared oppose the way he settled scores with the old Leninist guard in 1923, outright anti-Semitism, hatred of the internationalist tradition of Rosa Luxemburg, obsessive fear of the Trotskyist opposition, the "May Error" at the time of Pilsudski's coup, the lead-up to an alliance with Hitler which the KPP would necessarily have sought to block? Whatever the case, this outcome illustrates the "tragedy of Polish Communism" in the words of Isaac Deutscher, excluded in 1932 as a Trotskyist opponent.[20]

If he had not left for France, would Matès have experienced Stalin's jails, after his time in Polish prisons? Would Matès have concluded in the end—as did the Jewish Communist writer Aleksander Wat, arrested by the NKVD in 1940 and jailed in Lubyanka—that "the Bolshevik conception of social relations" consisted of "killing man's inner life"?[21] Would he have been lured to Moscow, sentenced to ten years in a penal colony, deported to a Kazakh concentration camp, sent out naked into the night in 30-below weather, like Moshe Zalcman, and like him, would he have wept, saying: "Yes, at the time, I dreamt that Communism would make our lives an unending celebration"?[22] Probably not, for Matès and Idesa were only second-tier cadres. Either the "technicians" of the Parczew KZMP were unaware of what was going on, or they simply dismissed it all as lies and slander spewed by the reactionaries. But if they did get wind of the purges, and had the strength to admit that the rumors were true, then I can only imagine their pain, the humiliation of betrayal by the man for whom they had sacrificed their best years. Their defeat would have been existential, a lifetime's dream shattered. With less than thirty revolutionaries executed in Poland in the 1920s and 30s, it is undeniable that the most dangerous anti-Communist dictatorship was not the Pilsudski regime, but the Soviet Union.

The same causes that had led to their joining the Communist Party—poverty, anti-Semitism and oppression—also prompted their departure into exile ten years later. Their decision to leave amounted to an admission of powerlessness and defeat: the revolution would not be taking place, not in Poland anyway. But where were they to go? A popular joke speaks volumes: a Jewish candidate for emigration goes to the community's mutual aid office. The clerk offers him a visa for Australia. "Australia?" exclaims the Jew with surprise. "But that's so far!" The clerk replies, "Far from what?"

As I write these lines, a summer storm has just burst over Paris. I go out onto the balcony to witness the spectacle, and a draft rushes into the apartment behind me, slamming a window shut so hard that the glass pane shatters. It has broken into 1000 pieces of all sizes, most of them landing in a 100-foot radius on the lawn at the foot of the building, the others propelled into my sitting room, some even under the couch cushions, while a few remain suspended in the window frame, like so many tiny guillotines. I rush down to pick the shards off the grass, taking care not to cut myself. A victimless incident, fortunately, and a serendipitous metaphor: bent over archival files, as I am now over this lawn, I have gone in search of Jewish Parczew, scattered to the four corners of the globe.

The writer Sholem Aleichem tried to rouse the famished shtetl-dwellers, who also happened to be his most avid readers. Look at how narrow-minded you are here! Escape! Leave for Hamburg, like the dreamer Menachem-Mendel, cross the Atlantic, like the cantor's son Motel! During the interwar period, nearly 400,000 Jews left Polish territory, heading to France, Palestine and the Americas.[23] From the early part of the century, Parczew's Jews made their *aliyah*, or "ascent" to Eretz Israel, with the help of several different movements: the youth group Gordonia and the Pioneer (*He-Halutz*) and the Young Pioneer (*He-Halutz Hatzair*) movement, the latter two established at Frog Street. In Yashinke, on the other side of the river, the candidates for *aliyah* learned how to hoe and weed at a local farm school, awaiting their departure for a real kibbutz. But in Parczew, as elsewhere, these Zionist utopias were harshly criticized. Convinced that the Messiah would return to guide them back to the Promised Land, ultra-orthodox Jews were scandalized by this demonstration of hubris. The middle classes, in their bid for social integration, rejected any notion of Jewish exceptionalism, especially Theodor Herzl's vision of a separate state. Bundists and Zionists hated one another, since class struggle opposed nationalism, and vice versa. (The leftist workers movement *Poale Zion* attempted to reconcile this opposition, but it was accused of being a tool of the Jewish bourgeoisie.) As for Communists like Matès and Henya, they would attack Zionists before taking on the bosses.

Settling in Palestine was no easy venture, moreover. Elkana Niski, Matisyahou Tempy, Yozef Henochs, Moyshe Goldstein, Moyshe Liberman, and a few others made a go of kibbutz life in 1925, but found life in the desert exhausting, and ended up back home, excepting Niski, who would be joined by little Rachel a few years later.[24] Thanks to the internet site JewishGen, I found out from an Israeli that a cousin of my father's, a certain Alter Jablonka, born in Parczew at the turn of the century, made his *aliyah* in the mid-1920s. A founding member of the kibbutz Ein Hashofet, near Haifa, he lived peacefully to the ripe old age of ninety. From the same generation, Shlomo, the son of Yoyne Jablonka, boarded the *Tiger Hill* on 3 August 1939, at the port of Constanţa in Romania. (He sailed alone, however: his sister Hinda, having missed the boat, went back home to Parczew, and this would cost her life.) Once in Palestine, Shlomo settled in Ramat Yohanan, another kibbutz near Haifa.

Of Matès's siblings, Simje was the first to leave. He boarded the *Conte Verde* in Genoa in 1931, at the age of twenty-seven, according to the Center for the Study of Latin-American Migration in Buenos Aires, a one-room office with wooden display cases and an old-fashioned desk.[25] He left on his own, having asked his parents to look after his young wife Raquel (the same one who had stood guard in front of the house while the police entered through the back and arrested her comrades). She would have to wait a full year before joining him. His adventure began with a long train trip: nearly 1,200 miles lay between Broad Street, with its kerosene shop and rain-soaked ruts, and the Italian city of Genoa, one of the Mediterranean's great ports. He had to travel by way of Krakow, cross Czechoslovakia, Austria and northern Italy, then find his way to the port and present his travel documents. The *Conte Verde* sailed along the Italian coastline, with stops in Naples and Palermo to take on more emigrants, then headed for Gibraltar. After a last stop in the Canary Islands, they set sail for the high seas, where he could breathe in the air and spray, the ship a mere dot on the vast curve of the ocean. Moving at a speed of fifteen knots, the massive vessel, with a registered tonnage of 18,000, two smokestacks and two masts flying Italian flags, transported the little Jew from Parczew, along with 1,000 emigrants crowded into steerage and a privileged few in first class, to one of the southern hemisphere's great metropolises.

An amazing land, this Argentina, where the Association for Jewish Colonization, founded by Baron Hirsch, had been sending Eastern European pioneers since the late nineteenth century. For the Jews of Warsaw's Krochmalna Street, the images that Argentina conjured up were not of the epidemics, hard labor and rough times that awaited these uprooted populations, but rather of the pampas, non-kosher red meat, easy money and the sweet kiss of red-lipped ladies of the night. Other promises made many a head spin among the customers of Lloyd Sabaudo, the Turin-based company that owned the *Conte Verde*: the chance for a fresh start and wholesome work on the land, like the biblical ancestors. The Polish state encouraged this movement, and in the early 1930s, after calling upon the Havre-based Chargeurs Réunis, or United Shippers, it created the Gdynia-Ameryka Linie, a national company that ran between Gdynia, in the north, and South America.[26]

Why Buenos Aires, and not France, the United States, Australia or Brazil? Because Simje was friends with a couple in Argentina, Yankel and Jume, both natives of Parczew (they helped one another out all their lives, and are buried together in the cemetery of the *Asociación Mutual Israelita Argentina*). There was likely an exchange of letters at first, but Simje left Europe without knowing exactly what he would find on arrival. After a thirty-one-day crossing, he landed in the middle of winter on 20 August 1931, in the crowded, cosmopolitan capital. With the help of his friend Yankel, who ran a small mattress-making business, Simje found work combing and carding wool. His letters, which were confiscated by the Polish police in 1933 during a raid on the Broad Street house, are tinged with melancholy:

> Dear parents, It's been four weeks now since I got your letter. All week, I have been down at the port counting the ships coming in from Europe, hoping to receive another letter from you. I just don't understand why you have written so little recently. . . . Over here, things are the same as always, we are in good health, and back together, as we always were. Raquel is a little less homesick now. . . . Let me know how you are doing, your health, your work and all. Hanukkah is approaching, or to be precise, by the time this letter gets to you, Hanukkah will already have passed. It must already be muddy and snowy where you are, you can tell me all about that. Over here, summer has just begun.[27]

Their first son, Benito, would be born in February 1934, not out on the pampas where the cattle roam, but in a hovel on Francisco Bilbao Street. At that time, Matès was serving time in the Parczew prison.

Reizl joined them in 1936. Her son Mauricio tells of an incident during the crossing: she thought she'd come upon some little chunks of chocolate—or were they prunes—arranged in a small dish. A real find, since she loved sweets. She bit into one, and immediately spat out the black olive. She would never in her life touch another black olive. Down at the port, Simje, who had taken the day off to meet his sister's ship, was getting impatient. The paperwork was endless, the customs agents could speak neither Yiddish nor Polish and Reizl spoke not a word of Spanish. But they were finally reunited. The new émigrée would be living with her brother's family on Francisco Bilbao Street. She had packed three gifts from their parents, a kind of dowry for her household in the New World: cheap silver spoons; a big down comforter called a *yberbet*, literally "bed cover"; and a new coat, the one originally intended for Henya. In Parczew, farewells had been long and tearful: Reizl suspected it was the last time she would see her parents, pious Shloyme and sweet Tauba. But they were the ones who urged her to leave, gently but firmly.

Three years later, the same scene was reprised with the two youngest, Hershl and Henya. In September 1939, Henya was released by her jailers, in their rush to flee the advancing Germans. In Parczew, once she was reunited with her family, her parents begged her to leave. But where to? "Go east. Last time, the Germans left the old folks alone, and just rounded up the young people and sent them to work camps. You need to get out of here." Shloyme and Tauba, forever prodding their children into exile, were to die without ever seeing them again. Shloyme's children by his first marriage, among them the half-sister Gitla, stayed behind in Parczew, perhaps because they had families of their own to support. All of them would be assembled on the *Rynek* in July 1942, and taken to the train.

At Brest-Litovsk, Hershl and Henya crossed over into Soviet territory (the USSR had invaded Poland two weeks after the Germans, recovering the western parts of Ukraine and Belarus). The siblings kept pushing eastward until they reached Novosibirsk. Why Novosibirsk, an industrial town in the middle of Siberia? Because it was the edge of the civilized world, as far away as they could get from the Nazis. Hershl joined the Red Army reserves, while Henya stayed in Novosibirsk. The war separated brother from sister.

Many other Jews, particularly Communists, left Parczew in a mad rush. This was the case for Mayer Rapoport, former leader of the local KPP, who left for Brest-Litovsk with his wife and their two boys. When the Wehrmacht invaded the Soviet Union in June 1941, he enlisted in the Red Army. When she learned that the tractor factory where Mayer worked was being moved further inland to begin producing tanks, his wife refused to leave the city. In Novosibirsk, where he had gone for a hand amputation, Mayer ran into Henya, that little girl he used to tease at the Broad Street house where he went to see his friend Simje. She was alone and living in squalor; he gave her money and food. In 1944, when the German army was in retreat, Mayer left for Brest-Litovsk to rejoin his wife and children. They were nowhere to be found. Even with the help of neighbors, he was unable to find the mass grave. Mayer and Henya left to live in Kowel, in Soviet Ukraine, some 125 miles east of Parczew, where their daughter Tamara was born in 1946. Six or seven years later, a telegram from the Red Cross informed them that Hershl was still alive and had been living in Baku since the end of the war. They rushed there to find him living with his wife and child in utter misery: a basement room where the child slept on a kind of wall ledge and the feet of passersby were visible through a dim window.

This is the fate of three Polish Jews, longtime Communists, who went over to the Soviet side. Another case of "Judeo-Bolshevism"? Collective memory in Poland pictures throngs of Jews in 1939 welcoming the Russian liberators with open arms and bouquets of flowers. Some Jews did heave a sigh of relief at the arrival of the Red Army. But can they be blamed given that, in the USSR at that time, there were no *numerus clausus* quotas, no pogroms? It was a matter of survival, after all: some 350,000 Polish Jews had fled to the east ahead of the approaching German troops. The problem of the refugees, of whom there were some 1.5 million in all, had the Soviet authorities on their guard, and most were deported in four successive waves between February 1940 and June 1941.[28] After the war, most of the Jews were repatriated, but some settled—Hershl died in Baku in 1989—or emigrated to Israel.

When I meet up with Tamara in a hotel bar in Faubourg Saint-Honoré in Paris, where she is staying briefly before leaving to tour the Alsace region, I'm anxious to show her the digital version of the Parczew *Yizkor*

Bukh that I have downloaded onto my laptop. She clicks through, some-what grim-faced at first, commenting on certain photos: there's Chaim-Leyb, son of Israel Jablonka, "the man of a thousand books," next to Shlomo, son of Yoyne Jablonka, both attending a meeting of the Friends of Parczew in Haifa during the 1950s. And here's that braggart from the Betar movement, a pioneer group, and a facsimile of a membership card for the Zion Youth, 1925. Tamara's face brightens. She's a short, curvaceous redhead, whose quick wit is not dampened by our less-than-fluent conversation in English. Her native intelligence is further sharpened by a knowledge of Hebrew, Yiddish, Polish and Russian. Matès was, in her view, like today's sabras: unfailingly generous, but don't rub him the wrong way. The first time her father Mayer happened upon a copy of the *Yizkor Bukh*, he paged through it, curious to see the contributions of his old friends. Nothing! Not a single Communist had been asked to contribute. No way would he buy a copy of this book! (With a sweep of her arm, Tamara pretends to knock a book off the table.)

A year later, it is her turn to greet me at the Tel Aviv airport. On the highway that takes us to her home, Tamara launches into proselytizing mode as she points to the cloverleaf overpasses flowing with the latest Japanese and American SUVs, the upscale homes in Herzliya, the mammoth construction projects, buildings that spring from the ground in three weeks' time, a grand choreography of cranes. All smiles, I remind her about the time her mother was sentenced to a year in prison in 1934 for breaking into a Zionist meeting, the "Jewish fascists" of Parczew. At first taken aback, she gives me a doubly tender look, inspired by my seemingly childish naïveté and by nostalgia for her deceased parents.

In 1956, in Kowel, Mayer had his Communist membership card taken away. Outraged, he left for Moscow to lodge a complaint (an act that would have cost him his life under Stalin), and against all odds, he actually got it back. But he was left feeling bitter: "If I'm not a good Communist, then this isn't the country for me anymore." The family left Kowel for Lodz, where Mayer, a former prison comrade of Gomułka's, became an apparatchik. On a trip back to Parczew, Henya encountered the policemen who, twenty years earlier, after arresting her, had insulted and beat her and led her around town on a leash. They all still had their jobs. Through a window, she could imagine Tauba's candles that used to illuminate their Friday evening prayers. After crying, cursing and tearing her hair out, she finally convinced her husband that they had to leave.

They chose Israel. In Haifa, Mayer worked as a doorman, and Henya as a chambermaid to a woman doctor, a *Pani Doktorova*, whose father had been a doctor back in Parczew. Henya would come home at night, after spending the day dusting, scrubbing, laundering and ironing, her feet swollen to twice their size. At barely forty years old, her body was broken, scarred by the torture inflicted in prison. The Polish government was the enemy of the Communists and Henya abhorred Zionism, but she would die Israeli, never returning to her native Poland crushed behind the Iron Curtain. Yes, dear Tamara, you are right, it's complicated. Today Tamara lives in Hadera, north of Tel Aviv, and her daughter is an attack helicopter pilot in the Tzahal. One of her fellow pilots is none other than the legendary Roni Zuckerman, granddaughter of Antek, hero of the Warsaw ghetto; she is Israel's first female F-16 fighter pilot. And Henya Jablonka's granddaughter flies a Cobra, a fighter helicopter she took into battle against Hezbollah in south Lebanon in 2006. Once, she was asked to represent the Israeli Air Force in a public relations event in Poland. The ceremony was to take place in Lublin, the town where Henya, Hershl and Matès had been imprisoned. When she learned this, Tamara wept. She could hardly imagine that her daughter would walk those same streets not only as a free woman, but as an officer in the Jewish army! The old wise men of Parczew would leap from their tombs, if they had had any.

I spend a week together with Tamara talking about the family. In the scorching heat of Caesarea, where we climb among the ruins of the hippodrome and walk out to the promontory overlooking the dazzling Mediterranean, we talk about Henya's new coat that Reizl took to Argentina with her. At the Hadera cemetery perched high above the town, I place a stone on Henya's grave, a white rectangle so like all the others and so perfectly aligned as to become indistinguishable at just a few paces. After a swim, we dry off in the sun, while Tamara tells me about the reunion of Simje, Reizl, Hershl and Henya in the late 1970s, after nearly a half-century of separation: in Buenos Aires, the Jablonka siblings were together again for that short while, but without their beloved brother. At an outdoor café in Tel Aviv, I meet Ahuva, the daughter of Chaim-Leyb and granddaughter of Israel Jablonka. After spending the entire war in Tashkent (another far-flung location), Chaim-Leyb immigrated to Haifa in 1949. He never spoke of the past, but at gatherings of Parczew old-timers, he would exude joy, greeting his old friends—Shlomo Jablonka son of Yoyne, Zonenshayn, and the whole *Yizkor Bukh* editorial committee— with bear hugs and pats on the back, laughing raucously at the tricks they had played on the *melamed* fifty years earlier. In the 1990s, Ahuva went to Parczew with Bernie Stern, a friend whose parents, Canadians today, had survived by hiding in the forest. They went together to the home of an old Polish couple. The wife asked them to wait: her husband was napping, but he would be up soon. The Pole came in a bit later, a large, heavyset man. He recalled that the Sterns had owned a mill, and Ahuva added that her own father had worked there as an accountant. Ahuva completes the story: "This Pole was a *Hasid umot ha'olam*, one of the Righteous among the Nations. I know the people he saved, they live here in Tel Aviv." I mention the name Ludwik Golecki, adding that I met his son Marek. She nods in approval: "He was quite ill. We left him a large amount of money, he was happy about that."

One afternoon, Tamara drives me to the Ramat Yohanan kibbutz, near Haifa, for a family reunion. In the parking lot, we meet up with Zohar, whom I had contacted two years earlier, with the help of the Jewish genealogical website JewishGen. She leads us along a cement path that weaves through the housing properties, mostly spacious single-story homes, with little gardens and an awning that shades a labrador napping next to the bikes and the lawn mower. Contrary to appearances, the kibbutz doesn't live off its large cattle ranch but, rather, from its community plastics factory, which produces a special kind of plastic that is exported worldwide. Zohar stops in front of a house where Israeli flags flying on the front porch filter the late afternoon sun. Inside await several cousins and Zohar's three brothers: two of them live on the kibbutz with their families, and the other, who lives much further south, made the five-hour drive just to meet me. From my generation, there is Reut, one of Zohar's nieces whom I had finally met on Facebook after writing to 100 different Jablonka/Yablonkas all over the world. And then, back in the dining room, sitting enthroned

in a foam armchair, a ninety-six-year-old man, removed from all the com-
motion around him, a sphinxlike character, seemingly disconnected from
reality, but who emanates an inexpressible gentleness: Shlomo Jablonka,
son of Yoyne, first cousin to my grandfather, the man who, aboard the
Tiger Hill on 3 August 1939, managed to evade the death trap.

I draw closer to him, not daring to take his hand. I am introduced in
English. Shlomo begins to cry. "Since his illness," says Zohar, "Dad is very
emotional."

I have so many questions to ask him! But Shlomo is feeble, and doesn't
hear so well. What's worse, I can speak neither Hebrew nor Yiddish. But
he addresses me in English, which suggests that he understands what's
going on around him. Zohar reminds me, almost apologetically, that he
left Parczew a long time ago and that his whole family was murdered. His
brother Meir was shot by the Germans on Pesach 1940 (the *Yizkor Bukh*
devotes a few lines to him), and the others were gassed at Treblinka. I show
him photographs of my grandparents on my computer screen. He doesn't
understand who they are. Trying every possible pronunciation, I repeat
"Matès Jablonka," and he finally nods in recognition. Reut, who knows
the man's story as well as any, since she is the one who filled out his Yad
Vashem forms back when she was still a schoolgirl, comes to me and whis-
pers: "His brother was also named Matès." She leans in to her grandfather,
tenderly takes his hand in hers, and says: "*Saba, Saba.*" Shlomo gazes back
at her, smiling.

"*Saba,* don't you remember Matès Jablonka, the other Matès?"

He just keeps smiling.

"*Saba,* do you remember your uncle Shloyme, Shloyme Jablonka?"

Shlomo lowers his head and answers in Hebrew, teary-eyed. Reut
translates for me:

"He had a *beyt merkhatz,* a sauna. Steam would rise to the ceiling, there
were wooden tubs."

Bingo! But it is getting late, and Zohar lets us know that it's her father's
bedtime. As I descend the porch steps, I etch into my heart the image of
this ancient man, so gentle and sure, who somewhere in the recesses of his
brain preserves the proof that my grandparents were once alive, that they
said and did things just like you and me, that they were young and happy,

just like Reut is today, that there was once a time when they still had their whole lives to live: their hopes and dreams, children of their own, and maybe, one day, a grandchild. I have met the last man, I have seen his eyes that saw them and that saw me today. Back at Zohar's house, over a cup of herbal tea, we talk about prewar Parczew. I explain that Yoyne was a member of the *Judenrat* in 1940, but the subject puts everyone ill at ease. Zohar's daughter shows me photos of Parczew that she took on a school field trip.

Shlomo died two months later, on 15 July 2010, the day after the thunderstorm that shattered my apartment window. Reut emailed to let me know. At times like these, it's hard to know what to say in reply. So, I write the first thing that comes to mind, something undeniable: we lost a truly exceptional man. On a more personal level, I could also declare that he brought back to life both my grandparents and Parczew, and that, although he left us bereft, his death hardly marks the end of a lineage. For he will forever be present in Ramat Yohanan, in Hadera, in Tel Aviv, in Buenos Aires, in Baku, and in Paris; and also in Montreal with Bernie Stern, in Johannesburg with Mordkhe Rubinstein, in La Paz with Berl Nelkenbaum: my shattered shtetl, scattering its shard-like stars over the world. It has become universal.

On the way home with Tamara, she and I talk about Matès. What does she think about his leaving for France in 1937? Tamara doesn't hesitate: Paris was just the first leg on the way to Argentina. Simje's departure in the early 1930s was part of a family strategy to send him as the pioneer to earn some money, after which he would send for the others: his wife and Reizl first, followed by Matès, then Hershl, Henya and the parents. As we now know, the plan succeeded only in part. But what about the YKUF? Little chance that a conference about Yiddish would have interested a KPP cadre: he was a Red, not a *Yid*. So why did he not go directly on to Argentina? The ticket was too expensive at the time. Well, why didn't he join his siblings later, then? Tamara doesn't know, nor do I, but I believe that, more than money, it was his police record that was the main issue. Among Simje's papers in Buenos Aires, I find, in addition to his passport, a stack of official documents, all duly stamped, certifying his good health, his work qualifications, financial status, etc. His certificate of good conduct attests that Simje had committed no "infringement of public order" within the previous five years. Same thing for Reizl, whose passport was a mass of blue stamps: from the district of Włodawa, from the Warsaw immigration inspector, from the Argentine consulate. Matès, on the other hand, not only had been sentenced to five years in prison for "crimes against the state," but was on the police's wanted list. And not to forget Argentina's circular 11, a secret text adopted in July 1938, which banned Jews and political refugees from entering the country. How could he have legally emigrated under such conditions?

Contrary to what my father had long believed, Matès and Idesa did not leave at the same time. Why did Matès agree to leave separately from his sweetheart? Perhaps because the police were less insistent with Idesa, or because she was trying to obtain her passport in Warsaw, a long and costly process. We can only imagine Matès, after two and a half years behind bars, hunted by the police, wandering from one hideout to the next at a time when the country was calling for the expulsion of Jews to Palestine or to some hypothetical African colonies. Where could he go? To America? The borders were closed. To Palestine? Never! To Buenos Aires? He lacked the money and the visa. France? Idesa had cousins on the Korenbaum side in Paris, the children of her Aunt Esther and of her Uncle David, the Maloryta forester. So many Jews had opted for the country of human rights: "As happy as God in France," as the Yiddish expression goes.

One weekday morning, under a steady rainfall washing over the deserted Bagneux cemetery, Colette takes me to see the burial vault of the Society of the Friends of Parczew. It is an utterly nondescript monument in dark marble, studded with little pebbles, flint chips and bits of broken glass set all around the photographs of the deceased. After delicately moving them to one side, and standing under Colette's umbrella, I take pictures of all the names engraved in stone. I suddenly stop:

"This isn't sacrilegious, is it?"

"Of course not!" assures Colette. "This is how memory gets transmitted. They would have enjoyed it."

Women on the left, men on the right, and in the middle, the founders of the Society. On the gravestone, to the right, the families deported from Poland, and on the left, those deported from France. There are the

Szermans, the Tenenbaums, the Pilczers, the Kenigsmans, and lots of Zlotagoras, Kaszemachers and Sznajders, including Icek Sznajder, 1901–1974. Colette's parents are also listed, Abram Fiszman, 1911–1971, and Malka Fiszman, née Milechsberg, 1914–2003, who died without ever managing to locate the Parczew house. Colette is certain that Matès and Idesa joined the Society as soon as they arrived in Paris. In so many cities, including Paris, Jewish immigrants gathered into *landsmanshaftn*, hometown societies based on one's shtetl of origin, which helped new arrivals to make the transition by finding them housing and work, organizing funerals, etc. Later, they would publish a *Yizkor Bukh*, or "book of remembrance," that piously recorded what they recalled as their happy lives before the great dispersion. Throughout the 1950s and 60s, the children were dragged to the annual event sponsored by the Society for the Friends of Parczew. The adults loved this heartwarming occasion, since it reminded them of their youth and gave them a sense of solidarity (not unlike similar occasions organized in Haifa during the same period). My own father attended once or twice, met some of the old-timers, and even received a 10,000-franc grant from a fund-raising effort, but he admitted: "I felt disconnected, not in the least bit curious about my own history." Colette and I make our way to the exit, and walk to a couscous restaurant on Avenue Marx-Dormoy where we have an excellent lunch, in the company of old immigrants and black-suited undertakers.

Parczew, summer of 1937. Could it be that Matès, freshly graduated from his prison education, found the shtetl even more indigent and petty than he had remembered it? Or perhaps he learned from a friend, or the *Trybune*, that a World Congress for the Defense of Jewish Culture was to be held in Paris. The whole world was talking excitedly about the news. One Polish immigrant in France had this to say: "It was all anyone could talk about. You can't imagine how much people were looking forward to it, so much expectation!"[29] This would be a major event for all those who believed that Yiddish culture had a role to play in the fight against all forms of barbarity. But Matès and Idesa wondered about France. After all, there had been the Dreyfus affair, and after World War I, General Weygand was sent to Pilsudski's Poland to make sure the Russian Revolution did not spread all over the continent. But times had changed. Since

1935, France and the USSR had been allied against Hitler. And wasn't France the home of the Revolution, the Commune, and the 17th infantry regiment, which refused to open fire on demonstrators in 1907? It brought Hugo and Zola into the world, Babeuf and Vallès, its watchwords were liberty and equality, universal brotherhood. So many outcasts had found refuge there! Gorki once said that all revolutionaries should go at least once in their lives to the Place de la Bastille. The French had emancipated the Jews, and even elevated one to the head of government—a Jew *and* a Marxist: Leon Blum.[30]

But is emigration actually a matter of weighing the pros and cons? Rather, I can picture Matès panic-stricken, his fight-or-flight instincts kicking in. The police were hot on his trail; he risked being captured, beaten and thrown back into prison. With the exception of the Scandinavian countries, Great Britain, Belgium, the Netherlands, Switzerland and France, Europe was going over to authoritarianism and dictatorship, with democracies such as Spain and Czechoslovakia increasingly bullied into fascism. In January 1937, the Polish government presented a plan for Jewish emigration/expulsion. That same year, on 26 April, the Spanish village of Guernica was bombed by Hitler's air power, resulting in over 1,000 deaths. In May: the Brest-Litovsk pogrom. August: the last bastions of republicanism fall in Spain. Goebbels would write in his diary on 1 August: "The trip with the Führer to the Friesenwiese was a triumph. One hundred thousand people. . . . An indescribable storm of acclaim."[31] With the forces of death closing in, what was the most secure asylum?

Right before separating, Matès and Idesa made their love official, getting married on 26 June 1937, in the presence of a rabbi of lesser rank—Rabbi Epstein, who had married Simje and Raquel six years earlier, was most likely deceased by then. The town hall records would report that a twenty-eight-year-old leatherworker, "of Mosaic faith," had married a twenty-three-year-old woman, also "of Mosaic faith."[32] Was this a moment of bliss before exile, their day of happiness when they could finally think of themselves, or was it just a quick religious ceremony to please their parents? Then came the good-byes, the well-wishing, words to remember for a lifetime. In Grodzisko, in Galicia, Ilex Beller's mother washed and mended his clothes, prepared his small satchel and hugged him for the last time: "Here in Poland, there is no hope for us, my child. You have to leave, to go someplace else where you can really live." Then the *yiddishe mame* wrapped her shawl around herself and watched as the wagon pulled away, eyes brimming with tears, gazing until it disappeared into the distance.[33] Another scene, between Faiwel Schrager and his parents, at the stop for the bus to Bialystok. His mother's eyes were full of reproach: "So you're abandoning us, too?" The father lashed out at her: "What did you think? That he would stay here forever, clinging to your skirts? This is his destiny! He's going to study and make something of himself." And the father solemnly handed over his *tefillin*.[34] But I doubt that Matès, who couldn't show himself in Parczew or Warsaw, would have gotten the chance to say good-bye to his family and friends, to bid farewell to the forest and river of his childhood, as was the custom. His departure was rushed, no passport or visa. I see only one plausible scene, in some secure place, with the woman who had become his wife only weeks before: "We'll meet again soon, my love, we will continue the struggle in a free country, you'll be happy, no one will hurt you anymore . . ."

I have no idea which overcrowded milk train he took, which express train he then caught, which deserted stations or hubs teeming with peasants he had to transit through. I can only imagine the strangers he encountered during this ordeal, the narrow alleyways he had to sneak down under cover of darkness, always on the lookout, in his threadbare suit. After Ilex Beller's farewell, he placed his fate in the hands of a *makher*, a go-between who took charge of him and 5 other emigrants. The German border was a river that they crossed waist-deep. On foot or by train, they travelled penniless, sleeping in Jewish community hostels, before finally arriving in Antwerp.[35] In 1939, Jean Améry, a literature student, slipped into Belgium with his wife via a contraband route: "It was a long way through the night. The snow lay knee-high; the black firs did not look any different from their sisters back home, but they were already Belgian firs; we knew that they did not want us. An old Jew in rubber overshoes, which he was constantly losing, clung to the belt of my coat, groaned and promised me all the riches of the world if only I allowed him to hold on to me now."[36] For Matès, all I know is what he declared to the police: that he entered France "via the Belgian border, on foot, in the company of three fellow Poles," after paying a smuggler 150 zlotys. By 30 August 1937, he was in Paris.

Idesa's odyssey, six months later, is a little better known to us. Two sources contribute to the narrative: a postcard addressed to Simje and Reizl in Buenos Aires and a passport that my aunt Suzanne would inherit after the war. The card, undated, is signed by Shloyme, Tauba and Idesa, which suggests that Matès, like his brother a few years earlier, had left his young wife in his parents' care. The card sent warm greetings from the parents to their two eldest and their grandchild, to whom they sent "a thousand kisses," though they had never met him, little Benito who was by then almost four. They expressed their hope that "things will turn out for the best, and that our misfortune will soon end. Or that at least the young ones will be released soon." (They were referring to Hershl and Henya, who had been jailed for a second time.) On the back, Idesa gave Matès's address, and asked Reizl to send him "the snapshot where you are standing next to your husband. We'd also like one. By the time it arrives in Paris, I'll be there, too."[37]

Idesa was in Warsaw around 22 February 1938, the issue date of her passport. Today, it is housed in my laptop as a digital file scanned page by page. Its midnight-blue cover bears in gold lettering the words *Rzeczpospolita Polska*, "Polish Republic." As we might almost have forgotten, Idesa was a Polish citizen. The inside front cover shows her married name, "Ides Jablonka," and the next page gives her particulars: average height, oval-shaped face, black hair, brown eyes. Her visas were valid only for Germany, Czechoslovakia and Belgium, and even those were only for transit or tourism. The black eagle, wings spread, grasping a swastika in its talons, is opposite other less-than-inviting stamps: "You are formally forbidden to seek employment in Belgium." On page 7, a red stamp by the Polish authorities specifies that the passport is "valid for a one-way exit to a foreign country."[38] No possible return to Poland, no access to the main exits from the continent, Italy and France, no granting of temporary stays elsewhere. In other words, Idesa had no right to live anywhere at all.

On 15 March 1938 in Warsaw, she changed some money, and the next day she entered Germany via Zbaszyn, with 60 zlotys, 50 Belgian francs and—noted by the customs officer on the last page of her passport—"a brown fur coat." It was winter, of course, and it was her most precious possession, apart from her wedding ring, perhaps. A young Jewish woman hounded out of her country, looking out the train window at the passing landscape, bundled up in her fur coat . . . Idesa dreams, Idesa smiles— I imagine her smiling. Brown fur coat, locomotive cutting through the countryside, clickety-clack of wheels on steel rails, fur coat, fur coat, fur coat. I could go on repeating these hollow syllables, echoing a millennium of exile; I could whisper them until I'm voiceless, for eternity, as the last link to the shtetl dissolves into the night, leaving behind parents, uncles and aunts, school friends and teachers, neighbors, Party comrades.

I'm intrigued by the Czechoslovakian visa. Located on the German-Polish border, Zbaszyn sits at about the same latitude as Berlin and Amsterdam, while Czechoslovakia is much further south. The shortest route to France goes through Germany and Belgium. Thus, three possible scenarios: either the railroad imposed a detour through Czechoslovakia; or Idesa had requested as many visas as she could get, though she would only use two; or, as a third possibility, she harbored the scheme of somehow getting to an Italian port, where she and Matès would set sail for Argentina. What actually happened, heaven only knows. Like Matès a few months prior to his arrival in France, Idesa made a declaration to the French police, who transcribed it thus: "Crossed the Belgian border on foot, and alone, she claims."[39] We have to take her at her word. She arrived in Paris on 18 April 1938, penniless, without a visa, knowing not a word of French. And there she was, standing on the esplanade outside the train station. Within the hour, she would be falling into her husband's arms, and their new life would begin. City of Light, cultural capital of tolerance, endless choreography of traffic on the boulevard, metro stops, modernity. France, homeland of human rights!

4

THE

UNDOCUMENTED

JEWS OF MY FAMILY

Two refugees among tens of thousands, two droplets in a sea of hardship: Italians fleeing fascism, Germans fleeing Nazism, German and Eastern European Jews driven out of their countries, followed in 1938 by ex-Austrian nationals, and by those from Czechoslovakia recently annexed by Hitler, and in 1939 by Spaniards escaping from Franco's terror. At that point, France counted some 60,000 Jewish refugees from Eastern Europe, 42,000 of whom were illegal, and a half-million Spanish Republicans.[1]

These uprooted masses were added to the 3 million foreigners already present on French soil (7% of the population), mostly Italians, Spaniards, Poles, Russians and Eastern European Jews, the *Ostjuden*. Used at first to fill the labor shortage in the wake of World War I, they then became increasingly undesirable, particularly when the economic crisis hit, and came to be seen as profiteers and parasites. In 1932, the parliament ruled that foreign workers could not make up more than 5% of the payrolls of companies with state contracts. In addition, quotas by sector and region were established. The Armbruster Law of 1933 required that all medical doctors have French citizenship. In 1934, naturalized citizens were excluded from the civil service and the bar—other professions would soon follow suit. The next year, supposedly "to protect French artisans from foreign competition," non-French artisans were required to have ID cards, which were granted very sparingly.[2]

Even so, the international crisis in Europe continued to force tens of thousands of refugees into France. Starting in late 1933, the government attempted to stem this flow. Applicants without passports, or those with only tourist visas, were rejected outright, and an expulsion policy was put in place. After sweeping the May 1936 elections, the Popular Front eased the restrictions, granting amnesty to refugees, issuing work permits and speeding up naturalization procedures. In the wake of the Geneva Conference, the Blum government created an "identity certificate" for German refugees already present in France, thereby shielding them from expulsion. But the agreement did not apply to other nationalities, and made no mention of future refugees. For them, France would become a transit point, not an asylum. Even so, from summer to fall of 1937, at the time Matès was crossing the border along with three fellow Poles, nearly 18,000 refugees from Eastern Europe—three quarters of whom were Jews—entered France illegally or on tourist visas, claiming they were visiting the Universal Exposition. Marx Dormoy, a socialist and the interior minister in the Chautemps government, which followed Blum's, stepped up repression by a notch: his circular no. 338 of 9 July 1937 ordered prefects "to be merciless in turning away any foreigner seeking to enter France without a valid passport or travel document." Particularly harsh treatment was in store for "the unemployed and the indigent in search of any kind of livelihood."[3]

Matès got to Paris on 30 August 1937. The first thing he did—even before attending the founding congress of the YKUF on 17 September, if indeed he did actually attend—was to request legal residency.[4] In order to obtain political refugee status, he worked through two different associations: *Secours populaire de France* or Popular Assistance-France, and the Liaison Office of the Committees on Immigrant Status.

Secours populaire, the French branch of *Secours rouge*, an international, Communist-linked organization, was set up by the French Communist Party to defend political prisoners and victims of fascism. As proclaimed in the 10 September 1937 issue of its weekly paper, *La Défense*, a "true right to asylum" should be granted to comrades who "have sought on our soil the kind of peace unavailable to them in their own countries that are being crushed by dictators or their lackeys."[5] Sponsored by prestigious intellectuals such as Romain Rolland and Paul Langevin and a membership, in 1937, of 140,000, *Secours populaire* provided refugees with legal, financial and material support. There is little doubt that Matès was sent there by the KPP or the MOPR, the Polish branch of *Secours rouge international.*

The Liaison Office of the Committees on Immigrant Status was a more ecumenical association. Created during the Popular Front to coordinate the actions of multiple associations, it demanded that refugees be welcomed with dignity, and that they be granted, in addition to the right to asylum, the "right to a decent life," which meant employment. The various gatherings that it sponsored, such as the international conference of 20 to 21 June 1936 at the town hall of the 5th arrondissement, or the World Assembly against Racism and Anti-Semitism on 10 to 12 September 1937 at the Mutualité, brought together the anti-fascist Left with hundreds of delegates from all around the world. In Paris, as in the voivodeship of Lublin, the time had come for unity. Refusing to pit class against class, the Communists supported Leon Blum, who governed from June 1936 to June 1937. Yesterday's enemies now fraternized within the Jewish Popular Movement: Bundists, *Poale Zion* on the left and right, trade unionists, Communists from the Jewish branch of the immigrant labor group MOI.[6] In a sign of the times, *Secours rouge* took the name of *Secours populaire de France.*

On 22 September 1937, at the request of the Liaison Office, the national security office of the interior ministry took up the case of "Mr. Jablonka Matys, Polish," who had arrived three weeks earlier and was residing at 37 Rue des Couronnes.[7] In early October, *Secours populaire* requested a foreign resident ID card, "which would allow him to live legally in France."

The Paris police prefecture carried out an investigation. On 24 December, the blade dropped in the form of a pink slip: denial of residency. Matès had to leave the territory within five days. He was stamped "E. 98,392," indicating that he was nearly the 100,000th person subjected to this "removal" procedure. The police prefecture, applying Marx Dormoy's circular no. 338 issued a few months earlier, ruled that: "With no passport and no family ties in France, [he] cannot demonstrate an ability to support himself." The police report goes on to say that, unfortunately, this foreigner had gone into hiding in early 1938, right after receiving his denial of residency. The prefecture had no idea that Matès had just moved to 11 Rue du Pressoir, behind Place Ménilmontant, only 100 yards away from his last address: it was this new address that Idesa sent to Reizl, and where she would go once she got to Paris.

In a tight spot now, Matès turned to a third association: *La Ligue des droits de l'homme*, or The League of Human Rights (LHR). Open to all nationalities and political leanings, whether republican, socialist, communist or pacifist, the LHR played a key role not only because it embodied the Popular Front's values of unity, but because its high profile and large membership—190,000 members in 2,500 sections—meant it could exert pressure on the interior ministry.[8] Although *Secours populaire* criticized the way it confined itself to judicial matters only, LHR sponsorship was highly valued, and Matès knew that very well. But here is where the problem arose: the challenge for the association consisted of sorting out political refugees, those persecuted for their opinions, from the bulk of immigrants who were "merely" fleeing misery, war or anti-Semitism.

Making the case could prove a real challenge. As explained in a 1938 issue of *Les Cahiers des droits de l'homme*, an LHR publication, refugees would first typically go underground in their own country, and "hide out at a friend's home, wander the countryside, through forests, and along back roads before finally reaching the border, without making a last visit home. Then they would cross into French territory, knowing not a word of our language, fearing above all that they would be turned away and sent back to their persecutors."[9] Matès had no way of proving the validity of his case, and the LHR employee who processed his request wrote at the bottom of his application: "He has the backing of *Secours populaire*.

I told him that this wasn't good enough."[10] Idesa, who had arrived in the meantime, came better prepared. At her first visit to the LHR, on 24 May 1938, she showed them the 1935 Lublin indictment and verdict (which is how I know about those); she also presented herself under her maiden name, which enabled her to call upon the witness of two other refugees: "Mr. Jablonka Mathis confirms that Miss Feder was persecuted by the police. Mr. Stol confirms that Miss Feder was released from prison due to a mental illness contracted in prison" (Hersz Stol, a Communist from Włodawa, jailed from 1934 to 1936, fled to France to avert a further trial).[11] This evidence was judged sufficient and, on 30 May 1938, Idesa received a certificate from the LHR attesting that she could "rightly claim the status of political refugee."[12] The same day, she filed for a foreign identity card from the Interior Ministry.

It is something of a miracle that I have been able to access such detailed information about their early days in Paris. When I first begin this investigation, after several sessions with my father, I take stock. Who were my grandparents? Jewish immigrants, like so many others. They lived on Rue du Pressoir, between Ménilmontant and Belleville, in the heart of working-class Paris where so many of the foreign-born resided. Earned a living doing odd jobs. Had two children, a girl, Suzanne, born in January 1939, and a boy, Marcel, born in April 1940. My aunt's date of birth indicates that Idesa must have gotten pregnant a few weeks after arriving in Paris. What else do I have, apart from these mundane details? No further course of action seems apparent. That's when a somewhat nebulous term I've heard, "the Moscow archive," resurfaces in my memory: during a seminar a few years prior, a colleague told of several miles of police archives from the interwar period that had just been returned to France from Russia. I get on the internet and discover that this collection contains a massive index of some 2.5 million individual records, all the National Security files at the interior ministry, where foreigners are listed as spies, anarchists, antimilitarists and other suspects. Confiscated by the Germans in 1940, sent to Berlin, seized by the Soviets in 1945 and left to collect dust in some secret service depot, the records were finally restored to France in the early 1990s and warehoused in an annex of the National Archives in Fontainebleau. Here, my good fortune is twofold: not only does this archive provide free access, but a name index is available on microfilm, which allows me to get to work immediately.

So here I am: armed with my laptop and a digital camera, I hop on an early train from the Gare de Lyon, ready to dig into the National Security files. The indexing system is distributed among thousands of cardboard boxes, each containing hundreds of individual cards, and each card refers you to that person's complete file made up of reports, memos, forms, ID photos, correspondence between the person in question and the police, the ministry and various associations, all this paperwork suddenly ushering me into the private, desperate world of people now deceased, Matès Jablonka and Idesa Korenbaum-Feder, but also Abram Fiszman, Colette's father, Icek Sznajder, betrayed by the traces of red paint on his coat lining, Gitla Leszcz, fingernails pulled out during a torture session, Hersz Stol, witness to my grandmother's depression in prison, and dozens more Polish Jews exiled in France, as well as French anarchists whom I'll talk about later. All these dangerous individuals had earned a folder in the file cabinets of National Security.[13]

I call my father to tell him that this archive is going to make him completely rethink the picture he has of his parents. Along with my mother, he comes immediately to Fontainebleau and, dumbfounded at the sheer magnitude of the discovery, all he can say is "Wow!" As it happens, my discovery results from a simple reformulation of the issue: Matès and Idesa were not first and foremost Jewish immigrants—Ménilmontant, sewing machines, Yiddish accent, and so on—but illegal aliens, which is why they were being watched by the interior ministry. The richness of this historian's paradox—you don't find because you search, but you search because you've already found—makes my book possible, and the National Security records, trundled from Paris to Berlin, and Berlin to Moscow, before their repatriation to France, to the delight of historians, provide me with a powerful tool, a wealth of revelations. Apart from ID records and other police questionnaires that provide the paper trail of their successive addresses, income sources and administrative formalities, our stock of photos is suddenly increased by 20%. My father wants to take them home with him, these tiny, black-and-white ID portraits taken in profile: Matès with a receding hairline, aquiline nose, jaws clenched, looking deeply worried, and

Idesa with her jet-black hair pulled back and her arched eyebrows, looking both chic and hardscrabble in tweed with diamond-shaped buttons. My father is about to steal these relics, but for me, it's clear the archive needs to be preserved as is. Time has passed between his generation and mine!

Most importantly, these records open up new research avenues. One might well imagine that the National Security files at the interior ministry would have matching records over at the Paris police prefecture, since the two institutions were constantly swapping information. I am soon disappointed, however: the priceless "central records" of the police prefecture (1.5 million files on foreigners residing in the Seine region) were evacuated by barge in June 1940, only to be captured by the Germans and pulped after the war. I hold out another hope—the various local associations—but after two years of searching and only a handful of return emails, I have to admit defeat: the records for *Secours populaire* between the world wars are nowhere to be found. The League of Human Rights archive, however, another Moscow returnee, is located at the university campus in Nanterre. Together, the National Security archive and the LHR records provide the bedding on which my grandparents' biography, that portion of their lives between exile and the war, humbly lies. My breaking and entering into their paperwork lives is at once painful, challenging and joyous.

On 4 June 1938, Matès and Idesa were summoned to the Paris police prefecture, by the unit in charge of foreigners and passports, to fill out forms addressing "identification of a foreigner discovered on French soil without valid documentation," four pages of data that would enter the records of the prefecture and the ministry. There is abundant eyewitness testimony as to the treatment of foreigners there, the face-to-face encounters between the shabby illegals from the shtetl and the freshly laundered paper-pushers of the Republic. The secretary general of the LHR describes it thus, in May 1938: "These poor wretches, summoned from on high, tremble as they wait their turn. Whole batches of them are shoved into a room facing anonymous functionaries who, with a stroke of a pen, decide their fate. No discussion or explanation is allowed: 'So and so? Residency denied, prepare to leave before such and such a date. . . . So and so? Expelled, you have forty-eight hours to leave (or twenty-four). . . .'"[14] Werner Prasuhn, a German socialist refugee in Paris, showed up at the prefecture hoping to obtain a work permit. "I climb the five flights of stairs—elevator forbidden to foreigners—feeling lighthearted. Suddenly I see before me a large doorway with two swinging doors. I enter, and immediately read the sign: Expulsion Department. I check the room number indicated on my summons, and this is indeed the place I am supposed to be." At the window, the clerk handed him "a green slip. This time, I didn't need a dictionary, the language was clear, a familiar vocabulary in these parts: 'The aforementioned person, residing at . . . is required by law to leave French soil within five days upon receipt of this notice. . . .' In the corridor, many remained, unable to take another step, discussing, waving their green slips. Among them, women who wept openly, children who wailed."[15]

I'll never know whether the undocumented Jews of my family proved defiant or deferential at their 1938 hearing; whether they had to endure, as did the Berliner parents of Claude Olievenstein, "the rants worthy of Hitler himself by functionaries who were, indeed, overwhelmed by the situation."[16] But I do know that they threw themselves into this lopsided battle against the state apparatus. The way they clung to the associations in desperate hope was proof of their tenacity, as was their choice to declare separately during their interrogation, as a way of protecting each other.

MATES JABLONKA
Born 10 February 1901 in Parczew.

Nationality: Polish.

Religion: Jewish (French administrators were asking that question well before Vichy).

Marital Status: married, no children.

To the left, under the ID photo, his description: 29 years old, 5'4" tall, reddish-blond hair, greenish eyes (like my father's), clean-shaven, receding chin, pale-skinned.

Last known foreign residence: Warsaw (his last hiding place?).

Family remaining in country: his wife (the truth is dusted with a hint of falsehood).

Past employment: upholsterer in Warsaw, unemployed in Paris.

Passport: none.

Consular Visa: none.

French references: none.

Motive for coming to France: Claims to have been persecuted in Poland and had to flee. Would like to settle in France.

Date of arrival: 30 August 1937.

Remarks: *Secours populaire* acknowledges him as a political refugee.

Decision: Temporary fifteen-day stay pending high-priority investigation of case.[17]

IDESA FEDER

Born 14 May 1914 in Parczew.

Polish, Jewish, unmarried.

24 years old, 5'1", light-brown hair, light-brown eyes, straight nose.

Speaks Polish, Yiddish and German.

Last known residence: Parczew.

Family remaining in country: mother.

Past employment: seamstress in Parczew, unemployed in Paris.

No passport or visa.

Available Funds: 150 francs.

Persecuted in Poland for her political opinions, and threatened with imprisonment.

In France since 18 April 1938.

Crossed into France over the Belgian border alone, she claims.

Would like to stay in France and work, if possible.

Has LHR backing.

Decision: one-month reprieve, pending investigation of case.[18]

Summer passed. The Popular Front had collapsed and the new Daladier government, formed in April 1938, intensified the hunt for illegal aliens. A new legislative decree on 2 May 1938 applied heavier sanctions against foreigners who entered or extended their stay in France illegally, who failed to apply for an ID card, who failed to carry their papers at all times, who changed residence without notifying the authorities. Persons indicted would lose their deferments and any attenuating circumstances relating to their case, and would be expelled from French territory after serving their sentence. On 12 November, a new law further forbade foreigners without a "merchant trade card" from exercising any commercial profession.

Naturalization would no longer confer the right to vote, and the process leading to loss of citizenship was streamlined. And finally, the law provided that certain foreigners could be placed in "special internment centers" whose purpose would be to "ensure that undesirable persons be rigorously eliminated." This set off panic in immigrant circles. Associations and Yiddish newspapers were inundated with requests from merchants without proper papers suddenly forbidden to do business, from whole families ordered to leave the country in forty-eight hours, from refugees sent back to prisons in their home countries.

Throughout 1938, Hitler was determined to stir up turmoil in Europe. On 12 March, Austria was annexed and state-sanctioned anti-Semitism was enacted immediately. On 3 October, France and Britain approved the annexation of the Sudetenland at the Munich conference. On 9 to 10 November, the Kristallnacht pogrom raged throughout Germany. Just as Poland had taken away the citizenship of émigrés (most of whom were Jews) who had spent more than five years outside the country, Romania and Hungary also embarked upon a program of denaturalization. Thousands of refugees flowed into France. After the Anschluss, France's National Security director, arguing that the country had reached a "saturation point," ordered that they be "ruthlessly expelled." In October 1938, Chautemps, vice-president of the advisors' council to the Daladier government, feared that an "influx of Jews might provoke racial troubles in our country."[19] In other words, the refugee problem was seen as more threatening than Mister Hitler and his admirers.

Once it had received Matès's ID forms, the interior ministry decided, on 10 October 1938, that "there are valid grounds to proceed with expulsion of this foreigner." Matès was then issued his second pink slip: he now had eight days to leave the country.[20] Ever determined, he returned to the LHR, bearing an affidavit from the Union of Sponsors for Polish Nationals, a certificate attesting to his release from Sieradz prison and a letter from his attorney, Winawer, summarizing the entire case. This time, the LHR agreed to acknowledge him as a political refugee. On 24 November 1938, it went before the interior ministry to plead for "a new, more clement examination" of his case. To improve his chances of success, Matès sent two letters in a row to the ministry, humble and awkward requests typed by a public letter writer, replete with "your kindly solicitude" and "most sincerely yours," in which he reiterates for the 100th time the narrative of his woes: "I had to leave my country after being sentenced to five years in prison for a political offense. As a Jew, I am forbidden to return to Poland, and to other countries as well. I would therefore be most grateful if you would grant me permission to reside in France, and I hereby declare that I am prepared to go wherever you decide is best. My spouse, with whom I am living, is in her seventh month of pregnancy."[21]

But time was running out. Subjected now to a second denial of residency, Matès had to hide, in the same way he had been obliged to slip away under cover of night without paying rent earlier in the year: "I am forced to flee my residence and to leave my wife eight months pregnant, alone and helpless in her current state."[22] Meanwhile, he placed his fate in the hands of yet another association: The Committee for the Defense of the Rights of the Jews of Central and Eastern Europe, often called the "Gourevitch Committee" after its vice president, which strongly advocated for the repeal of the 1938 laws. On 10 December, the Gourevitch Committee attempted to attract the minister's "kind attention," but to no avail.

Over a single year, Matès made the improbable move from the ex-*Secours rouge* to the Committee for the Defense of the Rights of Jews, a slippery slope that changed this rock-solid Communist into a beggar, a *schlimazel*, an eternal loser. Did he look elsewhere for a solution? On 5 December 1938, the Swiss legation in France gave this response: "Your request for an entry visa into Switzerland cannot be considered at this time." The same day, the British Passport Control Office gave a similar answer. On 6 December, the Swedish consul in Paris, Raoul Nordling, returned a flat refusal, stating that in order to gain an entry visa, the applicant would have to present "a valid ID . . . bearing a return visa to France."[23] Though it might not appear to be the case, these three requests for emigration show that Matès actually did want to settle in France with his wife and child. Article 11 of the law of 2 May 1938 did in fact stipulate that a foreigner who "is unable to leave French soil" would not be issued a warrant for expulsion, and this "inability" was shown based on the denial of visa requests from three different consulates.

But the interior ministry could not be bothered with such details: on 8 March 1939, it asked the police prefecture to "proceed without delay with the expulsion of this foreigner." Ten days later, it ruled that Idesa was also subject to circular no. 338 of 9 July 1937 and again ordered that the police "proceed with the expulsion of this foreigner." Then it was Idesa's turn to receive a pink slip: mother of a two-month-old, she became overnight "E. 114,560" and was given eight days to pull up stakes.[24] At this same time, the Yiddish magazine *Oyfn sheydveg* (*At the Crossroads*) wrote in its first issue: "We are living in a period of the impending liquidation of the era of emancipation with its humanitarian and democratic principles. We have become a nation of refugees facing closed doors."[25]

They stayed. They stayed because the law, however repressive, contained loopholes that worked in their favor. In his 1936 dissertation, a legal expert found it regrettable that expulsion rulings were so often ineffective because of leniency toward offenders. It was his view that "without direct repatriation, expulsion is just an illusion" that never really achieves its desired outcome. It is true that the interior ministry would often grant illegals the benefit of an inquiry and a "renewable deferment." Multiple warning notices would lead to a series of inquiries and appeals, and the process would drag on, much to the displeasure of the police prefecture which, even in the best of cases, had no way of verifying whether expulsion orders had been carried out once they had finally been pronounced.[26]

But these flaws (or rather, protections) did not prevent undocumented foreigners from living in a constant state of anxiety. Take the case of Ilex Beller in Belleville, after a stay in Belgium. Deprived of working papers, living in a hotel for *grine*, or newcomer Jewish immigrants, he did odd jobs for a grocer. On this particular day, a Sunday, he left his room to go out and get some fresh air on the boulevard. The Jews whose papers were in order had peace of mind, they would be out strolling, talking boisterously.

> You see some that seem to be in a hurry. . . . Always weaving through a crowd, looking worried about something. Watch them closely. . . . They never go any further than a certain intersection, and once there, they turn around and retrace their steps. With one eye, they're looking to see if someone they know is there, and with the other, they scan the passersby, trying to detect a plainclothes policeman hidden in the crowd, to sense

whether an ID check is about to take place. At the slightest alert, they disappear: these are the ones who have received their expulsion orders.[27]

In the book *The Jews of Belleville*, published after the war, the Yiddish writer Benjamin Schlevin (born in Brest-Litovsk in 1913) gives us a glimpse into the squalid life of Kraindel, a poor Jewish woman who ekes out a living from needlework. In her quest to obtain an ID and work permit, she entrusts her fate to a go-between from Bessarabia who helps with her paperwork while relieving her of the little money she has. When she gets served with an expulsion notice, she shuts herself into her hotel room, working by candlelight, but she has trouble delivering her cumbersome wares, and risks arrest if she steps outside.[28] To this fictional story, we can add a very real one: the arrest of young Abram Solarz. Born in Parczew in 1917, he arrived in France with no passport or visa at the age of eighteen and worked for his father making hats at an address on Rue Vieille-du-Temple in the Marais district (the rest of the family, the mother and three other children, stayed behind in Parczew). On 12 November 1936, according to a police report, Abram was apprehended for "failure to produce an ID and fleeing a police officer." This resulted in a pink slip, denial of residency "E. 77,605."[29]

Clandestine life was a full-time activity, where fear seeped into and corroded every aspect of life. Illegals had to avoid public places where they risked roundups, flee the "swallows" (the officers on bicycles who monitored immigrants), learn to jabber some French, make contacts in the garment and shoemaking trades, work undeclared while avoiding the worst exploiters, take care not to fall ill or get injured and be ready to pick up and move at a moment's notice. The paperwork alone could occupy a large part of one's days. As Werner Prasuhn tells it, "I went begging for deferments and grace periods. Every week, I would climb to the fifth floor of the prefecture and, from morning until closing time, I would wait for the sound of that stamp that would allow me to exist for a bit longer."[30] Matès, a case in point, would spend all his time between the police prefecture on the Île de la Cité, *Secours populaire* at 97 Rue Lafayette in the 10th arrondissement, the Human Rights League at 27 Rue Jean-Dolent (14th arrondissement), the Gourevitch Committee at 48 Rue François I (8th arrondissement), the translator who certified his documents in Polish at 38 Rue Hallé (14th arrondissement) and the various consulates that turned him away, not to mention the mounting costs for paper and envelopes, stamps, translator's and typist's fees and the like.

If they stayed and endured all this hardship, it's because they had nowhere else to go. The last democracies of Europe and America had closed their borders. Their passports were not in order. And even if they managed a visa for Argentina, the fare would be beyond their means. On Matès's ID form, under the heading "Available Funds," one reads: "120 francs on his person, and 80 francs weekly plus rent from *Secours populaire*," which amounts to roughly 5,000 francs a year, a quarter of an average worker's earnings.[31] Communist solidarity helped thousands of people: from 1935 to 1937, *Secours populaire* received some 8.2 million francs from both party members and other contributors, enabling the organization to distribute 109,000 days' worth of aid.[32] The association also found odd jobs for the refugees, as in the case of Louis Gronowski, expelled from Liège in 1929, who managed to get work in a Paris restaurant as a dishwasher and cellar master. I have no way of knowing whether Matès and Idesa dined at any of the soup kitchens that were springing up in the 20th arrondissement, but in these tough times there was no shortage of customers: in 1936, six soup kitchens distributed a total of 710,000 meals, while eight clinics carried out 48,000 consultations.

While visiting the Society of the Friends of Parczew, after the war, my father heard from one of the old folks that Matès had worked as a glover in Paris. A saddler knows how to cut and sew leather, so he would probably also be able to make gloves; this meant that, in addition to his meager income from *Secours*, Matès could also make a little on the side from selling leather articles. It probably didn't amount to much, as we might conclude from the expulsion directive transmitted by the police prefecture in 1939, which states that Matès "has no steady employment." Who was his boss? Where did he get tools? Between his arrival in Paris and the end of 1937, Matès was living at 37 Rue des Couronnes, at the corner of Rue Vilin, and then, until July 1939, at 11 Rue du Pressoir, some 100 yards away. An oft-heard story; apart from the Marais, Jewish immigrants tended to concentrate in an area bordered by the Père-Lachaise cemetery, Rue des Pyrénées, Rue de Belleville and Belleville and Ménilmontant Boulevards.[33] This was the heart of the garment and leather district of Paris, two sectors where immigrants could find work: Armenians, Turks, Polish Jews and the like. In the mid-1920s, out of some 16,000 active Poles (three quarters of whom were Jews), 4,600 worked in the garment industry, 3,000 in leather and pelts, 2,300 in retail commerce and a few thousand in peddling and secondhand shops, the trades reserved for the most recently arrived, and therefore most insecure, immigrants.[34]

By pure coincidence—but can we really speak of coincidence here?—at the time I begin my research, I am living on Rue du Pressoir. Today, at number 11, the place where my grandparents landed in 1938, the tenements are gone; not a single vestige remains for my generation to visit. In their place, there is a concrete high-rise from the 1970s, identical to the building where I now live with my wife and two daughters, just a few doors down. In the neighborhood, Jewish workshops have given way to Chinese sweatshops, and stuffed dates and honey-soaked pastries have replaced the jars of pickled gherkins. The rooming houses that remain are full of elderly North Africans, bent over with rheumatism. 37 Rue des Couronnes, across from my daughter's nursery school, no longer exists either. The building was torn down when Rue Vilin was widened and extended, today reaching all the way to Belleville Park. In its place, there is a center for medical imaging with opaque glass in its front windows. On my way home along Rue du Pressoir, I often pass in front of number 11 and imagine Matès and Idesa up on the second floor, sharing a baguette and some black radishes.

But since these daydreams are just depressing and don't really get me anywhere, I go to the archives of the City of Paris to consult the prewar census figures. The last one is dated 1936, unfortunately. At that point, Matès and Idesa were still in prison back in Poland. For 37 Rue des Couronnes, the census indicates with stunning precision that a certain Mr. Laurens, a fifty-two-year-old hotel owner from the Aveyron region, lived there with his wife and children; an Armenian, a dishwasher in a restaurant, cohabited with an unemployed Polish woman. I also find an Algerian laborer and a whole flock of Poles. There are many bachelors, so it must have been a hotel, the one belonging to Mr. Laurens. From numbers 37 to 40 on Rue des Couronnes, the census counted 102 foreigners out of 596 persons, or 17% of the residents. At 11 Rue du Pressoir there lived Albert Mariottini, a fifty-six-year-old Italian, an unemployed shoemaker; and Zela

Sheinbaum, a forty-nine-year-old leatherworker, married to a Romanian woman; but there were also such names as Maurice Boucheron and Léon Carpentier, Roger Mortreuil or Jeanne Poirier, with occupations such as baker, metalworker at Billancourt, store clerk at Trois-Quartiers, polisher or lithographer.[35] Some of these may well still have been there a year later when Matès Jablonka arrived, a twenty-nine-year-old Polish saddler soon to switch to making gloves.

Even though the 20th arrondissement was one of the most Jewish areas of Paris in the 1930s, right up there with the 18th (8,500 Jews) but behind the 11th (more than 13,000), the Belleville-Ménilmontant neighborhood was nothing like a ghetto; rather, it was a patchwork of ethnicities, a tower of Babel spread over three square miles. Born-and-bred Parisians rubbed shoulders with freshly arrived provincials, such as our hotel owner from Aveyron, over on Rue des Couronnes; but also North Africans, sub-Saharan Africans, foreigners both legal and undocumented, refugees, Italians, Czechs, Romanians, Poles, Jews, Turks, Armenians, all of them working to turn raw materials into finished goods, either at a shop or at home; they strolled along the boulevard, sipped coffee at an outdoor café, stood in line at the butcher's and crossed paths in their stairwells. Like Romain Gary in *La Vie devant soi* [*The Life Before Us*], like Thierry Jonquet in his thrillers, the Armenian writer Clément Lépidis made himself the bard of this international village: "Some of them [the Eastern European refugees] had such awful accents that the folks of Belleville had trouble telling the difference between all the various races among them, easily confusing Jews with Armenians and Armenians with Greeks."[36]

Matès probably worked at home, as a kind of informal subcontractor. Nothing very original there. A Belleville boot maker recalls: "Every home is occupied by a room full of workers, always ready to perform any task; there was no shortage of suppliers of leather, pelts and accessories."[37] Arriving in Paris in 1929, Moshe Garbarz's parents lived in a 30-square-foot attic room where they worked, cooked and slept. They later managed to move into a "palace" in Belleville, two rooms, running water and a toilet on the landing. But the sewing machine over which they slaved from dawn until late into the night took up all the extra space. "Once it was in place, there was no room to move."[38] It must have been a very similar experience for Matès and Idesa, except that there were three of them: my aunt Suzanne, Soreh in Yiddish, was born on 23 January 1939 at the Rothschild Hospital. Diapers would have been drying over the sewing machine, pairs of finished gloves piling up on the duvet used at night as bedding for the child. Matès was clever enough to find outlets for some of what he produced, but who buys gloves in the summer? Without any form of welfare to offset their losses, they must have suffered greatly during the slow season. Did he ever try switching to belts or wallets? On my father's birth certificate, in April 1940, it says the father's profession is "upholsterer." The old man from Parczew didn't mention any such occupation, but who knows whether his information was accurate to begin with.

Working at home was a last resort, and usually meant that the worker was poorly integrated, didn't know much French and was living on the edge, economically and socially. Like the other 10,000 pieceworkers in Paris, Matès had no access to the world of workshops or factories. French workers were already hit hard by unemployment during this time, but in any case, Matès didn't have a work permit. On the other hand, he managed his raw material as he saw fit, and was free to organize his own work schedule, but this is the "freedom" of the day laborer of prerevolutionary France, when a man was paid for his day's work, never knowing what the next day might bring, or whether his family would have enough to eat at day's end. A reservoir of cheap, "flexible" labor, in today's parlance, pieceworkers were tied to their bosses by a verbal agreement whose clauses—shipment, quantities, quality control, wages—remained purposely vague, and this often resulted in exploitation of the worst sort.[39] As was the case in Parczew, workers were involved in a preindustrial scheme of production, which could nonetheless become confrontational. But in Paris, fear of the police, the squalor of daily existence, the language and nationality barrier combined to extinguish their combative spirit. In 1938, Hersz Stol, having arrived a few months earlier via Basel and been almost immediately declared "E. 98,824," lived in Villa du Parc, in a one-room flat "furnished very modestly with items belonging to him. . . . He works as a tailor out of this home. After declaring that he made trousers for a merchant in the 4th arrondissement—he knew neither his name nor address—he asserts today that he is in business for himself, and sells the same trousers at a stall in the

Carreau du Temple. It would appear that he is working illegally for some boss he doesn't want to name." This work earned him about 150 francs a week (in addition to the 65 francs he got from *Secours populaire*). The police report bears a handwritten remark in red across the page: "This foreigner is one of many who are undermining our local industries."[40] Like Matès.

Aid from *Secours populaire* and the occasional sale of gloves allowed the household to survive. In the early days, perhaps they also got help from the three children of Esther Korenbaum, one of Idesa's maternal aunts. These cousins, Frime, Sroul and Dina, who had immigrated to Paris in the early 1930s, lived in a two-room-plus-kitchen apartment at 88 Avenue d'Italie. As it was explained to me by Sroul's son, who used to watch them in the cavernous basement workshop down stairwell C, the two women worked as "furrier mechanics." Sroul's job was to nail the pelts to a board, cut them into fine strips a few millimeters thick, then stretch them gently before machine-sewing them back together. The three furrier workers were too poor to help out their Parczew cousin in any substantial way, but they may well have supplied them with a little food or secondhand baby clothes.

In her declarations to the LHR and the interior ministry, Idesa claimed to be receiving "money from America." She said as much again in a letter to Simje and Reizl, dated 9 May 1940: "I wrote you a card when I got the 250 francs. . . . You really don't need to send money since you yourselves have so little to live on. You're just workers, and I know how hard that is. I get money every so often from America. They are helping us out. They can afford more than you."[41] What surprises me here is not so much the existence of these anonymous benefactors as how insistently Matès and Idesa refer to them when dealing with the authorities, almost as if this were a point of pride, proof that others had preceded them, that they had relatives in the *goldene Amerika*. I find myself caught up in the search for their identity. On the Jablonka side, there was no one in the United States, and in any case, the money was always intended expressly for Idesa. So I turn to the Korenbaum branch. A very distant cousin, Richard Coren, spent several years digging through records and contacting strangers who might share some of the same DNA, all for the pleasure of establishing the Korenbaum family tree, a genealogical masterpiece branching out from Chaim Korenbaum (1784–1866) all the way to the generation of my daughters, born in the 2000s, and including, along the way, Idesa, Frime, Sroul, Dina and dozens of great-grandparents, great-aunts and countless cousins.[42]

Originally from Maloryta, not far from Parczew and Brest-Litovsk, the Korenbaum family today is scattered throughout twenty-eight states in the United States, as well as Canada, Israel, France, Belgium and Germany. Abandoning his native Russia during the bloody pogroms, Chaim Korenbaum, great-grandson of the ancestor of the same name, set sail in 1905 on the steamer *Kensington* heading for Quebec, then pushed further south to Pawtucket, Rhode Island, where he settled, going to work as a peddler. Chaim had left behind in Maloryta his parents and six siblings, Esther, David, Rushla (my grandmother's mother) and the three youngest, Baruch, Henya and Basha. About Esther, I know nothing. David, who became a woodsman, spent his whole life in Maloryta, where he died peacefully in 1937, never again to see his seven daughters, who had left to seek their fortune in Palestine and France. Rushla ended up in Parczew, following Feder who, like a feather floating on the winds of history, vanished into thin air. As for the youngest, Baruch, Henya and Basha, they eventually joined their brother in Rhode Island and, a few years later, they were American citizens.

In early 2008, I send an email to the grandchildren of Basha "Bessie" and Henya "Annie" Korenbaum, Idesa's aunts. Both agree that Annie was the one who stayed in contact with the family in Europe, and that she was a generous person. According to one of Bessie's granddaughters, she traveled to Palestine in 1937: "I was very young at the time, but I clearly recall my parents talking about Aunt Annie's trip, and later on, I remember Annie herself talking about it. Maybe they went to Europe on the same trip." One time while I am visiting New York University, I go up to Boston to meet one of Annie's granddaughters. I'm having trouble finding my way in a suburban grid composed of neat gardens and deserted streets, where walking is considered a suspicious activity. Finally, Annie's granddaughter opens the door and greets me warmly. She is a lovely, dark-haired woman, who speaks a little French. Her husband is a psychoanalyst with an office in the basement. Also a Francophile, he has read his Lacan and Ariès. We talk about the war, about Jews and France, and then we move to the topic that is our common interest, the Korenbaum family saga. In Rhode Island, Annie and her husband ran a furniture business. They weren't wealthy, but had enough, undoubtedly, to be able to send "money from America." Annie wasn't the kind of person who put the past behind her. Did she know Idesa personally, her niece in Paris who was born after her departure for the United States? No, not unless the 1937 trip led to their meeting in Parczew or in Maloryta. I need to preserve a trace of this soul who shone like a beacon while the Old World was about to collapse, so Annie's granddaughter lets me take a snapshot of a framed photograph in her living room, showing Annie listening to her daughter play the piano. She is staring forward, a little dreamy-eyed, her white hair pulled back in a bun, while the young woman at the piano seems transported by the music. Her son, a slim boy, quite elegant in his jacket, stands attentively at his sister's side, ready to turn the page of her score. A fine-looking pair.

Matès and Idesa undoubtedly had backing from other sources and networks as well. Let us first observe what the *Ostjuden* could expect from the French Jewish community. Picking up the rhetoric of the ultranationalist Croix-de-Feu, the Patriotic Union of French Jews demanded that something be done about the "Jewish question" in France. Raymond-Raoul Lambert backed the liberal position and, on the eve of war, joined the Gourevitch Committee in demanding that the Daladier laws be repealed at once. But the majority position was best expressed by Jacques Helbronner, vice-president of the central consistory and a delegate to the High Commission for Refugees of the League of Nations: France could not continue to take in "the riff-raff, the rejects of society, the elements who could not possibly have been of any use to their own country," those individuals who were "a bunch of non-entities of no use to any human agglomeration." Not surprisingly, Helbronner advised the government to close the borders and turn everyone away, with the exception of 100 or 150 intellectuals. Anyone who managed to slip through this net would be sent back, by military force, to the country whence they came. Helbronner's reasoning was not so much that of a middle-class Frenchman inconvenienced by the unwashed masses as it was that of a loyal Jewish Frenchman who respected the nationals/foreigners divide, the simple us/them binary. Adopting a different logic, the Germans later loaded him onto a cattle train, in November 1943, and murdered him in a gas chamber.[43]

The more important issue is that of political connections. In Paris, Matès and Idesa reconnected with many of their old comrades: Abram and Malka Fiszman, Colette's parents, who were their closest friends; Gitla Leszcz, born in Dębowa-Kłoda, near Parczew, who would attest to my grandfather's morals at the Père-Lachaise police commissariat in 1939; Hersz Stol, Idesa's witness during her dealings with the LHR. There is evidence that my grandparents knew these four people, and it's hard to believe they would not have also come across Icek Sznajder, he of the paint-stained coat lining: born in Parczew in 1901, militant with the KZMP in the early 1930s, arrested and sentenced in 1933, he arrived in Paris in February 1937 and managed to subsist thanks to *Secours populaire*.

Here lies the mystery that remains unresolved to this day: once in Paris, did Matès and Idesa continue their militant activities? My instincts tell me that they settled down, a high-profile association with the Party being too risky. But not as risky as in Poland, of course: the French Communist Party (FCP) was a legal party, a mass movement, and refugees fresh from their home country's jails were stunned at how openly the French comrades went about violating the basics of underground activity, drawing up membership lists, demonstrating under police protection, singing "The Internationale" in public and so on. Still, the last thing an undocumented refugee attempting to legalize his situation needs is to associate with "subversive" organizations. For the Republic, this alone was grounds for denial. Hersz Stol's record met with this kind of suspicion from the very start. As the police prefect self-righteously pronounced, he "seems to take a special interest in extremist parties. In such conditions, I will leave it to you to determine whether there is any reason to authorize this foreigner, this so-called political refugee, to take up residence in France."[44] In 1929, Moshe Zalcman, a Communist figure in Zamość and later on in Warsaw, left Poland on a fake passport, with the address of *Secours rouge* Paris in his pocket. Hired by a workshop in the Marais, he insisted on being paid the same day. The boss sized him up: "As I can see, you're one of the 'little comrades,' aren't you?" And he added, in a patronizing tone: "Trust me, that stuff won't get you anywhere around here. This is Paris, so you'd best forget all that nonsense."[45]

My intuition is also based on the fact that, in late 1937, the FCP experienced some born-again patriotic zeal. In a climate of rampant xenophobia, the Party joined the pack, denouncing opportunistic immigrants, proclaiming "France for the French" in the columns of the Communist newspaper *L'Humanité*.[46] And the Jewish branch of the MOI, now a cumbersome embarrassment, was dissolved. In Paris, Shlomo, a Polish Jew from Płock, was an activist with *Secours rouge* until the FCP's chauvinism started making him uneasy. He then opted for the soup kitchens of Belleville instead, before dropping his activism altogether and settling down in 1937.[47] Elsewhere, the economic crisis put enormous strain on worker solidarity with immigrants, assuming there had ever been any in the first place. In Le Havre, in 1934, a "group of French workers" sent an anonymous letter to the interior ministry to denounce Yankel Niski, a Jewish tailor from Parczew, who would very shortly be issued an expulsion order:

> We, French workers, who toil to keep our children fed, who have gone without work for years, listen to your fine speeches that ask us to be patient, to wait a little longer until the crisis is over. There are no jobs. Could you tell us, then, how it is that Mr. Niski, a Pole, who has no right to be working in France, has managed to find a job with the Charles Goldstein Co., located in Le Havre, at 94 Cours de la République, which has him make men's suit jackets to measure for 20 francs each, where a French worker would be paid 70 francs at least for the same work?[48]

And finally, the great purges in the USSR shook the convictions of many. Faiwel Schrager, the head of the Jewish branch of the MOI, the founder of the Jewish Popular Movement and a journalist at *Naye Presse* (the Yiddish counterpart of *L'Humanité*), began to "doubt the truth of Communism" and broke with the Party in 1937, at the time of the Moscow trials.[49]

Was this the end of militancy, then? I prove my case by an absence of evidence, in fact. There is nothing in the archives of the French Communist Party or the MOI, no testimony, either direct or indirect. One might very well object that three years' worth of financial support from *Secours populaire*, which was a satellite organization of the Party, implied more than mere proximity: it meant loyalty. As soon as they arrived in Paris, many immigrants would start doing freelance writing for *Naye Presse*, work in the Jewish branch of the MOI or the Jewish Inter-Union Committee run by Dorembus-Warszawski, and would get involved in the *pa-tronatn*, support groups for political prisoners allied to the international *Secours rouge*. Paris was full of progressive Jewish organizations back then, social clubs, solidarity groups and anti-fascist centers. There was the Jewish Workers' Athletic Club (YASK), the Jewish Workers' Theater (PYAT), the Belleville Workers' Club and the *Arbeter-Ordn*, which involved two health dispensaries and an office for legal counsel, in addition to the famous YKUF congress. The most active community center was *Kultur Liga* on Rue de Lancry in the 10th arrondissement. Athletic clubs were headquartered there, along with workers' unions and *patronatn*, run on the side by the Communists; it housed a Yiddish-language library, a chorale, a theater troupe, conference rooms and a welcome center for new arrivals to France. Gronowski, who used to go there after his work-day at the restaurant, declared that it was "at the same time a cultural organization, a clearinghouse for jobs and housing, and an information bureau for those seeking work permits and ID cards, etc."[50] When he got to Paris in 1932, Faiwel Schrager "naturally" headed straight for Rue de Lancry, where he crossed paths with many other immigrants: "Some were political refugees wanted by the Polish police, many of whom had already spent time in prison."[51] In these crowded locales, I have no trouble imagining Matès and Idesa seeking advice, running into friends in the bitter-sweet brotherhood of exile; maybe they would dance, attend a lecture by Jacques Duclos, or a gathering in honor of the "three L's." It is possible, then, that they were active without being militants, like Moshe Garbarz, who ruled out joining the Party in any official capacity, for fear of expulsion, but who was a regular at Rue de Lancry, never missed an issue of *L'Humanité* or *Naye Presse*, took part in all demonstrations and gave what he could for the cause.[52]

But is it really conceivable that two KZMP cadres, accustomed to eluding the police and remaining defiant during interrogations, sentenced to five years in prison for "crimes against the state," would have been content to attend progressive cultural soirees? Could they have just sat back while Hitler was railing against Bolshevism and international Jewry, while Spanish republicans were being massacred and anti-refugee hysteria was reaching a fever pitch? In February 2008, I write to Adam Rayski, who was the director of the *Naye Presse* on the eve of the war and later head of the MOI. I get no answer, and it turns out that this great resistance figure is to die a month later. Paulette Sliwka, another resistance figure at the MOI while Rayski was director, agrees to meet with me at her home. She sits me down at her kitchen table, on the fourth floor of a subsidized apartment block in Montreuil, and asks me rather abruptly what it is that I want. I reply that I am trying to find out about my grandparents, whom no one seems to know much about.

"I'm sorry, but I can't help you."

"Oh, but I think you can. My grandparents were Polish Jews, born in a shtetl at the turn of the century, Communists, exiled to Paris. It's exactly the same profile as your own father. If you can say something about him, I'll better understand their life."

Paulette Sliwka stares at me, taken aback.

"Don't tell me you're going to pattern your grandfather's story after my father's!"

"No, of course not, but their paths do bear a certain resemblance to each other. For instance, from what you know, does it make sense that my grandfather would have stopped being a militant?"

"How would I know? I never met him!"

"All right, but we can assume that a KPP militant, once he arrives in Paris, would start spending time at Rue de Lancry, or with the *Naye Presse* people, that kind of thing."

"Stop imagining, will you? How do we know he didn't go over to the other side? It can happen, you know."

"What I mean is that you would have been more likely to find him hanging around labor groups like the MOI than the synagogue, or some far-right group." I keep going without letting her respond. "Put yourself in his place. He gets to Paris in August 1937. What does he do?"

She looks pouty for a moment, then answers: "He must have some address in his pocket, a friend, the *landsmanshaft* of his shtetl, someone to help him get on his feet, find some place to flop, a boss who hires illegals. No one lands here with nothing at all."

"The archives show that he got help from *Secours populaire*. Could you see him continuing his political activities?"

"I'm telling you, I have no idea! All I can say is that my father was a militant, he would go to the *Arbeter-Ordn*, and he sang in the chorale."

"And what about women?"

"For them, there was nothing but 'in sorrow you shall bring forth children' and life as a housewife."

"But in Poland, my grandmother went to prison, just like the men did."

"Well, maybe so, but in Paris, that's not how it was."

"A man like Joseph Minc was a Party militant—in Poland, then in France—from 1924 to 1967. In fact, he learned French by reading *L'Humanité*, and used to hang out with Communist students. His girlfriend became treasurer of a Party cell. He said something that I often think about: 'When you join the Party at sixteen, and go underground, constantly threatened with imprisonment or worse, the decision to leave can only be a long and painful one.'[53] So now, what if I told you that my grandfather, once in Paris, got close to the Jewish leatherworkers joint union, and that he passed out anti-fascist pamphlets on the streets every Sunday . . . ?"

Paulette Sliwka just shrugs her shoulders. I don't dare propose an even more doubtful scenario: could Matès's political leanings have accounted for how poor he was, or why he wasn't able to succeed as a saddler, or upholsterer or glover? Where some *Ostjuden* managed to open their own businesses, Matès may well have dismissed the idea of becoming a boss— not unlike Reizl, 6,800 miles from there, who, after coaxing her husband to start a business that eventually failed, realized that they were meant to live like good proletarians.

On a shady café terrace in the Recoleta neighborhood of Buenos Aires, I open up to Benito, Simje's son. He never knew Matès, any more than I did, but his own life story—three jail sentences, abiding loyalty to Marxist-Leninist values—has given him some experience in the area. Is it possible, I ask him, that a professional revolutionary like Matès would break with the Party once in France?

"Unthinkable," says Benito.

"I get the feeling you're projecting your own story onto Matès."

"You asked, so I answered. Your grandfather never let go. Communism was everything for him. He went to prison for it."

"Once in Argentina, *Tío* Simje dropped his militant stance."

"He was different from Matès. But he did stay Communist his whole life."

"Even after the purge of the generals, the dissolution of the KPP, the German-Soviet pact?"

"Of course! Being a Communist is a kind of identity, no matter what Stalin or the Party did."

All immigrants experience xenophobia and misery, all are vulnerable to varying degrees. But compared to Parczew, where you could get five years in prison for displaying a banner, where you couldn't hold a demonstration against pogroms for fear of arousing your neighbor's anti-Jewish sentiments, Paris must have seemed like a haven of tranquility. Here, we have to remember that Matès was born into the Czarist empire, where Jews didn't have the right to live in the city, buy land, practice certain professions or leave the "residence zone" that covered Congress Poland, Ukraine, Belarus, Lithuania and part of western Russia. Paris was the land of liberty.

But it was also a hive of activity. Narrow streets and alleyways were open-air markets for sock, umbrella and sponge vendors, for upholsterers, glaziers, shoe-shiners, knife-grinders, all the most marginal trades that were less indicative of some mythical picturesque Paris than of life's everyday precariousness, the daily slog. The hubbub of Ménilmontant Boulevard, conversations in twelve languages, the cries of the scrap peddler, iceman and coalman, car horns honking: this was the cacophony of the world that was Paris, reminiscent of Krochmalna Street in Warsaw, but certainly not the backward Podlachia of saddlers and rutted streets. In Roger Ikor's *La Greffe de printemps* [*The Grafting of Spring*], Yankel explores the capital, marveling every step of the way: "So many houses! So many people in so many streets! . . . How gigantic this city was! Sometimes he would wander onto a street that was ten times, twenty times wider than the widest street in Rakwomir."[54]

And life carried on as always. After hanging around the prefecture all morning, Matès would go collect some orders from his boss, lunch on a bagel and pickled herring at Café Warshawski, at the corner of Belleville Boulevard and Rue de l'Orillon; or maybe he would stop and shoot the breeze with Abram Fiszman, who worked for a cousin as a tailor; or maybe

he would just wander up and down the boulevard, like Schlevin's protagonists, "woefully idle," while mothers would go to Jewish cafés and beg for
a glass of milk for their undernourished babies, who got nothing but a
"shriveled breast."[55] Certain sociological studies show that women actually adapted and flourished far better than men, who were slaves to their
machines, humiliated by long stretches of joblessness and their inability
to provide for their families. Matès was not the kind to just lie down in
defeat, but in this early part of 1939, I picture him dispirited, haunted
by self-doubt, embittered. He wasn't a *luftmensch*, one of those impracti-
cal contemplative types, half dreamer, half tramp, living from day to day,
like a Charlie Chaplin character; but he was certainly also no longer the
charismatic leader from Parczew who galvanized the town's youth with
his street-corner harangues. His defiantly clenched fist was now an out-
stretched hand. After failing to rally Poland to the grand union of the
Soviets, he was living off subsidies in a bourgeois country, reduced to peti-
tioning its all-powerful bureaucrats.

Thus do I feel justified in stating that Matès's life in France was actually harder than it had been in Poland. It was not so much that he missed
his family, or the warm embrace of old-world neighborliness, like Gold-
man, Wolf Wieviorka's character in *Est et Ouest* (1936) [*East and West*], who
suddenly feels "awash in love and nostalgia for his native village that had
once been so repugnant to him."[56] The fact is that Matès's suffering was no
longer transcended by an ideal that made sacrifice worthwhile. The police
weren't harassing him because he sought to build a new world, or because
he was the salt of the earth, a freedom fighter hounded by the fascists in
a struggle of global dimensions. Rather, he was rejected as a foreigner,
an "undesirable," so that France might be protected from this "endless,
mass invasion of ill-chosen elements that surely constitute a threat," in
the words of some pen-pusher for *Le Petit Parisien* in 1939.[57] The fearless,
blameless revolutionary had been reduced to a diaspora Jew. The Polish
Communist was stripped: he now had nothing but his bare humanity, un-
protected, stateless, an outcast from Parczew to Paris, from Stockholm to
Rome, from the far right to the French Communist Party. Underground
in Poland, underground in France, twice absent from the world, though
the underground life in Poland had nourished the hope of being useful to

humanity, turned danger into mission, torment into sacrifice and left him with a sense of fulfillment. France, by comparison, was dull and overcast, absurd, a maze of countless dead ends. I would be so curious to know how Matès felt about the Nazi–Soviet Pact of 23 August 1939. "It is only on the rarest of occasions," writes Arthur Koestler, "at its darkest hours that humanity has been abandoned with no particular belief to live or die for."[58]

I have trouble picturing Idesa as a matronly housewife, secure in her identity and feeling right at home in her new country. Torn from her egalitarian world of political militancy, where men and women ran the same risks and paid the same price, she was now up to her neck in the cares and woes of daily existence. Rosa Luxemburg in an apron, she had to take care of feeding and changing Suzanne and do the shopping, searching for the cheapest produce and buying a little meat from Szloma Niremberg's, the butcher at 22 Rue des Maronites, just at the end of Rue du Pressoir. This uneventful life is surely not what Idesa had wanted, but after her years of activism, where one forgets to be oneself, after her month of wandering around Europe, a break may have been welcome. I tell myself that she experienced these housewifely days as a convalescence of sorts, after her "mental illness contracted in prison." And despite the long lines at the prefecture, the disillusionment, the money not coming in, the bad news from Poland, the tiny apartment with its dingy furnishings, there were still glimmers of hope, moments of happiness: getting her certificate from the LHR, watching the baby grow, having friends over to share news.

A photograph dating from 1937 or 1938 shows a front view of cousin Sroul at a fairgrounds shooting gallery, aiming his rifle as onlookers gape. To the right, standing in the background, is Matès, forehead wrinkled and eyebrows raised as if in surprise at the sound of gunfire, or at the shooter's skill. He is wearing a jacket and finely striped tie, looking less intimidating than the Parczew man of marble whose winter coat, stiff as a breastplate, tended to cast gentle Henya and good Hershl into the shadows. Cousin Sroul worked long hours, day in and day out. On Sundays, after spending the week ruining his eyesight in the poorly lit basement at the bottom of stairway C, bent over his stitching machine—two notched disks pull the fur forward, a *greyfer* catches the thread, a horizontal needle stitches together the strips of fur—he would go to Place d'Italie, to a particular stand at the fair. Whenever someone hit the bull's eye, the camera shutter would click open automatically, and a few hours later, you could come to collect your photograph. Sroul's son has kept several of the same kind of shot: olive-skinned, black hair swept back from the forehead, with a Mediterranean air, he looks focused as he closes his left eye, aims and shoots, as the stunned crowd looks on. He was such a good aim that the showman would call him over to come shoot again, since his exploits had the effect of attracting other paying customers.

But it was becoming increasingly obvious that they were not going to make it: they were still undocumented, they had no legal work and France wanted them out. On the CD-ROM that contains all the naturalizations granted in France from 1900 to 1960, there are all kinds of further selection criteria, and when I type Parczew, I find that all the other occupants of the Bagneux burial vault—the Kaszemachers, the Sznajders, the Zlotagoras— eventually became French, for the most part between 1946 and 1948. But before attaining the holy grail of naturalization, there was a whole series of obstacles that Matès and Idesa couldn't get past. Fresh out of prison, Abram Fiszman arrived in Paris in October 1936 with no visa or passport. Having legally deposited the lordly sum of 10,000 francs in a cousin's account, however, he obtained his foreign resident ID card in March 1937, on the condition that he not work a salaried job.[59] Gitla Leszcz got to Paris by way of Germany and Belgium in February 1937. Like all the others, her case fell under the purview of circular no. 338, but her relationship with a French hardware dealer, Raymond Gardebled, allowed her a three-month reprieve to "carry out her matrimonial plans."[60] The same held true for Idesa's cousins, Annette and Jascha Korenbaum, daughters of the Maloryta forester: they married, respectively, Constant Couanault in 1936 and Maximilien Charriaud in 1939, two French anarchist tradesmen. In September 1939, Rywka Szerman, a twenty-five-year-old Parczew native, slipped into France illegally via Italy with 25,000 francs in her pocket. Housed by her sister and supported by her brother, both of whom had all their papers in order, she got a passport from the Polish consulate. The prefecture noted that "it is no longer possible to send this foreigner back to her country."[61]

These contrasting examples demonstrate exactly what Matès and Idesa were lacking: proper documents and money, but also references, family

and friends who were already settled, a French spouse, a clean police record. Compared to such assets, political refugee status was practically useless; in fact, it may well have proven a liability. In 1938, the French consul
in Warsaw wrote to the minister of foreign affairs regarding Icek Sznajder,
who was *non grata* in both France and Poland:

> One might say that he embodies all the conditions that qualify him for
> immediate expulsion: irregular entry without proper visa; questionable
> identity, since he has been only temporarily admitted as a Pole by the
> Paris consulate; without any financial resources whatsoever, claims he has
> no source of income, though he must surely be working to keep himself
> alive; an appalling record, since he admits having done time in prison.
> He claims he was a political prisoner, not a common criminal. This re-
> mains to be proven, however, since it is so far an empty claim.[62]

Matès and Idesa's situation exactly.

But most importantly, they arrived in France too late. In December
1936, the Communists withheld their vote of confidence for Blum because
of his nonintervention policy in Spain. In June 1937, they were not accepted into the Chautemps government; Matès didn't get to Paris until
3 months later, at the end of August, too late to benefit from either the
temporary respite provided by the *Front Populaire* or the influence of the
FCP within the majority. Alongside all this, the Jewish Popular Movement,
a support group for Jewish immigrants, was starting to fall apart. The suppression of the Jewish branch of the MOI indicated to the Communists
that it was time to leave the anti-Nazi struggle to the French working class.
Everywhere, hostility toward refugees was making a comeback.

On the morning of Thursday 11 May 1939, Matès and Idesa were strolling along the boulevard with Suzanne when a policeman demanded to
see their papers. Placed under immediate arrest, they were sent over to
the police prefecture at 11:00. Idesa was released, since she had a Polish
passport, or because she had a child in her care, but Matès was locked up.
I can see the prison register before my eyes, a large volume resurrected
from the police archives and entitled "Street Traffic: Foreigners," and I see
"Feder Ideta, 11 Rue du Pressoir, residency denied," and "Jablonska Matès,
ditto," at the bottom of pages 390–391, framed by an Armenian living in

Alfortville on an "expired residency card," and a woman from Montreuil, also "denied residency card."[63] I see them, and I feel their fear. The next day, Matès was issued a detention warrant and taken to a cell in the Santé prison.[64] Based on this information, we can assume that he would have appeared in court a few days later. I ask my father to meet me one morning at the Paris city archives, near Porte des Lilas. In an unfortunate Freudian slip, he forgets to bring any ID, something I had made extra sure to remind him to do, and he is refused entry. We argue back and forth with the registration clerk, hoping to soften his heart. In the end, my father is authorized to go up to the reading room with me, as long as I vouch for him, so to speak. The prison records confirm that Matès Jablonka, "upholsterer" by profession, and curiously registered as having "no known address," was incarcerated from 12 to 19 May 1939, at which point he was transferred to the Fresnes prison. We then move on to the register of the 16th chamber of criminal courts for the Seine region. We page through the volume feverishly, our emotion at a peak: there he is.

I believe that I became a historian so that one day, I could make that discovery. The distinction we make between our family stories—our personal histories—and what we like to call History, with its pompous capital H, makes little sense. They are in every way the same. There are not, on the one hand, the powerful of this world, with their scepters and televised speeches, and on the other, the ebb and flow of daily life, full of anger and unfulfilled hopes, anonymous tears, the faceless masses whose names rust away at the base of some war monument or in some out-of-the-way cemetery. There is only one freedom, one finiteness, one tragedy to make of the past both our richest gift and the poisoned spring that floods our hearts. To do history is to lend an ear to the pulse of silence, to attempt to replace an anguish so intense as to suffice unto itself, with the sweet, sorrowful respect the human condition inspires in us. This is my work. And when I run my hand over these court registers, allowing my eyes to follow the flow of the clerk's cursive script, I feel an indescribable sense of relief.

On 17 May 1939, my grandfather was sentenced to a month in prison and fined 100 francs for infringing the 2 May 1938 law, that piece of repressive legislation cosigned by Edouard Daladier, then head of government, and Albert Sarraut, interior minister, that sorted all these new arrivals into "good-faith foreigners" and "undesirable foreigners." Matès fell into the latter category: "Jablonka was found residing on French territory, even though he had been denied residency and been officially ordered to leave the country," an offense punishable under articles 2 and 13 of the law.[65] Another refugee, Werner Prasuhn, recalls a similar experience: "Whispered consultation, one rap of the gavel and it was over. The sentence was pronounced so fast that I missed it, and soon I was being led out, handcuffed, down a corridor. The officer holding the leash had to explain it to me: 'Two months in jail. You got off easy!'"[66] Similarly, Matès was shuttled from the prefecture to the prison, from the prison to the courthouse, from the courthouse back to the prison, from the Santé prison to the Fresnes prison, staring out the barred window of the paddy wagon at his wife and daughter in the distance. He remained at Fresnes until 11 June. In the Val-de-Marne departmental archives, I come across the prison registry as well as his release record. The only interesting item there: "Speaks no French."[67] What was Idesa doing all that time? Did she ask for help from her cousins Frime, Sroul and Dina, the three furriers at Avenue d'Italie? Two weeks after Matès's release, the law was amended in a way that allowed the accused to benefit from attenuating circumstances.

Prison, yet again. If some Jews moved from the ghetto to citizenship, Matès went from one jail cell to the next, never shedding his outlaw status. As one jurist wrote in 1938 in *Les Cahiers des droits de l'homme*, "I have seen on countless occasions those poor wretches who practically spend their whole lives behind bars. They leave one prison, get sent over the border to a neighboring country where they will soon be locked up once again."[68] Matès should have been a political refugee to whom France would proudly grant asylum. Instead, his imprisonment shows how pointless it was to distinguish between "good-faith foreigners" and "illegal aliens" that get fused into the category of delinquents.

According to article 2 of the 2 May 1938, law, Matès was punishable with expulsion upon his release from prison, but article 11 provided that foreigners with nowhere to go could be merely placed under house arrest. At some point in June, probably on the advice of an association, Matès submitted a request to the interior ministry to be placed under house arrest "in the provinces." When the ministry failed to act on the request, the prefecture also delayed any action. Still waiting for an answer, Matès and Idesa moved to 3 Rue Désirée, a stone's throw from Père-Lachaise. Here is where my father was conceived, around August 1939.

How careless can a system be, or how long can it procrastinate, allowing yet more illegals to slip through the net and stay a while longer? Tens of thousands of foreigners denied visas or issued expulsion warrants were languishing in the Seine region alone, a situation that drove the prefect to turn to the interior minister in the late summer of 1939 and ask that he "relieve the congestion" in Paris: "The presence in greater Paris of so many undesirables is threatening to disrupt national security and public order. The military government of Paris also believes it is absolutely crucial that we clear these individuals out of the Paris area. It is ready to make available to us, on a temporary basis, a staging camp that it has planned for placing foreigners." At that point, are they not just a step away from setting up "concentration camps" to bring together dubious stateless persons, whether they are under expulsion warrants waiting out their extensions, or fugitives from justice?[69] I don't know how the minister answered, but the prefect's wish was soon granted: the "scum of the earth," in Koestler's words, would soon be sent out to rot in eighty different camps scattered throughout the country, from stadiums in the Paris region—Roland-Garros, Buffalo, Colombes—to the worst of these cesspools, Le Vernet in Ariège, just a few notches better than Dachau on the scale of suffering and humiliation.[70]

This short month in prison might seem like a lark compared to what Matès had experienced between 1934 and 1936: constant transfers, inedible food, hunger strikes and punishments. But because France was a liberal democracy, unlike Pilsudski's Poland, this incarceration amounted to a far more traumatizing ordeal. The process by which a refugee landed in prison, starting with the police record, then the denial of residence, the arrest and trial, was aimed not at his supposed criminal acts but at his very person. In other words, the undocumented refugee in Ménilmontant is no longer the *technik* of Parczew: the latter won't be bothered anymore if he ceases all illegal activities, but the former is guilty by definition and will remain so, since his status means he can neither leave the country nor stay. Beyond the alleged offense, the real targets of all this repression are the uprooted, the intruders, the Jews no one wants, the innocent that have to be painted as criminals. Nathan Tropauer, a Polish Jew legally settled in France since 1925, experienced this Kafkaesque nightmare. Served with an expulsion warrant, never given an explanation as to the cause, he finally packed up and left, heartsick. Then, adding insult to injury, the Polish consulate refused to issue him a passport. In August 1938, wracked by anxiety, he pled his case to the LHR:

> And so it was that two officers came, at seven o'clock in the morning, shaking me from my sleep and dragging me off to the Santé prison as if I were the lowest crook or most dangerous criminal. *Reason given: refusal to comply with an expulsion warrant!* Since when is it a crime to be foreign, and Jewish at that? Is it my fault that my country's consular officials denied me entry into Poland, for racist reasons? For two whole months I bitterly endured the shameful stain that prison represents for an upstanding worker like myself, and began to wonder whether the freedoms and sacred principles of human rights proclaimed by the 1789 revolution were nothing but a fiction in today's democratic French republic.[71]

This short reflection brings us to the heart of an important issue: the continuity between the Third Republic and the Vichy regime. The Republic's concentration camps set up to contain Spanish, German or Austrian refugees, as well as Jews hounded from their homes all over Europe, constituted a breeding ground from which the Nazis and the Vichy officials would be able to take their pick. The Daladier laws paved the way for Marshal Petain's legislation targeting naturalized citizens and foreigners in July to September 1940, and Jews starting in October. By then, France had been discriminating against foreigners and hunting down illegals for several years. The reports compiled by National Security on Matès and Idesa represent priceless historical material, and it is a powerful emotional experience just to scroll through them on my laptop. But this material heralds the persecutions to come. During the brief *Front Populaire* period, the National Security records were managed by a young, up-and-coming civil servant, René Bousquet, who would become general secretary of the Vichy police and organizer of the Vél' d'Hiv' roundup. In 1940, after they had been evacuated by river barge, the "central records" of the prefecture were returned to Paris where they were reactivated by the Department of Foreigners and Jewish Affairs. Heading this office, André Tulard organized a separate set of exclusively Jewish records that October, based on census data taken in occupied France. Having spent his entire career policing foreigners at the prefecture, he had been well trained for the job.[72]

These records, the envy of police departments throughout the world, proved a highly effective instrument—both microscope and scalpel—for whoever might seek to purify the nation. The Germans knew it full well, as did their French collaborators. Even though laws from the 1930s were not explicitly anti-Semitic, there was indeed a "Vichy before Vichy" fermenting in the Republic. Appalling continuities, bleak prospects. For France was still the European country where refugees stood the best chance of finding help.

FIGURE 3. Matès, Henya, Hershl, undated (© Ivan Jablonka, family archives)

FIGURE 4. Idesa and Marcel, late 1940 (© Ivan Jablonka, family archives)

FIGURE 5. Interwar Poland (© PAO Seuil)

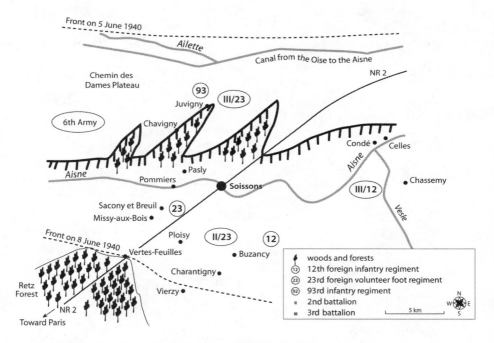

FIGURE 6. The Battle of Soissons, 5–8 June 1940 (© PAO Seuil)

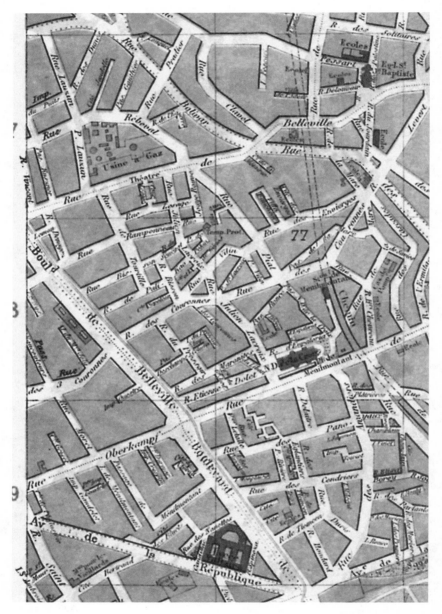

FIGURE 7. The Belleville-Ménilmontant quarter, Paris, in the 1930s. (Paris, plan et listes des rues, 4ᵉ partie, P. Joanne, Librairie Hachette & Co., map 14)

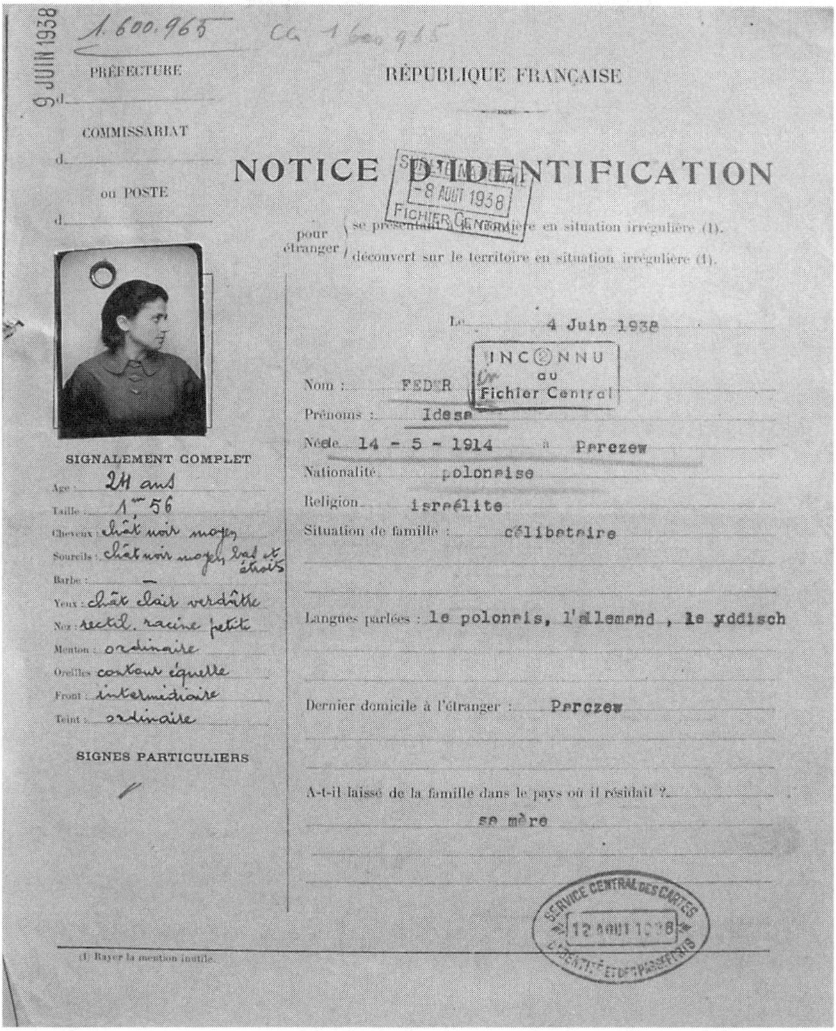

9 JUIN 1938

1.600.965

CG 1 600 965

PRÉFECTURE

d

COMMISSARIAT

d

ou POSTE

d

RÉPUBLIQUE FRANÇAISE

NOTICE D'IDENTIFICATION

SERVICE DES ÉTRANGERS
-8 AOUT 1938
FICHIER CENTRAL

pour étranger { se présentant à la frontière en situation irrégulière (1).
découvert sur le territoire en situation irrégulière (1).

Le 4 Juin 1938

INCONNU au Fichier Central

Nom : FEDER

Prénoms : Idesa

Né(e) le 14 - 5 - 1914 à Perezew

Nationalité polonaise

Religion israélite

Situation de famille : célibataire

Langues parlées : le polonais, l'allemand , le yddisch

Dernier domicile à l'étranger : Perczew

A-t-il laissé de la famille dans le pays où il résidait ? se mère

SIGNALEMENT COMPLET

Age : 24 ans

Taille : 1m 56

Cheveux : chât noir moyen

Sourcils : chât noir moyen, bad et étroits

Barbe : —

Yeux : chât clair verdâtre

Nez : rectil. racine petite

Menton : ordinaire

Oreilles : contour équelle

Front : intermédiaire

Teint : ordinaire

SIGNES PARTICULIERS

/

SERVICE CENTRAL DES CARTES D'IDENTITÉ D'ÉTRANGERS
12 AOUT 1938

(1) Rayer la mention inutile.

FIGURE 8. Identification record, Idesa, June 1938. File of Idesa Feder, ref. 19940445/57, Sûreté générale du ministère de l'Intérieur, Archives nationales (France)

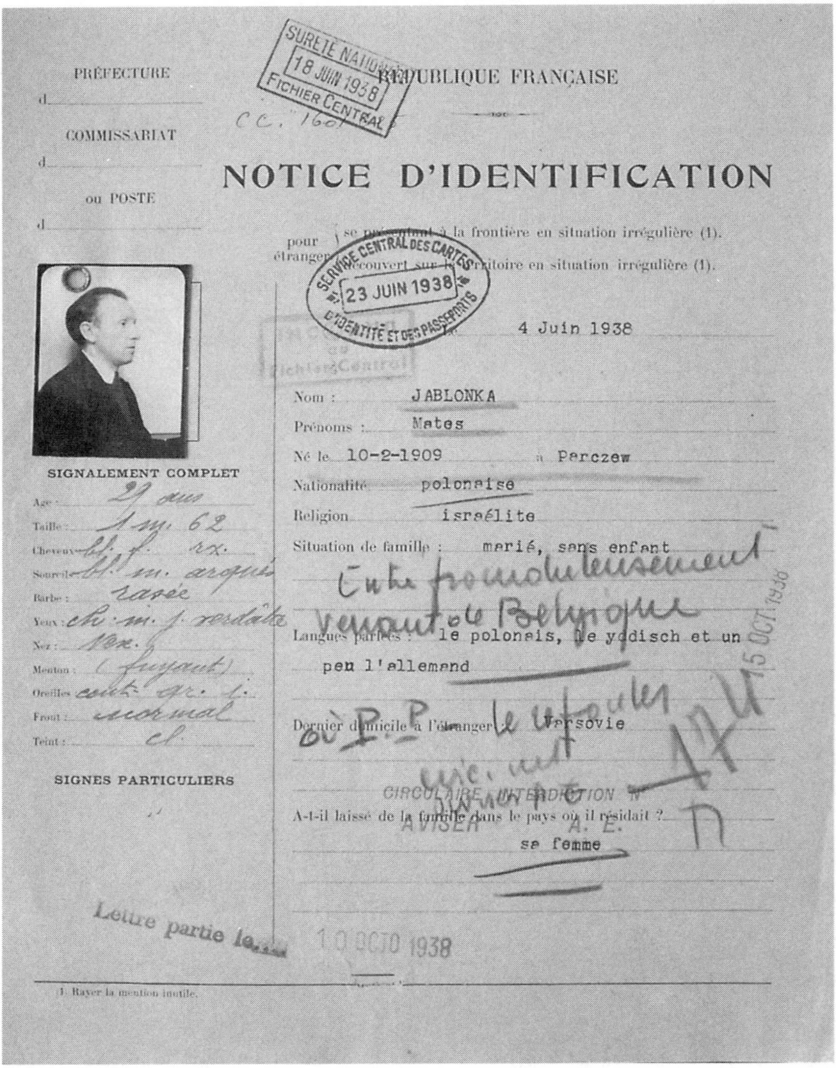
SÛRETÉ NATIONALE
18 JUIN 1938
FICHIER CENTRAL

PRÉFECTURE
d

COMMISSARIAT
d

ou POSTE
d

RÉPUBLIQUE FRANÇAISE

CC. 1601

NOTICE D'IDENTIFICATION

pour étranger { se présentant à la frontière en situation irrégulière (1). / découvert sur le territoire en situation irrégulière (1).

SERVICE CENTRAL DES CARTES D'IDENTITÉ ET DES PASSEPORTS
23 JUIN 1938

4 Juin 1938

Nom : JABLONKA

Prénoms : Mates

Né le 10-2-1909 à Parczew

Nationalité polonaise

Religion israélite

Situation de famille : marié, sans enfant

Entré frauduleusement venant de Belgique

Langues parlées : le polonais, le yddisch et un peu l'allemand

Dernier domicile à l'étranger Varsovie

CIRCULAIRE INTERDICTION N°

AVISER A. E.

A-t-il laissé de la famille dans le pays où il résidait ? sa femme

15 OCT. 1938

SIGNALEMENT COMPLET

Age : 29 ans

Taille : 1 m. 62

Cheveux : bl. f. rx.

Sourcils : bl. m. arqués

Barbe : rasée

Yeux : ch. m. j. verdâtre

Nez : rect.

Menton : (fuyant)

Oreilles : cont. qr. l.

Front : normal

Teint : cl.

SIGNES PARTICULIERS

Lettre partie le 10 OCT 1938

(1) Rayer la mention inutile.

FIGURE 9. Identification record, Matès, June 1938. File of Mates Jablonka, ref. 19940454/1, Sûreté générale du ministère de l'Intérieur, Archives nationales (France)

AUTUMN 1939:

THE FOREIGNERS

ENLIST

On 18 October 1939, Matès wrote to Simje and Reizl in Argentina. The most recent letter he had received from Parczew was dated 28 August, four days before the German invasion. No news since from the parents. "Despite the current tense situation," he wrote, "we're all doing well. Yidess [*sic*] takes care of the house and child, which involves lots of effort. As for me, I get work every once in a while, I haven't had much luck. . . . I have a good little baby, her name is Sizanne [*sic*] and she'll soon be nine months old. She can already stand." He refrained from mentioning that he had just spent a month in jail, nor did he say anything about Idesa being three months pregnant; he closed by asking for their news and adding this affectionate Yiddishism: "*Farbleybt mir gezunt*," or "Stay in good health for me." The addresses were written in French: the sender's, in the upper left-hand corner, "M. Jablonka, Rue Désirée 3, Paris 20th"; the addressee's to the right, beneath the stamp, "S. Jablonka, Buenos Aires, Montiel no. 2731, Rep. Argentina." At the bottom of the letter, like a rudder affixed to this skiff of words, a trivial post-scriptum indicating a change of direction: "I sent you a copy of my civil status record. If you still have it, could you please send it back?"[1] Ten days earlier, Gitla Leszcz and her husband, living at 7 Place Auguste-Métivier, adjacent to Rue Désirée, had vouched for Matès so that he could be issued a certificate of good conduct by the Père-Lachaise police commissioner's office, which would in turn allow him to enlist in the military. To complete his application, he needed an official copy of his civil status record, and this is why he was asking his brother and sister to forward it. Suddenly, new prospects were on the horizon: not the joys of domestic life, nor the hope of a new start in the Americas, but impending war.

A month and a half earlier, on 1 September 1939, Hitler had launched his armored divisions against Poland. On the 3rd, France and Great Britain entered the war. On the 9th, an accord signed between Poland and France ordered "all Polish citizens . . . to appear before a review board."[2] While Warsaw was being bombed and French troops were testing the strength of the front in the Sarre and the Vosges regions, the Polish ambassador announced the creation of a Polish army unit in France. Nazism had to be pushed back to the Rhine as well as the Vistula. On the 17th, the Red Army entered eastern Poland, overtaking seven voivodeships as well as most of the oil wells. In accordance with the secret plan adjoined to the Nazi–Soviet Pact, Poland was divided between its powerful neighbors, just as it had been in the nineteenth century.

Apart from its official conscription campaign, the French army was also facing a large influx of volunteers. Over 80,000 foreigners enlisted during an eight-month period, joining tens of thousands of Italian, Spanish or Polish workers sent into mines, arms factories or "service jobs" that involved setting up camps or consolidating the Maginot Line.[3] Jews were not to be outdone. They rushed to barracks and to the Ministry of War, but also to recruitment offices opened for that purpose. On Rue de Lancry, where the Union of Jewish Volunteers of 1914–1918 was headquartered, over 10,000 volunteers signed up in ten days, and a further 12,000 enlisted at the International League against Anti-Semitism.[4] A month earlier, they had been dodging the police to avoid expulsion.

On 6 October 1939, Hitler visited Warsaw with great pomp and ceremony. Terror reigned in recently vanquished Poland. In Parczew, the Germans extorted a "tax" from Jews of 50,000 zlotys; the Gestapo forced a number of inhabitants to jump naked into the icy waters of the Piwonia; others were taken to the town baker's where they received orders to undress and climb into kneading troughs filled with dough.[5] In France, only a few clear heads were able to learn lessons from Poland's collapse. Colonel de Gaulle handed a memorandum to his superiors, entitled "The Coming of Mechanical Force," in which he repeated what he had been crying in the desert for years: the future belonged to tanks, airpower, towed artillery, motorized units and speed; France had to constitute armored divisions immediately. For millions of French people, however, nothing was happening. Back in the barracks, no one knew which way to turn: France had declared war on Hitler, who said he wanted peace. On 8 October, Matès showed up at the Père-Lachaise police station with his guarantors, Gitla Leszcz and her husband, Raymond Gerdebled, an anarchist metalworker under surveillance by National Security.[6] On 18 October, he wrote to the Argentinian relatives for the copy of his civil status record.

"S. Jablonka, Buenos Aires, Montiel no. 2731, Rep. Argentina." Benito, Simje's son, takes me to visit the Mataderos neighborhood, the "Slaughterhouses," with its empty lots, noisy motorbikes, the carts of the *cartoneros* filled with scrap of all sorts, clusters of purple flowers spilling over crumbling walls, legendary boxers, hair slicked back—Justo Suarez, "el torito de Mataderos"—its abandoned factories, its football stadium with a painted image of an enormous bull's head among the bleachers. Benito parks and turns off the ignition. Bags of rubble abandoned against a tree have left long chalky trails on the pavement. The air is full of lilac and sewage. Three adolescents are sitting outside a shop, leaning against its metal shutters. The boys, bare-chested and with their arms covered in tattoos, and the one girl, obviously pregnant, all glare with distrust. Benito jokes with them, the way he does with all strangers he meets, and they start to laugh. The ice is broken. Benito explains that I am a tourist; the two boys get up, and showing off their shoulders, ask me to take their picture. At the entrance, on a freshly replastered wall just above the rust-swollen lintel, a white enamel oval bears the number 2731. Montiel no. 2731. Next door lived Yankel and Jume, the friends who had coaxed Simje to come over to Argentina. Who lives there today? I poke my head inside and can just make out, in a tiny courtyard, a stack of boards and a filthy refrigerator, with plastic bottles of some dubious-looking liquid piled on top.

When he arrived in 1931, Simje set up house on Francisco Bilbao Street, where he welcomed his wife Raquel a year later: the same dismal two-room flat, no amenities, is where Benito was born in 1934. Two years after that, the toddler had to share his room with *Tía* Reizl, just arrived all the way from Parczew. Next, Simje moved the whole brood to another hovel, Avenida Bruix, closer to his place of work, while Reizl, now pregnant, left to live with her companion. When Mauricio was born, she stopped working. Her household—whose most luxurious items were a down comforter and a set of spoons—was not a wealthy one, but she was not complaining: proletarians are made to work with their hands and by the sweat of their brow, and not to own. Reizl and her husband rented a room from some Armenians who worked, illegally, in a neighboring shop. They had no space, no privacy, no peace, no money. Benito smiles: "Oh yes, that's what it was like, *la vida de los inmigrantes!*"

In the late 1930s, Simje and his family moved to 2731 Montiel Street, in the slaughterhouse district. Yankel had work for Simje: by machine, Yankel would cut open used mattresses and pull out the wool, which Simje would then card. The children had a happy childhood. Benito, his brother and sister had books, but no toys. Their father would occasionally give them some small change to go buy a little something. They ate bread and onions, which they washed down with a little wine, unbeknownst to their parents. And that was life on Montiel Street. Every so often, a letter arrived from Paris. Borges, who at the time was a modest librarian, had this to say: "In those days, there was not a single Argentine whose Utopia was not Paris."[7] But letters from Matès told of a life just as bleak as theirs in Mataderos. The letter of 18 October 1939 says it all: "Yidess takes care of the house and child, which involves lots of effort. As for me, I get work every once in a while, I haven't had much luck."

Matès went to the Clignancourt barracks on 8 November, bearing his certificate of good conduct issued by the Père-Lachaise commissariat. I try to imagine the scene: orderlies in blockhouses, blacktopped paths crisscrossing at right angles, a long queue in front of a building, offices teeming with men in uniform at the Foreign Legion recruitment station, where he'll be kept waiting a while longer. Finally his turn comes. At the end of his medical checkup, the physician concludes that Matès has no major ailments or disabilities, and that he is "strong and well-built" (after all, although he was only 5'4", he weighed 143 pounds). In another office, an underling slips a blank form into his typewriter, types his name, date and place of birth, his address, profession and particulars, rolls out the form, stamps it a few times and reads out the statutory texts, thereby making official "the enlistment of M. Jablonka, who has sworn to serve with honor and loyalty for the duration of the war." The new legionnaire signs at the bottom, a solemn act that betrays none of his doubts to me as I pore over this document today, scrutinizing every line, stamp and bit of spidery scrawl.[8]

In the enlistment rolls of 1939–1940 (the appropriately named "onion-skins," made of some kind of tracing paper that today crumbles at the merest touch), all nationalities are represented: Spaniards, Italians, Poles, Yugoslavs, Czechs, Hungarians, Romanians, Germans, Russians, Bulgarians, Greeks, Turks and even Luxembourgers. Inexplicably indexed under two serial numbers, "Seine central no. 1753" and "no. 13641" (perhaps an earlier enlistment was postponed awaiting a copy of his civil status record), Matès is lost in the listing among dozens of other Poles.[9] His comrades-in-arms were probably all Jews, because, since September, Catholic Poles had been handled by the government in exile. Those who opted for the Foreign Legion were those whose country wanted nothing more to do with them, or who refused to serve under anti-Semitic officers.

Once all the paperwork was complete, Matès was given his individual Foreign Legion soldier's record, class of 1939, as an EVDG, a "voluntary enlistee for the duration of the war." Whether he enlisted of his own free will or because his back was against the wall, this enrollment does clarify certain things. As I have already said, the question of whether Matès distanced himself from Communism remains a mystery to me. But one thing is certain: by enlisting in the army of a bourgeois state, he was turning a page. His do-or-die ideal was no longer revolution, but the fight against Nazism. He was now a soldier for democracy under siege, not for the international proletariat. For Communists refused war. In September 1939, all Jewish organizations issued the call to fight Hitler and opened recruitment offices—all, that is, except the Communists. Gronowski justified the Nazi–Soviet Pact before his comrades at the *Naye Presse*, and until the very end of August 1939, the paper was hedging. Even though they voted to fund the war, the French Communists adopted the defeatist Soviet attitude: this imperialist war was not their business, unless it could lead to revolution as in 1917. Calling for civil disobedience and sabotage, the now underground *L'Humanité* reprinted Molotov's speech, which the Germans had already reproduced on tracts that they dropped from airplanes over Paris: "The goal of this war of Western powers, which is to annihilate Hitlerism, . . . is nothing short of criminal."[10] Arthur Koestler, interned at the Vernet camp, sharply criticized this turnabout. For his Communist co-detainees, uniting to fight fascism was now out of the question; their duty as proletarians was to struggle against the bourgeois enemy within the country, and not to serve as its cannon fodder.[11] On 26 September, the French Communist Party was dissolved. Party head Maurice Thorez deserted. Dozens of parliamentarians were arrested in Paris and the provinces. More than 300 Communist municipalities were suspended.[12]

It would appear, then, that my grandfather's enlistment probably involved some serious soul-searching. The events of autumn 1939 must surely have been both welcome and terrifying for him. On the one hand, the Soviet invasion and assimilation of western Poland into the USSR fulfilled one of his dearest wishes, dating back to 1933 ("Long Live the Soviet Polish Republic," proclaimed one of the banners); and Stalin, whose fleet was carrying out manoeuvres in the Baltic, was preparing to "protect" the Baltic states and Finland. On the other hand, Matès had no news of his parents, who were stuck in Parczew while the Wehrmacht was ravaging the country west of the Bug River, bombing open cities and mowing down columns of fleeing refugees. Yet coming to their rescue, engaging in the fight against Hitler to crush his barbarity and anti-Semitism, would involve embracing France, the "host country" hostile to anti-fascist refugees but ready to rush into battle to help Rydz-Śmigły's anti-Semitic Poland.

Anyone enlisting in November 1939 was agreeing both to turn his back on the USSR and to fight in the same camp as the French bourgeoisie, the Polish generals and the Hassidim of Frog Street.

Tens of thousands of Polish Jews volunteered. The spirit of sacrifice! The love of France! But I don't like how those words sound. There is something annoying about the golden legend of "fighters for right and justice" marching lightheartedly into battle. The alternative hypothesis, that these enlistees were nothing but opportunists looking for a way to become documented, is just as distorted. In Arnold Mandel's *Les Temps incertains* [*Uncertain Times*] (1950), a bitingly ironic narrator goes to the headquarters of the Friends of the French Republic, in Belleville, where a recruitment stand has been set up. The officer in charge, a bald veteran covered in medals, examines each candidate's paperwork, then barks: "Sign here. Next!" One man waiting in line remarks: "Tell him that we Belleville Jews are going to fight for liberty, equality and fraternity, and then for an ID card, since what we're hoping is that once we're war veterans, they'll finally give us proper papers and a work permit."[13]

How could Matès not have been tempted by the prospect of at last obtaining valid ID papers? Even his enlistment document from the Foreign Legion bore the number that had haunted him for almost two years now, his denial of residency, "E. 98,392." Once these refugees had enrolled, the government cleverly switched its policy of control and expulsion to one of extended visas and dispensations, holding out the hope of fast-track naturalizations.[14] On 15 November 1939, a week after Matès's enlistment, the French president deferred the 100-franc fine that the Seine criminal court had imposed on him in May.[15] In spring 1940, right after his son was born, second-class legionnaire Jablonka Matès, roll number 5132, 43rd company of the Legion, asserted his six months of service in a request that the interior minister annul denial of residency "E. 114,560" which still loomed over his wife.[16] Becoming legal was no longer an end unto itself: the goal now was his children's naturalization. A few days later, the ministry informed the prefecture and the Gourevitch Committee that, "in light of the circumstances," Idesa would now fall under the regime of quarterly deferments, "with the possibility of renewal." Wives of legionnaires were not to be expelled.

But enlisting is a serious matter, and this personal calculation alone may not explain his decision. Many foreigners felt compelled to follow the crowd, out of team spirit or fear of reprisal, knowing that the French themselves had been mobilized since 1 September. "The ID card seems devalued," wrote Spanish volunteer Léon Aréga. All that mattered was enlistment, one's military status, and anyone who was still on the fence had some explaining to do. They were constantly reminded of "the bread that you have been eating in France."[17] This meant that certain Communist Jews ended up in the Legion, but called themselves "CV," or compulsory volunteers.[18] In his October 1939 letter to the Argentines, Matès writes: "With regard to my presence at home, you must certainly have read in the papers that what has already happened to many foreigners is going to happen to me, too. And I'll be finding out sooner rather than later."[19] This cryptic statement, referring to what sounds like moral pressure, is perhaps referring to the internment of "suspects" in camps around the Paris region and down south, or to the 9 September accord between Poland and France.

So, which was it? A patriotic call, a Machiavellian scheme or just passive resignation? Though he may well have enlisted reluctantly, Matès did agree to risk his life in order to better provide for his family, waiting back in their tiny flat on Rue Désirée, in order to offer them a world free of oppression and anti-Semitism and the right to live in that world. This road to betterment started among the saddlers of Parczew and led to the Clignancourt barracks. Matès must have enlisted out of both conviction and self-interest: because Hitler was threatening the working masses in general, and his family in particular; because he needed money; because everyone around was enlisting; because he wanted to live in France with his children; and not least, because he undoubtedly preferred life in the barracks to life in an internment camp. Matès enlisted in 1939 in the same spirit as that with which he emigrated in 1937: free will steered by necessity.

The naturalization process, the reward for blood spilt in battle, was now underway. But as long as he had not yet been anointed with citizenship, an undesirable was still undesirable. As of April 1939, a decree authorized foreigners who had resided in France for ten years or more to enlist in the same regular regiments as the French. But the military was reluctant to apply this decree, demanding more "stringent selection criteria." They denied entry to those who enlisted through associations and discouraged candidates by requiring endless paperwork, in the hope of ridding their ranks of all kinds of imaginary enemies: German and ex-Austrian refugees, *Ostjuden*, Spanish republicans, "fifth-column" infiltrators, and so on. But in the end, volunteers were arriving in such numbers that the army finally had to open its ranks. Still, as in 1914, these undesirables were relegated to the Foreign Legion, that army of mercenaries with a discipline of iron, that den of nameless criminals, created in the nineteenth century to colonize Algeria. Although volunteers had early doubts, the army asserted that "if at first, the name 'Foreign Legion' scares off some foreigners, they will surely be glad in the end to have joined, just as their elders from 1914 were, and they will be proud to have belonged to such a glorious corps."[20]

Nevertheless, to make sure that contact with foreigners didn't sully the "genuine" legionnaires, the government isolated them in reserve units, the *Régiments de marche des volontaires étrangers* (RMVE), or foreign volunteer foot regiments, numbered starting with twenty so as to avoid any harmful confusion. As it happened, the 21st, 22nd and 23rd RMVE, formed in October 1939 at the Barcarès camp, were joined by the 11th and 12th foreign infantry regiments along with the 13th semi-brigade, which distinguished itself in April 1940 at Narvik.[21] Today, the Legion considers the RMVE fighters true "veterans" and is pleased to enshrine the "memory of their sacrifice," as printed on the form letters I have received. Time having reconciled everyone, the military records of tattooed hulks who bragged of their desert experiences and showed off their biceps lie side by side in a warehouse in southern France with those of bespectacled gefilte-fish eaters. But early in the war, the army was taking a different tack, preferring to sideline the anti-Nazi Germans, the Italians opposed to Mussolini, the Jews hounded out of their homelands, the stateless wanderers in search of asylum and the former members of the International Brigades who, however Jewish or Communist they may have been, were prepared to march against Hitler in a confrontation that some had been waiting for since 1933. This error in judgment had a great deal to do with the catastrophes to come.

Around mid-November, Matès was sent to the Foreign Legion station in Sathonay, near Lyon. Benjamin Schlevin, also an enlistee and future war prisoner, describes the train trip, under guard by Senegalese infantrymen, in

Les Juifs de Belleville: "The atmosphere was heavy with melancholy in this convoy of lost souls." The recruits were taken to their barracks on a chilly autumn afternoon. The bugle sounded the assembly for dinner. A petty officer called out roll: "He stumbled over every complicated Jewish name before finally producing a decent pronunciation. . . . He looked visibly contemptuous as he stared out at that gang of civilians in tattered clothing. He had inquired as to the recruits' professions, and burst into a laugh: 'So everybody here's a tailor, or what?'" The first night in barracks was spent on moldy straw against damp walls. At icy dawn, the men crowded around the only faucet, after which they were given an ungenerous bowl of coffee and were led, after roll call, to their medical checkup.[22] A while later, they were taken to be fitted for uniforms at Vancia, a sinister fortress one can only see in photos today, with its rubble-stone walls, iron grating, tunnels and cellars. Each recruit got trousers, a greatcoat, a shell jacket and a cap. He was now a legionnaire.

From Fort Vancia, Matès was sent to La Valbonne, where he began his training (he had no prior experience, since he had never done military service[23]). It was in this camp during the *drôle de guerre*, or "phony war," the first eight months when no major operations took place, that Matès learned the basic rules from petty officers and reservists: how to salute properly, march in step, disassemble and reassemble a gun, make a bed with hospital corners and so on. Living conditions were undoubtedly very poor. The winter of 1939 was a harsh one. The army was still short about 2 million pairs of shoes and 1.5 million blankets. Soldiers didn't have a change of clothes, and barracks were underequipped for cold weather.[24] As Manès Sperber tells it in *All Our Yesterdays*, the volunteers ate cold meals, got sick from sleeping on damp straw and wasted time and energy on makeshift exercises, wearing uniforms that had already served in the trenches of a previous war.[25] Once in La Valbonne, did Matès at least begin to experience the benefits of national solidarity? For instance, did he learn some rudimentary French, he who was hardly a polyglot intellectual like Manès Sperber? The Foreign Legion likes to define itself as a melting pot where soldiers from the world over converge, having jettisoned their national, ethnic or religious baggage. But in 1939, it definitely sorted and labeled according to origin: in La Valbonne, you'd find the Italians, nationals from neutral countries not counting the United States and Poles not serving in the Polish army (Jews, in other words); Sidi Bel Abbes in Algeria took Germans, ex-Austrians, Czechs not recognized by their own government and former legionnaires from those countries; at Coëtquidan, there were the Poles serving under the Polish flag.[26] Throughout their training, Eastern European Jews were insulted and harassed. For the Legion was corrupt to the core with an anti-Semitism worthy of the Dreyfus affair at its height. Some highlights:

Testimony from Zosa Szajkowski, enlisted on 2 September 1939 for the duration of the war: at La Valbonne, officers and noncommissioned personnel called them all Solomon and kept shouting at them that "this is the Legion here, not the synagogue!"[27]

Excerpt from a confidential report made by chief warrant officer Mazzoni, a forty-nine-year-old Corsican, retired from the Legion and in charge of the Barcarès camp annex (25 January 1940): though they are loyal, the Jews "enlist for the sole purpose of speeding up their naturalization. . . . Although there are exceptions to this, I don't believe we can invest much hope in this category of enlistees."[28]

Werner Prasuhn, sent to Algeria: "Jews and stateless persons are made to bellow out Nazi songs on the order of an officer on horseback, and anyone who refuses gets eight days in the slammer. . . . We accidental warriors get called dodgers, traitors, reds and kikes. . . . The Legion was like some annex of the Third Reich."[29]

In February 1940, two encoded telegrams from an officer in Algiers to a Paris headquarters emphasized the "damage caused by the disproportionate influx of Jewish foreigners enlisted for the duration of the war. . . . As colonel of the 11th Foreign, I feel that this imbalance is liable, in the short term, to seriously modify the spirit and values of the Foreign Legion. I insist that measures be taken without delay to reduce this proportion."[30]

Excerpt from a report by the officer in charge of postal communications in the region of Clermont-Ferrand (regarding foreign Jews at La Valbonne):

> This is an unreliable lot, both physically and morally, but you can be sure that they will be *boasting later on about their bravery in the field*, even though *they never left the barracks*, since these fellows are worthless for even the most menial work behind the lines. They have praised their 1,500 "war dead" from the last war, but to be fair, they never spoke of

men "killed in action," since their dead all died in the hospital, which makes sense since 99% of them have physical disabilities, and most were granted pensions for what amount to congenital defects, having never seen action at the front except at the movies.[31]

Those at the receiving end of these demeaning attitudes learned that foreigners would not be joining the national family any time soon, and that even the soldier's uniform would not protect them from their status as aliens. This is where Matès, the Polish Communist who had rallied to France, would yet again feel the sting of anti-Semitism. In March 1940, military reconnaissance intercepted and transmitted to a circle of generals a letter that a Lebanese legionnaire stationed in Sidi Bel Abbes had sent to his father a few weeks earlier:

> We're not even men, as far as they are concerned. They treat us like convicts or men with a shady past who have come here to hide out and forget. . . . Those of us from friendly or neutral countries, free men with no military obligation to France, who have enlisted of our own free will, you would think we'd be welcomed more courteously, with more respect for our human dignity. We deserve better treatment than what we're getting from the Foreign Legion.[32]

Meanwhile, back at Rue Désirée, Idesa was on her own with little Suzanne. Eight months pregnant, she managed as well as she could, living off the 8-franc military allocation and, I would imagine, the "money from America." On 28 April 1940, Matès hurried home from La Valbonne on a thirteen-day leave, and got there just in time, for on that same night, Idesa was admitted to the Rothschild hospital where she gave birth to little Marcel, Moyshe in Yiddish, his grandfather Feder's name.[33] Like his sister a year earlier, my father was born in this temple of wealthy Jewish philanthropy. For children of Communists, it's a bit embarrassing, but it hardly matters: for generations, the poor Jews of Paris had been entering and exiting the world through that hospital on Rue de Picpus, founded in 1852 by the famous baron. I can imagine her, feeling those first contractions, supported by Matès, now back in his civvies, stating his identity to the desk clerk; I am at this moment looking at the page of the hospital

intake register for 29 April 1940, which I photographed at the archives of
the welfare bureau, with both my parents at my side. It is interesting to
compare it to the page for 23 January 1939. Where Suzanne-Soreh bears
the name Feder, the name of her mother (who herself was an illegitimate
child), Marcel-Moyshe is called Jablonka from birth[34]: since Idesa had received notice of her own denial of residency in the meantime, there was no
longer any need for the unwed-mother stratagem.

In a single instant, all thoughts of the barracks were swept away: the
exercises, lowly chores, roll calls, insults and that war that couldn't seem to
get off the ground! The voluntary enlistee was back with his wife and little
daughter, after a six-month separation. He was able to be present at the
birth of his son. While on leave, he lived with the furrier trio, Frime, Sroul
and Dina, in their apartment on Avenue d'Italie. It was an easy metro
ride to the hospital, eight stations from Place d'Italie to Picpus. The son
was most likely circumcised while still in the hospital, and registered by a
Rothschild employee at City Hall in the 12th arrondissement, under the
name Marcel.[35] Was it the employee who suggested that transcription to
the parents? After all, Moyshe could also have been translated as Maurice.

Conversations with my father have taken a different turn: he is now
part of the historical record. There he is, tucked into one corner of a larger
picture, even though he has no consistent memory of those times, only stills,
sentence fragments and flashbacks, by nature difficult to situate in time and
place. This one, for instance: one day, while waiting inside a building, he
remembers jumping down the stairs, though he doesn't recall which building or when. My father reads me a letter that Idesa wrote to the Argentine
siblings on 9 May 1940: "My dearest ones, I am announcing that I have
brought a little boy into the world. I'm sending you this card from the hospital. I'm doing very well, and the child is fine. His name is Moyshele, in
French Marsl [sic]. . . . Here's hoping our little boy will bring us lots of joy."[36]

I love this letter. Not so much because it clarifies the circumstances
of a birth that will in time lead to my own, but because each sentence
radiates joy and a zest for life, revealing the bubbly, fun-loving woman
beneath the KZMP "technician" who once stored political posters in her
hallway, then denied ever having done so. I owe a debt of gratitude to
my translator, Bernard, who pointed out the humor in her short text, its

chatty, playful tone, written in the flow of the moment, exuding a kind of jubilation that still gets to me, even seventy years after the fact. The child is "fine": the Yiddish word *laytish* means "well-formed physically," but it can also mean "well-behaved," usually used to describe a child of six or eight who is always nice, doesn't annoy his mother and so on. She is playing on words, presenting the newborn as one would a good little boy at a family gathering. "If you can, write to the folks back in Poland that I have had a boy and that we now have a pair": a couple of fledglings, girl and boy, Sizanne and Marsl. "As you can see, we've been trying to catch up with Simje and Raquel," an allusion to their two boys, Benito and his brother, six and two years old, which put the Argentines ahead of the French in the baby race. "Tomorrow, they're having me leave the hospital," with the verb *traybt* meaning literally "they're tossing me out," but without any dramatic connotations. She is simply happy to be going home. And then she ends in the imperative mood: "So what's happening with you? Write soon!"

A somewhat out-of-focus snapshot shows her about six months later with little Marcel in her arms. They are in some unidentified locale, in front of what looks like a stand of trees or an ivy-covered wall. With his sparse black hair in evidence, the baby is closing his eyes, opening his mouth wide, clenching his tiny fists. You can't tell whether he's crying or yawning. Idesa is gazing up into the lens, creating a shadow that seems to widen her eyebrows, giving her a provocative look. She is firmly gripping the baby's white overalls. Her smile exudes a mother's pride, a dimple in one cheek, and seems to be saying: "Oh no you don't, little guy, you're not getting away from me!"

On 10 May 1940, the day his wife and son left the Rothschild Hospital, Matès respectfully applied to the interior ministry for the "naturalization of his two children born in Paris: Suzanne, born 23 January 1939, and Marcel, born 29 April 1940."[37] This application, involving two such French names, would seem to indicate that Matès and Idesa were planning more than ever for a future in France. On that same day, toward the end of Matès's furlough, the Wehrmacht invaded the Netherlands and Belgium. In accordance with plans made by General Gamelin, chief of staff of French armed forces since 1931, France's best armed divisions were sent to the rescue. Between this concentration of troops in Flanders and the fortifications along the Maginot Line in Alsace-Lorraine, there were the Ardennes uplands, where a few ill-equipped reserve units were stationed. Why had this sector been so un-dermanned? Because it was considered impassable. On 7 May 1940, General Huntziger, commander of the 2nd Army, was still reassuring the mayor of Sedan that this was so: "I do not believe that the Germans would ever consider an attack in this region." Not an inch of barbed wire was protecting the banks of the Meuse, bunkers were still under construction and the tanks of the 3rd armored division were scattered over several units. Marshal Pétain, the hero of Verdun, former Minister of War, the inspiration behind France's defensive doctrine between the wars, decreed that if the enemy were to venture into the Ardennes, "we'll nip them on their way out."[38]

Yet this is precisely where Rommel's and Guderian's surprise tank attacks took place on 13 May 1940. The first crossed the Meuse at Dinant, while the second swung further south and crossed at Sedan, pushing forward without waiting for infantry reinforcements. The French leadership was stunned. At the generals' headquarters, General Georges, commander in chief of the northeast front and Gamelin's right-hand man, collapsed into a chair and wept.[39] On 15 May, Gamelin reported to Daladier, the head of the government, that the French army was heading for disaster. The next day, the German panzers reached Laon: Paris was now two days away by road. Panic swept through the government, and they set about burning archives and reinforcing the mobile guard in case a revolution were to break out. In an unexpected turn of events, however, instead of heading toward the capital, Hitler's generals drove on toward the sea, attacking the armies engaged in the north from behind. Heading up two panzer divisions, Guderian took Amiens on 20 May, Boulogne on 22 May, Calais on 23 May and stopped before Dunkirk on the express orders of Hitler himself. After driving from Dinant to Arras, Rommel began tracking north. The trap was now closing around a million soldiers, whom the Allies began evacuating through Dunkirk.

Since not much could be expected of them, foreign volunteers were sent to the front earlier than the French. On 6 May, the 22nd RMVE left the Barcarès camp for Alsace. On 11 May, the 12th Foreign left La Valbonne heading for Maux and Château-Thierry.[40] The 23rd RMVE was formed the day of the German offensive. Created on paper the previous autumn, it had since then been a ghost regiment, since it had served basically as an instruction unit for the 21st and 22nd, which received the 23rd's theoretical numbers.[41] But the situation had become dire enough to require that a real 23rd RMVE be placed on war footing. On 16 May, 1,000 men, including Matès, who had just returned from his furlough, were sent from La Valbonne to Barcarès, where the new regiment would be put together. Imagine, at the other end of France, near Perpignan, a spit of sand stretching out between a salt lake and the sea. On this peninsula battered by the winds from across the mountains, imagine the remains of a former internment camp built right on the sand, with no floor or windows, bales of hay for mattresses, fleas everywhere, sea water to wash up with. This was Barcarès. Here, Jewish tailors and Spanish republicans carried out manoeuvres under the surveillance of noncommissioned officers whom they couldn't understand, doing battle against imaginary Germans and very real squadrons of mosquitoes, hauling crates of weaponry across miles of beach, attempting in vain to keep sand out of their food and their pants.

Two days after the breach at Sedan, the 23rd RMVE was immediately bolstered "by personnel, especially Jews, coming from La Valbonne."[42] In Barcarès, as recounted by Ilex Beller, who had been there since late 1939, the news caused a stir: finally, some "real" legionnaires as reinforcement! Everyone got shipshape to welcome them in style. But instead of legionnaires, the new arrivals turned out to be the old friends from Belleville.[43] Lieutenant Colonel Aumoitte, commander of the 23rd RMVE, was equally disenchanted: the new arrivals had been poorly trained, were "clearly inferior" to the other soldiers and hardly a one had ever even fired a machine gun. The bulk of them were "former tailors, cloth merchants and hosiery dealers, or clerks of one sort or another. These men will be needing some serious training if they are to prove useful in any way."[44] On 17 May, Matès was assigned to the 23rd RMVE, private second class.[45] With his back to a hostile Mediterranean, a body of water he was seeing for the first time in his life, along whose shores he dragged his pack full of gear, he must have lifted his eyes toward the plains and rivers, the valleys and hills, to France, threatened by invasion, and up north, to the flagpoles in the ports of the English Channel all flying the swastika.

During this time, defense strategies were being devised. At first, a counterattack was proposed to destroy the panzer divisions that had advanced so boldly, in order to reestablish the connection between the armies of the north and south. But in the end, the generals fell back on their old defensive reflexes from 1915. Once again the man of the hour, seventy-two-year-old General Weygand, Foch's former chief of staff, went to great lengths to form an unbroken front line, right over the scars of the previous war: the Somme, the Aisne and the Chemin des Dames. In preparation for the stand that was to save the nation, he set up support bases in villages and forests, closed up gaps in the infantry and artillery, and ordered everyone to hold their positions, making it clear that retreat was not an option. Some sixty divisions were deployed over a 150-mile front between the English Channel and the Meuse River, with a series of fallback echelons that further subtracted from the troop count at the front.[46]

In this human dike, the 23rd RMVE would serve as a stopgap. In late May 1940, it received orders to prepare to move to the front. But here was the problem: nothing was ready. Or rather, the Legion had been so neglected as compared to the other French regiments that it could not possibly withstand the power of the blitzkrieg. The foreign volunteers had trained with guns dating back to before World War I. Mortars and machine guns were in short supply, kit items were missing or mismatched, with oversized trousers or undersized caps, etc. This ill-equipped band of refugees, at the very bottom of the military heap, some of whom went into battle wearing espadrilles, wooden clogs or no shoes at all, were dubbed the "rope regiments," since their gun straps were replaced by a length of twine. Because of constant rotation and the arrival of the inexperienced recruits from La Valbonne, the officers never got to know their men. The legionnaires of the 23rd RMVE had to wait until the very end of the month to find out how to use their new MAS-36 rifles, and to become familiar with antitank guns and 81-mm mortars, delivered just a few days earlier. As for field telephones and optical equipment, they never arrived at all. In his report issued on 31 May 1940, the Barcarès commander communicated these concerns to his superior: the 23rd "still has to learn how to use all the materiel. . . . It's important to train the troops and get them adjusted gradually by having them perform increasingly difficult missions, for they are currently unprepared to go straight into battle."[47] It is in this state of unpreparedness that, on 4 June at dawn, Matès and his fellow soldiers went off to face the army that had just crushed Poland, Belgium and the Netherlands, and had humiliated the French generals. In other words, they were being sent to slaughter.

The legionnaires of the 23rd RMVE marched all the way to the Rivesaltes train station, twenty miles from Barcarès. There, they piled into specially prepared cattle cars, the kind that hold forty men and eight horses each. During the trip, they sang, told jokes, played cards; but as the regiment's medic, Dr. Danowski, tells it, all the lightheartedness was masking something else, for their thoughts went to their wives and children left behind in Paris.[48] As I imagine the men snoozing in the air heavy with tobacco and sweat, jostled by the train's relentless rhythm, a poem by Aragon comes to mind:

> We set off for God knows where, it's like a bad dream
> We'll soon be snaking along the line of fire
> At some point it's no longer a game
> The boys out there await relief.

They arrived on the night of 5 to 6 June 1940, in silence, at a small switching station. The sky was red, the thunder of cannons shook the ground underfoot. The soldiers marched through the night, then camouflaged busses drove them to their positions.[49] They were near Soissons, on the Aisne River, in the sector of the 7th Army set up to cover Paris. Battle had been raging for twenty-four hours. Back in the capital, the exodus had just begun. And here I am, sitting at a table in the Defense Ministry's history department at the Château de Vincennes, where thousands of volunteers waited in line in the fall of 1939. The generals' papers, the officers' reports, the maps, and the regiments' logbooks are spread out in front of me.[50]

As soon as they got to the combat zone, the 23rd RMVE was broken up, its battalions deployed to other regiments: its 2nd battalion (the II/23 in military parlance) was sent to the 12th foreign infantry regiment, billeted in the sector for the previous two weeks, and its 3rd battalion (the III/23) ended up with the 93rd infantry regiment, in charge of holding Ailette, to the north of Soissons. This reinforcement battalion was supposed to attack at the fore, but after its commander Digoine du Palais argued that they were lacking "supplies of all sorts," their participation consisted of plugging gaps to the east and west of Juvigny, where the command post of the 93rd infantry regiment had located. On 6 June in the morning, French positions were battered north of the Aisne. The German Stuka planes dive-bombed, sirens screaming, the ground collapsing under the impact. After this overture, the German infantry launched an assault on Juvigny. Out of ammunition, the supplements located in a forward position fell to the enemy, but reinforcements of the III/23 helped push back the attack until noon. Captain Talec's 10th company installed machine guns at entry points to the village. On the left, their flank was protected but on the right, a mile-long wooded ravine separated them from the 9th company. The Germans started infiltrating around noon.

South of the river, the defense of Soissons was incumbent upon the Foreign Legion, represented by the 12th Foreign and what remained of the 23rd RMVE. The mission of the two regiments, composed mainly of Polish Jews and Spaniards, was to "prevent the crossing of the Aisne," the last blockade on the road to Paris. To the west of Soissons, Aumoitte took command of the sub-sector that led to the Pommiers bridge. At 10:45, Lieutenant Colonel Besson, commander of the 12th Foreign, entrusted the recently allocated II/23 with a number of support missions: to station themselves at Vertes-Feuilles, on the edge of the Villers-Cotterêts forest; to hold the national highway leading to Paris; to carry out reconnaissance as to the possibility of bivouacking in Charantigny and Buzancy, south of Soissons; and to find support locations for establishing a rear blockade at Missy-aux-Bois and at Ploisy, situated on either side of National Route 2. And there was a word of warning to all: "Watch out for enemy aerial reconnaissance."[51]

At the same time, to the east of Soissons, the legionnaires of the 3rd battalion of the 12th Foreign (III/12) were facing an ambush on the opposite riverbank. Trained at La Valbonne and commanded by battalion chief André, the battalion was made up of twenty-nine nationalities, from Chinese to Polish Jews, not to mention Norwegians and a strong majority of Spaniards, all trained by noncommissioned officers from the Legion. Starting around 11:00, low-flying aircraft began methodically bombing the positions. Dozens of panzers came rolling down the slopes of the Chemin des Dames, along with other tracked vehicles. Without antitank guns or armor-piercing ammunition, the battalion had no way to stop them. All it had available was seven machine guns, three of which were missing their mounts. Military doctor Lieutenant Levy, working in an open-air rescue post, was shaken by an explosion, but refused treatment even when he started spitting up blood. By then, he had treated and evacuated 161 wounded. Lieutenant Perez refused to surrender when his company was surrounded, and led the Resistance until he was killed while trying to force passage.

The Germans advanced by infiltrating the whole sector. Throughout the day, the 12th Foreign's radio receivers were receiving messages from the three infantry divisions engaged to the north, between the Aisne and the Ailette, reporting that the enemy was advancing and that their own forward posts were surrounded and running out of ammunition. At 18:30, Lieutenant Colonel Besson addressed the II/23 from his command post: "Because of how the situation is evolving, the rear blockade will be occupied by nightfall." He praised "the effort made by the units of the 23rd RMVE, and ask[ed] that everyone make every effort to set up overnight and by morning be sheltered from aerial bombardment and ready to use their automatic weaponry."

The evening of 6 June. North of the Aisne, the situation was worsening. On the outskirts of Juvigny, fighting was hand-to-hand and losses were heavy. The 93rd infantry regiment was overtaken around 20:00. Preceded by an artillery bombardment, the Germans entered Juvigny with machine guns in hand. Some men from the 93rd resisted in the castle, while the regiment's command staff took advantage of the cover of night to slip away. The Germans advanced through the woods to the south of the village. Chief Warrant Officer Soulisse, section leader in the III/23, showed bravery and composure under automatic weapon fire, shelling and Stuka attacks. His own machine guns, in position to the south of Juvigny, were able to hold back the German assault in the near term, and later covered the retreat of the 93rd infantry. A quartermaster of the 10th company, sent out to get munitions, came across Digoine du Palais, commander of the III/23: the officer was wandering in the wilderness, in a state of shock, unable to say what had happened to his battalion. He told the quartermaster that he'd received no supplies, that his positions were surrounded and that the situation was hopeless. Around 22:00, the French infantry division fighting north of the Aisne was given the go-ahead to cross the river.

For the night of 6 to 7 June, the 12th Foreign received new orders: hold the bridges over the Aisne, "retreat not an option," to allow for the infantry divisions engaged in the north to fall back; after that, the engineer corps would blow up the bridges. In defensive positions to the north of Soissons, the III/23 was covering the French regiments being pushed back, but having received no orders, it had to fall back in the direction of the Aisne. The Pommiers and Pasly bridges, the three bridges of Soissons, the railroad bridge and the one at Venizel were all blown up between two and four in the morning. The Gambetta bridge of Soissons had just been blasted when the French saw some latecomers emerge on the opposite bank, begging for a boat to bring them back to the other side. Some legionnaires of the III/23 improvised ways to get across; the colonel of the 93rd infantry swam across; to the north of the Aisne, hundreds of soldiers of various companies and regiments pulled back in utter disarray. Samuel Maier and other men of the 10th company of the III/23 were up all night in the midst of gunfire, the sky ablaze with rockets and explosions. In the absence of anti-aircraft weaponry, the sky was buzzing with German planes.[52] After fierce resistance, the Juvigny castle fell at dawn. The 93rd infantry was no more. As for the 12th Foreign, it had lost half its men.

What was Matès doing in this reprise of Waterloo? Knowing that a regiment includes between 2,000 and 3,000 men, divided into three battalions, a weaponry regiment and non-rank administrators, I figure it will be like looking for a needle in a haystack to try and find him. The 23rd RMVE was fighting north of the Aisne with the 93rd infantry, and to the south with the 12th Foreign, but also to the west under its commander, Lieutenant Colonel Aumoitte. As is specified in the "copy of the individual military card standing in for ID," which I am finally able to wrest from the Office of the Veterans of the Legion after much begging, Matès was posted to "CA2" commanded by Lieutenant Recht, the initials standing for "accompanying corps of the 2nd battalion," therefore the II/23, a corps that focused on heavy artillery, according to specialized websites: sixteen 8-mm Hotchkiss guns divided over four sections, two 25-mm antitank cannons and two 81-mm mortars. There is no way for me to know which materiel was used by legionnaire Jablonka. If we opt for the 81-mm mortar, he might have worked for his gunnery chief as aimer, loader, blaster, supplier, gun transporter or munitions carter; since these last two occupations required draft horses, they might have thought a man with experience in saddle-making would be best qualified for the job.

I'm looking through officer files, especially that of Reserve Lieutenant Recht, commander of the CA2 of the 23rd RMVE: born in Buenos Aires in 1905, a bulk grocery salesman in Paris, he came out as a "militant, antimilitarist Communist" in August 1936, in the early *Front Populaire* days. After the armistice, he would be decorated with the Order of the Regiment for "staying calm and keeping his wits about him when leading a section during the violent combat of 7 to 8 June. Through example, he was able to rally a core of elite fighters."[53] There is nothing to stop me from imagining as many glorious scenarios as I wish. But a more likely one would have had Matès behind his machine gun covering for his comrades, who were no more experienced than he was, sent into action against panzers with their antiquated guns and their grenades, to give the French troops time to flee. I imagine him billeted south of Soissons with the better part of his regiment, and in just forty-eight hours, going from the humdrum life of Barcarès to the chaos of bombardment, the sirens and screams, body parts torn away, headless corpses, horses lying among their own spilt viscera. Following the orders of Lieutenant Colonel Besson, commander of the 12th Foreign and the II/23, he probably went to Buzancy on 6 June with the whole CA2. The next day, he likely took part in the defense of the Soissons-West sector.

Bombing continued uninterrupted throughout the whole day of 7 June, throwing units into disarray, cutting off communication, killing men and horses, spreading terror in the ranks ("the Spaniards were uncontrollable whenever there was an aerial bombardment," writes Lieutenant Garandeau of the 12th Foreign[54]). Soissons was battered unremittingly by plane and artillery. Young, bare-chested German soldiers were chanting "*Ein Volk, ein Reich, ein Führer*," as they attempted to cross the river under French gunfire.[55] To the east of the town, the legionnaires under battalion chief André were given the mission to hold the Condé locks and a bridge over the Aisne. It was eight in the morning, the fog was rising: panzers were coming down from the high ground. An hour and a half later, a column of German infantrymen entered the town of Celles, on the north bank of the Aisne. Four machine guns mowed them down; the corpses remained in the village square all day. Around 13:00, the enemy crossed the river at two locations, unimpeded. Samuel Maier and his comrades of the 10th company marched all the way to the northern outskirts of Soissons, where they were likely warned by French soldiers: "There's no use, all you volunteers, you won't be able to get over; all the bridges have been destroyed." After being bombed yet again, they swam across the Aisne at the foot of the Soissons bridge. The small band headed for the Montgobert crossroads where the other survivors of the III/23 were gathered: there were only 150 of them left.

The afternoon of 7 June. Lieutenant Colonel Besson tried to secure the banks of the Aisne. Engineers were sent back to Gambetta bridge, damaged but still serviceable, to complete the job. At the junction to the railroad bridge, German soldiers with megaphones urged the legionnaires to surrender. But having already pushed back several German infiltration attempts, the legionnaires answered this exhortation with a volley of grenades. The soldiers billeted at Buzancy were deployed to the captain commanding the Soissons-West sector; they were sent to Ploisy, where they were to hold the rear blockade. To the east of Soissons, a 100-man reinforcement turned up with no weapons or munitions and went to battalion commander André. By late that afternoon, German rockets were exploding over Chassemy: the enemy had managed to cross the Aisne to the west and east, and were now threatening to surround the battalion. The locks came under heavy fire. Leaflets were being dropped from planes, summoning civilian and military authorities to surrender, or else the town would be burnt to the ground. Telephone links were cut: between 23:30 and dawn the next day, Lieutenant Colonel Besson lost all contact with his division general and with his units. That night, he learned that the sappers had not been able to get near the Gambetta bridge, since the enemy had the area covered by heavy guns and grenade launchers. Infiltrations were taking place on the eastern outskirts of Soissons.

By the morning of 8 June, the Aisne had been crossed at every point. Retreating to the south, the French attempted to regroup. With a retreat back to the Ourcq seeming imminent, Digoine du Palais, commander of the III/23, received orders to form a unit with what remained of his battalion and to move back to the front. Heading up three sections of light riflemen and a section of machine gunmen, he took position to the north of Missy-aux-Bois. The formation was immediately pounded by Stukas and German artillery fire. The entire 23rd RMVE, in conjunction with the 12th Foreign and the 237th infantry regiment, fought southwest of Soissons, at Vaux,

Missy-aux-Bois, Saconin and Breuil, under a relentless bombing campaign. Faced with multiple assaults, the regiment lost half its numbers.[56]

Here is an account by the physician Danowski:

> The dead and wounded are pouring in, and the battalion's emergency post is proving inadequate for this level of need. The stretcher-bearers are doing a good job. Then suddenly, one of them begins singing and dancing. He no longer knows what he's doing or where he is, becoming the ideal target of an enemy shooter. The *danse macabre* ends abruptly, and soon he is dead. . . . During these tactical retreats, officers often suffered nervous collapse. In one case, a crazed officer picked up a rifle, gathered together a dozen men and ordered them to form a "resistance line," an order which made no sense, since the enemy was nearby, overwhelmingly superior in men and firepower. An order is an order. And the men were decimated. This was how a certain Jewish enlistee was to die, mortally wounded by gunfire, who dragged himself to the emergency post seeking shelter, bleeding profusely from a severed carotid, arriving only with the greatest difficulty. But his hemorrhage was too serious for us to save him without surgery. His face drained, his eyes sunken, nose pinched, tears of pain veiled his eyes. In his delirium, his words were soon incomprehensible.[57]

Henri Ribera, of the 23rd, posted at Ploisy for artillery cover, was sent to the regiment command post to request orders. Order to withdraw. On his way back, he found the road so clogged with refugees that he had to abandon his bicycle and get back to post on foot, running through fields in his cape and puttees. He was then ordered to go alert the groups of gunmen in position above Ploisy. On the way back, caught in enemy gunfire, he jumped into a hole already occupied by a young Polish legionnaire. Utterly exhausted, they both fell asleep amidst the crash and bang of explosives.[58]

This 8 June 1940 proved a true baptism of fire for Matès. Numb with fatigue, gnawed by hunger, pushed to the point of exhaustion where the body switches to automatic pilot—shoot, reload, carry munitions, huddle behind a hillock, crawl, run—he would get sniped at again and again, and tasted death with every whistling bullet, with each flash of artillery fire from the other side. Maybe he was crazed with fear. Maybe his nose was bleeding. Maybe he was cursing France and all its Missy-aux-Bois that meant nothing to him. Or perhaps he swore to go down in glory performing a deed of great bravery, something to make his children proud. Seen from a bomber overhead, he was an ant among thousands of ants, busy moving a blade of grass. He didn't have enough ammunition to reload his gun, but in any case, he was too inexperienced to make good use of the thing. A similar complaint was expressed by Second Lieutenant Bertholay, commander of the CA1: the field artillery and guns were always too far forward on the infantry's line of resistance; they should have been 700 to 1000 yards away in order to perform most effectively.[59]

To the west, most of the 23rd had been destroyed and Soissons was crushed by bombings, while the 12th Foreign had to beat a retreat. The III/12 commanded by battalion chief André was showered with shells coming in from Chassemy to the south, which indicated that enemy artillery was now taking the battalion from the rear. Following a particularly heavy bombardment, the 100 men sent as reinforcements were now on the run. Fighter planes were machine-gunning the ground, followed by bombardiers that destroyed positions in six successive waves. By the end of the morning, the division general telephoned Lieutenant Colonel Besson to inform him that "the situation in the east no longer allows for local consolidation." The 12th Foreign received orders to withdraw around noon, but due to the distance of the command post, and to general disorganization, the orders brought by liaison officers did not reach the units until between 14:00 and 16:00, which meant that the withdrawal lasted into the evening hours. At Condé, the men of the III/12 ceded ground a yard at a time, with the officers, gun in hand, the last to leave. Lieutenant Veyrunes had the locks blown up while gunners attempted to delay the German advance. At 18:00, the battalion fell into an ambush (six enemy gunners appeared a short distance away); André ordered that guns and mortars be dumped into the river, and then the detachment surrendered.

In the Soissons-West sector, the legionnaires of the 12th Foreign, boosted by the II/23, withdrew to Vierzy, ten miles to the south. The withdrawal of artillery pieces was noticed from enemy aircraft overhead, and until 21:00, the columns of the 12th Foreign were shelled and machine-gunned by squadrons of fifteen planes over each withdrawal itinerary. Since the fields allowed the soldiers to scatter, there were few casualties, but anything horse-drawn was "massacred," as Lieutenant Colonel Besson put it. By the afternoon, the 12th Foreign had lost thirteen of its fifteen portable field kitchens, nearly all its small vehicles and 130 of its 173 horses. The regiment regrouped at Blanzy between 19:00 and 23:00, when fresh orders arrived for a withdrawal to the Ourcq.

On 8 June, late in the day, remnants of the 23rd surged back chaotically toward Vertes-Feuilles, at the edge of the Villers-Cotterêts forest. Five officers had been killed, and Lieutenant Colonel Aumoitte was wounded. While some were still waging a rear-guard battle in the forest, others were fleeing south out of Vertes-Feuilles. In the forest infested with German patrols, Second Lieutenant Bertholay, commander of the CA1 of the 23rd, received a warning shot from 100 paces. The undergrowth protected him, but since the shots had alerted the other patrols, he had to hide in a thicket until nightfall. Around 21:00, a column of German vehicles pushed into Villers-Cotterêts via the National 2. To the north, parachutists were drifting out of the sky. At dawn, Second Lieutenant Bertholay arrived at the railroad bridge, where he was met with machine-gun fire.

On the morning of 9 June, the 23rd RMVE, decimated and practically leaderless, was melded into a single battalion under the command of Captain Talec. Along with elements of the 12th Foreign, in punishing heat and without supplies, it withdrew on foot to the Ourcq canal to defend the Mareuil area. Taken to a German camp, battalion chief André and the survivors of the III/12 received their first food since the morning of 7 June: a cup of toasted barley.

The front had become entrenched by the Aisne, but also by the Somme, in Picardie and in Champagne. Cut off from tank and air support, left without orders ever since communications with the command post had been cut, clinging for dear life to their defensive positions, but without reinforcements or munitions, the French infantry took a beating for forty-eight hours, desperately attempting to keep "plugging the holes" until the entire blockade fell to pieces. On 9 June 1940, Marshal Pétain concluded that the war had been lost. The next day, the government moved to the castles of the Loire. Paris was eerily empty.

Look at the land now, so peaceful! I'm gazing out over fields, green and golden, undisturbed countryside as far as the eye can see, with a little copse in the distance, a farmhouse, some high-tension lines barely visible. We walk through Missy-aux-Bois during the siesta: a quiet village, streets shaded by plane trees and ancient walls covered in climbing roses. As we turn a corner, we come upon the monument to the 23rd: set into an enormous bush pruned to form a crypt, a stone column rises out of a mass of white flowers and roses. Atop the column, a winged angel (or is it a woman draped in a mantle?) is supporting an inanimate soldier, whose head tips toward a shoulder. The pedestal is inscribed with gold letters: "In memory of their comrades of the 23rd Regiment of Foreign Volunteers." A cemetery is tucked away at the foot of the church. A graveled grave topped by a grey cross bears the inscription "Second Lieutenant A. Lonjon, 23rd RMVE, 9 June 1940, died for France." A freshly shaven elderly gentleman in a shirt and tie comes out of a house. Born right after World War I, he has always lived in Missy-aux-Bois.

"Every year, there used to be a ceremony in front of the monument, followed by refreshments served at the school, but this year, no one came, everyone's getting too old. Their command post was set up way over there, in the quarries. Out that way was the landing strip. There wasn't much fighting here, nothing compared to Chemin des Dames in 1917."

He placed his hand on my arm, and in a low voice:

"You know, those foreigners, an unreliable bunch, always raising hell, stealing from farms. The Germans occupied the village, but they really weren't so bad."

We take the National 2 north, cross the Aisne and track left toward Juvigny. This smaller road runs along a crest: to the north, fields and the Chemin des Dames plateau; behind me, a wooded ravine, the one that separated the 9th company from Captain Talec's 10th. The guns were camouflaged behind this mound, in a thicket, ready to gun down every living thing, while the bulk of German tanks could be seen on the horizon . . . This is what it means to be stuck back in the twentieth century: you see the poppies in the wheat fields, but suddenly they're being crushed by panzers; you can't enjoy the clear summer sky, because you're trying to imagine it raining down iron and fire. You wonder whether you should play with the children in the grass, or try to make them understand all this.

A few moments later, I ask my wife rather abruptly to pull over to the side of the highway: I have just noticed a monument over on the right. It's a half-buried granite rock in which a three-foot-long bronze sword is planted. Bolted onto the rock, a plaque recalls that the 7th infantry division, fighting along a fifteen-mile front, "had received orders to defend the Ailette and the Aisne without looking back. This it did generously on 5, 6 and 7 June 1940 in fierce combat, vastly outmanned by the enemy, in a gesture of boundless self-sacrifice." The 93rd infantry is mentioned, but not the Foreign Legion. I jog back to the car and we drive off.

The elderly gentleman at Missy-aux-Bois was right, of course: the three-day battle for the Ailette cannot be compared to the inferno of Verdun, the universal slaughter, four years lost in the mud and blood of trench warfare. Still, I don't believe that the volunteers of 1940 proved unworthy. For Captain Appolinaire-Esteux, whose company defended a crest to the southwest of Villers-Cotterêts from 9 to 10 June, the legionnaires of the 23rd "handled themselves very well under fire" despite "rather poor military training."[60] Cited for honors, the battalion of Digoine du Palais is described as a "superb unit of young troops."[61]

And yet, their courage did not earn them equal esteem. Lieutenant Garandeau of the 12th Foreign put it this way: "the Polish Jews, not particularly courageous by nature, did their duty."[62] The brave Yids! You can make something out of them after all, like Frydberg of the III/23, a model driver, full of energy, indefatigable, always ready to join the fighters on the front lines, "entirely devoted to France, which he served faithfully," recommended for honors, but to no avail.[63] Or Akerman and Wajsblum of the 22nd RMVE, who died for France at Marchélepot, south of Péronne, clutching their old Lebel rifles, after waging a resistance fight that earned them 400 individual citations, a collective citation by the Order of the Army and even compliments from German officers.[64] And what of the legionnaires of the 21st, used as cannon fodder to spare the French forces, and whose sacrifice, near Sainte-Ménehould in Champagne, would inspire one general's victory cry: "Five hundred Jews the less!"[65] Using the Jews and getting rid of them all at the same time: a masterstroke! Léon Aréga, a fighter in the 22nd, sharply criticized the French on behalf of his fallen comrades at Soissons, Villers-Carbonnel and Marchélepot: "The war has relieved you of 'Polish' leatherworkers who lived on nothing and worked for even less. Henceforward, fine Parisian leather goods will regain their lost splendor, from before the alien invasion. . . . They're gone now, dead and buried, never to return."[66]

This disastrous attempt at holding back the German advance signaled the final act of France's campaign. General retreat was ordered on 12 June. Two days later, the Wehrmacht entered Paris, declared an open city. On the other side of the world, the *Sydney Morning Herald* wrote: "The shadow of tyranny now looms over France; one of civilization's lights has gone dark."[67] Along roads and rivers, France was flowing with tainted blood: Rommel's panzers crossed the Seine at Rouen; Von Kleist's group headed due south out of Reims; Guderian tracked the Marne, heading for the Swiss border. Within ten days, Cherbourg, Brest, Nantes, Poitiers, Bourges, Moulins, Clermont-Ferrand, Saint-Étienne, Lyon, Besançon, Belfort and Nancy had been reached.

Together with the 12th Foreign, which followed the same basic itinerary, the 23rd RMVE remained at a rear-guard position for the 6th Army, covering its fallback, until the armistice. On the Marne, around 11 June 1940, heavy bombardment met resistance for three more days; columns of German soldiers marched down the slopes of Nanteuil singing as they came under artillery fire.[68] The sappers blew up Champigny bridge too early, cutting off hundreds of legionnaires who were then taken prisoner, though some were able to swim across or get over by boat. In his notes to his division general, Lieutenant Colonel Besson was constantly asking for food supplies, maps of the region and munitions for his two remaining guns. It was "absolutely impossible," he said, to keep his men from falling asleep: "As soon as an officer has passed by a soldier, he will find him back asleep again moments later."[69] While the retreat was turning into a free-for-all, every man for himself, and Pétain's government in Bordeaux was preparing to demand an armistice, the 23rd RMVE had been holding back the German advance at Pont-sur-Yonne for two days. On 15 June, Szajkowski took a bullet to the chest; the men in his unit walked right by without helping him because he had left the Communist movement.[70] French author Georges Perec's father, Icek Judko Perec, born in Lubartów near Parczew and a legionnaire in the 12th Foreign, was wounded in the abdomen. A German officer hung a sign on him: "To be operated on immediately." He died of his wounds the next day, in a church serving as a hospital, at the age of thirty-one.[71]

The road from Pont-sur-Yonne to Cheroy was strewn with dead horses, mostly showing no visible signs of wounds, fifty yards from the bomb crater. On 16 June, units from the 23rd RMVE were captured in Montargis, already occupied by the Germans. Legionnaires in full flight walked day and night, under bombardment, caught between the Wehrmacht's oncoming crush and various infantry elements that had moved in from the south, so that they sometimes had to hide in swamps or cross German blockades dressed as civilians. While the men of the 23rd were marching south along the train tracks, those of the 12th Foreign were attempting to make their way among the carts full of refugees, the overloaded automobiles, the bicycles and even baby carriages that were clogging the potholed roads that led to the Gien bridge over the Loire. The city had been bombed; at the entrance to the bridge, trucks and houses were on fire, slowing down the traffic considerably.[72] The vanguard managed to cross the Loire during the afternoon of 17 June, but most of the 12th Foreign was a mile or so further north, blocked at a railroad crossing where German soldiers in disguise were spreading panic among a column of refugees. On the radio, Marshal Pétain, the new head of the government, called for a "cessation of combat." The French blew up the Gien bridge at 20:00, ceding to the enemy whatever transport materiel the 12th Foreign had left behind. On the morning of 19 June, the Germans crossed the Loire at Sully on a floating bridge. The 23rd received a further mission to hold the Quincy bridge, working with the 12th Foreign posted a little further up the Cher.

Thus, what remained of the 23rd RMVE was swept from one water line to the next: on the Ourcq 10 June, on the Marne the 11th, on the Seine the 14th (south of Paris's latitude), on the Yonne the 15th, on the Loire the 17th, on the Cher the 21st, on the Indre the 23rd. In other words, from Soissons, a forced march of 250 miles in two weeks. It was in Berry that the hobbled 23rd RMVE finally descended into hell. On 25 June, as the armistice went into force, they were scattered between La Châtre and Châteauponsac.[73] In the Alps and the bunkers along the Maginot line, French soldiers were refusing to lay down their arms.

There remained fewer than 700 men in the 23rd RMVE and 300 in the 12th Foreign. In a six-week campaign, 100,000 men had been killed (an average that was higher than that of World War I) and the Wehrmacht had taken two million prisoners. I don't know whether Captain Talec was right when he reported that the 23rd was one of the "rare regiments that was still flying the French flag the day of the armistice, paying it the homage it deserves."[74] For, in those June days, there wasn't much else to be proud of. Still, there were a few who managed to save the country's honor: the North African *spahis* who charged against Guderian's tanks, Colonel de Gaulle's armored unit at Montcornet, the Saumur cadets refusing to abandon their positions and—seemingly—the foreign volunteers, admirable in their determination and scrappiness, even until the final rout. The generals at headquarters might have been very surprised, along with the country notaries, the gossips, the pen-pushers for the daily rags and all the Munich-backers, if they had been told that the ragged Jews and Spaniards of the "rope regiments," those undocumented illegals that the republican police were to have escorted to the border in all urgency, had brought back to life the legend of the volunteers of 1792—"that army of vagabonds, tailors and shoemakers," writes Michelet—at the heart of the worst defeat France had suffered in all its history. They knew why they were fighting, unlike the reservists of the 71st division, who disbanded on 14 May 1940 on the Meuse heights and went home, leaving behind their guns and kits. Sociologically, I am more similar to those runaways, those thirty-five-year-old husbands and fathers from the greater Paris region, than I am to the undesirable Jews whose blood flowed in the furrows of France; no one can predict whether the grandson would have proven worthy of his grandfather.

Between armistice and Matès's demobilization on 28 September 1940 in a camp in the southwest, three whole months went by. Nothing is known of this lost summer except the demobilization certificate itself, a single sheet that my Aunt Suzanne obtained from the Veterans Bureau back in the 1970s. Next to the line that reads "Address where interested party is returning," a first answer has been scratched out:

Châteaumeillant (Cher) at Mr. Châtaigner's.

A bit further down, another item scratched out:

Demobilized upon presentation of work papers from Mr. Châtaigner.[75]

Châteaumeillant has kept my father and me busy for several weeks. This town of 2,500 is located twelve miles from La Châtre, which corresponds perfectly with the withdrawal itinerary of the 23rd. But why was the answer to the question scratched out? A few days after writing to the Châteaumeillant town hall, like sending a message in a bottle, my father gets a phone call. At the other end, a former municipal councilman. He has a clear memory of Mr. Châtaigner, with his stiff leg, living on Avenue de la République. He worked as a saddler in his own shop. What about a regiment of foreign volunteers in 1940? No, he has no memory of them. A while later, a woman from the town hall calls: you have to write to Ida, who was hiding out in Châteaumeillant during the war, and who had a memorial plaque placed there for The Righteous.

December 2008. Ida invites us into her living room, decorated with paintings in bright patterns of blue, vermillion, lime green and canary yellow. At sixty, as bright and lively as her paintings, she wears glasses with spiral frames and a brooch made of multihued moons. Her father, Samuel Rozenberg, a Polish Communist Jew, was a cabinetmaker in Faubourg Saint-Antoine. He enlisted as a volunteer on 9 November 1939 and fought with the 12th Foreign. After his demobilization in August 1940, he and his family withdrew to Châteaumeillant, where some 100 Jews were in hiding. By 1944, only three had been arrested. How to explain this miraculous figure? Ida believes there was local complicity, a network formed by the carpenter, the grocer, the photographer, etc. One gendarme, Raveau, who knew everything that was going on at the local Saint-Amand prefect's office, served as scout. Certain evenings, he would drop by the butcher shop and utter the code phrase: "Nasty business tonight." This was the alert for the Jews, and meant that men should go immediately into hiding. Châteaumeillant had had a long welcoming tradition since early in the war, when families from Ivry and the 11th arrondissement of Paris—including Ida's mother—had gone there to seek refuge. A list dated December 1939 that surfaced in the departmental archives of the Cher region attests that dozens of women with children—a few of whom were Jews—had lived there while their husbands were off at war. Was there some kind of pairing going on between the 11th arrondissement and Châteaumeillant? Ida believes there was. During the exodus, the town took in 600 refugees, and a charity committee took charge of finding them housing and food.

This further evidence makes the following scenario plausible: certain soldiers of the RMVE took advantage of contacts that their families had made in the region, during the evacuations of the "phony war," to hide out during the Occupation. I have no reason to think that Idesa had established ties among the Cher tradesmen. But I can well imagine that Matès found himself in Châteaumeillant at the end of the fighting, around 25 June 1940, and that he stayed there for a while. But unlike the Rozenbergs, he was not able—or perhaps the notion never occurred to him—to hide out there with Idesa and the children.

The correspondence of a Romanian legionnaire in the 23rd RMVE, Izu Abramovici, which his daughter was kind enough to share with me after we met at a conference on Jewish volunteer enlistees, shows that he wandered from village to village before settling down in Morlac in mid-July, some thirteen miles from Châteaumeillant. For those who made it out of the debacle alive, these weeks left them in a kind of limbo: demobilization was taking place at a scandalously slow pace, but it was summer, they could finally sleep all they wanted, bathe in the rivers and creeks, have a drink with friends at the local bistro, write to their families, enjoy just being alive. The reprieve was short-lived, however: the occupation authorities were starting to go after Jews, and the Vichy regime, established on 11 July, aimed its attacks at both foreigners and naturalized aliens. On 22 July, Izu wrote to his fiancée from Morlac: "It's possible that my demobilized status will allow me to return to Paris, but I wonder if that's the wise thing to do right now, since I'm a foreign volunteer and a Yid. I guess you read the papers and have figured out that various purges are going to be starting soon. So it might be safer to avoid walking right into the lion's den."[76] What kinds of things were these papers saying? *Le Matin*, a supposedly tasteful republican daily, published a report about the Marais in its 4 August edition: kinky-haired children playing with garbage in the gutter, butchers in soiled aprons chatting with gossipy matrons, a woman behind the delicatessen counter, heavily made-up but with filthy nails, bearded men in long overcoats speaking in hushed tones, rabbis, hustlers, all these characters living in this neighborhood where "everything is Jewish." The article concludes: "It is astonishing, at a time when we are supposed to be fighting against germs, that we would allow this ghetto, a repulsive stain in the heart of Paris, to continue to exist."[77]

Matès's demobilization papers were drawn up in Caussade, in the Tarn-et-Garonne region, hundreds of miles from Châteaumeillant and Morlac.

It was a while before I understood that Caussade was the train station for the Septfonds camp and that Matès, like Izu and thousands of other foreign volunteers, was being held there. His release papers state that legionnaire Jablonka would be going to stay, not with Mr. Châtaigner, as it turned out, but with "L. Mur, in St-Antonin, region of Tarn-et-Garonne," who also provided him with work papers. With that, my father and I start our investigation. The granddaughter of Lezin Mur describes for us a shoemaker, owner of a tiny vineyard, too poor to hire another worker but perfectly capable of signing phony work papers. "That sounds just like the sort of thing he'd do." And Septfonds? Just a camp like all the others, on the small side and completely forgotten today, originally intended for Spanish refugees. Early in the war, it was a Foreign Legion depot, then, after the French defeat, it became an internment camp for foreign volunteers.[78]

The camp's archives were destroyed after the war, which means that I have to rely on two personal accounts, one in Joseph Ratz's *La France que je cherchais* [*The France I Was Seeking*] (1945) and the other in Conrad Flavian's *Ils furent des hommes* [*They Were Men*] (1948). A Russian refugee and trained engineer, Ratz enlisted in the Foreign Legion out of love for "Eternal France." He was sent to Septfonds, a few dozen flea-ridden shacks with inedible food and barbed wire everywhere, even though these men had enlisted of their own free will. After the armistice, he found himself once again at Septfonds, as did Flavian, a Romanian lieutenant in the 23rd RMVE, who witnessed the arrival of survivors "in a pitiful state." Demoralized by weeks of retreat and aimless wandering, they could not be officially demobilized without orders from Vichy. By then, French soldiers had returned to family and workplace, but the "voluntary enlistees for the duration of the war" were doomed to rot away indefinitely in this ill-fated camp.

The tedium of day-to-day existence settled in. August 1940: the armistice had been signed a month and a half earlier, and still no demobilization orders. Ratz comments: "Everyone agreed that the situation had become unbearable."[79] They decided to go on a hunger strike. The camp commander, Edgard Puaud, an officer of the Legion who was a bit too fond of the bottle, and who had wanted to resist on the Tarn river, was of two minds: he could not agree to negotiate with rebels, but if the situation got any worse, he would have to call in the prefect of Montauban, or worse, the Germans. But the orders from Vichy were ironclad: not to demobilize, because this bunch of undesirables was to be sent to "foreign worker companies" where they would perform some sort of forced labor or other. The hunger strike was suspended when Puaud, violating orders, agreed to demobilize the older soldiers, fathers of large families and anyone with working papers. When Vichy did finally agree to demobilization in principle, it placed so many qualifying conditions on the men—requirements having to do with work, living arrangements, family and money—that it became practically impossible for "men who were not French and had, besides, just completed a thirteen-month campaign."[80]

While forced enrollment was beginning under the direction of Commander M., sent by Vichy, Puaud decided to send home as many enlistees as possible. His office was mobbed, and "anyone whose documents were more or less in order was demobilized. . . . Blatantly forged employment affidavits were accepted without question."[81] Puaud himself procured "work documents for these legionnaires, and had relatively substantial sums of money paid to some of them to help with their readjustment."[82] Up to 100 demobilizations were being processed daily. Commander M. was furious, and tore up the demobilization orders; he was of the opinion that foreign Jews should not be released from duty, but detained and carefully guarded. Izu Abramovici managed to get demobilized, and soon left for Nice with his fiancée, who came to join him. On 13 September, the demobilization of Flavian's company was complete. Puaud signed his own personal affidavit and recommended that he keep his revolver on him, to continue the fight.

I now have a better understanding of why Matès acted as he did. He wrote urgently to his old acquaintance, or boss, in Châteaumeillant, Mr. Châtaigner, to ask for a work affidavit. Either it never arrived, or it did and was rejected, one of the two. So, he submitted another request to Lezin Mur, the shoemaker of Saint-Antonin, located a few miles from there. This time, it worked. After having fought for France for eleven months, the saddler-glover from Parczew, thirty-one years old, father of two, was finally returned to civilian life. He left Septfonds and got himself to the Caussade train station, with the princely sum of 200 francs in his pocket, his demobilization bonus. The date was 28 September 1940. The next day, the underground Yiddish paper *Unzer Wort* [*Our Word*], successor to the outlawed *Naye Presse*, wrote: "The Jewish soldiers of the Sept-Fonds [*sic*] camp report that the French government concentrated them into camps as if they were murderers or common criminals, good for nothing but cannon fodder. It wasn't enough that thousands of them had fallen in battle for France; those who survived had to be shut up in concentration camps and labor camps."[83]

October 1940. At this point, there were only 600 men remaining in the camp, but the situation had become critical. Having gotten wind of Puaud's insubordination, the interior ministry turned over the duty of overseeing demobilization to the police, and Puaud was transferred to Montauban. There, he went about setting up a federation for veteran volunteers, with local associations all over France, to support war widows, comrades imprisoned in the stalags, and the like. This came to the notice of Vichy: an association of Jews who fought against Germany! Ratz and Flavian each joined the Resistance. And what about Puaud? You might think that he would have backed the cause of freedom, with his courage and rebellious spirit. But in 1944, he took command of the Legion of French Volunteers against Bolshevism, and the one-time protector of Jewish soldiers at Sept-fonds disappeared on the eastern front, wearing the stripes of a *Waffen-SS* general.[84] As for the foreign ex-volunteers who were not so fortunate as to have had someone like Puaud on their side in the fall of 1940, they were either moved into "foreign groupings" (the law of 27 September prescribed that "foreigners who are redundant in the national economy" be sent to work camps") or interned at Pithiviers or Beaune-la-Rolande. From the 23rd RMVE alone, there were fifty-six ex-combatants in the first camp and forty in the second.[85] Now that the short combat chapter of their lives was over, they were back to their basic identity: Jews. In 1944, Izu Abramovici was deported in convoy 73 from Drancy and shot in Lithuania, at the same time as Kalme Chimisz, a volunteer enlistee in the 23rd, who was wounded in the leg on 6 June 1940 during the fighting at the Juvigny castle, awarded France's War Cross and honorably discharged due to his wound. Back in Paris after many weeks at Septfonds, he had written to his camp commander to ask respectfully for authorization to wear his medal.[86]

6

THE

PROVIDENTIAL

DENTIST

Gitla Leszcz is in the last stages of life. Her spindly arm, nothing left but veins and tendons, emerges from her yellow "Hospitals of Paris" bedsheet. Her skin is translucent, her muscles melted away. I shake her hand and she stares back with a look of suspicion. Her nails have long since grown back, but her son Serge explains that she never completely regained feeling in her fingers, which was a problem since she was a seamstress.

Serge lives in the suburbs, at a bend in the Seine. We arrive at his place about forty-five minutes late, after getting lost somewhere around the Levallois bridge. Traffic is heavy; my father is cursing the lack of proper signage. While he parks, I dash over to a nearby pastry shop and buy three small pastries. Serge greets us at the door.

"I'm deeply touched," my father says, shaking his hand warmly. "We read a lot of names on paper, but now yours is no longer an abstraction."

Our interview is somewhat scattershot, with my father constantly interrupting with new questions, even though we had agreed back in the car on how we would conduct things. "You take the lead," he insisted. While talking to us, Serge is digging through some boxes belonging to his mother, and pulls out stacks of photos, letters, bank statements, tax returns, utility stubs and lab results, all those pieces of accumulated evidence that prove a person exists. He hands me a text in which his mother tells of the torture she suffered at the Kowel prison in 1933, as well as his father's autobiography, entitled *Trompe-la-mort*, or "death dodger." Raymond Gardebled belonged to the generation traumatized by World War I, and was therefore fiercely antimilitaristic; and yet, when the Spanish Civil War broke out, it made his blood boil, and he signed up with the International Brigades. He refused to call himself an anarchist (though when I checked the National Security archives, I found that he was on file for this opinion-related offense.[1]) He wasn't really a hardware dealer; rather, he'd worked for one, but once returned from Spain, he had no job at all, since his bosses refused to take him back. In 1938, he married Gitla Leszcz, a young Polish Jew recently arrived from Dębowa-Kłoda, to save her from being deported. The wedding took place at the Neuilly-sur-Seine town hall, Communist at the time. Love at first sight, or marriage of convenience? Whatever the case, things didn't work out. On the eve of the war, Raymond and Gitla lived at 7 Place Auguste-Métivier, right over the bakery (which is still there today). So, why did they agree to attest to Matès's good conduct at the Père-Lachaise police department on 8 October 1939?

"Helping folks out," said Serge, "that was just part of our family values. Everyone was welcome at our table, even if my mother complained about it later."

Gitla's and Idesa's lives were amazingly similar. One was born on 14 September 1913, the other on 14 May 1914, in two shtetls connected by a small country road. They were both Jewish, Communist, were jailed at age twenty, and each sought exile in Paris upon her release, in the late 1930s. Rue Désirée is a two-minute walk from Place Auguste-Métivier, by way of

Avenue Gambetta. I can even imagine that it was the Gardebleds who got my grandparents to move to the neighborhood, after Matès was released from Fresnes in June 1939. Père-Lachaise must have meant a change of scene after two years in Ménilmontant.

Serge takes us to his mother's bedside. What if she actually remembers my grandmother, recognizes her face? We walk through the geriatric ward, where the acrid smell of urine is overwhelming. The corridor is lined with elderly women, seated, sometimes done up nicely, bobbing their heads. In their rooms, old men are snoring or grumbling in front of their television screens, sound blaring. From her bed, Gitla greets us with a hostile stare. I smile back, unintimidated. This haggard body, now devoured by cancer, these hands that some torturer once crushed, these piercing eyes belong to a great resistance fighter. The self-portrait she wrote in the 1950s for some Party commemoration takes the reader from Pilsudski's jails to the round-ups of the Occupation.

> By late 1941, the Paris comrades had set up a mimeograph machine in our little apartment to print our tracts. While they were doing that, I would go to the park with my child; later, I would deliver the tracts, hidden in the baby's clothes. In 1942, someone informed on me as a supposed "Jew" who wasn't wearing "the star," which was a violation of the new laws in force. The police arrived early one Saturday morning to question me. I proved to them that I wasn't Jewish, and asserted that they could go to the prefecture to find a document proving (supposedly) that I was Christian Orthodox. Frankly, I was petrified during this police interrogation, because right behind the chair I was sitting on, there were twenty-five packets of tracts, weighing over ten pounds each! We used to print out the tracts on Fridays, and our liaison people would come collect them on Saturday. It was only 5 a.m., and I hadn't been expecting anybody that early. I was really very lucky that the police didn't seem interested in what was in the apartment. The inspector left, warning that he was going to the prefecture to check out what I had said, and that in the meantime, I was not to leave the apartment. Once I was alone, I let the comrades know what had happened, and they immediately evacuated the machine and the tracts. I then left the apartment carrying my child. That was in March 1943.[2]

As Serge films us with his digital camera, I write down names on a notepad and show them to Gitla. She examines each thoughtfully and nods her head at "Parczew" and "Jablonka." I show her a photo of my grandmother on the screen of my laptop. She cries out "*Oy!*" and her eyes light up, before falling back into her lethargic state. "Matès" does not ring a bell. I shout into her ear "Idesa" and "Parczew," but these names trigger no reaction. Serge shows her a picture of himself as a child. When she says "My son!" he points to himself, as if to explain that the picture is him. She doesn't seem to get the point. Suddenly, I sense that something, near my arm or behind me, is arousing her interest. She's pointing at me, but I don't understand why; she keeps pointing, I lean in, and she finally points out a tiny hole in my sweater, around the elbow—it's the seamstress in her speaking—and tries to poke her cold, pointy finger through it. Before we leave, my father says to her "*Do svidania*" and "*Do widzenia*," meaning "good-bye" in Russian and Polish. The next day, Serge sends an email: "I watched the video footage from yesterday. My mother's reaction to the name Jablonka and the town name, and also to the photo of your grandmother, is really quite telling. Even without that, I am now convinced that my mother must have known your grandparents, nothing hypothetical about it anymore. I think the evidence points to it."

My memory of Annette is of another kind altogether. I knew her well. She was tiny and frail, a wrinkled old lady but warm and friendly, and as a child, I remember being struck by her accent that would roll and distort the simplest words. Her husband Constant was a force of nature, with a strong build, big nose, pale-blond hair combed back, a Jean Gabin type. If he stood in front of Annette, she would disappear. Apart from the fact that I can't imagine one of them without the other, what I felt—although unconsciously—is how very different they were from our normal context, the milieu of a French public teacher. Constant also spoke with an accent, though I'm not sure whether it was a rural accent or a working-class Ménilmontant one. My father has a whole series of anecdotes about him: Constant wallops some street thug, Constant tells his anti-Semitic neighbor to go to hell, Constant mocks clerics and employers, Constant scolds cowardly kids. Early in the war, after much hesitation, Annette went to register with the census. The commissioner asked: "Are you Jewish?" Constant broke in: "From what standpoint, religious or ethnic?" The commissioner: "How long have you known words like that?" Constant: "Sorry, sir, I didn't go to college like you." Furious, the officer could barely speak: "You'll be hearing from me!" Constant was a nonconformist, an *anar*, or anarchist, my father says, and I learned to respect that word very early, even though I was too young to understand what it meant. At family gatherings, he would speak loudly and used swear words unabashedly, which made quite an impression on me as a young boy.

Constant and Annette were my father's and aunt's guardians. They lived in northern Paris. We would see them from time to time. They were always there for Christmas and birthdays. They brought my brother and me presents, but very odd presents; or rather, it was the fact that they brought us presents at all that I found odd, since I knew they had a daughter (born in 1943) and a real grandson. We would occasionally go spend a Sunday with them at their little cabin in La Celle-sur-Morin, where my brother and I would be dying of boredom. We would flee the cramped quarters to play outdoors with our guinea pigs, or we'd head over to the railroad tracks and put 10-centime coins on the rails and wait for a choo-choo to come by and flatten them. With Constant and Annette, my father was always cheerful and considerate. I can see him, out in the garden, kitchen glasses set on a wobbly metal table where the aperitif is being served; he jokes, gets everyone's news, engages with everyone. So why is it that I always felt uneasy around them? Where did this guilty indifference come from? They were good people, after all, practically family: as my father would explain to me whenever I asked, Annette was his mother's first cousin, Annette's father and Idesa's mother were brother and sister, they were both Korenbaums. But I couldn't quite visualize this family tree. I felt I ought to make an effort to show Annette and Constant an affection that they didn't show toward me. A good deal consisted in sending them a postcard whenever we went on vacation. But that's over now: they died some fifteen years ago.

Annette Korenbaum, son of David, the forester of Maloryta, arrived in Paris in the mid-1930s. Her older sister Maria had been living there for a few years with her daughter Sarah. At first, the two sisters lived at 88 Avenue d'Italie with their cousins the furriers, Frime, Sroul and Dina. Maria fell in with the anarchist circles, which is how Annette met Constant Couanault, a likable loudmouth, leatherworker by trade, originally from Fougères, in Bretagne. Constant took a liking to the little sister freshly arrived from the shtetl, undocumented, like so many others. In 1936, they signed marriage papers to make her situation legal, and for their supposed honeymoon, they went to Spain, where Constant was to cover the political situation for *Le Combat Syndicaliste*—a fact noted in his National Security file, since he also had a record as a "militant anarchist trade unionist," and his name appeared on a list of suspects that was periodically transmitted to the interior ministry. A regular customer at the leftist bookstore *La Librairie sociale internationale*, known for his libertarian views which he aired openly at rallies, Constant was one of the leaders of the CGT-SR, an ultra-minority revolutionary wing of the more mainstream General Confederation of Labor, created in the mid-1920s, and whose newspaper was *Le Combat Syndicaliste*.[3] Back from Spain, Constant and Annette set up house at 106 Rue Saint-Maur, in the 11th arrondissement, also the address to which *Le Combat Syndicaliste* directed comrade workers in leather and pelts to write if they missed an issue of their federal bulletin.

At the National Library, I have no trouble finding Constant's reportage, entitled "What We Saw in Spain," a travel diary of his trip in late 1936 with his young wife, at the invitation of the CNT, the large Spanish anarchist trade union organization. Enthusiasm was in the air in Catalonia, its revolution in full swing: tanneries and dairies were organized, headed by workers' committees made up of delegates from each entity; oil was distributed to factories by farmers from Aragon, who in exchange received cement, coal or sugar; there was a brotherly welcome from anti-militarist soldiers from a Barcelona barracks, who replaced "the servitude they experience daily in the capitalist fascist regime's army" with more useful activities; the Puigcerda church, whose only purpose was "continuous brainwashing," had been transformed into a public park where children could play; public utilities and transport were under the control of the unions; and there was a general welfare system in place.[4] For Constant, this was the ideal society, with neither God nor master, where man no longer has the right to exploit his fellow man—before it was destroyed by the Catalan authorities and the Stalinists, even before Franco's victory.

I have trouble imagining Constant and Annette as anything but old folks, the substitute grandparents that I am supposed to love, so that today, as I read the surveillance reports on "the anarchist Couanault Constant," or when I write that Annette was born in Maloryta in 1906, I can't help but feel how strange this life before my life is. But at the same time, it saddens me to think that I so completely missed out on knowing them better, their life commitments and struggles, all those complications that are so often kept from children. A family photo from 1910 shows Annette at age four with her sisters and parents, dressed in a little skirt and smock, her angelic curls held back by a white headband. She's holding hands with her sister Maria, six years old and just as blond. Their father, David Korenbaum, still a young man, is sitting in a chair, ramrod straight. His face, framed by a visor and clipped beard, is the picture of dignity. In the background are spindly, leafless trees, what looks like waterlogged ground, and a fence running the length of the photo; in other words, a typical rural shtetl. "Life was idyllic in Maloryta," asserts Sarah, Maria's daughter, an Auschwitz survivor like her mother. Although theirs was an arranged marriage, David Korenbaum and his wife adored each other. She would serve meals but never sit at the table herself; she gave birth to one boy and seven girls sent from God. David worked for local Polish princes as a forester, deciding which trees were to be pruned and which ones chopped down. He would then check that the work was carried out according to orders. The children would take turns, by twos and threes, accompanying him through the forest in his troika, bundled in their fur overcoats. The sleigh bells jingled in the biting cold, and noisy crows would take wing, causing clumps of snow to drop from their perch. An enchantment![5]

The boy died young, the girls grew up. Maria was being courted by Moises Lichtsztejn, son and nephew of rabbis, polyglot, fine Hebrew-speaker, anarchist, half painter, half poet. He had her reading Kropotkin and Bakunin, she renounced Communism for him, and she got pregnant. She was sent away to Danzig to hush things up. It was in this city—claimed unequivocally as their own by the Nazis—that Sarah was born in 1928. Once settled in Paris, the couple made friends in anarchist circles, such as Constant, as I have already pointed out, but also Carmen Torres, a Spanish woman who lived in Blanc-Mesnil in a bungalow built amidst the workers' vegetable gardens. Moises, Maria's husband, was a strange character.

Enrolled in the Conservatory of Arts and Crafts, he owned a Singer sewing machine and, according to the National Security report, "a mannequin that allows him to make clothes for his fellow Poles." He was a faithful reader of *L'Humanité* and *Le Libertaire*, got home late every night, had a bad reputation and failed to respect "the most basic rules of hygiene." Their breakup took place in 1935: he left his wife and child, and went back to Poland. Maria became Mother Courage, working as a seamstress at home, but was worn down by so many denials of proper ID papers. Her case attracted the attention of Jacques Doriot, ex-Communist parliamentarian for the Seine region, who was able to get her an authorization to stay in France, a clemency measure that also benefitted her husband, who was now back in France.[6] This didn't keep Moises from continuing to live day to day, doing odd jobs, and that would have been my lasting impression of him if his daughter Sarah did not speak of him, starry-eyed, as an extraordinarily good, highly cultivated man. In one photo, sitting between her mother, the pale, dainty dressmaker, and her father, in a suit jacket, a shock of hair, looking pensive and holding a cigarette, she looks like a mischievous sprite emerging between two trees, smiling ear to ear.

In 1937, Annette and Maria went back to Maloryta to bury their father, the forester with the magic sleigh. They were reunited with Jascha, now twenty, the youngest of their siblings, and with the other sisters, who had returned from Palestine for the occasion. The sisters took their widowed mother back to Eretz Israel, but Jascha immigrated to Paris in 1938.[7] There were no more Korenbaums left in Maloryta now, that many Jews saved from the coming slaughter. Jascha was also a character from my childhood, but because she was grumpy, and had deprived my father of orange juice when he was young, I didn't care much for her, unlike her husband, Maximilien Charriaud, called Poulot: another anarchist, a jokey, bushy-haired type, always making puns, who taught me to play tic-tac-toe on a wooden board at his house in La Celle-sur-Morin, a stone's throw from the house of Constant, his inseparable friend. Despite the occasional quarrel, they were lifelong friends, married to two sisters, to seal the deal! Wives as well as husbands, Polish Jews and French anarchists, all were on file at National Security.

Raymond and Gitla Gerdebled, Abram and Malka Fiszman, Moises, Maria and their little Sarah, Constant and Annette, Poulot and Jascha, these were my grandparents' friends in the early days of the Occupation. The closest were the three Korenbaum sisters, Maria, Annette and Jascha, and their husbands. But why such a late start to these friendships? Logically, Idesa should have sought out her cousins as soon as she arrived in Paris in the spring of 1938. But Annette tells my father with certainty: "I'm sure it was later. You were already born when I got to know your parents." Among the husbands of the three sisters, Constant was the most generous and devoted, as his story will later prove. He had an aversion to Marxism, but this leatherworker, with a self-taught interest in all things political, a brilliant speaker at his anarchist-revolutionary union meetings, who didn't give a damn about bourgeois conventions, had quite a few things in common with Matès. As I walk by Père-Lachaise along Avenue Gambetta, I think of those workers, who winced at the very mention of a foreman, a cop, a warrant officer or a cleric, but who were not above helping an undocumented Jewish immigrant woman by marrying her, for love or otherwise, and would help out any friend in need, no questions asked. What good is a French ID card if not to help out those who don't have one? Anarchists, libertarians, Reds, socialists, republicans, it hardly matters so long as they fight together against fascism. Heirs to a legacy that goes back to the *sans-culottes* of Faubourg Saint-Antoine, to Proudhon, to the French labor exchanges, these workers were cooperating, whether they knew it or not, with the League of Human Rights to help refugees that born-and-bred Frenchmen, whether Catholic or Jewish, accused of coming to France to sponge off its citizenry.

I turn left onto Rue Désirée, paved in cobblestones for 100 yards, and find myself in front of number 3. A gate with an intercom prevents unwanted intrusions into a neat little courtyard, bordered on one side by a row of plane trees, on the other by flower boxes set in front of ground-level bay windows and, at the very back, by a low stone wall. The atmosphere puts me immediately at ease. In this little square of greenery in the middle of Paris, everything exudes charm, nothing is out of place: a fine building, windows open to the soft breeze, a patch of grass with folding garden chairs and a coiled garden hose, an easy walk to Père-Lachaise. I would guess about 800 euros per square foot. What's left of the slums of 1939? I buzz a few names on the intercom, at random. No answer: some are gone for the weekend, others don't want to be bothered on a Sunday morning. So I go off to try out a few different itineraries, two minutes from Rue Désirée to Place Auguste-Métivier, three minutes from Rue Désirée to the Père-Lachaise police station, and so on, as I invent new ones to try.

At the archives of the City of Paris, the population censuses of 1936 and 1946 show that number 3 Rue Désirée housed six families, which I assume must have meant two families on each landing in the small, three-story building. Both before and after the war, the tenants were almost exclusively Polish Jews. I copy down all the names, and once back home, I enter the last names into the online directory, limiting my search to the greater Paris region and excluding such recently popular first names as Vanessa and Sébastien. With the data gathered, I send out some forty letters that start like this: "I am writing to you in the hope that you are related to the such-and-such family, who used to live at 3 Rue Désirée in the 20th arrondissement in [1936 / 1946]. My grandparents lived in this building before the war, etc." I receive only one reply, via email: "I have just received your letter, and am very moved to read these few lines about your grandparents, who lived in the same place as my parents, brothers and sisters." The email is signed Charles Raduszinski, a name I find right away in the 1946 census:

> Jojna Raduszinski, born in 1913, Polish, tailor
> + his wife Myriam, born in 1915, Polish
> + their children: Berthe, born in 1937
>   Fanny, born in 1940
>   Charles, born in 1943
>   Bernard, born in 1945[8]

We begin a long-distance conversation. Charles's parents had close ties with another family from the building, the Jagodowicz family, originally from Minsk Mazowiecki, a little town between Warsaw and Siedlce. And indeed, the 1946 census shows the following entry:

> Becalel Jagodowicz, born in 1914, Polish, cobbler
> + his wife Kajla, born in 1916, Polish
> + their children: Élie, born in 1938
>   Liliane, born in 1943

Charles agrees to put me in touch with the Jagodowicz children and with his own older sister, Berthe, who might be a better source of information.

A sports bar in the 13th arrondissement, early afternoon. I let the owner know that I'm waiting for a lady named Berthe. He points her out to me, on the terrace, chatting with some old acquaintances. When she sees me, she jumps up and kisses me on both cheeks. Berthe is a warm, passionate person. She has had a "charmed life," as her father Jean promised her she would (Jean is the French version of Jojna). She wants to tell me about her college years, her travels around the world, but I keep nudging the conversation toward the war years, again and again, and not only that, the war years as seen through the narrowest of lenses, the spatial setup at 3 Rue Désirée. Finally yielding to my insistence, she cooperates, though not without a few side trips to the fun-filled 1960s. As she explains, there was a porch with front steps that led into the building, which was ancient and falling apart, "disgustingly filthy," with shared toilets in the central courtyard and a rat-infested stairwell. Her father's workshop was one floor up: a room for the machines, an ironing board, and a kitchen. The family lived in a two-room apartment—one for the children, the other for the parents—in another building. Jablonka, no, that name doesn't ring a bell, nor does her sister Fanny recollect it. Maybe my grandparents lived in the other building, she ventures.

A few days later, I have a long phone conversation with Liliane, the Jagodowicz daughter, born in 1943. She also has a vivid memory of the building, because her family lived there during the war: a square porch with an iron railing, two steps up from street level. A dark hallway links the two buildings. A paved courtyard. On either side of each landing, a tiny room for each family. She doesn't remember the name Jablonka, it wasn't one her parents ever mentioned to her. All this would seem to demonstrate that the families were not very close, or that Matès and Idesa had become extremely discreet by the eve of Vichy, fearing arrest. But then again, they didn't live that long at Rue Désirée, only from 1939 to 1942, and the Raduszinski and Jagodowicz girls were still very young then.

Whatever the case, it was in this fleabag of a building that Matès, just released from Septfonds, was reunited with his wife, their daughter Suzanne-Soreh, and their little baby, Marcel-Moyshe, whom he hardly knew.

My father was five months old by then. How did he greet this "stranger"? With screams and tears? And what was the happy father saying to himself? "Later on, you'll go to a French school with a book bag I'll hand-tool for you, and you'll become a man." Matès was now in Paris, Matès was back with his family, and Matès had just jumped feetfirst into the lion's den. It was late September 1940, and the Germans had just ordered a census of Jews in the occupied zone. On 3 October, the Vichy government passed the Jewish status laws, banning Jews from access to assembly, the courts, the civil service and cultural professions. The text was signed by Marshal Pétain and half of his government, including General Huntziger, who had been in charge of the Sedan sector in the spring of 1940. The following day, a law authorized the internment of "foreigners of Jewish race."[9]

It is hard to know whether Matès and Idesa realized how serious the situation had become. Others, after all, had made the reverse decision: the demobilized soldier would stay in the free zone to the south, and his family would come to join him. This is what Izu Abramovici and his fiancée did, for instance. Or this variation: after his demobilization from the 23rd RMVE on 16 August 1940 in Septfonds, Moises Ingwer, a Jew from Lens, met up with his wife and children in a tiny town in the Loire valley where they had been waiting for him since May 1940.[10] We know how the story ends, but they did not, which is why I try not to reason in terms of foresight, lucidity or winning strategies. First of all, to leave home, it takes money, connections and somewhere to go. It is unclear whether Matès would have felt close enough to Mr. Châtaigner, the saddler in Châteaumeillant, or to Lezin Mur, the cobbler-winegrower in Saint-Antonin, for him to move in with his wife and children. In the case of the town of Lens, a statistical study of such departures proves that most were undertaken by young, childless adults, whereas families and the elderly tended to stay put, at least in 1940.

So, what about Paris? The census began in early October and would give rise to the "Jewish file" at the prefecture, a monument of police know-how, André Tulard's brainchild: 150,000 persons, 600,000 individual color-coded file cards (blue for French, orange or beige for foreigners or stateless persons) divided into four sub-files by alphabetical order, nationality, street and profession.[11] Since this gigantic filing system was destroyed at Liberation, I am unable to confirm whether or not Matès and Idesa were listed in it. But it is highly likely that they submitted to the census, like the overwhelming majority of Parisian Jews and like a large number of Communist Jewish Poles who should have known better, given their previous experience living underground. Recall the case of Annette, defended by Constant when the unfortunate rookie census taker asked her whether she was Jewish: "From what standpoint, religious or ethnic?" As further evidence, Matès's name is in the prefecture's "family file" (a different set of records now preserved at the National Archives) with the following mention: "Jewish file number 56,339."[12] And one final indication: during the Vél' d'Hiv police raids, the officers, who based their arrest warrants on the Tulard files, went to 3 Rue Désirée knowing exactly where to knock. What were Matès and Idesa thinking, filling out a census form in 1940 as undocumented Jews, threatened with internment! But for them, it was just one more instance of the bureaucratic red tape they'd come to accept. And anyway, everyone else was doing it, so what could they possibly be risking? And then, they wouldn't dare come after women or war veterans, would they?

For Matès, life went back to normal, though it was much harder than before the war: he had to find someone who hired illegals, then work cutting and stitching from dawn to dusk, distribute the goods without being spotted, pay the rent, feed the family. But at this time, leather was in very short supply, and economic oversight inspectors were always on the prowl. I can only presume that Idesa waited in line at the grocer's and the baker's, and took care of the children. In 1940, Rue Désirée wasn't this completely deserted street where I have been pacing, in the hope of coming across an elderly lady who will turn out to be the neighborhood's memory. The business directory from before the war shows a grocer at number 3, an outlet for paint and plate glass at number 5, a radio shop at number 7, the Hotel Désirée at number 13, across the street from the Hotel Dahlia, at number 4, and finally, at number 6, a wine merchant.[13]

Sarah, Maria's daughter, who was only twelve at the time, made herself useful by taking Suzanne out to the park, and was rewarded by getting to finish off Marcel's cans of Nestlé's sweetened milk. Another story, from Colette this time, and therefore secondhand: her parents, Abram and Malka Fiszman, often got together with Matès and Idesa. They would visit, chat over a cup of tea, marvel at Marcel's babbling. They made a very close-knit group. Right around this time, Matès began to make friends with Constant and Poulot, the (French) husbands of Annette and Jascha. In the 1970s, Annette described her memories of Matès for my father: a cheerful, active, helpful person, always ready to lend a hand. One day, Poulot had to transport a mattress. Matès showed up to help, even though nobody else even knew who he was. When did this happen? I reread notes I typed out after interviewing my father. For the year 1941, I've written: nothing.

The plane is in its descent; a rattling sound under my seat says that the landing-gear bay has just opened. After several sleepless nights—my book is nearly done, my grandparents are about to be murdered—this trip feels like a release. At last, I'll be meeting the mythical Argentinian family! My father's cousins come out to greet me at the airport: Benito and his sister Celia, on *Tío* Simje's side, and Mauricio, on *Tía* Reizl's. We all hug out in the parking lot, on a hot summer's day. That evening, before sitting down for supper, Benito helps me work through the particulars of our family history, how the bath can be both a *mikvah* and a *bod*. He shows me old Shloyme's *tefillin*, which he inherited from his father, though he considers himself a Communist before being Jewish. Mauricio tells me of his 4 years in prison under Videla. At Celia's, as I dig through a shoebox full of photos and letters, I come upon a letter written in Polish in a lovely hand. It is a letter from Parczew dated 26 November 1940. Here is what their good mother Tauba, with her very fragile health, writes to Simje and Reizl: "Back here, nothing special is happening, we're all feeling fine, as are Gitla and the [half-]brothers. We get cards from Hershl and Henya. . . . Unfortunately, we have no news from our Matès and Idesa and their daughter. I would praise the heavens to get some news from Matès." What follows is more news of this and that, and exhortations to write more often.[14]

Upon reading this letter, Simje and Reizl could not have suspected the underlying tragedy, which the *Yizkor Bukh* today brings to light: the Jews of Parczew and surrounding villages were shut into a ghetto; many households were starving; local thugs roamed the streets to make sure no one was milling grain; men were being rounded up for labor camps; Meir

Jablonka, son of Yoyne, was shot by the Germans on Passover.[15] But this letter must have nevertheless troubled its Argentine readers. Why was it written in Polish, for one thing? So that the censor could read it? Because Yiddish had been outlawed? At the same time, life seemed to be going on as always. "Papa is working on the farm as usual," Tauba writes, not making clear whether she is talking about the family home or someone else's farm where the old man was hired after he gave up studying the Kabbalah. Either way, we at least know that Shloyme was still alive at that point. To sum up, family news was still circulating, but just barely: Simje and Reizl wrote, but not enough; Hershl and Henya, refugees on the Soviet side, seemed to be safe. From Paris, on the other hand, "we have no news from our Matès and Idesa and their daughter," which means that no one even knew yet that they had a seven-month-old boy.

The next day, as we drink a piping hot yerba mate out on the patio, Reizl's daughter brings me a preprinted postcard on Red Cross letterhead, all crumpled and dog-eared, which she found in her attic. It's a letter from Simje to Matès: the *"demandeur—Anfragesteller—*enquirer," Simje Jablonka, Montiel 2731, Mataderos, Buenos Aires "would like to hear from you." The *"destinataire—Empfänger—*addressee" is I. Jablonka, 3 Rue Désirée, Paris 20th, France, but the reply is signed by Matès: "I, my wife and my two children Suzanne and Maurice [*sic*] are all well, and we are working a little. Let us hear more from you. Matès, 8 February 1941." Alarmed by the letter from Parczew, Simje had thus taken the lead and written to his brother. He probably thought Matès was in hiding, or was still in the army, since the letter was addressed to Idesa. Like the Jews corralled into the ghetto in Parczew, Matès and Idesa say nothing of the war, the census, the hardships, the ration tickets, the black market, the ID checks at the metro exits, the arrests in the street in broad daylight. It's true that the Red Cross did not encourage lengthy introspective missives: as specified on the card itself, "twenty-five words maximum, family and personal news only." Matès managed with only twenty-four, not counting the date. Thus, it is only in passing that the Argentines learn of the birth of my father, Moyshe-Marcel-Maurice. I find the concision of this letter interesting for what it does not say, and all the more moving: real suffering can find no words.[16]

A further discovery for this year 1941. One of my Aunt Suzanne's old files contains a letter from Constant, written after the war on behalf of the children, addressed to some German indemnity commission, I don't know which. "In 1941," writes Constant, "when Jews were first being arrested, the police made a house search at their place [Rue Désirée] for the purpose of arresting the husband. Since I had gotten wind that these arrests were taking place, and since I knew of a room for rent at 17 Passage d'Eupatoria, I did the necessary paperwork and signed the lease for the room in my name, as both domicile and workplace. Mr. Jablonka lived in that room and worked in relative safety."[17] Passage d'Eupatoria, an alley in the 20th arrondissement: two streets over from where we are living today; fifty feet from my daughters' kindergarten.

There were three big police roundups in Paris in 1941. The first took place on 14 May, Idesa's birthday. The so-called "green slips" that were sent out to the domiciles of thousands of Jews summoned them to come forward for a "review of their situation." The 3,700 men who fell into this trap were sent to Pithiviers and to Beaune-la-Rolande.[18] Among them was Moises, Maria's elusive husband, but he managed to escape, covering some sixty miles on foot before making a stop at Constant's country house. He then returned to Paris and lay low at the same Passage d'Eupatoria. This was not the roundup that nearly caught Matès, since Constant talks specifically in his letter about a house search. Since the 12 December roundup was aimed mainly at Jewish notables, I figure that the dragnet of 20 to 24 August is more likely, the one carried out first in the 11th arrondissement before spreading to the rest of the city. (The Drancy camp started receiving its first Jews at this point.) The morning of 20 August 1941, a young woman left home to stand in line at the unemployment office in the Japy gymnasium, and ran right into some French and German policemen: "Our first thought was that the 20th arrondissement would be next in line, and we attempted in vain to warn the husband of my mother's younger sister to go spend the night with any non-Jewish friend willing to accept him."[19] This was precisely when Constant, who lived on Rue Saint-Maur in the 11th, warned Matès and rented him the room at 17 Passage d'Eupatoria, behind Place Ménilmontant. This was all happening in late August 1941.

Back at Rue Désirée, Idesa was once again on her own, as she had been during the "phony war" and the French campaign. Hunted now not as an illegal but as a Jew, Matès managed to escape first an internment camp, then a roundup, the two antechambers to deportation. Thanks to Constant, he was out of harm's way, at least temporarily. But it would have been very dangerous to step outside because of all the ID checks. Who brought him food? Did he slip out, under cover of darkness, to go tuck his children into bed? Was glove-making enough to earn them a living? They were certainly not candidates for the Aryanization campaign[20]—there was nothing to be stolen from this kind of Jews! "Working a little" wrote Matès in February 1941, somewhat reassuringly. But the situation had evolved since then: he was banned from public places, forbidden to go out after 8 p.m., to use a telephone, to own a bicycle. By law, he had to ride in the last car of the metro and do his shopping between three and four in the afternoon (when there was nothing left to buy in the shops). As of 1 June 1942, all Jews above the age of six had to wear the yellow star.[21]

On 16 July 1942 at dawn, teams of policemen deployed in the Père-Lachaise neighborhood. Noiselessly, they filtered into streets, hallways and courtyards, making use of the data on record. They climbed the steps of still-slumbering apartment buildings and began pounding on doors until someone opened. "Take only the bare minimum and come with us!" The mothers gathered a few items and went to wake the children. The families were then escorted to "first-stage assembly points" as bystanders looked on and merchants rushed out and stood by their shop fronts. Some were herded into the Bellevilloise, an auditorium where, ten years earlier, a conference had been held in preparation for the European Anti-Fascist Workers Congress. Others, lugging bundles of clothing and even mattresses, transited through a parking garage before piling onto busses that were still displaying their customary destinations. This is what happened to Maria and her daughter Sarah, who had just been arrested at their home on Rue des Pyrénées.[22] The weeping and cries of anguish, writes eyewitness Clément Lépidis, were drowned out by "the passing police vehicles and motorcycles, and the busses fitted out by the authorities to transport the 'captive human material' to Vél' d'Hiv."[23]

It was early, on this 16 July 1942, but the summer heat was already oppressive. In this densely Jewish neighborhood, the police had their hands
full. On the Rue Désirée sidewalk, a boy watched as two of his school
friends passed by—Alfred Szyper and Marcel Gandelman, both twelve
years old—and was unable to bid them good-bye:

> I went down to the street where I live, around eight-thirty in the morn-
> ing, and realized immediately that there was an unusual commotion.
> There were squadrons of police officers and inspectors entering homes
> and coming out fifteen or twenty minutes later with whole Jewish fami-
> lies, children included, carrying with them what they could. They were
> taken to Avenue Gambetta, where a line of busses stood waiting along a
> square where I used to play with my schoolmates. I thus witnessed the
> departure of my friends Alfred and Marcel, who lived at 15 Rue Désirée,
> fifty yards away from our place. They were leaving with nothing but a
> small bundle each, surrounded by police. They were clearly ashamed and
> didn't even dare look my way. They followed their mothers, who were
> carrying the younger siblings in their arms.[24]

At Vél' d'Hiv, children, the elderly, pregnant women, women in labor, the
ill and ailing, all were dumped onto the velodrome track along with their
meager luggage and randomly chosen effects. Nurses struggled to make
rounds through this sea of humanity as police kept shoving in new arrivals.
The two boys appear in Klarsfeld's *Mémorial*: convoy no. 20 of 17 August
1942 for Marcel, convoy no. 68 of 10 February 1944 for Alfred, his mother
and younger brother.[25] One month after that day in July when Marcel Gandelman was trotting behind his mother, he would be gassed at Auschwitz.

My father is forty, and it is the first time he has questioned Annette
with such tenacity. In the past, she would go all the way back to the start
of the war, make dozens of digressions, get tangled up in details, hop from
one unrelated topic to the next, and in the end, my father would just tune
out. But this time, he persists. Annette makes an effort to really focus:
3 Rue Désirée, at the top of the stairs, the police pounded on the door,
Idesa was alone at home with the children, and we now know why, since
Matès had been living at Passage d'Eupatoria since August of 1941. Despite
strict orders to the contrary (arrest Jews "without any idle talk or com-

ment"), the police yielded to Idesa's begging: "Get yourself ready, and we'll be back." As soon as they were gone, Idesa grabbed the children and fled. Since the whole neighborhood was cordoned off, she plunged into the metro and went to her dentist's, clear on the other side of Paris. The concierge watched as a woman with two young children approached: "Madame, it's still early, the office isn't open yet." Idesa replied in her Yiddish accent: "I'm in too much pain, I'll wait."

This is the most intense moment in all of the interviews that I conduct with my father. He has an aversion to psychoanalysts, but here, he confesses that he saw one when he was young. The recollected scenes he recounted during his sessions became etched into his memory, so that today, he remembers less the original scene—he was only two years and two months old in July 1942—than his memory of telling it as an adult. The analyst: "Do you have any childhood memories?" My father: "No." The analyst: "Really? Not one? Tell me one memory, it doesn't matter which." My father: "I don't have any, I'm telling you. Anyway, that's all just bullshit, it doesn't mean anything." The analyst persisted, but my father retreated into silence. Not to be discouraged, the analyst kept at it until something rose to the surface. "We're at home. I'm with Suzanne in one room, our mother is in the other. I'm anxious because Suzanne says that Mommy is crying, and that there are two men at the door. There's a table, and I can barely reach it." Another memory, apparently unconnected, but also revealed to the analyst, comes up during one of our sessions: I type furiously on my laptop keyboard so as not to lose a single word, and to keep my brimming emotion from altering his own. "I am in the metro. My mother is there. It's very crowded. The train lets out a strident 'toot!' and I'm feeling increasingly anxious. A little later, there is a set of stairs. I play at jumping from one to the next."

Where was this dentist's office located? I have no idea, but I imagine it was in one of the upscale neighborhoods ("clear on the other side of Paris," said Annette, which means as far as possible from the 20th arrondissement), where the metro line 2 or 3 takes you from either the Père-Lachaise or the Gambetta station, located less than five minutes from Rue Désirée. I sometimes think of this frantic flight of Idesa's with my father and aunt when I take metro line 2, with the station names flashing by like markers of their life's trajectory: Ménilmontant, that's where you'd get off to go to Rue du

Pressoir or Passage d'Eupatoria; Couronnes, to go up the street of the same name where Matès landed in August 1937, with no visa or passport; Colonel Fabien, hero of the Communist resistance, today the location of French Communist Party headquarters; Stalingrad, the victory so long in coming; Barbès, where the same Colonel Fabien shot a German officer cadet on 21 August 1941, two months after the invasion of the Soviet Union.

But although the neighborhood was crawling with policemen, before getting on the metro, perhaps Idesa preferred to just stroll along the street as if nothing were happening, picking streets at random, going nowhere in particular. . . . Whatever the case, she needed a combination of luck and self-possession, what's called survival instinct, to weave through so many obstacles, two children in tow: police officers on foot and motorcycle, inspectors in civilian clothes, rounded-up families, the Szypers and the Gandelmans, the busses parked along the avenue. A year later, after hearing from her husband who was being held at Drancy that the police would be coming to arrest her, Anne Wellers would make the same bold move: "I left the apartment, holding my two children's hands, carrying nothing, just my handbag, as if we were going to the park."[26]

Sixty-eight years later to the day, I attend a commemoration of the rounding up of Jews at Vél' d'Hiv in the 20th arrondissement. The event includes representatives from the mayor's office, deportee associations, the Committee of the Rue de Tlemcen, various resistance groups (FFI, FTP), all gathered in front of the Bellevilloise auditorium, with maybe fifty people come to attend. The crowd, the speeches and the tricolor flags fringed in gold attract the surrounding neighbors, who lean on their balcony railings to watch. Someone reads from the 13 July 1942 circular: "Every Jew arrested, man or woman, has a file on record. . . . The teams in charge of making the arrests must move with the greatest speed, without any idle talk or comment."[27] One woman tells of her escape from the Bellevilloise, of the last words she exchanged with her mother, how her mother slapped her because she was afraid to leave all by herself, her escape through the emergency exit, the police guard who looked the other way. A plaque is unveiled, standard-bearers stand at attention, the flags are lowered, the guard stands at ease, wreaths are laid. Next, our procession moves to the town hall of the 20th arrondissement, and we arrive at a side entrance, now sealed up, to what used to be the Père-Lachaise-Gambetta commissariat where, on 11 February 1943, dozens of elderly men were brought after a raid.

To close the ceremony, we go to Édouard-Vaillant Square and stand at the plaque dedicated to the children. Eleven thousand children were deported from France during the Occupation, one thousand of them from the 20th arrondissement alone. Here are engraved the names of 133 little ones who weren't even old enough yet to attend school: "Passerby, read their names, for your memory is their only tomb." A few people take turns reading out all the names. The litany brings tears to our eyes: Bella Altman, six years old, Rachel Altman, four years old, Colette Anzlewicz, one year old, . . . Danielle Gryner, nineteen days, . . . Maurice Rozenberg, ten months, . . . Jacques Zelazo, four years old, Chaya Zylberg, four years old. This list might have included, indeed should have included Suzanne Jablonka, three years old, and Marcel Jablonka, two. But today, my father is attending the national commemoration being held at the Bir-Hakeim metro stop, where the Vél' d'Hiv used to be located, the very place where Sarah, followed by her mother, backed into a group of onlookers after asserting to a policeman that she was not Jewish, and that she had just come to see someone.

The roundup netted 12,884 arrests. This was fewer than what had been predicted, but plenty to fill the boxcars that pulled out of Drancy at a steady pace.

Let me keep reading from Constant's letter to the German indemnity commission: "On 16 July 1942, the police returned to Rue Désirée to arrest the wife Jablonka and her children, but the officers took pity on the woman and let her leave with her two little ones. I took care to have the children placed in safekeeping outside the city limits, and Mrs. Jablonka returned to join her husband in the room in that alley, Passage d'Eupatoria."[28] What about the Jagodowicz family, the neighbors at 3 Rue Désirée? They were warned, Liliane tells me, as they always were whenever a raid was impending, by a policeman friend of theirs. It was probably around this time—I cannot be certain, since all the witnesses were then under five years of age—that the Jagodowiczes and the Raduszinskis went to hide at number 5, in a room whose tenant had left for the United States (according to Liliane) or been deported (according to Charles). The fathers worked in the attic. In the evening, chairs were hung from the ceiling to make room for mattresses on the floor. Once a week, the children got a bath in a basin. Three children in one family, two in the other. "You can just imagine how hard it was," Charles writes me in an email.

The two families got their food supplies through the concierge, who had an understanding with the local merchants. The concierge's name? Marguerite. If she hadn't died a few years after Liberation, her name would be listed today with The Righteous among Nations. I have found her name in the 1946 census: Marguerite Lévêque, thirty-two years old, three children.[29] Keeping my momentum, I send Charles a list of all the inhabitants of Rue Désirée, before and after the war. Regarding the grocer at number 3, he writes: "My parents spoke of her often. It was thanks to her that Marguerite was able to get us food without our having to provide ration tickets." The disappeared tenant, the compassionate policeman, the concierge, the grocer: this was an impressive network of solidarity. But how did those not benefitting from such networks fare? Either they were arrested, or they dropped everything and fled. This proves, first of all, that it was possible to remain at Rue Désirée throughout the entire war, and secondly, that Matès and Idesa were not as well integrated as other Polish Jews who had arrived in similar conditions (Becalel Jagodowicz, for instance, who arrived undocumented in France in February 1937, according to his National Security file[30]).

I'm standing with my back to the gate at 3 Rue Désirée. Three escape routes are available to me. Avenue Gambetta, on the right, is full of busses and police vehicles. In front of me, a street goes up toward the 20th arrondissement's town hall. On the left, Rue Désirée runs into the sinuous and aptly named Rue des Partants—from the verb *partir*, to leave—and this is where I believe they must have headed. It's starting to sprinkle. Instead of taking the metro to get to "the other side of Paris," I walk down the whole length of Rue Sorbier, without stopping in front of the school for boys. I skirt Notre-Dame-de-la-Croix, built in the nineteenth century in an effort to re-Christianize the working class in this factory neighborhood, and I enter Rue d'Eupatoria. My daughters' kindergarten is closed today. Their playground is separated from Passage d'Eupatoria by wire fencing. This is where Idesa and the children met back up with Matès on the evening of 16 July 1942, after their day at the dentist's. I bet that the 200 parents who drop off their children every morning at this school are unaware that this alley even exists. And how could they know, since it is now a cul-de-sac, sealed off, about twenty yards in from the street, with graffiti-covered cinder blocks. Only vagrants answering the call of nature would venture into such a place, or perhaps the tenants of the surrounding buildings, slated for demolition, whose distended outer walls are about to burst. Some lanky vegetation is flourishing just inside the fence of the school playground. In the 1940s, the alley made a sharp, 90-degree turn to the right and snaked along the fences bordering tenements and factory walls. This is the heart of Ménilmontant, a name deriving from Mesnil Maltemps, "foul-weather abode": in the thirteenth century, a hamlet buried in the midst of woods and vineyards.

A few centuries later, in a differently foul political climate, my grandparents were holed up like rats at 17 Passage d'Eupatoria. This is where the police eventually found them, on a February morning in 1943. Nothing remains today of that room rented in Constant's name. The people were destroyed first, followed by the walls they had hoped would conceal them. It was long after the war, in the 1960s, that the bulldozers rolled in and razed everything: alleys and stairways torn apart, along with sheds, chicken coops, rabbit hutches and drystone walls; hotels, hotel bars and notions shops disappeared, clearing the way for the building cranes that were soon spinning overhead. They finished the job by knocking down the old apartment buildings, the wrecking ball breaking through boarded-up windows, exposing wallpaper and broken floor tiles. And finally, they bulldozed the last creaky old houses with their propped-up walls, out on the edge of the vacant lot where the poured-concrete apartment complex I currently live in is now located. Number 37 Rue des Couronnes, my grandfather's first hovel, maybe some kind of flophouse, disappeared when Rue Vilin, the street where the writer Georges Perec grew up, was widened; Rue Vilin in turn has since been shortened considerably to make way for the Belleville park flower garden, an urban oasis where I read Perec's *W, or the Memory of Childhood* while my daughters dash around the park with their little friends.

I resort to the tried-and-true method: processing population data from 1936 and 1946 at the archives of the City of Paris, recording the names of

the people who lived at 15, 17 and 19 Passage d'Eupatoria, then searching the directory for possible descendants. To speed things up a bit, I
decide to phone the 100 or so strangers who appear to be living in the Île-
de-France region whose last names correspond to those wartime tenants.
Apart from the few who mistake me for a phone solicitor and hang up,
they all show interest in my research, but regret not being able to help, either because they have no connection to the tenant in question, or because
they are such distant cousins that the family connection has been lost, or
sometimes because they're simply not interested, or never got the chance
to be interested as their family legacy unraveled. By the time I finish this
investigation of the neighboring tenants, which I have expanded at the
suggestion of various people, I have found five reliable witnesses: Robert
Erpst, born in 1933, who grew up at 17 Passage d'Eupatoria with his parents and brother; Robert Vazghir, eighty years old, his mind still sharp as
a tack, inveterate globetrotter, with a working knowledge of everything
from the Angkor Wat temple to the sapphires of Sri Lanka, and who has
such fond memories of his childhood that he agrees to get together and
talk about what school was like in 1936 to 1937; Ginette, whose mother
Hannah Brochsztejn was in hiding at no. 19 at the start of the persecutions; and finally, the daughter of a café proprietor on Rue d'Eupatoria,
whom I met through someone currently living in the alley and who recalls
those times "with great nostalgia, because back then, people respected
each other, there was solidarity and friendship." To these witnesses, add
Sarah, daughter of Moises and Maria, fourteen years old in 1942, student
at the Lycée Hélène-Boucher, who is well acquainted with the microcosm
of the Passage d'Eupatoria, since her own father hid there after his escape
from Pithiviers. Her mother later set up her shop there, after the war.

In what follows, I present a digest of their testimony, cross-referenced
with the census data I processed, and will attempt to paint a picture of the
years 1942 to 1943, a necessarily hypothetical one, since, like all the slums
and tenements the world over, people's lives there are unstable, they come
and go. So here is Passage d'Eupatoria, a user's manual.

Passage d'Eupatoria: the surroundings

To begin, let us walk back up Rue d'Eupatoria, and imagine the scene. The right-hand sidewalk is occupied by a church, Notre-Dame-de-la-Croix. From one of the stained-glass windows, a fabled fox and a stork once looked out on the children of Polish, Hungarian, Romanian and Latvian Jews as they came home from their school on Rue Julien-Lacroix (today, there is a plaque in their memory, but back then the school principal complained about the growing number of foreigners). Then, according to the business directory of the day, we would walk past a wine merchant, a hairdresser's, a florist's, a laundry and another wine merchant. The Passage d'Eupatoria opened up on the left, about level with the church transept. On the corner, there nested a nameless café—people would just say let's meet *chez le bougnat* (at the coalman's)—a place where men would go play cards on Saturdays when the wife needed room back home to bathe the children. You could also buy charcoal there for cooking and heating since, it goes without saying, none of the buildings had gas.

Passage d'Eupatoria: the buildings

Here we are in the alley itself. At number 1, a shoemaker. At number 3, the Jeanne-d'Arc parish school for boys. After the sharp turn, in the place where my daughters' school would one day be located, there was a set of low-rise buildings, filthy and crumbling. Three of them created an ensemble, set behind a grating: no. 15, off to the side; no. 17, where the concierge lodges were located; and no. 19, the last building in the alley. Ground-level tenants had gardens, where they grew flowers or vegetables. These three buildings looked out on a peeling wall, the back of the Garnier factory, specializing in "affordable kitchen stoves" (made of poor-quality metal) and fronting onto Rue d'Eupatoria. At this point, the alley got so narrow, reduced to the width of a few tilted paving stones to create a rivulet, that you could stand in the middle and touch the grating of 15-17-19 with one hand and the factory wall with the other. Before the war, the lamplighter would pass at sundown, and later, the town hall had electricity installed (but not in people's homes). Further on, the alley opened onto Passage Notre-Dame-de-la-Croix, which led to a garden set at an angle to the church of the same name. The garden is still there today, but I never take my daughters to play there; it's too small.

Passage d'Eupatoria: the surroundings (continued)

After going up both alleys, dark and filthy but full of life, we're back on the Rue d'Eupatoria, at the other end of the street, a stone's throw from the Garnier factory, the Rousseau grocery and snack shop, a thermometer manufacturer and a dressmaker's shop.[31] The Rousseaus had large wine vats, where you could bring your empties, stick them in the bottle filler, and get a liter of rough red table wine, the kind that stains so awfully. For meat, you had to go to Ménilmontant, where there were no fewer than seven butcher shops, each with its specialty: beef, pork, poultry, horse, tripe and so on. Before the war, to find kosher meat, you had to go to a butcher's at 22 Rue des Maronites, or to the one on Rue Julien-Lacroix, across from the school for boys. At the top of Rue d'Eupatoria, there was a gutter where the children used to launch little paper boats down the stream that flowed all the way to the *bougnat* café. On the church side, behind a low wall, a dirt path sloped down to a basement window hidden behind brambles: these were the "dungeons." Further on, behind the Ménilmontant station, at the top of Rue des Couronnes, you came upon vacant lots bristling with rusty scrap metal, dilapidated shacks and stunted trees covered in vines that the kids would attempt to smoke. "We were all a little sickly," recalls Robert Vazghir, as he ponders the graffiti tags smeared across the shutters of the ex-*bougnat*, as if deciphering runes. At the nursery school, they would serve them beef hash and scrub them head to foot. The children living in the alley and on Rue d'Eupatoria were always at one another's apartments, and were raised like one big family. Those children included Camille Jourist, seven years old in 1942, living at 2 Passage d'Eupatoria; Abraham and Régine Hirsz, fifteen and eight years old, 15 Passage d'Eupatoria; Maurice Gutfrajnd, nine years old, 15 Passage d'Eupatoria; Simon Felner, eight years old, 13 Rue d'Eupatoria; Michel Adler, thirteen years old, 17 Rue d'Eupatoria; Paulette and Esther Kosiorowski, six and twelve years old, 17 Rue d'Eupatoria; Fanny Rozenbaum, eleven years old, 17 Rue d'Eupatoria; the three little Cybula children, between ten and fourteen, 17 Rue d'Eupatoria: all of them were deported in August 1942.[32]

Passage d'Eupatoria: stairwells and interiors

The rooms of the alley buildings had no water or electricity, not even the most basic amenities. In the tiny courtyard of 15-17-19, there was a little fountain. On each floor, there was a spigot and a squat toilet. Since the timer on the hall light was always out of order, you had to feel your way up the stairs. No account fails to mention the rats: they would scurry down the stairs, and could be heard squeaking under the risers. Some visitors would not venture in without calling from the courtyard for someone to come down with a flashlight. And yet (or perhaps for that very reason), the interiors were spotless, both extremely poor and extremely clean. Among tax records for independent professions, I came upon a widow named Farnet at number 17 who rented "furnished rooms."[33] She may well be the one Constant contacted after the August 1941 raid. "Furnished" rooms? Furnished with what? People owned next to nothing, perhaps a table, some chairs, a bedframe if they were among the better off. Most had nothing at all, especially when they had been forced out of their previous hovel with no warning. The alley was full of illegals, often Eastern European Jews, all tradesmen. No one was religious. The men wore work caps, never yarmulkes. They ate matzo, but you'd never find them at synagogue.

15 Passage d'Eupatoria: ground floor

To enter the building, you first had to walk through a small courtyard. In the mid-1930s, the Vazghir family, which included five children, lived on the ground floor, in a kind of semi-basement lit by a kerosene lamp, whose only window looked onto the courtyard. The father, a Latvian Jew, was a painter. His wife was Romanian. Three quarters of a century later, Robert still remembers the names of the neighbors, all confirmed by the 1936 census. Also living on the ground floor: the Reimsbach family, whose gramophone played the same record over and over, "Beneath the Mantillas"; above, the Gubovics, Hungarians who would soon go back to their country. But the Vazghirs moved in 1937, so this picture does not apply to the Occupation, except in regard to the Hirsz family.

15 Passage d'Eupatoria, first floor up:
the Hirsz family and Nachim Krepch

Up on the first floor, Robert tells me, lived the Hirsz family, which in-cluded three daughters and a son, Abraham, called Henri, his "little buddy," who, I informed Robert, was deported in August 1942, a few days before his mother and sister. Sarah remembers a different detail, "a French woman who was always shouting," and a friend of her father's, Nachim Krepch, a Polish Jew, in his fifties: "Krepch, we called him Kreppl, we were always giving him a hard time, but he was always joking around, too. He would pretend to berate the Odryzinskis' baby, the neighbors at 19: If you're not good, I will spank you!" For my part, I will add the Gutfrajnds, deported the same year as the Hirszes, and a French family, the Colins, who are listed in the census of both 1936 and 1946: it would appear that they spent the entire war in the building. The father worked at Simca. I don't know which floor they lived on.[34]

15 Passage d'Eupatoria, second floor up (?): Calel Sommer

One key character that Sarah recalls very distinctly is Calel Sommer, a tailor, then in his forties, married and father of a son. As detailed in the report by two intelligence inspectors, of Intelligence Section 3, Calel Sommer was arrested on 7 October 1942 at 17:00, at the corner of Rue de Belleville and Rue Piat. Not only was this individual "of Jewish race and religion" not wearing the requisite yellow star, but he was carrying forged documents—a fake ID card (purchased for 3,000 francs), a fake naturalization document, a fake civil status record, a ration card issued by the town hall of the 20th arrondissement in his fake name, coupons for tobacco and clothing rations also issued in his fake name.[35] By consult-ing various records available to them, the officers found that Calel Som-mer had been denied residence under the file number E. 101,549, spent a month in prison in October 1938 for infringement of immigration law, and been issued an expulsion order in May 1939.

Paging through his national security file, I feel an immediate kinship with him. A black-and-white snapshot taken at the time of his trial in 1938 shows a pale-eyed man with curly blond hair slicked back, his narrow nose and strong chin giving him an eagle-like appearance. Calel Sommer arrived in Paris in January 1937, with no passport. He fled Poland, he explained to the interior ministry, because he was being persecuted "for being a JEW and for having always held 'left-wing' opinions." What followed were denial of residence, prison and an expulsion order. On 29 August 1939, on the eve of war, Calel Sommer wrote to the Minister of the Colonies, Georges Mandel, to ask that his stay be extended for an extra three months. What I find so touching, almost heartbreaking, about this comically unreadable letter is that it could easily have been written by my own grandfather, if he hadn't preferred to hire a public writer, and that it underscores the tragic banality of daily existence for these immigrants who would have only a few more years to live.

> Dear and Noble Sir Minster, I beg you pardon that I permitt myself of again writt you, dear Sir Minster. Since you alreddy done letter to Sir Minster Interior on behaff stay in France and send the anser that the rekwest to Sir Police Prefek to examin thoze afairs, I am go to prefek to extended my stay the prefek say no to me and I muse leev imidiatly and beecoz the situation and I have not pasport I kant go, and yestrady I red artikal in France soir many minsters and also Minster Mandel that National Sekurity and police handels foreners for ID paper, and beecoz I not hav paper, they katch me and I go to jayl.[36]

The letter was, of course, never answered, and Calel Sommer had to remain underground. He was rounded up during the "green slip" raid in 1941 and interned at the Pithiviers camp, but managed to escape; he went back to live in the Passage, where he'd stayed two years earlier. Detained for questioning on 7 October 1942 by Intelligence Section 3, nicknamed the "Jewish department," he was sentenced to six months in prison for forgery and falsification of documents. A special report was sent to SS Captain Heinson, liaison officer of the occupying authorities with the police prefecture. Calel Sommer was jailed at the Fresnes prison on 29 October 1942. The prison register indicates that he lived at "15 Passage de Patoriat." He claimed to be Catholic.[37]

17 Passage d'Eupatoria, ground floor: Mr. and Mrs. Georges

Everybody remembers them, and for good reason: they were the concierges for the three buildings. They always spoke in grunts and mumbles; she was uncongenial and he was boorish. Their little garden was decorated with scallop shells. In the evening, they would "pull on the string," that is, they would open the door from their bed. They were said to be Protestants. Regarding the tiny vegetable gardens at the foot of the building, Mrs. Georges used to repeat to Mrs. Vazghir: "You may not be rich, but you'll never go hungry!" The 1936 census shows that Mr. Georges was born in the Haute-Savoie region, and that his name was Armand, even though the name all the witnesses gave me was Désiré. His wife, Marie-Louise, was originally from the Pas-de-Calais region. In 1942, they were sixty-nine and sixty-five respectively. A digitalized photo at the Center for Contemporary Jewish Documentation shows them posing in front of a blackened stone wall, between an overturned metal basin and a bit of scrap fencing, looking as if they had been forcibly removed from their lair and stood up straight, long enough to take a photograph. Mr. Georges looks like a scarecrow in his baggy, threadbare jacket, hair unkempt, brow furrowed. Mrs. Georges is smiling, but with the twisted grin of a toothless crone.

Why is there a place in the Center for Contemporary Jewish Documentation for this unlovable concierge couple who look as though they have just wandered out of the woods?[38] Because, during the war, they went to each Jewish tenant to warn them every time they got word of an imminent police raid. They would climb the stairs, scratch at the door and go away without a word. Several families, on several occasions, were saved in this manner. Mr. Georges also helped mothers take the train to go out to visit their children hiding out in the countryside. He died in 1962 at a ripe old age, and his wife followed a year later. For the apartment buildings, they were guardians, but for their tenants, they were guardian angels.

17 Passage d'Eupatoria, first floor up: a French couple

Sarah has a vague memory of a French couple, a man and a woman with no children.

17 Passage d'Eupatoria, second floor up: Mrs. Erpst

The Erpsts and their two boys are listed in both the 1936 and 1946 census. Robert, the older brother, lives in the Paris suburbs today. After the war, he worked as an apprentice tailor with Poulot, Jascha's husband and Constant's brother-in-law, whose "libertarian lessons" left a huge impression on him. Over the phone, he speaks of him with gratitude and heartfelt emotion. My father lets him know that Poulot has slid into dementia. A pity: he would have liked to see him again. In the early days of the Occupation, Robert, seven years old, was friends with the son of the butcher on Rue Julien-Lacroix. On Thursdays and Sundays, they would go hang out in Belleville or around the Place de la République. The Erpsts were Jewish, but not religious. The mother was Czech, the father Polish. A polisher by trade, he enlisted as a volunteer, was imprisoned in 1940, spent the entire war in a German prison camp and returned to France a paralytic. On her own with the two boys, Mrs. Erpst called upon the underground Jewish assistance network, the Rue Amelot Committee. The social worker who helped her noted in her file: "A very skittish sort, does not seem to like being questioned or counseled." In January 1943, she asked the Amelot Committee to hide her children; her record informs us that the boys' board would "be paid by a donor."[39] Robert explains that these expenses were met in fact by the priest at Notre-Dame-de-la-Croix, who placed the boys with nuns. Shunted from one convent to another, the two brothers ended up in a castle in Normandy. One day, some soldiers knocked at the door there: they were Americans.

Mrs. Erpst, however, spent the whole war back in the alley. Robert has no idea how she managed. Moises was a neighbor, living at number 19. After the Vél' d'Hiv roundup, Maria hid with Sarah on Avenue de la République. One day in 1944, Maria and Moises took their daughter to see a movie at the Ménil-Palace cinema, on Rue Ménilmontant, in the company of Mrs. Erpst. Such public entertainment was forbidden to Jews, but life did go on, however tenuously. On their way out, the little group was stopped by two policemen in raincoats. At gunpoint, Moises stuttered: "I'm an artist, a painter, I'll give you some paintings." Taken away by the officers, Mrs. Erpst was released a short while later.

17 Passage d'Eupatoria, third floor up: the Pole

A man all by himself: the "Pole," as Sarah calls him (if she refers to him thus, it's clearly because he was not Jewish). He was always disheveled, a big head of hair. "When he was young, he looked like some kind of sixties leftist." In Sarah's eyes, he was a hero.

17 Passage d'Eupatoria, third floor up: Mr. and Mrs. Jablonka

Matès had been hiding out here since the raid of August 1941, which he had managed to escape thanks to Constant's intervention. Idesa joined him a year later, on the night of the Vél' d'Hiv roundup, with Suzanne, three and a half, and Marcel, a little over two. Rented in Constant's name, the room was too small for a couple with two children, and the situation was dangerous. Annette (or Maria) provided Idesa with the address of a Spanish woman in Blanc-Mesnil, Carmen Torres, who agreed to house children. Here is Annette with my father, in the 1970s, taking an ironic tone: "Your mother was a good mother. To prove it, she went to Blanc-Mesnil every day to bring you milk." Years after Annette's death, Sarah refuted this testimonial: "It would have been impossible for your mother to go every day; it involved a major expedition, not to mention the risk of being arrested, or the expense. At most, she would have gone out there once a week. And once there, she would hide behind some bushes until she was absolutely sure that no one would see her enter the house. She used to accuse Carmen of stealing your powdered milk."

Because I keep insisting, and with the help of Constant and Annette's daughter, my father has been able to find Carmen's son, who very openly tells us his parents' story, sending us two photos. Born at the turn of the century in Almería, his father, Juan Torres, left his town when he was only fifteen and walked across Spain into France, and all the way to Paris, where he went to work as a mason. With Carmen, he bought a piece of land in Blanc-Mesnil where he built a little shack. Juan and Carmen were anarchists. Their house was a kind of refuge for comrades from all over: Spaniards threatened by the suppression of trade union action, Italians fleeing Mussolini and the like. Moises, Constant, Poulot and his father all gravitated around this core group, a fine sampling of the European Left just a few years ahead of the

Front Populaire. Maria, whom everyone called "Maria the Jewess" to distinguish her from all the Spanish Marias, joined the merry band in 1934, around the same time she met Constant, her future brother-in-law. The first photo shows a tall mustachioed man in a beret and an overcoat, holding a brown-muzzled nanny goat on a leash. Next to him, Carmen, a middle-aged peasant woman in a smock, wearing a scarf around her head and neck. The man was a Kabyle, an anarchist and antimilitarist who had come to Blanc-Mesnil to let his goat graze. In 1936, Juan left to fight in Spain, abandoning Carmen and their son. She subsisted on what she earned doing laundry. In 1939, Juan passed back into France, and was interned at the d'Argelès camp, then handed over to the Germans, who deported him.

During the war, Carmen's house continued to serve as a hideout for all manner of refugees, Spanish republicans, but also Jews (after his jailbreak, Moises slept there in a hole under a lean-to). *La casita de amistad*, "the little house of friendship,"[40] can be seen in the second photograph. It's a sort of bungalow built out of cinderblocks, a big cube with a window and a door, as makeshift a dwelling as the house where the three little storybook pigs sought shelter. In the small adjoining garden is a young woman, her face out of focus, half concealed by bushes, leaning over, perhaps to toss grain to her chickens. This is where my father and aunt spent the summer of 1942, right after they escaped the Vél' d'Hiv raid. They slept in the same bed as Carmen. Her son, fifteen years old at the time, would often travel around France to work, which explains why he has no memory of the two children. Who took them to Blanc-Mesnil in this month of July 1942? Nowhere is Constant's name mentioned in this matter. Maria had also just slipped through the net and was in hiding.

Knowing that one's children are in the hands of a stranger, far away, is unbearable for any parent. At one point, Idesa couldn't stand it anymore, and went out to bring them back to Paris. And there they were, in the single room at 17 Passage d'Eupatoria, far from the fresh country air. In the 1960s, at another session with his analyst, my father recovered another image: "In the bed with Suzanne, I see my mother hovering over us, crying. She shows me her breast and says: 'You see, I don't have any more milk.'" Does this shred of memory mean something in this particular context? Historian Saul Friedlander, taken from his parents at age ten, says:

"When knowledge comes, then comes memory."[41] This is not the way my father sees it. When we read, he says, when we seek understanding, our stored mental data suddenly prove so tenuous, so insignificant in the picture reconstituted only an instant ago, that they are practically weightless and simply float away. When knowledge comes, memory is erased. My father says all this as a way of handing over the baton to me now, to the historian that I am. But given the dearth of firsthand testimonials that I have to work with, my father's flashes of very early memory are of crucial importance. At any rate, there is no reason to assume that Idesa wouldn't have nursed her little boy as long as possible, if only to spare the expense of buying milk. When the children left for Blanc-Mesnil, this would necessarily have led to weaning, and Idesa did seem worried about the powdered milk she suspected Carmen of diverting from its purpose. And when the little boy finally did come home to Passage d'Eupatoria, she had no more breast milk.

Matès and Idesa made an arrangement with the Pole, their neighbor across the landing: the children would spend the night at his place. Thus, Suzanne and Marcel would be sleeping near their parents, but not with them. Speaking as a father, I can't say I like the idea, since I would always be anxious about whether they were covered, or were waking up after a nightmare without a parent's reassuring presence. But in late summer 1942, at the height of the police raids, it was for their children's protection that they were placed elsewhere for the night. It would undoubtedly have been possible for all four to sleep in the same room (entire families were often packed into 150 square feet, like the Raduszinskis and the Jagodowiczes, in their hideout at 5 Rue Désirée), but the wiser option was to entrust them to a goy neighbor. What could they do to thank the Pole? Annette to my father: "I told your mother that she should at least offer to feed him." Does that mean that Idesa had enough food for three adults and two children? I don't know how they kept themselves alive, but they did. Could it be that they had forged ID papers and the ration tickets that such documents granted, as did their neighbor at number 15, Calel Sommer? Or perhaps they were helped out by the Jewish Communist solidarity programs, at the canteen on Rue de Saintonge or at the clinic on Rue de Turenne. Maybe they were regulars at other community centers, like the canteen on

Rue Vieille-du-Temple which was set up on the Bund premises, or the one on Rue Béranger, funded by the left-leaning *Poale Zion*.[42]

Sarah used to come visit them, just as she did when they were living at Rue Désirée, especially since her own father was living in the next building over. But today, we are at my parents' home, on a Saturday, having tea together. With her steel-grey crew cut, still so pretty and well-groomed, still a twinkle in her eye, Sarah is a smart and vibrant woman for her ninety-plus years, full of the fire that burns within all Auschwitz survivors.

"Thirst was worse than hunger," she recalls. "In the open-air coal cars that evacuated us out of Bergen-Belsen in January 1945, we tried to swallow the snow that was falling around us, but it had no effect. Without saliva, you couldn't get your bread down. I say bread, but it was barely a crust."

Sarah is taking my research very seriously, and thinks hard about each scenario I submit for her to examine. She's the one, for instance, who put me on the trail of Henya "Annie" Korenbaum, the aunt behind Idesa's "money from America." I have so much affection and admiration for Sarah, but I don't really know her; she was not a part of my childhood world in the way Constant and Annette were, or Poulot and Jascha. I do know that she is very active: she gives talks in high schools as a war witness and survivor and has written a book entitled *Chassez les papillons noirs*, (chase away the black butterflies), a refrain from an Edith Piaf song that she would sing to herself in the camp to lift her spirits. And here she is today with us. She paints a picture of Passage d'Eupatoria and the room where Matès and Idesa lived. "A little room. A big bed, an armoire, a table, since that's where they would eat. There was no noon meal." Do you remember them well? "I visited them many times. Matès was at his machine by five in the morning, and he worked very hard. When I came by, Idesa would make me tea." What about the children? "They were next door."[43] Did Matès take part in the strike by the Paris glovers that resulted in a deficit of 160,000 pairs of gloves intended for the eastern front?[44] There is no way of knowing.

The family tells many stories that cover this period:

The day after the Vél' d'Hiv roundup, Matès and Moises broke into Maria's apartment on Avenue de la République, after it had been sealed off by the police. They recovered Maria's sewing machine, Sarah's violin and Moises's poems.

Little Suzanne was very smart and talkative. One day, the laundry woman stopped by. Idesa didn't know the French word for "bedsheets," so Suzanne translated for her.

Sarah tapped on little Marcel's tummy: *"Vuss iz duss? A barl, duss?"* ("What is this? a pot belly?"—literally, a little pear). Marcel, who speaks only Yiddish, answers, *"Yo, a barèlè!"* ("Yes, a little belly.") I am wondering whether he was called Moyshele or Marsl.

19 Passage d'Eupatoria, ground floor (?): Mrs. Kohn

A Jewish lady whose husband had been deported. She had 3 sons: 2 older ones, including an apprentice coppersmith, and a little 5-year-old. She would eventually return to Hungary after the war.

19 Passage d'Eupatoria, first floor up: the Odryzinskis

Listed in both the pre- and postwar census, Yankel and Rywka Odryzinski had one son, Samuel, five years old in 1942. Like all the others, they have a file at National Security that I can consult. Working as a cable layer in radio communications, originally from Drohiczyn, a shtetl near Siedlce, Mr. Odryzinski declared to the authorities that "he ha[d] lost all hope of returning to Poland, where life for Jews ha[d] become too difficult." The intelligence was favorable in their case, he was in a relatively highly skilled profession, and was earning a decent salary, so that in late 1937, the interior ministry agreed to start processing their documents.[45] The Odryzinskis had both rooms on their floor, separated by an icy landing that had to be crossed to get from one room to the other. On one side was Samuel's room, and on the other, the "living" room, with a tiny kitchen area—a sink with utensils up on a shelf—separated by a curtain from the dining area, which consisted of a table covered by an oilcloth and a couch that folded out for sleeping. A basin filled at the sink allowed them to wash, but in two phases: the "upper" body in the morning, and the "lower" at night. Once a week, they went to the public baths. During the war, the Odryzinskis were saved several times by the concierges, Mr. and Mrs. Georges. Samuel was sent away to the country with the help of the Amelot Committee. Since Mr. Odryzinski never went out, for fear of arrest, Constant handled all the administrative paperwork for him. After the war, Samuel became an engineer, though some say he was a physicist. In the 1970s, he turned up as the French consul in Aruba, an island paradise off the north coast of Venezuela.

19 Passage d'Eupatoria, second floor up: Moises Lichtsztejn

Sarah's father, Maria's occasional husband, Moises Lichtsztejn was an anarchist poet who, according to National Security, failed to respect "the most basic rules of hygiene."[46] He had been in hiding in the alley apartment ever since his escape from Pithiviers in 1941. Carmen Torres's son paints a very negative picture: "He was living off Maria, thought he was some kind of big intellectual. . . . It's a miracle that he was never caught." But Sarah always speaks lovingly of him, like a little girl who adores her father, and that's what counts for me. He stayed put even after the war. The 1946 census says:

> Moises Lichtsztejn, born in 1903, Polish, alterer
> + his wife Maria, born in 1904, seamstress
> + their daughter Sarah, born in 1928, student.[47]

19 Passage d'Eupatoria, third floor up (?): Hannah and Freydke

Hannah and the poet Schulstein were husband and wife, but I always think of them as the lovers in the haystack: a 1938 photograph shows them sitting on a bale of hay in a field bordered by plane trees, at high noon. With a wry smile, wearing an immaculately white shirt, he is holding Hannah in his arms, her blond hair tossed in the wind, her skirt hiked up to her knees. They are young and beautiful, it is summer and the war has not yet separated young lovers. Ginette, Hannah's daughter with her second husband, welcomes me to her magnificently remodeled farmhouse deep in the Brie region, where a fire crackling in the fireplace provides relief from the bitter wind blowing off the fields. She offers tea and the piece of cake she had promised in an email: "I'll make you a little *gleyzele* of tea with a slice of *leykekh*, if you can muster up the courage to come see us someday." She then brings out the birth certificates, the photos, the letters and we take a trip together back in time.

Hannah Brochsztejn was born in Warsaw in 1915. Her father was cantor at the synagogue, her mother sold herring and pickles. It was at a

Communist Youth meeting that she first met Schulstein. The boy's parents had decided that he would be a tailor like his father, but the poor child was all thumbs, and only art and poetry could interest him. Hannah invited him over, supposedly to shorten a winter coat. Her father, sensing something going on behind his back, found an excuse to enter the room without knocking. Schulstein was in the process of sketching a charcoal portrait of Hannah. The coat to be shortened was tossed across the table. Schulstein leapt from his chair, grabbed the coat and, searching for something to say, blurted out: "Hello Mr. Brochsztejn! Would you happen to have a pair of scissors to lend me?" The flabbergasted father could not believe a tailor would have no scissors, but then he looked and saw the drawing: "*Oy*, it's my Hannele! How beautiful she is!"

In May 1937, wanted by the police, Schulstein went into exile in the land of Voltaire and Hugo. Fearing that she might corrupt her sister, who was soon to be married, the parents agreed to let the girl join her lover in France. Equipped with an 8-day tourist visa, Hannah arrived in Paris on 6 August 1937, saying she was visiting the *Exposition Universelle*, and moved in with Schulstein in Villa du Parc, near Buttes-Chaumont. She immersed herself in intellectual Yiddish culture, made friends with Chagall and Soutine, became close to Freydke, companion of the writer Benjamin Schlevin, and played cat and mouse with the police until they finally caught up with her and sent her to the Petite-Roquette prison for a few weeks. Her National Security record supplies the specifics: Polish nationality, Jewish religion, entered France "by way of Belgium in a bus, unaccompanied and unaided, she claims"; denial of residence "E. 103,935."[48] The photo in the haystack dates to this period. Schulstein is squinting slightly, but he has a real charm. Like his friend Schlevin, translator into Yiddish of Balzac's *La Cousine Bette* and future author of *The Jews of Belleville*, Schulstein had made a certain name for himself. He belonged to the Jewish intelligentsia in exile, and spoke at the founding congress of the YKUF in September 1937. After the war, he wrote a poem, "A Doll in Auschwitz":

> Here sits a doll on a mound of human ash
> Sole relic, only sign of life.

Alone now, she is the orphan of a child
That loved her with all her heart, all her little soul. . . .
The doll survived, for she was but a doll.
How lucky to be a doll, and not a child.

But, Ginette continues, while enjoying my passion for her *leykekh*, Schulstein was "wild as the wind," both paranoiac and neurasthenic, always sick with something; life with him must not have been a bed of roses. When Hannah decided to leave him, she was summoned by a circle of Jewish artists and intellectuals, a kind of family court: they asked her to stay a little while longer with him, for fear that too sudden a split might worsen his condition. But in the end, Schulstein was committed to a sanatorium, which probably saved his life. When the persecutions began, Hannah went underground and moved to 19 Passage d'Eupatoria. Exactly when, we don't know, but in any case, by 1941, she was there. She met up again with her friend Freydke, who had been alone since Schlevin enlisted with the 23rd RMVE (he would spend the entire war in a German prison camp, which is how he survived). Their situations were similar: Polish Jewish women in occupied Paris, consorts of writers, alone but helped out by their boyfriend/lover. They both worked at home as "sweater stitchers," a job that consisted of machine-sewing sweaters that came to them unassembled. In 1940, during various alerts, they took shelter in the metro with Claude, Freydke and Schlevin's son. Hannah left for the free zone to the south in late 1942, but Freydke left later.

19 Passage d'Eupatoria: the other tenants

All those I have no knowledge of, French and foreign, Jewish or not, the good, the bad, the funny, the introverts, the pessimists, the big families, the workers, the children, all those ghosts.

19 Passage d'Eupatoria:
the surroundings, last chapter (after the war)

I've just dropped my daughter off at kindergarten, a model establishment, airy and surrounded by greenery, built on the lot where the old "affordable kitchen stove" factory used to stand. As always when I walk back down the Rue d'Eupatoria, I glance to the right into the alley. A delivery truck is parked there. Water is dripping from a balcony.

Another time, at the end of a workday, I turn into the alley, taking my time. Strains of some reggae rhythm rock the twilight. Up on the first-floor balcony, friends are smoking and enjoying the music. It is a fine spring evening in 2010.

BARE

HUMANITY

Matès and Idesa were arrested at 17 Passage d'Eupatoria on 25 February 1943, early in the morning, the hour of milk trucks and street sweepers.

I could conjure up the sound of footsteps on the stairs, the loud knock at the door, the rude awakening. But I want my narrative to be incontrovertible, based on evidence or, at least, on hypotheses and deductions. To honor this moral contract, I must embrace these uncertainties as full partners in the complete narrative, while at the same time resisting the lure of pure imagination, however conveniently it serves to fill in the blanks. My story will begin, therefore, with Sarah's testimony.

Going on fifteen, she had just started high school at the Lycée Hélène-Boucher. Thanks to the headmistress, this school was a haven of peace, but outside its walls, one was constantly at the mercy of dragnets and ID checks. For this reason, Sarah carried forged papers and never wore the yellow star. On that particular Thursday, she was going to see her father, Moises, who was hiding out at 19 Passage d'Eupatoria. It was about 8 in the morning. The young girl left her apartment on Avenue de la République, where she had been living with her mother ever since the Vél' d'Hiv raid. She went up Rue Oberkampf, crossed Place Ménilmontant and started down Rue Étienne-Dolet, whose view is blocked by the Notre-Dame-de-la-Croix church. As she walked along the right-hand sidewalk, she caught sight of the Pole, Matès and Idesa's neighbor, on the opposite side of the street, holding Suzanne and Marcel's hands, the two children crying and looking utterly distraught. The man was moving quickly, and the children had trouble keeping pace. Sarah understood immediately that something was wrong. Given the direction they were heading, they could only be on their way to Constant and Annette's, Rue Saint-Maur, a few hundred yards away. When Sarah got to her father's, she found him in a state: "They've arrested people! We heard the police shouting, they've taken people away!" A bit later, Sarah went over to Constant and Annette's. There were the two children, clearly still in shock. Six months pregnant, Annette was in a state of nervous agitation. Constant and the Pole were trying to keep calm, but in fact, everyone was in a panic.

In Stalingrad, Marshal von Paulus's 6th Army had just capitulated, and the Soviet counteroffensive in the Caucasus had begun. As the Paris police prefecture's biweekly report stated, all eyes were focused on the Russian front, "even though the public was expecting an Anglo-American attack against Europe at any moment."[1] The Laval government was slipping ever deeper into collaboration with the Germans. On 17 February 1943, forced labor was mandated as a contribution to the German war effort. On 22 February, by way of compensation, the government announced a relaxation of the demarcation line, the elimination of the "forbidden zone" in the north, the release of some 50,000 prisoners of war and the attribution of worker status to 250,000 others. The French population was feeling the pinch of food scarcity: no meat or poultry, no sugar or coffee, except on the black market. There were root vegetables like Jerusalem artichokes and rutabagas, but it was hard to cook without any oil or butter. The weather was chilly, "with occasional rainy warm spells."[2] What else was happening on 25 February 1943, the day the police raided Passage d'Eupatoria? A law was passed establishing a 500-yard protected area around historic monuments; a drunken German soldier was apprehended on Rue de Sfax for shooting off his firearm in the middle of the night;[3] at Porte de la Muette, three partisans tossed a grenade into a squad of German soldiers;[4] on his London-based radio broadcast, General de Gaulle declared that the enemy "besmirches our soil, poisons our atmosphere, dishonors our homes and insults our flag";[5] at Brive-la-Gaillarde, resistance fighter Edmond Michelet was arrested by the Gestapo.[6] In other words, an ordinary day during World War II. Another nonevent took place that day: my grandparents exited the world of the living.

Their arrest fit the pattern of growing persecution. On 9 February 1943, Röthke, head of the Gestapo's anti-Jewish unit, addressed a polite message to the Paris police: "I would kindly ask that, over the next few days, you arrest all the Jews in the Seine region whose nationality already allows them to be deported according to currently existing legislation." The Jews in question had to be over sixteen, but there was no upper age limit. A man of experience, Röthke advised that the operations be carried out "suddenly, keeping them secret until the very last moment, so that the target population will have no prior warning."[7] The department handling foreigners and Jewish affairs at the prefecture, under the direction of André Tulard, architect of the census of Parisian Jews, sprang into action during the night of 10 to 11 February. Dozens of elderly men were rounded up at the Rothschild Hospital.

On the evening of 13 February, two Luftwaffe officers were killed on the Pont des Arts on the way back to their hotel. In retaliation, Ernst Achenbach, head of the political section of the German embassy, demanded the deportation of 2,000 Jews. The task was to be carried out by the prefects of the former free zone and, in Paris, by the police prefecture.[8] On 20 February, the director of the city police informed all commissioners in Paris and the suburbs that, "upon orders by the occupying authorities, further ID checks on a certain number of foreign Jews (men only, aged sixteen to sixty-five) will be implemented. The Jews at issue will be those who have already undergone previous interrogations and who, until now, have not been arrested." The logistics were to be the same as for the 10 February operation: transmission of the records of the Jews to be arrested, "thorough investigations" of each, formation of teams, rounding up of arrested persons, and transfer to

Drancy by bus. The arrest quotas were set according to arrondissement. The municipal police of the 20th received 932 records out of the overall 6,421, or 15% of the total. The operation began the same evening.[9]

On 24 February, the chief of staff to Leguay, one of the top brass in the national police force, informed Röthke that "more than 1,500 able-bodied Jewish men aged sixteen to sixty-five" had been arrested throughout France (in Grenoble, the Italians blocked a few dozen arrests). We don't know much more than this, but we would have to conclude that, more than ten days after the Pont des Arts shooting, the French police had yet to reach its target of 2,000 Jewish arrests. Did Leguay take the blame? Was he pressured to step up the operations? Did he express his discontent to the Parisian municipal police? Whatever the case, the next day at dawn, police officers arrived at 15-17-19 Passage d'Eupatoria and arrested my grandparents along with other tenants. This was a police raid, and not a major roundup. The results were very small. No archive refers to the raid, no report provides a trail and the only documents that give any direct information are the police blotters at the Île de la Cité prefecture, where those "foreign Jews" were transferred. One of these logs tells us that they were brought from the "P.M. 20th arrdt," i.e. the municipal police of the 20th arrondissement.[10]

If it is true that the arrest of Matès, Idesa and other Jews on 25 February 1943 was somehow connected to the Resistance's execution of two Luftwaffe officers, this arrest still did not help the French police meet the specified quotas: the prefecture's biweekly report shows evidence of fifty-one arrests of Jews from late February to early March 1943. Out of the twenty-nine made available to the occupying authorities, eleven foreigners fell under the "circular concerning gatherings of Jews of certain nationalities."[11] For its part, Intelligence Section 3, in charge of hunting down Jews who had escaped roundups, reported ten raids and fifty arrests for the last week of February.[12]

Nobody is left to describe the scene to me, the first morning light of that 25 February 1943. Was it raining? Was the only street lamp in the alley still lit, the one behind the Garnier factory? As the police wended their way into the buildings, were they horrified at the squalor, at the broken-down rat-infested stairwells and the squat toilets on the landings? Were they proud to be smoking these Yids out of their spider holes, or were they sickened at having to do the state's dirty work? Did they kick in the Jews' doors? Constant and Annette, who took in the children that same morning, learned what they could about the circumstances of the arrest from the account given them by the Pole, but my father took no interest in this story after the war, and today there remains only a scrap of testimony, namely, that the police arrested "the whole stairwell" of number 17. Sarah, who didn't arrive on the scene until everything was over, brings another fact to bear: when the policemen saw Suzanne and Marcel in the Pole's room, the latter logically claimed the children as his own. According to Constant and Annette's daughter, he had been given instructions to that effect, and he knew where to take them if the worst were to happen, and despite his panic, he didn't miss a beat: he dressed them and dragged them, in tears, to Rue Saint-Maur. The *bougnat*'s daughter from Rue d'Eupatoria, only fifteen at the time, has no memory of any arrests for the entire war period. The only things she recalls vividly are the strict rationing ("250 grams of bread and 25 grams of butter per day"), the fighting that took place at the Ménilmontant station in August 1944, during which five resistance fighters were killed on the footbridge, and the bombing of Rue Boyer, an explosion so powerful that it sent her mother rolling to the other end of the hallway.

Without direct witnesses or police reports, I find I have to fall back on conjecture. My hypotheses have to take into account a fact attested to by the police prefecture archives, one that leaves me wondering: in the three buildings of 15-17-19 Passage d'Eupatoria, that nest of foreign Jews in hiding, the police made only three or four actual arrests (at number 15, Nachim Krepch and perhaps Calel Sommer, and at 17, Matès and Idesa Jablonka). But what of the others? Was the police uninterested? Were the records missing, were the people not home by some stroke of luck, or had they been warned by their concierge and were already on the run? Whatever the case, more than 10 people slipped through the net that day: at number 17, Mrs. Erpst, and at 19, Mrs. Kohn and her boys; the Odryzinskis and their son Samuel; Moises, who was waiting for his daughter's visit; and Freydke Schlevin and her son Claude.

1. An Unfinished Operation?

By situating my grandparents' arrest in the context of retaliatory measures ordered by Ernst Achenbach, I have linked two series of events, so it is important to realize that this association is itself an interpretation on my part. The first hypothesis: following the killing of the Germans on Pont des Arts, in accordance with instructions issued on 20 February 1943, and in order to meet arrest quotas, a team of municipal police from the 20th arrondissement went to Passage d'Eupatoria. They arrested one or two tenants at number 15 and "the whole stairwell" of number 17, except for the Pole, who was not Jewish, and Suzanne and Marcel, his ostensible children. A plausible scenario, if we assume Mrs. Erpst was absent or forewarned.

If such is the case, then the police team happened upon my grandparents through mere chance, since the record sent to the commissariat of the 20th arrondissement could only have indicated their official address, 3 Rue Désirée, which had been sealed off since the Vél' d'Hiv roundup. The fact that Idesa was also arrested and taken away, even though the 20 February instructions targeted males only, should not be too surprising. But how exactly do we explain that the policemen, under pressure from their higher-ups and perhaps ideologically complicit (several were purged from the force after Liberation), did not go after all the Jews in the building, in number 19 in particular? We know for certain that Moises was at home that morning.

2. Targeted Arrest?

Sarah gives an altogether different account, which she must have gotten from her father or from the Pole. According to her, the police were coming to the alley apartments exclusively for the Jablonkas. A day or two before, they had followed Idesa as she was buying bread, several baguettes at once, it seems. She didn't look French, was not wearing a yellow star, and was out shopping at an hour when Jews were not allowed to do so. The police knew who they were looking for when they got to the alley. They didn't go after Moises or the Odryzinskis or any of the Jewish neighbors. No one else had anything to fear. As it turns out, police archives prove that, on this last point, Sarah's story got it wrong: Nachim Krepch, called "Kreppl," did in fact get arrested that day. But overall, her description fits the facts: it was a blitz operation that prevented the concierges from spreading the word in time.

I have uncovered some interesting documents at the police prefecture: the municipal police for the 20th arrondissement had a special mobile "stop-and-question" brigade that involved ten plainclothes police officers working the streets, including Officer Bourniquey and his fellow officer, Berger, both of whom stood trial after Liberation for arresting a Jew not wearing a star and three Resistance fighters, who were "pistol-whipped about the face and head."[13] This brigade was headed by Émile Petitguillaume, deputy chief inspector at the commissioner's in the 20th, who in 1944 was honored for making an "important arrest," only to have the award revoked, along with his pension, in 1945.[14] Did they spot Idesa coming out of the bakery with all those baguettes? Did the sound of stitching machines in the alley arouse their suspicion? It's not out of the question that the brigade intervened based on a tip-off. Did the presence of all those Jews somehow exasperate or disturb some anonymous Frenchman?

The *Ostjuden* were easy targets. Socially and economically vulnerable, speaking little or no French, clustered into the same neighborhoods, the same streets and buildings, often with no outside support system, they were visible even as they attempted to hide. If they had entered France illegally, they were on file with the police, starting in the 1930s, and were considered social parasites and political troublemakers. The Vichy regime, sensitive to nationality above and beyond its anti-Semitism, had even fewer qualms about handing Jews over to the Germans when they were Polish, Russian or Romanian (the 20 February 1943 ruling was aimed at foreign Jews only). Their helplessness can be summed up by the respective deportation rates: 43% for foreign Jews, as compared to only 17% among French Jews.[15]

I shall posit another scenario, a variation on the one given just above: on that day, they were arrested as "terrorists." If we assume that my grandparents had never stopped their militant activities, it is possible that they joined the Resistance after the German invasion of the Soviet Union. As early as 1940, Paris was flooded with home-printed leaflets in Yiddish, Russian and French denouncing the Vichy regime and the Nazis' "unspeakable crimes." From a political and sociological standpoint, Matès and Idesa presented the typical profile of the foreign resister: Polish Jews, Communists, craftspeople, living in the 20th arrondissement. A few prototypes: Joseph Minc, born in Brest-Litovsk, immigrated to Paris in the early 1930s, worked at MOI and participated in founding the UJRE, the Jewish Union for Resistance and Solidarity, in May 1943.[16] By 1941, Gitla Leszcz and her husband Raymond Gardebled were running a small rotary printer at their apartment. As Gitla tells it in her autobiography, she was visited in March 1943 by a police inspector, while bundles of tracts were stacked up on the floor behind her. Yankel Handelsman, a Polish Jew, organizer of the Paris glovers' strike, was arrested on 12 February 1943 along with his wife at their residence on Rue Oberkampf.[17] During their tailing operations, did the intelligence officers spot other Communist glovers, too? If so, then on that 25 February, the police might well have come to arrest members of the Resistance. But here's the hitch: neither Annette, nor Maria, nor Sarah ever mentioned this kind of activity.

In the kitchen of her Montreuil apartment, Paulette Sliwka serves me tea and cookies. We've been talking for 3 hours now about Jewish Communist immigrants, the cafés of Belleville and the little tailor shops, the MOI and the *Kultur Liga*. Now, we move on to the topic of the war itself, the reason I've come to see her.

"What was your life like in 1943?"

"It was very dangerous to go out, because of the ID checks. To get ration tickets (bread, butter, meat, clothing, tobacco, there were coupons for everything), you had to have your ID papers in order. Otherwise, you bought on the black market, but everything was so expensive there! Some had contacts with Solidarity, an organization that supplied either real or forged food coupons, or provided milk to mothers whose husbands had been sent to the Beaune-la-Rolande internment camp. There were people without a penny to their name."

When she was nineteen, Paulette Sliwka worked for the MOI under the false name Martine. This involved tracts and underground publications, a highly compartmentalized structure, hideouts, and absolute discretion—I couldn't help thinking of the young militants of Parczew. With her companion Henri Krasucki, she was part of the second generation of Jewish Communist resisters: politically inexperienced but eager to act, these young people became Communists within—and by way of—the Resistance, whereas their elders, the likes of Louis Gronowski and Adam Rayski, long-time militants, had entered the fray out of loyalty to an ideal.[18] The police began trailing suspects in February 1943. These operations were carried out by a special brigade made up of police officers driven by anti-Communist sentiment, anti-Semitism or sheer personal ambition. Their work consisted of following the resisters, either on foot or in a van, to "house" the target, i.e., to discover the person's hideout. Arrested in late March 1943, a month after Matès and Idesa, Paulette Sliwka was transferred to the police prefecture. There, she dealt with Commissioner David, head of Special Brigade no. 1. Here, Paulette Sliwka cuts her story short. She need say no more, for I know that those interrogations made ample use of clubs and whips against handcuffed resisters as they lay in pools of their own blood. She was deported to Auschwitz in convoy no. 55, on 23 June 1943, along with some fifty of her comrades.

"So, if my grandparents had resisted, they would have been arrested by the special brigades, or the Jewish Affairs section or the like."

She gives no answer.

"In any case, they wouldn't have sent the municipal police into the 20th arrondissement, right?"

Still no answer.

3. The Sommer Lead

But which police service was in operation that day? On 7 October 1942, Calel Sommer, the neighbor at 15 Passage d'Eupatoria, was arrested by Intelligence Section 3 (the "Jewish department" in charge of "seeking out Jews in breach of laws, decrees or ordinances, or engaging in any commercial or political activity"[19]) and was sentenced to six months in prison for use of forged ID papers. Incarcerated at Fresnes, he was released on 23 February 1943, two days before my grandparents' arrest.[20] He didn't have time to enjoy his newfound freedom, since he was picked up again almost immediately by Intelligence Section 3.[21] Though we don't know the exact date of his arrest, between 23 and 25 February, it's quite possible that it could provide the key to the whole story.

Here is one way things may have unfolded: whether he was released too soon (he had served only four months of his six-month sentence) or was bound for internment no matter what, once he had served his sentence, Calel Sommer was recaptured by the same inspectors who had arrested him in October 1942. With three strikes against him now, as Jew, foreigner and outlaw, he was a fine catch for the "Jew department" of French Intelligence. If he truly was arrested in Passage d'Eupatoria on 25 February 1943 (and not, for example, on the 23rd outside Fresnes prison), we can imagine a cascade of events culminating in the arrest of Matès and Idesa. An inspector from Intelligence Section 3 who has come to arrest Calel Sommer comes upon Idesa in the courtyard and asks to see her ID; not a French-speaker, arms loaded with baguettes, she is caught off guard. Or perhaps Calel Sommer, intimidated by the inspectors, denounces the Jews in the building that he has helped by supplying forged ID papers. Or an informer notifies the police that Calel Sommer is the tree hiding the forest. It was just this sort of chain of events that led to the arrest of Louise Jacobson in 1942: officers from Special Brigade no. 1, who had arrived on the scene because of some Communist brochures, were told by neighbors that the sixteen-year-old high school student was failing to wear her yellow star.[22]

But one point remains unclear: though Intelligence Section 3 did make house calls, they mostly operated out in public, through ID checks and trailing. How then do we reconcile Calel Sommer's arrest by anti-Semitic intelligence officers with that of my grandparents by beat cops from the 20th arrondissement who, when not transferred to questioning, were usually busy arresting pickpockets and petty black-marketeers? The archive is unambiguous here: for Calel Sommer, Intelligence Section 3; for my grandparents, the municipal police of the 20th arrondissement. Was the police raid of 25 February 1943 a joint operation? By June 1942, procedure provided that Jews arrested by Intelligence be sent to the arrondissement commissioner.[23] Given that, why wasn't Calel Sommer taken to the prefecture with all the others? One way around this problem is to assume that Sommer was nabbed as he left prison on the 23rd, or at his residence on the 24th, and that the intelligence officers gave the alley address to their colleagues at the 20th arrondissement; or that this operation, led by plain-clothes intelligence officers, required the intervention of police officers because of some incident. And indeed, there was an "incident" that day: my grandfather's "rebellion."

Here are a few lines drawn from the registry of the police prefecture where the Jews of Passage d'Eupatoria were taken on 25 and 26 February 1943:

ORDER NO.	NAME, DATE OF BIRTH, ADDRESS OF DETAINEE	ENTRY DATE	AUTHORIZER OF ENTRY	MOTIVE FOR ARREST	EXIT DATE	AUTHORIZER OF EXIT	DESTINATION
2612	Krepch Machin Born 21.11.92 In Nessiz, Poland Jobless 15 Passage d'Eupatoria Paris, 20th	25.2.43 14:30 (Gérardin)	Municipal police 20th arrondiss.	Foreign Jew	25.2.43 (Gérardin)		Drancy
2613	Jablonka Idesa Born 14.5.14 In Parczew (Poland) Jobless, residing at 3 Rue Désirée	25.2.43 14:30 (Gérardin)	Id.	Foreign Jewess	25.2.43 (Gérardin)		Id.
2614	Madjanska Doba Born 15.7.13 In Sokolow (Poland) Jobless, living at 13 Rue de l'Orillon, Paris 11th	25.2.43 14:30 (Gérardin)	Id.	Id.	25.2.43 (Gérardin)		Id.
[...]							
2632	Jablonka Matès Born 10.2.09 in Parczew (Poland) upholsterer, residing at 3 Rue Désirée	26.2.43 0:15 (S. Banier)	Belleville [Police Commissioner's]	CP Jew, undocumented, Rebellion			DC 26.2.43 No. 110
[...]							
2677	Jablonska, Mates Born 10.4.09 In Puchezh (Russia)	26.2.43 20:00 [signature illegible]	Domestic Intelligence	CP	27.2.43 9:30 (S. Banier)	Taken by Inspector [signature illegible]	Philippe Domestic Intelligence Section 5

SOURCE: APP, register of temporary consignments at the police prefecture jail (25 and 26 February 1943). Abbreviations and transcription errors have been preserved. Nachim Krepch was born in Niecicz.

My grandparents were domiciled at 3 Rue Désirée, their "official" address, the last one known to the police. This is why I have also reported
the arrest of Doba Madjanska, who was taken to the prefecture by the
municipal police of the 20th arrondissement the same day, at the same
time. She may well have also been apprehended at Passage d'Eupatoria,
if she had been hiding there ever since her domicile at Rue de l'Orillon
had been sealed off. Unlike Nachim Krepch, the neighbor at number 15,
Calel Sommer is missing. Nor is his name listed on any other date in the
register, probably because he was taken directly into custody by Intelligence Section 3. Taken to the prefecture around 2:30 in the afternoon,
Krepch and Idesa were interned at Drancy that afternoon, a few hours
after being dragged out of bed. Not Matès, though, who wasn't taken to
the police station until quarter past midnight, on the night of 25 to 26
February, by officers from the Belleville commissioner. This discrepancy
is confirmed by the Drancy records: Idesa was interned there on the
25th, Matès not until the 27th.[24] Why this forty-eight-hour separation?
The answer is spelled out in the prefecture's records: not only did the
Jew Jablonka have no ID papers, but at the time of arrest, he was found
guilty of "rebellion," something akin to resisting arrest. Consequently,
he was locked up at the Belleville station, which didn't hand him over to
the prefecture until just after midnight. According to clerks working at
the prefecture archives, the term "rebellion" is exceedingly rare. In fact,
I haven't found it mentioned anywhere else in association with the hundreds of persons, Jewish or not, taken into custody at the police prefecture. Because of his disorderly conduct, Matès went from the register of
"provisional confinement" (CP) to that of "detainees in custody" (DC),
involving a longer detention. He is listed here for the date of 26 February 1943, with the following charges:

— infringement of article 3 of the legislative decree of 2 May 1938 regarding
   the policing of foreigners (foreigners who "fail to solicit . . . the issuing
   of an identity card" will be fined "100 to 1,000 francs" and are liable for
   "imprisonment of one month to one year");

— infringement of articles 209 and 219 of the penal code (in the paragraph
   titled "Rebellion," the articles refer to "any attack, any violent resistance

or assault" toward a representative of the state, and any "gathering of rebellious elements" accompanied by violence or threats "by defendants, whether indicted or sentenced");

— infringement of the German ordinance of 28 May 1942 requiring that Jews in the occupied zone wear the yellow star.[25]

These facts make it possible to piece together my grandparents' arrest on 25 February 1943. Whether they were being pressured by the Germans and their own higher-ups following the Pont des Arts attack, or had been notified of Calel Sommer's release or tipped off by an anonymous letter, the police made a dawn raid on the courtyard of 15-17-19 Passage d'Eupatoria. At number 15, they arrested Nachim Krepch, and possibly Calel Sommer; at 17, the Jablonkas, without their children. Here is what Sarah tells me in a calm, collected voice, in my parents' living room, as she takes a back seat to the protagonists of her story: the police enter the Pole's apartment and ask who the children belong to. "To me," the man answers. The parents don't flinch: a harrowing, heroic silence. The police press no further, and go about leading Matès and Idesa downstairs, alone.

When did the violence erupt? From the start, because the couple refused to open the door to the police? A little later, because they wouldn't go quietly? Did they get the neighbors involved, did they resist along with other tenants? In its 15 January 1943 issue, the underground paper *Unzer Wort* gave the following instructions: "If the police come to your door, don't open up, but alert the neighbors, call for help. . . . We mustn't let them arrest us. We shall consider it a case of legitimate self-defense, as we would if we were attacked by robbers. The lives of our wives and children depend on our steadfastness."[26] Thus, it was in that pathetic 1-room apartment/workshop where he manufactured gloves to survive, or in the stairwell of that rat-infested slum, or between the courtyard fence and the factory wall, or maybe even in the middle of the street outside, as they were loading him into the police van, that Matès "rebelled," according to article 219 of the penal code. Sound and fury, scream of rage, punches thrown, and I can image it taking several brawny officers to pin him down. Sarah adds that Idesa hurt her leg trying to escape—an unverifiable episode. What is certain, however, is that the police force in general, from intelligence to local municipal officers, had been marked as a right-wing institution since the late nineteenth century, extending its tradition of violence, beyond Vichy, from the Clichy incident of 1937, when police fired on demonstrators, to the massacres on 17 October 1961 and in the Charonne metro, the latter two connected to the Algerian War. It is equally obvious that Matès and Idesa, as foreigners, Jews and "Reds," embodied for many the quintessential enemy.

I would give anything to know exactly what took place at dawn on 25 February 1943, back in that alley, Passage d'Eupatoria, gone today, in the exact spot where my daughters sleep in the peaceful nap room of their kindergarten. Suzanne and Marcel were sleeping too, for it was still early; their childish slumber concealed from them what they were meant never to see. My father is still kicking himself over this, since all he would have had to do, back in the 1970s, was to go see Moises, Mrs. Erpst or the Odryzinskis, and ask them about what happened. The arrest would necessarily have been violent and brutal because the Jews knew that their lives were at stake. This time, the officers showed no pity. I imagine them behaving the way they had when they arrested Goldale, the widow of an enlisted volunteer of the 21st RMVE killed in 1940:

> Goldale, in her nightgown, thin, sickly and shivering, first attempted to reason with them: "Let me be, my husband fought and died for France, I have a young child to raise!" When they dragged her down the stairs, Goldale struggled. She cried out for help, swore at her captors, wept and finally began to beg for her life: "I haven't done anything wrong, I'm just a poor seamstress, let me be." Then, two of the sturdier officers picked her up and took her away. . . . She was deported from Drancy to Auschwitz, never to return.[27]

Once they had gotten Matès and Idesa under control, perhaps the officers decided that that was enough for one day and wound up their investigation then and there, without moving on to number 19, where Mrs. Kohn, the Odryzinskis, Moises and Freydke were huddled in anxious anticipation.

Did the noise and shouts finally awaken the children? Did they see the police beating their parents? My father, at any rate, has no memory of those events. This blank could be interpreted in two opposite ways: either he saw nothing, or he saw everything but has suppressed the memory. By 8:30 that morning, it was all over. While the Pole was evacuating teary-eyed Suzanne and Marcel, and Sarah was arriving at her father's to find him in a panic, and the police van was on its way to the station with Krepch and Idesa (and perhaps Calel Sommer), Matès was being held at the Belleville commissariat, Rue Ramponneau. This is the commissariat where, as Koestler tells it in *The Scum of the Earth*, the old man Poddach, a Czech refugee, is slapped by a policeman because he can't understand what he is being told.[28] Unfortunately, the blotters for the entire war period are missing.

In 2009, I am summoned to that same police commissariat for an identity theft issue. The walls are lime green, a young policewoman is answering the phone behind a counter, there is a "user's charter" posted on the wall and a rack full of pamphlets about drugs and spousal abuse. I have no idea which cell was the one where they kept Matès on 25 February 1943, while his children were waiting in a daze at Constant and Annette's and his wife, sick with worry and maybe even wounded, had just been shown to her straw-filled mattress at the Drancy camp. But I leave the police station like a good, law-abiding Frenchman, without daring to ask whether I might visit the cell where they had locked up the volunteer soldier of 1939, the Jew charged with failing to sew a yellow star to his jacket and resisting arrest. This incident fit a pattern of his, in fact: in 1933, he had been convicted by the Parczew courts for insulting a civil servant. "Rebellion," says the penal code; "rebellion," writes the orderly into his ledger at the police station; "revolt," Camus would have said, man's ontological *no* shouted at the world, his claim to dignity.

At a quarter past midnight, Matès was locked up at the police prefecture, where he spent the night. Did he know where Idesa was, and who was taking care of the children? The next day, 26 February, he underwent questioning. About this, I know nothing: unlike Calel Sommer, Matès has no file at Domestic Intelligence. That evening, at 20:00, he was taken back to his cell, where he spent a second night. On the morning of 27 February, he was taken by Inspector Philippe for interrogation to Intelligence Section 5, the service that feeds into the prefecture's "central records," where Matès had been on file since 1937.[29] For if Matès was a Jew, he was also an illegal alien. How did this interrogation go? In the absence of archives or witnesses, it is impossible to know. Still, Inspector Philippe, purged in disgrace after Liberation, does have a record that tells us he was thirty-one in 1943, three years younger than Matès, and that he was "a notorious opportunist, never having particularly patriotic motivations for what he did." Coming before a commission in charge of postwar purges, an elderly gentleman, arrested in 1942 for possession of a couple of pounds of barley and a sizable sum of cash, tells how he was treated by Inspector Philippe:

"'Are you French?'

'Yes.'

'Where is your star?'

'I haven't got it.'

'And what about this barley? Are you dealing on the black market?'

He slapped me across the face. Then he asked me to turn over everything I had, including my wallet. He saw I had 20,000 francs.

'You, a Jew, with 20,000 francs? You have no right. Where did you get this money? Whose is it?'

He took the wallet and put it in his own pocket, and we were off. On the way, he said:

'Don't try to escape. I'm armed so watch out. No fast moves!'"

Later, Inspector Philippe let the man's wife know that he would be released in exchange for a large sum of money.[30]

After his interrogation, Matès was interned at Drancy. His record, dated 27 February 1943, shows that Vichy's anti-Semitism had absorbed the categories of Republican repression: this Jew was still being denied residency, his "E. 98,392" issued in 1937 still stood. Interned at Drancy "by order of the German authorities," in this case by SS Captain Heinson, liaison officer to the police prefecture, Matès was reunited with Idesa.[31] The previous day, Darquier de Pellepoix, Commissioner for Jewish Affairs, had declared: "The French people must understand that the measures taken against the Jews by the French government are not acts of persecution, but of self-defense."[32]

The Drancy camp was set up in a horseshoe-shaped low-rent housing project still under construction. The buildings were far from complete: the floor was cement, plumbing was exposed and windows didn't shut properly. From balconies and the large courtyard, the street beyond was visible, that unreal world where people could still move about freely. Internees could even wave to loved ones who ventured out to the double row of barbed wire fencing guarded from watchtowers.[33] Upon arrival, the Jews were assigned numbers and searched. Doba Madjanska, taken to the police station at the same time as Idesa, had to surrender 1,500 francs (money which, for lack of heirs, would be turned over to the Deposits and Consignments Fund a few months later).[34] In this late February 1943, the camp was packed. The influx of new internees was relieved by three convoy departures between 9 and 13 February. A Red Cross nurse describes the arrival and departure of the elderly rounded up at the Rothschild Hospital on 11 February:

> Some were ambulatory, but many were being carried on stretchers, while others were limping and needed assistance to walk. Volunteers were asked to take care of these poor men and help carry their meager belongings. Already so close to death, these panicked old men asked, in their trembling voices, if it was true that they were being deported. They were physically and emotionally exhausted, fearful of what was to come. Without a moment's rest, they were taken to be searched, and were stripped of whatever little they had brought with them.[35]

Life at Drancy was more or less the same as in other internment camps: the wake-up bell at 06:00, the scramble for a place in the latrines and showers, the endless roll call in the courtyard, the distribution of bread, coffee and gruel. Because of his delayed arrival, Matès was not housed in the same room as Idesa, at least not at first: she was on the fourth floor, stairwell 15, and he was on the third floor, stairwell 9.[36] Their stay at Drancy lasted just a few days, but they probably crossed paths with people they knew. Krepch and Calel Sommer were present at the camp the same time they were. But I don't picture them chatting, playing cards or doing laundry. What was on their minds, after being hauled out of their rooms, dragged down the stairs, separated from their children and told they were being deported? Were they clinging to life or staring into the void?

The debate over "who knew what when" is complex and painful, an anachronism for the most part, for it assumes that people back then knew, as we know today, that there was something to know, to find out, to figure out, to suspect. Still, we can legitimately ask how much had come to light by 1943 regarding the massacre of Jews. The question allows us to approach those dark Drancy days from another angle. Just like the T-4 operation that organized the "euthanizing" of disabled Germans early in the war, the existence of killing factories in occupied Poland was a state secret that only a handful of insiders knew, a small circle of top-level figures close to the Führer, crematorium designers and experts like Kurt Gerstein, the disinfection specialist of the *Waffen-SS* in charge of delivering Zyklon B to the camps. Thus, very few people knew of the Reich's plan to annihilate Europe's Jews, as it assassinated millions of men, women, children and infants, young and old, in trucks or in gas chambers. As time passed, the truth emerged: in the summer of 1942, the Swedish consul in Stettin referred to the gassing of Jews in an official report, while Kurt Gerstein notified the nuncio and the Swiss legation in Berlin.[37] In the Warsaw ghetto, Czerniakow committed suicide in July 1942 when he understood that all the Jews were going to be killed (thanks to "their excellent secret service, they knew more than we did," declared one of the Nazi administrators of the ghetto in the movie *Shoah*[38]). But overall, the "Final Solution," as a program of extermination with its own logistics and know-how, remained a well-kept secret until the end of the war.

Nevertheless, a large part of Europe did witness, at the very least, the disappearance of the Jews. In shtetls and towns, in Poland and Ukraine, in Belarus and the Baltic states, civilian populations were aware of massacres because they were taking place before their eyes, as in Parczew, or even with their consent and participation, as in Jedwabne.[39] German soldiers took part in this mass murder: it was the local Wehrmacht commander, for example, who ordered a commando of *Einsatzgruppe C* to kill all the Jews of Bjelaja Zerkow, south of Kiev, in 1941. Letters and souvenir photos from soldiers were sent to families inside the Reich, revealing scenes of collective humiliation, punishment and murder. Or in the other direction, hundreds of women would travel to Auschwitz every summer to visit their husbands who were working as guards at that camp or others like it.[40] The German population benefitted directly or indirectly from the plundering of the Jews, who disappeared from one day to the next, never to be heard from again. Arrested in Berlin on 27 February 1943, deported to Auschwitz and replaced at the factory by Polish workers, the Samuels and their daughter Marion left behind an apartment and all their effects—table, sofa, baby chair, lamps, clothing—all of which was inventoried, turned over to a merchant and distributed to needy Germans or bombing victims.[41]

So, what about France? No one could be unaware that Jews were being excluded from public life, or that they were being required to wear a yellow star, that their homes were being raided, that entire families were being rounded up and deported east. Deportation did not in itself signify extermination, however, since it was not yet common knowledge that "evacuation" was Nazi code for "immediate execution." It was only during his detention in Berlin, in spring 1942, that Sadosky, chief of France's Domestic Intelligence Section 3, was to learn the truth firsthand from a petty SS officer. Georges Wellers, a medical researcher working at Drancy, described scenes of distress and hysteria when families were separated, but explained that not a single internee in 1942 imagined that children, the elderly or infirm would be harmed: it was "a widespread conviction that was simply not up for discussion."[42] Was it optimism, trust in the French authorities to do the right thing, a denial reflex against a truth too abominable to admit or a normal attitude among people for whom such a crime was simply inconceivable? Whatever the case, there was nevertheless a rash of suicides at Drancy in the summer of 1942; women were jumping out of upper-story windows.[43]

As time went on, it became increasingly clear to the Jews that they were under a death warrant, even though the truth came distorted by all manner of rumor. In one of her diary entries for November 1943, Hélène Berr referred to "asphyxiating gas that the convoys were subjected to at the Polish border" and admitted that she was terrified of being murdered in Upper Silesia (the Auschwitz region). Three months later, commenting on the arrest of a woman who dropped to her knees and begged the police to leave her child behind, she wrote: "You have to have a pretty clear sense of what awaits you to get to the point where you're begging them for permission to *abandon* your child."[44] Hélène Berr, daughter of the vice-chairman of Kuhlmann and Co., probably did not have the same information sources as immigrant Polish Jews. But here is what *Unzer Wort* wrote on 1 February 1943, three weeks before the police raid on Passage d'Eupatoria: "Hitler would like to complete the extermination of Jews in 1943. . . . From Holland and Belgium, nearly all the Jews have been deported to the east, and most have been exterminated."[45] Matès and Idesa, who were highly politicized, who read the Yiddish press, who had done time in prison, who had been fighting fascism for years, had left their relatives back home in Poland. Postal communications had been cut off, as Matès deplores in a letter dated October 1939, but were reestablished later. Liliane Jagodowicz, daughter of their neighbors at 3 Rue Désirée, tells me that her mother received letters from her own mother in the Warsaw ghetto urging her never to trust the Germans, never to respond to their summonses, etc. By February 1943, it had been six months since Rushla Korenbaum, Idesa's mother, Shloyme and Tauba Jablonka, Matès's parents, or his half-brothers or his half-sister Gitla had shown any sign of life. So long a silence was nothing but ominous.

Shortly before her transfer to Drancy, on the afternoon of 25 February, Idesa underwent a brief interrogation. Her record, preserved, like Matès's, at the National Archives, contains all the standard data: name, date and place of birth, address, but one detail brings tears to my eyes: the officer has written "*M.O.E.*" or "married, no children." This declaration provides incontrovertible proof that Suzanne and Marcel, entrusted every night to the Pole, had been left behind on purpose in the apartment building at the time of arrest. Mere hours after leaving them, their mother affirmed that she was "married, no children." *M.O.E.* These three letters would covertly underpin my father's entire life, both the miracle of his survival and the wound that would remain forever unhealed: his mother abandoned him so that he might live, her love culminated in rejection, in negation. For I ask myself the question, and I ask you the same, as did Hélène Berr: what would it take for you to part with your young children in a foreign country that you are about to leave, to be delivered to a hate-filled state bent on your destruction? Or put differently, how dangerous would a situation have to be for you to choose not to take your children with you to an unknown destination?

Two postcards. On the left-hand side, in pale blue ink, one can read along the arc of the police prefecture's circular seal "Drancy Internment Camp" and "Censorship Office." On the right-hand side, a burgundy-colored 1.20-franc stamp bearing the image of Marshal Pétain, canceled, and a postmark that makes it clear: Drancy, 2/3/43. An hour before the deportation got underway, Jewish employees of the camp made the rounds of the rooms to hand out a postcard to each deportee. They were filled out hastily, written on a neighbor's back or a wall, for want of a flat surface: hurry up, there aren't enough pencils to go around, the employees will be back any minute now.[46] It was five in the morning on this 2 March 1943: "My dearest children, we write you this card as a farewell . . ." Matès and Idesa could not write in such good French. The script of the bilingual friend who agreed to write out their last wishes took up the entire surface of the card, out to the very edges. He made a few spelling errors, which I have corrected in the transcription, the way one smooths the face of the dearly departed prior to burial.

The final letters from Drancy are often breathless with anguish and urgency, making little sense, mingling despair with reassurance that "we're keeping our spirits up" and "we'll be seeing you soon." Kisses and final salutations collide with mundane concerns that need addressing before departure: settling a debt, handing over keys, sending or receiving clothes, food and money. These bewildered sentences, these jumbled words reflect the anxiety of people torn from their lives; and yet, the letters still speak life. But this is not true of Matès and Idesa's. Theirs are written by innocents facing their death sentence, and I can scarcely bring myself to read them. They speak of bare humanity in all its starkness, and when I find the strength to stare into them, the world stands still, I fall into a timeless, bottomless sorrow, I feel stricken by some incurable ill. Matès and Idesa are taking leave of life. They do not know with the knowledge we have in hindsight, but still they do know. They are on the threshold of another world—not necessarily death, but a hopeless, futureless, joyless place where existence as a human being is no longer possible. On this threshold, their voices rise one more time to speak to the children, embrace them, console them, beg their forgiveness, instill enough love for a lifetime. Despite privation and exhaustion, despite a departure "with no personal effects or provisions," the children are their only concern, how the children will manage without them. Such self-denial among people facing imminent annihilation fills me with a holy terror.

The first card, the one from my grandfather, is addressed to "Mr. and Mrs. Constant," that is, Constant and Annette, at 106 Rue Saint-Maur, the place where the Pole brought the children on the morning of 25 February. Matès begs them to take good care of the children. The second card, unsigned but written on Idesa's behalf, is sent to "Mr. Charriaud," that is, Poulot, Jascha's husband, at 111 Rue Oberkampf, the same apartment where my father visits him now, when the poor man has lost his mind and no longer recognizes anyone. The letter is intended not for Poulot but for the children. Though she tries to end on a note of hope, it is indeed a farewell letter. Every phrase—"little orphans," "absent parents," "something to remember us by," "suffer our fate"—sends the children a message of sorrow and regret, pride and love, in a letter that is at the same time her will and testament, a letter that they will read later, when they are older, when they might understand, perhaps. "We are brokenhearted at having to abandon you at such a young age."[47]

Why were two postcards sent to two different couples? Just to be safe, no doubt. And why send them to two cousins of Idesa's, Annette and Jascha, and their husbands, Constant and Poulot? My grandparents had other friends besides them. But while the Gardebleds and their fellow workers were friends, they were not family. As for Frime, Sroul and Dina, they were all in hiding in Ariège. The choice to entrust the children to Constant and Annette was, beyond friendship and trust, a matter of the parents' desire for the highest guarantee of protection. "We implore you to take good care of our dear children so that they are not completely parentless." Constant's character would increase their chances of survival: he saved Matès in 1941 by signing the lease for the room on Passage d'Eupatoria; and even more important, Constant is French, a goy. They wouldn't lay a hand on him.

The day before their deportation, the internees were taken to a special stall to be searched. The judicial police inspectors (the special police for Jewish affairs had been relieved of their jobs after embezzlement charges were brought) checked all their bundles, felt around their clothes and un-stitched their hems, and skimmed what they wanted off the top.[48] Jewelry, watches, knives, leather wallets, scissors, medications and perhaps even the "brown fur coat" that Idesa was wearing when she left Poland. There they were, shivering in their underwear, humiliated one last time before the departure. And here they are, in front of me now, yellowed sheets of prefecture stationery bearing the header: "Monetary amounts seized from departing internees deported on 2 March 1943," with hundreds of typed names: Schwartz Anna, Kobler Roberto, Leonoff Mazal, Jablonka Matès, Ogzeret Regina . . . In the "Amount" column and the "Foreign Currency and Jewelry" column, there is nothing but dashes, which means "none," for each deportee. The various camp employees would then sign and stamp: "Seen by head inspector so-and-so," or "Certified accurate, camp cashier,"[49] and so on. They left the search stall with an X scrawled in chalk on their backs.

The place where Matès and Idesa spent their last night is known, since it is indicated on their postcards in the box marked "sender": fourth floor, stairwell 2. Their rooms were now completely bare. The moldy, flea-ridden straw mattresses having all been burned for health reasons back in November 1942, people had to sleep right on the cement floor, ninety to a room. A few buckets served as toilets.[50] I cannot imagine how anyone managed to sleep. Some spoke of their determination to escape at some point along the train ride.[51] At dawn, the employees entered the rooms and distributed cards and pencils. Matès and Idesa dictated their letters to a companion in misfortune.

SENDER:
Mr. Jablonka Matès
Stairwell 2, 4th floor
Drancy Camp
Seine

ADDRESSEE:
Mr. Couanault
106 Rue Saint-Maur 106
Paris 11

Drancy, 2 March—morning

Mr. and Mrs. Constant,
We are writing to you right as we
are leaving for Germany and we
implore you to take good care of
our dear children so that they are
not completely parentless. We do
not know if we will have the joy of
ever seeing them again someday.
You are soon going to have a child
of your own, so you will know
what a mother's heart is, and how
much it is suffering. All our hopes
are with you, and we are so very
grateful to you both. We are leaving
with no provisions or effects, but
this is hardly our concern. All our
thoughts go out to the children.
Please be happy, and know that we
thank you from the bottom of our
hearts.
Jablonka Matès

SENDER:
Mrs. Jablonka
Stairwell 2, 4th floor
Drancy Camp
Seine

ADDRESSEE:
Mr. Charriaud
111 Rue Oberkampf 111
Paris 11

Drancy, 2 March—5 in the morning

My dearest children,
We are writing this card by way
of farewell so that you will have
something to remember us by, for
in a quarter hour, we will be leaving
for Germany. We are brokenhearted
at having to abandon you at such
a young age. Although you will
remain little orphans, we hope that
Mr. Charriaud and Constant will
find it in their hearts to help you,
and to replace your absent parents.
We are trying to be brave and to
face our fate in the hope of someday
seeing our dear children grown up
and proud. Be good, be thankful to
your benefactors. Your Mommy and
Daddy send you warm kisses.

What followed is known to us through Georges Wellers's account of events:

> The convoys of deportees left the camp at first light. The deportees left their rooms around 5 a.m., while it was still dark. They were gathered into a barbed wire enclosure in the middle of the courtyard. Around 6, the camp inspectors arrived, and soon after, a few Germans. Behind a long table, by the light of a hurricane lamp, they quickly called the name of each deportee, who would then move toward the exit set up on the far south side, near the departure stairs.[52]

The busses were waiting.

We are all here—my parents, my Aunt Suzanne, my brother, my wife and I—on this rainy 2 March, 2003. The ceremony has been organized by the Sons and Daughters of Jewish Deportees of France, Serge Klarsfeld's association. Among the umbrellas, we catch sight of the "forty-and-eight" boxcar, forty men and eight horses, which has been set to stand as a witness, all by itself in the middle of the courtyard of this low-income apartment complex. At the foot of some sculptures in ochre stone, we take turns reading the list of the 1000 Jews who made up the convoy. The names tick by slowly, one by one: a large majority of older adults, 395 in their sixties and seventies, 317 over seventy, but also young adults: Matès and Idesa Jablonka; Yankel and Chana Handelsman, arrested on 12 February at their home on Rue Oberkampf; Joseph and Pesa Dorembus, arrested on 20 February at their home on Rue Piat; and thirty-five children, among whom the little Kagan children: Leon, fourteen, Rachel, nine, and little Maurice, only two. Poles and Russians accounted for 80%, with very few French.[53] At the Bourget-Drancy station, they walked to the boxcars, escorted by Lieutenant Gamet's men.

Here I am at nine, young Rachel Kagan's age when she died. My father receives regular mailings from the FFDJF (*Fils et Filles de Déportés Juifs de France*—Sons and Daughters of France's Jewish Deportees). At the time, I don't know what the acronym stands for. I think it sounds like some sports federation. I make fun of my father, saying he's just got another letter from the FFFJJJ or the FJFJFJ. He smiles, opens the envelope cleanly with his letter opener, as always, and removes the leaflet: it is a newsletter or a fund-raising plea. He leaves it on his desk on top of a pile of other papers to be filed away, and we go play a game of chess together, or we have dinner, or we watch television, or go for a walk in the neighborhood, looking for something "fun" to do—I'm the one who chooses the itinerary, which I enjoy, and my father follows along willingly, also enjoying it.

Access to the train was guarded by French gendarmes and German soldiers. Did the loading involve violence and shouting? How long did it take to load several hundred old, disabled or sick people? Finally, the doors were slid into place and sealed. The convoy then started moving forward; it was the forty-ninth to leave France. Back in his office, Röthke sent three telexes, one to the anti-Jewish department of the Reich's central security bureau in Berlin, one to the Oranienburg camp and one to Auschwitz, to let them all know that a convoy of 1,000 Jews had just left the Bourget-Drancy station.[54] "We are brokenhearted at having to abandon you at such a young age."

8

BEHIND

AN EVERGREEN

HEDGE

The children stayed at Constant and Annette's from late February through May of 1943. Suzanne and Marcel dried their tears and life went back to normal in the little two-room apartment at 106 Rue Saint-Maur. Space was made for the children, they were fed and clothed, taken out to play in the park and tucked in at night. When he left his parents in 1942, at the Montluçon hospital, Saul Fried-lander clung to the bars around the bed and his father had to force his fingers open,[1] but he was ten years old. At four and three years old, could Suzanne and Marcel really understand what was happening to them? One night, they were sleeping at the Pole's, and the next morning they were woken up to be taken over to Constant and Annette's. Their parents were gone, and now it was up to Annette to care for them. And that's all there was to it.

A series of photos shows them dressed alike in grey striped overcoats that expose their plump calves, hiked-up socks and little black boots. They are standing in front of a pond, like the one in the Luxembourg Gardens, but without the little sailboats. My father is chubby-cheeked, his head a mass of blond curls. In one of the photos, the children are sitting on the edge of the pond, between Poulot and Jascha. Looking at this picture, I experience a time gap: I have known Poulot only as an elderly man, telling his pleasant though often unsubtle jokes at his bare-bones lodgings in La Celle-sur-Morin; the young man in the picture with his arm around the children to keep them from falling back into the pond is an athletic fellow in a dark suit, handsome, square-jawed, with daring, dark looks that say he means business. Jascha looks like a real *Parisienne* in her long, pearl-grey coat, white scarf tied in a bow at the neck, black gloves, patent leather shoes and a leather handbag. Do her shoes and bag come from Constant's leather shop? Did Matès give her those gloves as a present? The sun casts the photographer's shadow across the pond's edge, there are leaves on the trees in the distance, so it must already be April.

I speculate as to whether these portraits of the children in their Sunday best have some connection to their being sent out to the countryside a few weeks later. Annette's baby would be due soon, and the place was too small for five people, to say nothing of the constant risk of keeping two little Jews in the house. Constant, a Fougères native, wrote to his sister, who still lived there, and asked her to find a host family in the area. Mr. and Mrs. Courtoux, a retired couple in Luitré, a village a short distance from Fougères, agreed to take them in. Meanwhile, Constant also got in touch with the Amelot Committee, the underground Jewish organization whose front was the "Mother and Child" clinic in the 11th arrondissement, 36 Rue Amelot: yet another risk taken to help the children whose parents he had already rescued in the past.

An outgrowth of the *Colonie scolaire*, or school colony, a Jewish charity organization founded in 1926 by David Rapoport and Jules Jacoubovitch, the "Mother and Child" clinic supported Jewish immigrant families. On 15 June 1940, when the Wehrmacht was just entering Paris and the 23rd

RMVE was making its last stand at Pont-sur-Yonne, several important Jewish figures met in secret to plan for the protection of the Jewish population. This social welfare bureau, undeclared to the authorities and soon to be known by the name "Amelot Committee," was one of the first resistance groups in France. As heads of the *Colonie scolaire*, Rapoport and Jacoubovitch went to great lengths to revive the prewar canteens, to ensure that families got medical care, to send packages to internment camps and—the underground side of their activities—to get children out of the cities and into the countryside, out of harm's way. Funding was provided at first by the Federation of Jewish Societies of France, then by the UGIF, the umbrella organization controlled by the Germans that the Amelot Committee finally joined in 1942, though it never abandoned its underground activities.[2]

Why did Constant go to the Amelot Committee for help, hosted as it was by Bundists and Zionist socialists? Several other groups were evacuating children to safety, the children of deportees and immigrants in particular. Though it is true that the OSE, an organization providing emergency help to children, operated mainly in the unoccupied southern zone, it did run a branch on Avenue Villars in the 7th arrondissement and a clinic on Rue Francs-Bourgeois, in the Marais. The clinic on Rue de Turenne, linked to the Communist Party, performed similar functions. In May 1943, Communist Jewish organizations came together within the UJRE, a resistance group that featured a separate committee for children's issues. Beyond just geographic proximity, however, Constant was perhaps aware that in January 1943, just a month before the police raid on Passage d'Eupatoria, the Amelot Committee had helped Mrs. Erpst hide her two sons. In any event, he went to the committee and explained that he had two parentless children at his house. A social worker visited them at Rue Saint-Maur. Annette's record, showing that she was a Polish Jew who had become "French by marriage to an Aryan," was created on 22 March 1943. The report from the visit:

> Mr. Couanault is a shoe-leather worker. Mrs. Couanault, pregnant, is looking after the two Jablonka children at the couple's home. The children look well cared for. We notified Mrs. Couanault that she could bring

the children to the clinic should the need arise. Mrs. Couanault has been looking after the children since 25 February. Mr. and Mrs. Couanault are kindly people. The children look clean and well fed. The family atmosphere is excellent. Their housing is small but well kept. The children are in urgent need of underclothes and shoes. Subsidies for these children must be found, for Mr. Couanault is a laborer and earns just enough to get his own family by. We will be asking for 1,200 francs per month for the two children.[3]

On 24 March, two days after the social worker's visit (and a month after the parents' arrest), Constant and Annette received one pair of children's shoes, a pair of long socks, a pair of ankle socks and a short-sleeved shirt, amounting to sixteen textile points on their ration card. This kind of aid was an important part of the Amelot Committee's resistance activity, as Jacoubovitch described it after the war: "We had a terrible time supplying enough underwear and clothing. Under the direction of Mrs. Youchnovetzki, our clothing distributor handled the demand. They performed veritable miracles to obtain huge quantities of merchandise in otherwise very tough times"[4] (which does not explain, by the way, where those very chic-looking jackets came from, the ones the children were wearing in the photo by the pond). The first cash payment was made on 30 March, in the amount of "1,200 francs for April." The social worker returned on 8 April, and her impression was again very favorable. Annette declared that "she intend[ed] to send the children to the country for Easter holiday and leave them there for the whole summer. She ask[ed] for undershirts for both children and shoes for Marcel." Once back at Rue Amelot, the social worker wrote "to the childminder to submit her request to the town hall of her locality."[5] This would clearly suggest that by early April 1943, the Courtoux, the retired couple in Luitré, had already accepted their mission.

In the Amelot Committee documents, two other children are constantly associated with Suzanne and Marcel: Samuel Odryzinski, son of the cabling specialist, and Claude Schlevin, son of Freydke and the writer, all living at 19 Passage d'Eupatoria. Did the 25 February raid hasten the evacuation of the other children? All four children were placed under Constant's responsibility. Claude Schlevin, three years old at the time, tells me the little he knows of his story, never mentioning Constant's name, nor the Amelot Committee. Hidden away with a farm family in the Sarthe region, he felt abandoned and miserable; Freydke went to see him when she could, but each time he would cry and want to go back with her. At the end of the war, his father, just released from the German work camp, showed up at the farm wearing a soldier's uniform, and despite his tender overtures, frightened the little boy, who failed to recognize his own father. In Benjamin Schlevin's *The Jews of Belleville*, there is a pipefitter named Constant. Though the resemblance is weak, I can't help thinking that the writer is honoring the man who helped save his little boy during the war.

In a letter he sent to the German commission after the war, Constant wrote: in May 1943, "I placed the Jablonka children with Mr. and Mrs. Courtoux who lived in the hamlet of Laleu, district of Luitré, in the Ille-et-Vilaine region." Constant's personal initiative must have come as a relief to the Amelot Committee, whose people were having trouble meeting the demand. "Most of our resources," writes Jacoubovitch, "were devoted to seeking out families, preferably out in the country, who were willing to take in children. . . . The children had to be provided with forged documents and transport to the host family location. We then had to keep tabs on them, making sure they had what they needed, clothing in particular, and to pay for their upkeep." Since it was Constant who recruited the Courtoux by way of his sister, it was up to him to ensure the follow-up. He also channeled the money to them: in Amelot Committee archives, Suzanne and Marcel are named in Constant and Annette's record, filed under "Paris," and the Courtoux couple, unlike other childminders, are not listed at all. In addition to clothing, the committee made twelve payments of cash between March 1943 and August 1944, for a total of about 30,000 francs.[6]

Suzanne and Marcel were sent off to Bretagne, then. An Amelot Committee document lists the various departments in France where some 500 children were in hiding by late 1943. If we group them geographically, we get the following breakdown, in descending order: around 280 children in Paris and the suburbs; 130 in the west (Perche, Maine, the Loire valley), sixty-four of those in Sarthe alone; thirty some in Picardie and the north of France; nearly thirty in Normandy, seventeen of those in La Manche; around twenty in Bourgogne; fifteen or so in Bretagne, two of those in

Ille-et-Vilaine, and I can only presume that these were my father and aunt.[7] This geography of rescue presents three remarkable features: the proximity to Paris, since practically all the children are placed within a 200-mile radius; the preference for rural family settings; and the resemblance with the placement map of the Seine region's welfare program. In the nineteenth century, this program ran a dense network of agencies from Bretagne to Morvan, and was hardly present at all south of the Loire or beyond Champagne.[8] In other words, the Amelot Committee, by recruiting childminders in the greater Paris region, was falling back on the choices that had been made by its predecessor, the old welfare program called *Assistance Publique*, which took advantage of the fact that those regions were already specialized in providing wet nurses for the Parisian bourgeoisie. Another constant was the preference of the foster family option over orphanages. This way, large concentrations of vulnerable children could be avoided (the counterexample being the children at the Izieu orphanage, who were loaded onto trucks by the Gestapo in 1944 and eventually sent to their deaths at Auschwitz). In early March 1943, the Amelot Committee evacuated its orphanage in La Varenne and scattered the children among foster families in the country.

Just as the Amelot Committee excelled at finding foster families, they also handled transporting the children: countless women served as escorts, including Annette Monot from the Red Cross, the Laborde sisters in Créteil, Mrs. Flamand from the Saint-Maurice hospital, and Micheline Bellair from the Paris prefecture, to name but a few, and would accompany the children to their destinations, pretending to be their mothers. Here again, the Committee was relieved of this task: Poulot and Jascha took charge of accompanying the children to Fougères by train. Why didn't Constant take them? Because at this point, he was about to become a father himself. Here is the story told 100 times at family gatherings: a train station, the train stops, German soldiers get on. Poulot and Jascha are scared to death because Suzanne is babbling away in Yiddish. She looks at the Germans and back at Poulot and Jascha, exclaims: "Hey, I understand what they're saying!"

Jascha claps her hand over Suzanne's mouth. They were actually just simple soldiers who weren't paying the slightest attention to what was going on around them. But for an instant, the shadow of death hovered.

Behind this simple Paris-Fougères trip lay the generosity of Constant and Annette, the courage of Poulot and Jascha. One could understand that the Korenbaum sisters would come to the aid of their Parczew cousin, but their husbands, those anarchist goys? Jacoubovitch puts it bluntly: "We could never have carried out these rescue operations of both children and adults without the help of the non-Jews."[9] Solidarity was alive and well at the Amelot Committee. Nearly thirty employees of the Committee, including David Rapoport, arrested on 1 June 1943, would be murdered by the Nazis.

Next, they changed trains at Fougères; then came the slow local, then the station at La Selle-en-Luitré. And finally, the village of Luitré, at the junction of Bretagne and Mayenne, far from the sound of boots and the eyes of intelligence agents. Where exactly were the children handed over? Were the Courtoux couple waiting somewhere at the station, photograph in hand? This clandestine transfer immediately arouses my interest, and it provides the first lead my father and I will follow together, in early 2007: he must write in all haste to the Luitré and La Selle-en-Luitré town halls to find out what he can about the Courtoux couple, whom he never saw again later in life. My father is reluctant, coming up with all sorts of reasons why it's useless, why no one will answer, why it won't work. But I insist, and in the end, he grudgingly relents, but is secretly happy, I believe, to be embarking on this discovery of his own past. Two weeks later, we get an answer from a certain Mrs. Hardy. My father's letter was forwarded to her from the town hall of La Selle-en-Luitré, where she has lived all her life. She is the Courtoux's niece. Here is what she writes, sixty-five years later:

> I have a very clear memory of those two children who had been placed in the care of my uncle and aunt. . . . There was a girl and a boy, they stayed several months, but soon some association or other came to get them. Everyone was deeply affected to see them go . . . Their foster parents gave the association an address and asked to be sent news about what was happening to the children, but unfortunately no news ever came, and they died without ever hearing anything.

My father gets all excited on receiving this letter, and calls Mrs. Hardy. She was twenty years old back in 1943. Her aunt, Mrs. Courtoux, worked in shoe manufacturing at Fougères and knew lots of people, which probably explains why she was approached by Constant's sister. The Courtoux were already elderly. They lived modestly, but had a cow, a sign of wealth (in the nineteenth century, it qualified you to take in a welfare child, as it proved you could provide milk, at least). Throughout the war, Suzanne and Marcel were the only foster children they hosted. They passed away a long time ago. Mrs. Hardy speaks of a cousin in Fougères, butcher by trade, who took refuge in Luitré after a bomb landed on his shop, and supplied meat to the "poor children."

"Why 'poor' children?"

"Because they were orphans, Jewish children. So sad, those poor little ones."

In May 1943, the Courtoux knew exactly what they were getting involved in. Either it was explained to them by Constant's sister, or they figured it out on their own (after all, Suzanne spoke Yiddish and my father was circumcised). Mrs. Hardy goes on:

"Marcel was a funny little boy, he went all over the place, was interested in everything. Suzanne was older."

I prevail upon my father once more, this time to write to all the Courtoux families in Bretagne. A few days later, the phone rings and it is Mireille, the Courtoux's granddaughter. She was born in 1944. Her mother, the Courtoux's daughter-in-law, had taken refuge in Luitré with her sister, because Lorient, where they lived, was constantly being bombed. The Courtoux were retired factory workers. She had worked in a shoe factory and he in glass manufacturing, at the *Cristallerie Fougeraise*. They owned a cow, but also pigs, chickens and rabbits, and they had two vegetable gardens, one in their courtyard and another some twenty yards from the house, on the other side of the road. Mireille describes the house to my father, who remembers it well: a large room with the couple's bed and the children's on either side of the fireplace. In the 1950s, Mireille spent all her vacations at her grandparents'. In what had been the pigsty, there was a stuffed hobbyhorse that no one was allowed to touch: it was Suzanne and Marcel's. The Courtoux still talked about them: Where are they now? Are they in good health? What's the name of that association that came to get them after Liberation? Old Mr. Courtoux, a former glass-worker, was ailing, bedridden; he stayed at home and his wife took care of him. After his death, she kept busy doing odd jobs, little sewing projects here and there, substituting for the train crossing guards around her area. The memory of Suzanne and Marcel was kept alive in the family. Years after the grandparents' death, their children decided to notify the television program "Lost from Sight," a show that helped find people one had lost contact with. They signed up, but the program went off the air before their turn had come up.

A year and a half later, we go to see Mrs. Hardy at La Selle-en-Luitré. From Paris, I catch the TGV train and go as far as Laval, then take a bus. At Fougères, where I meet up with my parents, we lunch on crêpes next to the Victor Hugo Theater, after which we head for the village, buried in the hedged countryside. All of a sudden, my father stops the car: he has just recognized the Courtoux's house, all the easier to spot since he'd already come out once in the mid-1960s with Constant and Annette (the Courtoux were deceased by then). Today, as with the first time, emotion runs high as pieces from the past fall into place and still images become moving pictures. "Perhaps this is what happens when there is childhood trauma. We need concrete evidence for our memories, since no one else is left to validate them." Thanks to a certain bend in the road in front of the house, to the way the stones fit above the window, to the particular angle between the roof and tree, to the depth of field as one looks out to the pastureland, his memories are authenticated, raised to the level of certainty. Yes, all of this was true. All of this really did happen.

There's no one around except the cat. The house, built of massive stone, with a slate roof, inspires a feeling of security. Much renovated, it is still recognizable thanks to four photos that my father has kept of his time in Luitré. The first three show Suzanne and Marcel on the far right side of the house, at the edge of the road, successively with Mr. Courtoux, Mrs. Courtoux and two women, one of whom is the Courtoux's daughter-in-law. Visible in the photos are a door and a window, edged in alternating brick and stone. Today, the door has become the window, and the window the door, but we have no trouble reconstituting the original arrangement. At the far left of the house, above a second door, a curtained window lets light into the remodeled attic (Mrs. Hardy says that that window was once used for loading hay). All the way in the back, the courtyard is enclosed by a hedge of evergreens that screens the area where the chicken coop and vegetable garden used to be. And beyond, cows are grazing peacefully in the pasture, which is brightened by a strip of white flowers running along a creek that my father remembers well. Further still, a curtain of trees marks the presence of a river, most likely the Couesnon, the natural border between Bretagne and Normandy.

We leave the way we came, and are back on the road. This is where the fourth photo was taken: it shows the children sitting on a little chair—Suzanne on Marcel's knees with her arm around his neck—in front of a rickety wooden fence, along with a pale basset hound, its snout lifted hopefully toward Suzanne ("It's Pyrame!" exclaims Mireille, the Courtoux's granddaughter, upon seeing the photo). The fence is now gone, but the stretch of road and the grassy slope in the background are identical. We make a stop at the Luitré town hall, where I have a look at the municipal archives, neatly filed and safely stored on an upper floor. Not a trace of the children or the Courtoux couple in the register of childminders or child protection files. Not surprising, since no one would have been foolish enough, in 1943, to declare guardianship of Jewish children. The archive of ration ticket distribution does not list anything either.

The fence gate is open. A dog tethered inside a shed barks as we pass. We walk through a courtyard almost completely taken up by a vegetable garden, surrounded by flowers, where cucumbers, potatoes, beans, cabbage, onions and squash grow in abundance. After knocking at the unlocked door, we enter somewhat timidly. "Please, have a seat," Mrs. Hardy says cheerfully, before serving us a glass of peach brandy with some peanuts. She is an elderly lady, but lively and warmhearted, with snow-white hair and big steel-rimmed glasses. She rolls her *r*'s, and when she talks about cows or calves, she adds, "begging your pardon," as if she had just said something vulgar. Her interior has not changed since the war: flowered wallpaper, oilcloth on the table, an enormous enameled stove with an exhaust fan, a sideboard topped with framed photographs of first communions and a bridal crown (her own mother's, married in 1907), a mantelpiece occupied by items of porcelain and a smoky blue hurricane lamp.

The Courtoux were selflessly devoted to the needy. During the war, they took in refugees from Fougères and the region: in the cellar behind the house, beds were set up in every available space. Lorient, a strategic port town, was bombed by the Royal Air Force as early as 22 August 1940, and suffered other air attacks in the fall of 1942 and in January 1943. Water, gas and electricity were cut, schools were closed by mid-January 1943 and nearly 30,000 Lorient residents fled the city.[10] The butcher who had fled Fougères would slaughter the calves people brought to him ("no pigs, they make too much noise") and sell the meat on the black market. Little Marcel would watch him work, but Suzanne, frightened away by the cries and blood, stayed in the house with Mrs. Courtoux. The butcher gave them bits of meat to keep them in good health, a considerable act of compassion in that context of nationwide scarcity (as of October 1941, meat rations, often of poor quality, were set at 100 grams—only 3.5 ounces—per week). In Luitré, apart from the one ambulance, only one other vehicle had the right to gasoline, and that was the mayor's. "Monsieur the Count," as he was called, a proud and haughty man. Children and adults wore wooden clogs, with socks in winter.

The Courtoux were very attached to Suzanne and Marcel. At Liberation, they nurtured the hope of being able to keep them, but that wasn't possible: they were poor, already getting on in age, and then there was that association to deal with. When did the children finally leave? Granddaughter Mireille was born on 2 January 1944. She has a scar from when she fell from a ladder once while Suzanne was supposed to be keeping an eye on her. Since she was walking at nine months, this takes us beyond September 1944. The last Amelot Committee payment is dated 2 August. In the Committee archives, an accountant has scribbled in next to the date 2 November 1944: "Share of Jablonka expenses (travel), 122 francs."[11] It would appear, then, that the children stayed in Luitré for a year and a half, from May 1943 to November 1944.

My father removes from their plastic sleeve the four photographs taken in front of the Courtoux home. Suzanne is a pretty little five-year-old. Her nicely combed chestnut hair is held in a barrette. She's wearing a sleeveless one-piece sunsuit in a light, white-flowered print. My father is dressed like a girl, in little shorts and an embroidered apron top. His hair is tousled—nothing like his neat curls in the pond picture—and he looks a little messy in his stained outfit. The children are not wearing clogs, but sandals. In the photo picturing Mr. Courtoux, he is wearing a straw boater and filthy-looking trousers held up by suspenders. He holds a child's hand in each of his (next to him, my father comes mid-thigh) and looks happy. In another photo, Mrs. Courtoux, in a long black cloth dress, looks ready to faint from the heat; she's wincing and the children's eyes are closed, as they seem to be squirming. Everyone looks a little grumpy in this photo, but it might just be the sun. My father is convinced that the pictures were taken by Poulot, whose camera had already served for the photos by the pond. One thing is certain: Constant and Poulot went to see the children at least once. While the Amelot Committee social workers were crisscrossing France to visit the children hidden away in villages, these two anarchist goys went up to Luitré to check that all was well. Sunshine, sandals, straw hat, sunsuit: this could well be the summer of 1944.

In these snapshots, the children look healthy and well cared for. But that doesn't prove anything. Escaping a police raid, fleeing with your mother across Paris, changing apartments in a panic, taking none of your things with you, watching your parents live in distress and anxiety, losing them from one day to the next, moving from one house to another before landing here with strangers: it's enough to shatter you for life. But then again, Suzanne and Marcel were too young to truly comprehend the enormity of what was happening to them; even the worst atrocities can appear as the normal course of events to a child who, like the children we see in Aharon Appelfeld's books, wanders alone through the forests of Ukraine after losing his parents. If Suzanne and Marcel did understand anything, it would not be with the clear-sightedness of the "Shoah children," but rather in the manner of that little girl taken to the La Varenne orphanage by an Amelot Committee social worker who, once she was bathed and combed, hugged the assistant and asked: "Would you like to be my mommy? I don't have a mommy anymore, you know."[12] According to my cousin, Suzanne transferred her affection onto a piglet she adopted and raised all by herself.

Suzanne and Marcel thus lived uneventfully with the retired couple in Luitré, and these children of Jewish immigrants, two Ménilmontant Yiddishland kids, tried their hand at living like little Bretons among the hens and rabbits. My father has much keener memories of this time than of the Vél' d'Hiv raid:

—A river ran behind the garden. Mrs. Courtoux used to wade across it with them. She would wash her laundry there, too. Years later, after the war, when his schoolteacher would talk about meandering rivers, watersheds and flow rates, this is the river that came to my father's mind. When he returned to Luitré with Constant and Annette in the 1960s, he went looking for that river of his childhood. He was astounded to find, 100 feet from the house, a pathetic little creek that barely moistened the surrounding grasses. Mireille, the Courtoux's granddaughter, confirms that there had indeed been a creek running through the garden, but because of some land reallotment, it was no longer on the property. We can see it now, further away, running through a patch of daisies and daffodils. A half-mile away runs the real river, the Couesnon.

—On the other side of the road, the neighbor owned a threshing machine. Just as little Marcel probably watched his father work at his stitching machine back in Passage d'Eupatoria, he must have also enjoyed watching this iron monster swallowing enormous bundles of wheat: the cylinders, pistons and belts would spring into action, making a clanking, labored noise as men oversaw the operation from up on a ladder, clouds of dust filling the air. One day, he cried because he'd missed the moment when they sounded the siren. During his trip with Constant and Annette, my father told the story to a neighbor, who corroborated it. The farmland of Bretagne was slow to mechanize during the first half of the century, and in the 1940s, a threshing machine was a real attraction.

—An outhouse, a hedge in the back of the barnyard. My father was learning French words like "hedge" back then (I believe that that was actually when he first learned French at all). He also learned to tie a bow, but on what? (Shoes? But weren't they wearing sandals and clogs? The mystery remains.) Personal hygiene, new vocabulary, everyday gestures: this was the age for learning all the basics.

—Marcel was cuffed one day for drinking water during the soup course. Another memory, which my father got from his sister ("The only thing she remembers better than I do"): entrusted one day with taking the cow out to pasture, they got themselves in big trouble when they lost it on the way. Taking the cows to pasture is one of the classic apprenticeships of rural youth.

—They would say their prayers by the fireplace. They went to church; Marcel has a clear memory of attending Mass. Awed by the decorum, he was completely overwhelmed: you had to stand up, sit down, stand again, sit back down, but you never knew when to do what. My father gives his account to Mireille. "Of course," she answers: Mrs. Courtoux was very devout, and as a child, she too had to go to Mass during vacation. They went on foot, and it was pretty far away. Like the childminders to whom the *Assistance Publique* entrusted children, the Courtoux couple took their educational role to heart. It consisted of setting limits, but also of teaching the basics, whether tying shoelaces or saying one's prayers. In general, in 1943 as in the nineteenth century, a foster parent's role consisted of both admonishing the children and setting an example for them, affection being optional (though in the case of the Courtoux, it didn't seem to be lacking). Furthermore, Bretagne experienced a religious renewal during the war period, when church became a way to socialize, but also a means of collective atonement.[13] Regular attendance at Mass, therefore, did not betray a desire to convert Jewish orphans. Still, there were cases everywhere in France where Catholics would have the children baptized to ensure their security, or in cases like the Finaly Affair, to gain souls for God.[14]

—Marcel was in bed. There were stirrings in the house. Adults were talking about "patriots in the forest." Somebody had hidden a bottle in a hollowed-out loaf of bread. Was it alcohol? Gasoline? A method of communication? By 1943, resistance groups were growing more numerous in Bretagne. The Parson network, one of the most important, was trying to scramble German communication lines and isolate ports. Arms and explosives were parachuted into Ille-et-Vilaine on eight separate occasions between July and December 1943. The first underground groups in the region, such as the Broualan group, small and mobile, were formed in late 1943.[15] Resistance fighters operated in the Ernée woods in Mayenne, not far from Luitré, under the supervision of the Le Donné couple, who were early Gaullists. This scene, all the more mysterious and exciting for the child who was assumed to be asleep, would suggest that the Courtoux were not content to merely hide Jewish children: they were also connected in some way to the region's resistance network.

Clearly, then, Suzanne and Marcel did not totally escape the war by leaving Paris, despite what we might assume. First of all, there were shortages of every kind in Luitré. The children had to be clothed, and those clothes had to be washed and mended, and winter meant they would need warmer wear. They had to be fed, beyond the occasional cuts from the good butcher of Fougères. They needed care when they got sick. The house had to be kept warm (English coal imports were interrupted, and supplies had to be brought in from the south of France). How was money from the Amelot Committee transmitted from Constant to the Courtoux? Were the payments enough? Most probably not. One day, Mrs. Hardy tells us, Mr. Courtoux went to the town hall to ask for food stamps "for two Jewish children."

"Oh really?" replied the mayor's secretary, pricking up his ears. "Are there Jews in the area?"

Mr. Courtoux, realizing his mistake, turned and left the building. You had to be careful of what you said in the village. This mayor, whose car never wanted for fuel, was not to be trusted. There was also B., a militiaman whom everyone in the area feared. One day, a farmer complained that resistance fighters were stealing his chickens. B. got wind of the issue from the local photographer's son and informed the *Kommandantur* (the German garrison headquarters). A resistance fighter was soon killed. B. lived in Luitré, in a place known as La Brebittière, where the train makes a stop after Vitré.

It's hard not to make the connection between this food stamp story, which Mrs. Hardy finishes pensively as she refills our glasses with peach brandy, and a scene that Poulot used to tell, in admiration, yet another illustration of Constant's moral fiber. On their visit to the children, most probably in the summer of 1944, Constant and Poulot stopped by the Luitré town hall. The mayor's secretary was sitting there, having his lunch, a beret on his head. Constant asked him for food stamps for Suzanne and Marcel. The fellow raised his head from his soup bowl absent-mindedly, replying that he couldn't give him any because "there's a war on," and went back to slurping his soup. Constant went right up to him and gave him a smack that sent his beret flying across the room.

"Since when is this a war against kids? And anyway, take your hat off when you're eating!"

Poulot's story ended there, which suggests that, however terrorized this fellow was by the feisty Parisian built like a tank, he still would not issue the food stamps. Had Mr. Courtoux told Constant his own story of failing to get the stamps, inspiring Constant to go back with Poulot, after taking the pictures of the children, determined this time to get the job done? The scene may have taken place around the time of the Normandy landing, after the Fougères bombing, on 6 and 9 June 1944: Constant had left Paris on a bicycle, heading out to join Annette, who had taken refuge in Fougères; the militias were losing their power.

In any case, the Bretagne countryside was anything but a peaceful haven. Early in my research, I imagined that Suzanne and Marcel were passing as the Courtoux's grandchildren, or as "little Parisians" sent out for health reasons. But the presence of militiaman B. in Luitré changed my perspective. In fact, the children were not so safe. The Courtoux knew they were sheltering little Jewish children, and that was probably common knowledge in the village as well. The surroundings were not as secure as in Châteaumeillant, and Ille-et-Vilaine didn't have its version of Mr. Ricordeau, the schoolteacher from Sarthe who watched over the Jewish children hidden away in the countryside. It took the combined efforts of three separate resistance groups to save my father and aunt: the anarchist milieu in Paris, the farmworkers of the Bretagne countryside and an underground Jewish committee. And even before all that, it had taken impressive solidarity to extract Matès from Vichy's grip in September 1940, to keep him clear of police raids and secure him a hideout in Passage d'Eupatoria in August 1941, to safeguard the family after the Vél' d'Hiv roundup, and to get the children out of Paris after the parents' arrest. One person supplied the work papers, another signed the lease for the room and got in touch with Jewish resistance groups, somebody arranged for the children's removal to the country, out of harm's way, and others hosted them at their farm for a year and a half. From Parczew to Luitré, from Châteaumeillant to Saint-Antonin, from Ménilmontant to Fougères, an internationale of craftsmen, an extended family of saddlers, tailors and leatherworkers came together during a certain period in the twentieth century, let's say 1930 to 1945, to defend the highest values of European humanism. All these nameless Righteous ones are gone now, and no narrative, no commemorative plaque attests to their courage. I wish I could see Poulot, Constant and Annette with my adult eyes, hear once again their rolled *r*'s and accents, whether rural, street-slangy or Yiddish. Their gruff humor that made me uneasy when I was a boy of ten, their contempt for bourgeois values, their cheekiness and short-tempered feistiness, and their integrity had everything to do with their willingness, in life-and-death situations, to come to the aid of those in need and save their children, unreservedly and without the slightest hesitation, not for money or medals or glory, but because it was the right thing to do.

On a trip out to Rennes, I stop off at the departmental archives to find out more about this militiaman called B. and his informer, the photographer's son, both of whom stood trial in 1944 in Ille-et-Vilaine. Here is what I find out.

In early June 1944, resistance fighters were sent into a wooded area called Forêt-Noire, near Larchamp, to recover items parachuted in by the British. One Saturday, fully armed, they went to a Larchamp farm to purchase cider. They returned the next day to notify the farmer that they had also taken two bundles of firewood and were prepared to pay for them. The farmer turned down the offer. A few hours later, the farmer went to Luitré to have a family portrait taken. People were standing around chatting before Mass. The farmer and the photographer's son, who was eighteen, agreed that the gendarmes should be warned that the Forêt-Noire was "crawling with terrorists." At this juncture militiaman B. arrived; he was on leave in La Brebittière, where his wife had taken refuge. Resistance fighters in the forest, you say? He immediately phoned his chief for instructions. Thanks to the directions provided by the photographer's son, B. went to Larchamp with a "security team." The militiamen entered the forest and shooting broke out. A seriously injured resistance fighter was finished off on the spot; two others were captured, and another two managed to escape. The militiamen left the corpse behind and headed to the farmer's for a bite to eat.[16]

This all-too-common story shows that, under the Occupation, the Luitré area was the site of deep conflict, bitter hatred and petty acts of cowardice. It was a shadow theater filled with German soldiers (called *Boches*), collaborators, the faint of heart, fence-sitters, hotheads and grouches, but also cool-headed retired couples, and "patriots in the forest," talked about in hushed tones after the children were in bed— the same children who had spent the day with Pyrame the dog, or with the pet pig, in the shade of an evergreen hedge. Militiaman B. and the photographer's son were arrested at Liberation. The militiaman, aged thirty-two, declared that he had chosen sides by May 1944: "I made no secret that I was in the militia, I would go see my wife in full uniform, and would always say that the militia worked with the police to suppress the black market, as my superiors told me to." The boy, on the other hand, tried to exonerate himself. He emphasized his ignorance of politics and his aversion to the black market, but the investigators spoke of his fanatical side, someone "inclined to follow the government of Marshal Pétain, blinded by silver-tongued speakers" like propagandist Philippe Henriot and others on Radio Paris.[17]

Leading up to the trial, Mrs. Le Donné, a garage owner and leader of the Resistance in the Ernée region, wrote a long report to be sent to the public prosecutor. Rescuing Jews was an integral part of her struggle against the occupiers. In January 1944, she agreed to house nine Jews, two of them children, who were "under threat of deportation by the Gestapo," and went to meet them at the coach stop with all their baggage, even though "there were Occupation soldiers all over the place." Friends of hers, farmers in a little village between Ernée and Luitré, agreed to host three of them, in full knowledge that these were "undocumented Jews." Mrs. Le Donné lodged the six others in a little house belonging to some farmers "who were also aware that they were Jews." On 15 April 1944, "on the day of a local cabal that I had great trouble quelling," the three Jews had to come back to join the other six. Several times a week, Mrs. Le Donné brought them bread and meat. They had to take enormous precautions: "A German soldier on guard duty one day at the factory gate—he'd been a bank director in Danzig before the war and was fluent in six languages—told me he had bet someone that he would kill five Jews, and he had won his bet!" After a string of arrests, the Le Donné couple had to leave their home with their four children and seek shelter at their farmer friends'. Mrs. Le Donné became a liaison officer, and it was in her capacity as the leader of the Resistance for Ernée that she arrested the photographer's son, in August 1944.[18] Epilogue: the young man was sentenced to ten years' hard labor. After attempting to slit his own throat, the farmer was acquitted; the militiaman B., sentenced to death by a military court, was executed on 24 November 1944.

By that date, Bretagne had been liberated for several months. The Americans entered Fougères on 3 August. One witness, sixteen years old at the time, recalls: "Over the days that followed, whole columns of American troops passed through Fougères. They had tanks, brand new materiel, they were well equipped, and very generous. As they came through, they passed out packs of cigarettes and chewing gum, they had more than they needed of everything, even coffee, which we hadn't tasted for four years."[19] The Americans got to Luitré around 4 August. It is my father's next-to-last memory of that time: "I was up on someone's shoulders. There was a crowd. A feeling of jubilation. Later (or perhaps another day), a train stopped at the crossing. Soldiers started throwing packages from off the top of the train cars." The American liberators were coming to resupply the overjoyed country folk who were still suffering from all kinds of shortages. According to Mrs. Hardy, that scene could only have taken place at the Alleu stop on the "little Mayenne line."

After thanking her for everything, and admiring her garden one last time, we go for a walk along the old railroad tracks, a straight, steeply embanked line that overlooks the surrounding country. The little gate-keeper's post is still standing, but it now marks a bus stop. Without rails or a crossing, without a train or even a single person in view, it's hard to imagine the Americans here, tossing bundles of supplies to the eager crowd. It was at a different stop, La Brebittière—a little white hut with red shutters and a brick roof—on a different line, that the children got on the train in late November 1944, accompanied by a social worker. The line is no longer in use. We follow the weed-choked rails and push through some thorny underbrush to discover, like enormous ochre flowers, the old rusty railway signage.

The war was ending. In the spring of 1944, 200 Jews emerged like wraiths from the forest of Parczew, cheeks sunken, tattered rags for shoes. Feygue Chtchoupak wandered through the streets of her shtetl in tears: here is where her parents had lived, her brothers, her aunts, her friends. The houses were empty, ransacked, some even burnt to the ground. The astonished Poles were practically scolding them for still being there: "What, you're still alive?"[20] The survivors settled back in as best they could, until the pogrom of 5 February 1946: against the backdrop of a civil war between Communists and nationalists, partisans disarmed the Jewish guards and ransacked their homes with the participation of the local folks, even students, who'd come to help the "resistance fighters" settle scores with the town's last Jews. Three deaths are recorded, and those who managed to escape fled the country.

From Parczew, they scattered to the four winds: to the USSR, Israel, Canada, the United States and South America, where they somehow patched their lives back together. Henya and Mayer found refuge in Kowel, in Soviet Ukraine. Hershl settled in Baku. In Buenos Aires, Simje and Raquel had three children by then. Simje had opened a shoe store in Mataderos, the slaughterhouse district. The family lived in the shop, a large room divided in two by an armoire: on one side, the display shelving, the shoes, mostly simple and inexpensive, a couple of stools for fittings, and a chess game for passing the time with customers; on the other, a bed for Benito and his brother, a table, a modestly stocked bookshelf. The parents slept in another room in the back, with the baby, Celia. By the time Reizl and her companion finally got married, yielding to social pressure and the benefits allotted to families under the Peron government, they already had two children. For their wedding, they gathered a few friends from the *Sociedad de Residentes de Parczew en la Argentina* and drank, sang and danced until dawn, but deep in their hearts, they were thinking of their departed loved ones, Shloyme and Tauba, Gitla and the half-brothers, Matès and Idesa, but also Suzanne and Marcel, all alone in faraway France.

Life was returning to normal in Paris. The Jews of Belleville, Ménilmontant and the Marais unstitched their yellow stars. "From April through August 1945," reads a commemorative plaque outside the Hotel Lutetia (which was then serving as a reception center), "a large proportion of the

Nazi concentration camp survivors were processed through this hotel, happy to be free again and reunited with the loved ones they had been forced to leave. Yet, their joy cannot erase the pain and anguish of the families who waited here in vain for the thousands who would never return." Passage d'Eupatoria was just as murky and flea-ridden as before. Freed from Bergen-Belsen, where they had been detained after the death march, Maria returned to her seamstress shop and Sarah was back at Lycée Hélène-Boucher in time to start the school year. Moises resumed his bohemian lifestyle. The Odryzinskis recovered their son, and Mrs. Erpst her two boys. Back from the Stalag, writer Schlevin went out to the Sarthe region to see his son. He separated from Freydke, remarried, moved to Belleville and wrote for Yiddish magazines. Constant and Annette still lived at 106 Rue Saint-Maur. Constant worked in a leatherworks shop and Annette stayed home with their little daughter. Frime, Sroul and Dina, the three furriers, returned from Pamiers, where they had spent the war. At first, they lived with Constant and Annette while they were looking for their own lodgings and taking steps to recover their expropriated apartment. Everyone went back to work, some with scissors, others with stitching machines. With busy hands and determination, it was possible to earn a living.

My witnesses were coming into the world, Tamara in Kowel, Celia in Buenos Aires. Serge was born in 1946 to Raymond Gardebled, the metalworker at Place Auguste-Métivier, and Gitla Leszcz, the seamstress from Dębowa-Kłoda whose torture sessions had caused her to lose feeling in her fingers—those ghostly fingers that had picked at the hole in my sweater that day in the geriatric ward of a suburban Parisian hospital. In 1947, Abram and Malka Fiszman, former Parczew Communists, became the happy parents of Colette; today, she tells me the story of her pilgrimage to the shtetl with her mother in the late 1970s, of her mother's childhood, of Polish schools, her German lessons, the anti-Semitic insults and the underground life of the KZMP. Hannah, the beautiful divorced wife of the poet Schulstein, "wild as the wind," married again; her second husband was an Auschwitz survivor, a shoemaker and singer in the local Jewish chorale. They had a child, Ginette, who invites me to her remodeled farmhouse deep in the Brie region, and standing in front of her fireplace, shows me the picture of her mother and Schulstein, sitting on a bale of hay in a tender embrace, so handsome and happy. The *Ostjuden* are no longer outcasts. The Sznajders, the Zlotagoras, the Kaszemachers, all the immigrants from Parczew, did the necessary paperwork to obtain— successfully—their French nationality. Icek Sznajder, the man with the paint stains on his coat lining, the quintessential outcast according to the French consulate in Warsaw, was naturalized in April 1947. Isn't the world simple and beautiful?

9

THE

OTHER SIDE

OF THE WORLD

Deportee convoy no. 49 left Bourget-Drancy station on the morning of 2 March 1943. At the border town of Novéant-sur-Moselle, French gendarmes turned the convoy over to their German counterparts and headed back into France. The train rolled on through the night and into the next day, 3 March, then all night again and into the next day, 4 March, until nightfall. The deportees thus rode for sixty hours in a sealed boxcar, crowded and dark, the air thick and stale, with nothing to eat or drink, no way to lie down, and one bucket to serve as a toilet among seventy to eighty people. Since convoy no. 49 was made up mostly of elderly people, some very old, we have to assume that the boxcar floor was strewn with their dying bodies (1,000 persons were counted departing from Drancy, with only 993 at arrival).

But all that was nothing, I believe, compared to the deep, wrenching sensation that made you want to pierce the night with your screams of helplessness. Children, family, friends, people who called you by name or knew your face, the living room, the bed, the machine, your daily activities, all of that was receding, slipping further away with each rhythmic jolt of the train. It belonged to your past life now, and you were alone, in this tangled mass of bodies living on borrowed time, steeped in their misfortune and the pain of having now gone over to the other side, no longer in the world of the living, the world where people got up and went to work, and then went back to bed, thinking of tomorrow. "Oddly enough, it was the hardships, the beatings, the cold, the thirst that kept us from sinking into bottomless despair, during and after the train ride," writes Primo Levi, deported from Fossoli a year later, in February 1944. He recalls the noisy quarrels, frayed nerves, the elbowing among total strangers who had nothing in common except for their being deported together.[1] And the journey went on and on. Through gaps in the boards or the one tiny window, Matès and Idesa could watch the landscape rolling by, the stations, towns, forests. Now the convoy was crossing a plain in total darkness. The cold had a smell that tickled the nose. The train began to slow down.

Rudolf Vbra, a Slovakian Jew assigned to sorting clothes between August 1942 and June 1943, describes a nighttime arrival in Auschwitz. The SS would line up along the ramp, guns drawn, searchlights blazing. The train would come to a stop, and the doors would slide open. The deportees would be wondering whether this was just another stop along the way. Then, the orders were shouted: *Alle heraus! Los! Los!* Every few feet an armed SS officer with a guard dog, and in the background, men in striped pajamas. Clubs and insults rained down (with the occasional sarcastic "Good evening, Madame. Would you be so kind as to step down?"[2]) Who helped Anna Schwartz, seventy-two years old, to get down from the train? How had the little Kagans fared? Were my grandparents still together at this point? People looked around for their relatives and friends. The order was given to leave all personal belongings on the platform, which was soon littered with suitcases, purses, various utensils, which Rudolf Vbra and his companions then collected. Terrorized, exhausted, weak with hunger and thirst, soiled with their own excrement, the deportees had been hurled into an undecipherable universe. At the end of the platform, a German officer showed them where to line up, on the right or the left.

As Auschwitz commander Rudolf Hoess explains, this selection gave rise to a number of incidents. Separation of husbands from wives, mothers from children, spread panic among the deportees: "The families wanted to stay together at all costs." Some would rush back to the end of the line, others would try to slip in with a family member, and all this confusion only delayed the operation.[3] Convoy no. 49 was composed mainly of the sick and elderly, traumatized by the journey, so that the sorting operation probably lasted longer than usual, and the SS had to come up with ingenious reassurances to keep people calm. Then, trucks would arrive and take everyone away into the night.

The Auschwitz museum provides the following figures: out of the 993 persons who disembarked from convoy no. 49 on the night of 4 March 1943, 100 men and 19 women were selected. The other 874 were gassed immediately.[4] These never entered the camp at all, since the gas chambers were located outside the camp proper. For them, Auschwitz was a terminus where they stepped off the train to their death.

We know that Matès was not gassed upon arrival. There is such a thing as truth in history. It exists, I have found it, and I cherish this certainty. Our first piece of evidence is a letter that Chaim Herman, deported in convoy no. 49 along with Matès and Idesa, wrote on 6 November 1944 and buried near Krematorium II at Birkenau, a few days before he was murdered. This letter, an "ultimate farewell," in which he asks his wife's forgiveness for all their past disagreements and urges her to remarry, is a staggering testimony from beyond the grave, registering detail with incredible devotion: Chaim Herman's letter describes his twenty months spent in the Sonderkommando, the "special team" of Jewish detainees in charge of emptying the gas chambers and burning the bodies in the ovens. "Dante's inferno is a colossal joke compared to the real thing here, and we are eyewitnesses, not meant to survive to tell what we have seen." The syntax in the original is choppy, betraying a deep anxiety: "We have heard them talking about our own execution sometime this week. Forgive my jumbled text, and my French; if you only knew the circumstances of its writing." Chaim Herman gives details: "100 persons were selected to enter the camp, myself among them, and the rest were sent to be gassed then burned in the ovens. The next day, after a cold bath, and deprived of all our belongings (apart from a belt, which I managed to keep on my person), we had our heads and faces shaved, and were then randomly selected for the notorious 'Sonderkommando.'"[5] A crucially important piece of information, since it matches that of the Auschwitz museum: 100 men from convoy no. 49, selected upon arrival at the camp, were assigned to the "special team" at Birkenau.

In Klarsfeld's *Mémorial*, I pick out all the men of working age in convoy no. 49; not very many, because of the large proportion of elderly people. Out of the 1000 names, if we select for men aged fifteen to fifty-five, we get 143 workers. If we limit the number to men aged twenty to fifty-five, the number goes down to 104, approximately the figure given by Chaim Herman. If we reduce the spread even further, to men between twenty to forty-five, only seventy remain. The conclusion of this macabre arithmetic is that Matès, age thirty-five, was among the 100 persons "selected to enter the camp," as Chaim Herman writes, and assigned to "the notorious 'Sonderkommando,'" for Matès was the very epitome of a man in the prime of life that the Nazis were seeking out on this 4 March 1943, with the four brand-new, latest-model crematoriums in Birkenau about to come onstream.[6]

What do we know about these men? By definition, they were all deported from Drancy on 2 March and all, therefore, had been living in France. The painter David Olère was one of the rare survivors of the convoy. Remarking his talent, the SS kept him close by to have him draw flowers on their love letters or address the envelopes for them in Gothic lettering. The pictures he painted after the war give a very exact idea of what the death camps were like, from the undressing room full of naked women and children to the enormous SS soldier blocking the entrance to a gas chamber brimming with corpses.[7] Apart from Olère, a few other names have emerged in handwritten texts "from under the ashes," buried outside the crematoriums: Chaim Herman's, for example, and the one written by his friend David Lahana, a Jewish merchant from Toulouse, an exception among all those Poles and Russians. We also know that the Sonderkommando revolt, on 7 October 1944, was led by two deportees from convoy no. 49, Yankel Handelsman and Joseph Dorembus, two Polish trade unionists who had been active in Paris between the wars.

All are of the same generation: Chaim Herman was born in 1901, David Olère in 1902, Joseph Dorembus and David Lahana in 1906, Yankel Handelsman in 1908; in other words, all were between thirty-five and forty-two years old. To identify other names, one need only go back to that age spread—twenty to fifty years old—that corresponds roughly to the figure given by Chaim Herman. Apart from Matès, born in 1909, then aged thirty-four, we also come across Calel Sommer, forty-two, and Zacharie Grumberg, forty-four, whose son would write two masterpieces after the war, works full of love, humor and memory: *L'Atelier* [*The Workshop*] and *Mon père, inventaire* [*My Father, an Inventory*].[8] The tattooed serial numbers of the 100 men run from 106,088 to 106,187. Yankel Handelsman became 106,112, Chaim Herman 106,113 and the slaves that David Olère depicted in his paintings after the war bore his own number, 106,144.

A letter from Annette written in 1946 to Simje and Reizl, whom she had never met, provides a further piece of evidence. My father has brought back the relic from a trip to Argentina. Sarah translates it, and just to be sure, I have Bernard retranslate it, and he identifies the standard Yiddish of Lithuania and eastern Poland (Annette was from Maloryta, some sixty miles east of Parczew).

Dear Friends,

Matès left me your address. I received your letter, and am now replying. Unfortunately, it pains me to tell you that we have some bad news for you. The fate of your brother and his wife is that of millions of other Jews. We managed to save their dear little ones. Hopefully, you will find in them some consolation. Please accept my sincerest and most heartfelt condolences in this terrible tragedy. I am a cousin of Matès's wife. In recent years, we have grown very close to your brother and family, and shared in their hardships during the years of Nazi Occupation. But fate did not spare them. They were deported on 27 February 1943 [*sic*]. Circumstances were such that we were able to save their children and hide them in the countryside. We continued to hope that at least Matès would return, since his health was good and morale high. But to our great sorrow, we have learned that he perished. We have no news of Idesa, but there is nothing to hope for.[9]

These last two sentences confirm that Matès and Idesa both died, but not in the same way. I have Bernard repeat these lines several times, to be certain: "We have learned that he perished," *"Mir hobn bakumen a gruss,"* some news gleaned in passing, spread by word of mouth, from someone met by chance in the street, probably an Auschwitz survivor—something very different from a Red Cross notice sent through the mail.

Paris 1946: neither Idesa nor Matès had come back, but Annette managed to obtain details, even tiny ones, regarding the latter's death. In other words, there were witnesses. In the Auschwitz context, death could come individually (execution, lethal injection to the heart, typhus, exhaustion, suicide) or by group execution within the Sonderkommando (as happened to Chaim Herman, who disappeared in November 1944). Either way, somebody saw, somebody heard, somebody could make a positive statement. "We have no news of Idesa, but there is nothing to hope for." From this most negative statement emerges one certainty: Idesa died quickly. Either she disappeared in the anonymous chaos of the gas chamber, a few hours after disembarking and filing down the *Judenrampe*, which would explain why there was no witness to transmit the news to her family; or she was singled out, like Matès, and this scenario is just as plausible, since nineteen women were selected from convoy no. 49 (serial numbers 32,277 to 37,295[10]) and since that convoy included very few young women (just as it included very few young men). If we adopt the more restrictive age spread, from twenty to forty years old, the result is only eighteen names. Idesa, at twenty-eight, would have entered the camp at the same time as Rebecca Lahana, thirty-three, wife of the Toulouse manufacturer who ended up in the Sonderkommando (in his letter, Chaim Herman informs us that Mrs. Lahana "died three weeks after getting here"). I'll formulate a conjecture within a conjecture: if Idesa was not murdered in the gas chamber on the night of 4 March 1943, she lived a few more weeks, perhaps months, but no more than that. Why? Because Maria would probably have found out, one way or another.

For Maria was deported to Auschwitz with her daughter Sarah on convoy no. 75 of 30 May 1944, one week prior to the Normandy landing. Arrested on a tip-off, they were interned at Drancy where they were stripped of all their money and valuables. On the eve of departure, they were fed lies meant to appease: "You'll see, you'll like it out there, it's not like it used to be; they have modernized everything, there's electricity, bathrooms and toilets. Especially for anyone with a skill and who wants to work, you'll be much better off there than in Drancy."[11] On the sunny morning of 30 May, they packed 1,600 people into twenty or so boxcars. Maria and Sarah's last letter is full of optimism. Thrown from the train, the letter indicates two addresses—that of Carmen Torres in Blanc-Mesnil, and that of Poulot and Jascha on Rue Oberkampf—to "whoever finds this letter." Some anonymous person took pity on the two deportees and the letter was delivered safely to its addressees.

On the ramp, an SS officer, switch in hand, would point each deportee toward one or another direction, to the left or to the right. Undressing, serial numbers tattooed in ink, showers, the secret smokestacks that lit up the night sky. Dressed in filthy tunics, the mother and daughter were assigned to hard labor: terracing, road construction and railroad building. This is where Sarah would sing Edith Piaf songs to herself to keep her spirits up: "Happiness will come greet you / Wait for it, don't give up. / As long as there is life, there is hope. / Don't let the dark clouds gather, chase away those black butterflies." As the Red Army was closing in, they were evacuated from the camp and marched to Bergen-Belsen. At Liberation, they were skin and bones, under eighty pounds.

At my parents' home, as we sit and have tea together, I talk to Sarah about my grandmother. Is it possible that she was sent straight to the gas chamber at twenty-eight?

"Of course, anything is possible. If she was hurt, unable to work. In the course of her arrest, she was shot in the leg as she tried to escape."

"Who told you that?"

"I can't remember. It was something the family always said."

"Was it your father who told you?"

"No. When I got to his place in Passage d'Eupatoria that morning, he was in an utter panic, and said: 'They've arrested people! We heard the police shouting, they've taken people away!'"

And the final pillar of my certainty: in the 1980s, my father says, Maria came to the house for dinner and asked: "Would you like to meet a man who saw your father in the camp?" My father declined curtly: "I'm not interested." Maria was a bit taken aback, but kept at him: "The man who saw your father is the butcher over on Rue des Maronites. Your father was an undertaker." It was only later, after seeing Chaim Herman's letter, that my father made the connection: Herman also referred to "undertakers," a euphemism used by the Germans, or by the Sonderkommando workers themselves.

Today, Maria is no longer with us. Nor is the painter David Olère or the five other survivors of convoy no. 49. Constant and Annette are both dead. All we can do is ask Sarah about the "butcher over on Rue des Maronites." His name was Niremberg. He has been dead for many years now, but Sarah knows his daughter. Thanks to the 1936 census, I already know that he had two:

Szloma Niremberg, born in 1902, Polish, butcher
+ his wife Frajola, born in 1903, Polish
+ their children: Marie, born in 1927
      Simon, born in 1925
      Cécile, born in 1932[12]

Cécile is the one Sarah knows. Again, because I insist, my father has her tell her life story in a tearoom on Rue des Rosiers.

When Niremberg left Warsaw in 1920, he was already working as a butcher. He settled with his wife in Ménilmontant, 22 Rue des Maronites, where it intersects with Rue du Pressoir. There are other butchers on the same street, but they are all French (the only other Jewish butcher in the neighborhood is on Rue Julien-Lacroix). Arrested in May 1941 during the "green slip" raid, Niremberg was deported to Auschwitz on convoy no. 6, 17 July 1942. Of his deportation and life in the camp, Cécile can say nothing, since her father chose to keep silent after the war. All she knows is that he worked in the camp kitchens (a survival factor) and that in 1943 he was transferred to Warsaw, his native city, to clear away what remained of the ruined ghetto. During the death march, he pretended to collapse during a group execution and then remained immobile for hours, beneath the dead bodies of his comrades. After stays in various camps, he arrived in France in June 1945. His wife and three children were alive; they had been hiding out in a village in Eure-et-Loire, with the help of the local population. The butcher shop reopened and life resumed.

First question: Did Niremberg simply come upon Matès in the camp, or would he also have been the witness capable of certifying his death, though unable to say anything about Idesa? Second question: Did he ever work at the gas chambers in the Sonderkommando, or did Matès ever work in the kitchens? Third question: What is the connection between Maria, Matès and Niremberg? Here is one plausible scenario: the two men already knew each other before the war, since my grandfather was living on Rue du Pressoir in 1938, and the nearest butcher's happened to be Niremberg's, at 22 Rue des Maronites. Rue Désirée is in another neighborhood, over by Père-Lachaise, and by the time Matès came back to Ménilmontant in August 1941, to hide out in Passage d'Eupatoria, Niremberg had already been arrested. After the war, Maria set up her atelier in the alley, and Niremberg's butcher shop was one of the closest. And it was Maria who first started doing the paperwork, at Liberation, to obtain Matès's "certificate of disappearance"; she was issued a document on 28 September 1945.[13] Maria had herself just returned from deportation, and people were missing everywhere, while survivors were constantly being asked whether they knew anything about this or that deportee. It was in this context, I imagine, that the death of Matès and Idesa became a certainty for the family: Maria went to buy meat at Niremberg's, they got to chatting, swapping news, recalling the deportation years, and Niremberg, the "man who saw your father in the camp," reported what he knew, firsthand or otherwise, about Matès's death. Despite the remaining information gaps, Annette knew enough by then to write to the Argentinians in 1946: "To our great sorrow, we have learned that he perished. We have no news of Idesa, but there is nothing to hope for."

On that 4 March 1943, two convoys arrived in Auschwitz: convoy no. 33 coming from Berlin and convoy no. 49 from Drancy. The first was transporting 1,886 Jews, among them a twelve-year-old schoolgirl, Marion Samuel, arrested in Berlin with her parents on 27 February. Deportee convoys would leave Berlin-Moabit station at 17:20, to arrive in Auschwitz the next morning at 10:48.[14] On this subject, Chaim Herman writes that his convoy "left Drancy on 2 March at dawn, and we arrived here at sundown on the 4th, in a boxcar without water; as we got off, there were already some dead, others had gone mad." The two convoys arrived at Birkenau six or seven hours apart. The mass murder began in the late morning, with convoy no.

33 from Berlin. While Marion Samuel's father, selected along with over 700 other deportees, was getting tattooed and being given his pajamas and clogs, his daughter and more than 1,000 other people were being gassed in Bunker 1 or 2, set up where farms used to be on the edge of a birch forest, a mile or so from the *Judenrampe*. The trip there and the undressing process (in a cabin near the bunkers) was to take place, explains Rudolf Hoess, "as calmly as possible. . . . Above all, no screaming or disorder!"[15] To avoid scenes of panic that might slow down the pace of things, the SS would announce a schedule of activities most likely to reassure people who were utterly distraught and exhausted: disinfection in that hut over there among the trees, cups of tea for everyone, then settling into the camp. The deportees would leave the undressing hut and walk the 100 yards or so, stark naked, between the hut and the bunker. One of David Olère's paintings depicts these mothers with their children, their breasts hidden behind their crossed arms, walking through the cold autumn landscape.

As soon as the screams ceased, the Sonderkommando men would unlock the bunker doors, allow the chamber air to clear, and then drag out the victims, from whom any valuable objects, including gold teeth, were removed; their hair was shorn by barbers. The corpses were then loaded onto flatbed wagons and dumped into large ditches, where they were burned: "first, the heavy wood was placed at the bottom, then increasingly small branches, and finally, kindling. . . . Once all the corpses had been transported from the chamber to the ditches, [SS soldier] Moll poured gasoline into the four corners of the ditch, lit a rubber comb and tossed it into the area sprinkled with gasoline. The corpses would burst into flames."[16] They would have barely finished this work when, at sunset, say around 17:00 in this late Polish winter, the club-wielding SS officers began overseeing the disembarkation of Matès and Idesa Jablonka, Chaim Herman, David Olère, David and Rebecca Lahana, Joseph and Pesa Dorembus, Yankel and Chana Handelsman, Calel Sommer, Zacharie Grumberg, hundreds of elderly people and three dozen children, including the little Kagans, aged two to fourteen. One hundred men destined for the Sonderkommando were selected on the ramp, at the same time as nineteen women. The others, including all the elderly and children, were gassed at Bunker 1 or 2, whichever one had not yet been used that day.

Immediate Fate of Deportees Arriving at Auschwitz II Birkenau on 4 March 1943

Convoys	Fate of deportees upon arrival at the camp			Total
	Gassed	Selected and assigned serial numbers		
		Men	Women	
Convoy no. 33 from Berlin (arrival 10:48)	1,169 (62%)	517 (27%)	200 (11%)	1,886 (100%)
Serial numbers		105,571 to 106,087	37,296 to 37,495	
Convoy no. 49 from Drancy (arrival 17:00 approx.)	874 (88%)	100 (10%)	19 (2%)	993 (100%)
Serial numbers		106,088 to 106,187	32,277 to 37,295	
Total	2,043 (71%)	617 (21%)	219 (8%)	2,879 (100%)

SOURCE: Danuta Czech, *Auschwitz Chronicle*, 344 ff.; Götz Aly, *Into the Tunnel*, 77–80.

Over 800 persons, or roughly one third of the total, escaped immediate death. It is only the 100 men from the French convoy who were assigned to the Sonderkommando, the "special team" of the gas chambers; the 517 men from Berlin and all the women ended up in regular work commandos, involving building embankments and other forced labor. Close scrutiny of the order of the serial numbers reveals that the men deported from France were tattooed after the Berlin deportees, which makes sense chronologically, but that for the women it is just the reverse: this means that the women coming from Berlin were tattooed after the arrival of the Drancy convoy, in other words, in the evening. At that point, 88% of the deportees from France had already been murdered, and a Sonderkommando team was working to empty the gas chamber of the corpses of people who, only three days earlier, had been playing, trying to get some sleep or signaling to friends and family from the Drancy balcony. By day's end, 2,043 lives had been reduced to barrows of ashes.

One might conclude that 4 March 1943 was just another ordinary day at Birkenau. But a major innovation was about to come onstream, which was the reason why 100 men from convoy no. 49 would become "undertakers" in the Sonderkommando: the Krematorium II, prototype of a new generation of gas chambers, was to be tested there before being put into more widespread use. Why was this modernization of the death machine taking place? Bunkers 1 and 2, which had served until then, were too small: there were two chambers in the first, covering an area of roughly 970 square feet, about the size of a tennis court; and four chambers in the second, with an area of about 1,300 square feet. Zyklon B was piped in through hatches set up in the old windows and, after the victims were killed, the space was ventilated naturally, which took too much time. In addition, evacuation of the bodies was cumbersome: in Bunker 2, the corpses were taken out through a second door in back, but in Bunker 1, there was only one door per gas chamber. The corpses were loaded onto carts and taken to the cremation pits, a further expenditure of time. Bunker 2 had a gassing capacity of 1,200 persons, which corresponded to the size of the Berlin convoy, while Bunker 1, with its 800-person capacity, was better suited to the French convoy.

Commissioned by Auschwitz's construction managers, the engineers of the company Topf and Sons, based in Erfurt, came up with innovative solutions to these challenges. Krematorium II was located inside the Auschwitz II Birkenau camp, which shortened the distance the deportees had to cross. The undressing room and gas chamber, both underground, measured 3,000 and 2,300 square feet respectively. Since it took a temperature of roughly 80 degrees F for the Zyklon B crystals to enter a gaseous state, the chamber was heated ahead of time and kept sealed. Powerful electric fans dissipated the Zyklon after use, which allowed the Sonderkommando to be sent in as soon as the victims were dead. Most importantly, Krematorium II was a rationally organized unit of corpse production and destruction: underground, the undressing area communicated directly with the gas chamber, and a freight elevator hoisted the bodies up to ground level, where they were incinerated in five triple-muffle furnaces (for a total of fifteen ovens), the actual crematoriums themselves. Where Bunkers 1 and 2 were made up of disparate elements cobbled together piecemeal—an old, sealed-up farmhouse, an undressing area 100 yards away, incineration pits dug out in the woods or open-air pyres—Krematorium II was designed from the outset as an integrated factory whose purpose was to transform life into death, human beings into nothingness, in other words, to destroy as completely as possible as many people as possible in as little time as possible, maximizing the productivity of all other inputs. When run at full capacity, the Krematorium gas chamber could kill 2,000 people at once (or, for a sense of scale, 400 families of five, or eighty classrooms of twenty-five children each). Corpse disposal was what slowed down the extermination rate, for, although Topf asserted that its five furnaces could incinerate up to 1,440 bodies per day, the SS noted that its own use yielded a daily incineration rate closer to 1,000 "items." Whatever the case, Prüfer, the Nazi Topf engineer, was proud of his invention, which he had patented.[17]

Krematorium II was delivered in working order on 31 March 1943, for a total cost of half a million Reichsmarks. In the same camp sector, to the west, three other crematoriums were under construction. Krematorium III, same model as II, was up and running by 24 June. On the other side of the "Kanada" warehouses, where the victims' belongings were stored, Krematoriums IV and V were being set up, featuring several gas chambers built at ground level. Other improvements were introduced later: looking ahead to the extermination of the Hungarian Jews, in the spring of 1944, a platform was built inside the camp itself to allow trains to stop much closer to Krematoriums II and III. The Nazis did not attain this level of criminal rationality overnight: from the moment when Hitler decided, in the fall of 1941, to exterminate all the Jews of Europe, they proceeded by trial and error, figuring out how to streamline their assembly-line death machine, and the four huge Birkenau crematoriums were the monstrous end product of a series of upgrades that led from the gas vans of Chelmno to the Bełżec "laboratory," from the outmoded Auschwitz Bunker I, soon to reach its full capacity, to Treblinka's "road to heaven" where the 4,500 Jews of Parczew were led into a gas chamber in July 1942, naked and beaten into submission. All of this culminated in the "Auschwitz Album," a series of photos showing a line of little boys in caps, little girls, old women in scarves, mothers walking briskly with babies in their arms, all of them on their way to the nondescript building of Krematorium II where they would be obliterated in a few hours.

It was on that day of 4 March 1943 that the engineers of death were making their final adjustments to Krematorium II. In February, in anticipation of its start-up, twenty or so deportees had been trained to run the ovens at the Auschwitz base camp. In early March, the survivors of that team, headed by *Kapo* Morawa, were assigned to Birkenau's Krematorium II. Among them, Henryk Tauber: "On 4 March, we were assigned to get the furnaces running, which we did, from morning until about four in the afternoon." The same day, a Nazi commission was to come out and check that Krematorium II was running smoothly, and it was in anticipation of this inspection that Henryk Tauber and his companions heated up the coke-fed furnaces that supplied the ovens. Soon, the SS officials from the political section and the camp's building management arrived on the scene, flanked by top brass from Berlin and civilian engineers from Topf. Prüfer, who arrived at Auschwitz the same day to test the furnaces and work out any technical issues, was also present. The trial run began, using as its subjects forty-five "well-fed and stout" men who had been recently gassed in Bunker 2 (could they have been the victims of convoy no. 33 from Berlin?). The forty-five corpses were distributed five per vent. The SS timed the operation: forty-five minutes, much longer than expected. "Once the incineration of this first trial load was over," Henryk Tauber recalls, "the commission members left the scene." The Sonderkommando men were escorted back to their quarters, near Krematorium II.[18]

These tandem operations—the gassing of 2,043 persons in the bunkers and the fine-tuning of the far more efficient killing complex of Krematorium II—enable us to reconstitute the broad outlines of that day's mass crimes at Birkenau, 4 March 1943. This schedule of events remains uncertain, however, based as it is on a number of hypotheses and deductions, but I don't believe there are that many gaps, apart from the obvious fact that we are dealing here with gas chamber deaths only, since no one is able to account for the hundreds of murders and deaths by exhaustion and sickness, or other forms of execution that occurred among the 50,000 detainees then present at Birkenau. But here is a plausible timeline:

Around 07:00 or 08:00, a Sonderkommando team that included *Kapo* Morawa and Henryk Tauber was transferred from the base camp to Birkenau. They began to heat up the coke-driven furnaces of Krematorium II.

Over the course of the morning, Prüfer, the chief engineer of Topf and Sons, arrived at Auschwitz to make some adjustments on the Krematorium II equipment.

Around 11:00, convoy no. 33 from Berlin unloaded 1,886 people onto the *Judenrampe*. Around 500 men and 200 women were selected; the men were tattooed within a few hours of arrival and admitted into the camp.

Sometime between 12:00 and 13:00, 1,169 people from convoy no. 33 were gassed (in Bunker 2?); 12-year-old Marion Samuel was among them.

In the afternoon, the corpses of convoy no. 33 were removed from the gas chamber by a Sonderkommando squad. Forty-five male corpses were then taken to Krematorium II.

Around 16:30, a Nazi commission attended a trial incineration in the Krematorium II furnaces.

Around 17:00, at sundown, convoy no. 49 coming from Drancy unloaded 993 persons onto the *Judenrampe*. One hundred men and nineteen women were selected, among them Joseph Dorembus, Yankel Handelsman, Chaim Herman, Matès Jablonka, David and Rebecca Lahana and David Olère.

Around 17:30, the Krematorium trial run was over; Henryk Tauber and his comrades were sent back to their barracks.

Between 18:00 and 19:00, 874 persons from convoy no. 49 were gassed (in Bunker 1?); among them were Anna Schwartz, seventy-two years old, Leon Kagan, fourteen, Rachel Kagan, nine, Maurice Kagan, two and (?) Idesa Jablonka, twenty-eight.

In the evening, the corpses of convoy no. 49 were removed from the gas chamber by a Sonderkommando team. The 100 men assigned to the Sonderkommando of Krematorium II were given their serial numbers. The women of both convoys were also tattooed.

Pallid light filters through the clouds. I am facing a square of turf, the same unoriginal green grass as in the Parczew cemetery-park. Just a peaceful lawn: so, this is where they died, amid screams and suffering, panic and terror, knowing neither where they were nor how they were being killed. There remains nothing of Bunker 1, not even the foundations, not even a shadowy rectangle visible from a plane, like the outlines of Gallo-Roman farms that I could make out as I flew over the fields of Île-de-France. The Foundation for the Memory of the Shoah has sent me on one of those quick turnaround trips that starts at Roissy at five in the morning, continues on a special bus out of the Krakow airport and casts you into the camp walkways, barbed wire security zones, wooden barracks and the ruins of the Krematoriums blown up in 1944 ahead of the approaching Soviet army, all of which you have little time to visit before the return bus leaves at 4 p.m., getting you onto a plane that is back at Roissy by midnight. You eat nothing all day, you lose all sense of time and place, you return from this trip into the world of the dead and back again feeling completely drained—which is exactly how it should be.

As soon as we get there, we go straight to the platform, not the one you see in the "Auschwitz Album," built specially for the extermination of Hungarian Jews, but the old *Judenrampe*, mostly forgotten today, located outside the camp proper, on the Vienna–Prague–Krakow line. This was where the selection took place, on 4 March 1943, at nightfall, between the boxcars and the cordon of SS soldiers: one queue for immediate death, with over 700 elderly people, a few adults and thirty-five children; and the other for death by exhaustion, sickness, mistreatment or summary execution, which included my grandfather, and perhaps my grandmother, separated from their children now for over a week. As in Drancy, all that remains today is a sample boxcar, alone on the rails. The platform itself, renovated by the Foundation, is a graveled strip bordered on one side by the rails and on the other by a dirt path and a warehouse. A set of rails branches off from the main one and heads into the Birkenau camp. Following the lead of Serge Klarsfeld, who is also on this trip, we follow, step by step, the rails whose curvature can be made out in the grass and which cross through some private property before arriving at the famous brick watchtower and gate entrance. There is a hen wandering around in the brush. Too weak to walk, the elderly and the very young were taken by truck to one of the two bunkers, a mile or so away, on the other side of the camp. The cold night was closing in, strange surroundings fed the anxiety of the exhausted deportees; the undressing room, the 100 yards to get to the cottage with its friendly-looking chimney and its sign *Zur Desinfektion*. And here I am. The rustling grass is soft to my touch. Since the four new Krematoriums were working at full capacity, Bunker 1 was decommissioned by the summer of 1943 and was completely dismantled, leaving nothing today but a grassy plot. Bunker 2, on the other hand, was reactivated in the spring of 1944, when the fast rate of convoys from Hungary meant that the camp had to operate on an as-needed basis. Today, a ground-level perimeter of stones recalls the bunker's outlines, at the edge of a birch forest.

Anne-Marie, the general secretary of the Foundation, is kind enough to allow me to pose the wreath. I set it at the foot of one of the stelae set up on the lawn. The vast expanse of the plain at night, the cold, the atmosphere of bewilderment and terror, the dogs, the farmhouse walls within which they would be asphyxiated, the cyanide-based gas, all of that is gone now. Am I on a pilgrimage? The dead were not put to rest here. This is no cemetery, but a meadow, like the one in Parczew, a meadow surrounded by a fence, a hedge, a white-curtained pavilion in front of which a car is neatly parked. This is no place for contemplation. He did not die here. Perhaps she did, but her body was incinerated elsewhere, over by those birches, at a place I'm unable to locate with any precision; later, the ashes were dumped into the Sola River. I raise my eyes skyward, as did Paul Celan in his poem "Death Fugue" or André Schwarz-Bart at the close of his *The Last of the Just*. It's cloudy.

Icek Sznajder and Abram and Malka Fiszman are in the Bagneux cemetery, in the burial vault of the Society of the Friends of Parczew, this grey marble monument drenched by rain that I manage to photograph from under Colette's umbrella. Henya, the darling little sister in her beret, the intrepid gamine who handed out tracts in the middle of a meeting of revisionist Zionists, is buried in Hadera, beneath a dazzlingly white stone slab. *Tío* Simje is with Raquel and his Parczew friends Yankel and Jume, at the cemetery of the *Asociación Mutual Israelita Argentina*, where the scorching summer air is refreshed by a cloud of droplets escaping from a leaky watering hose. Simje, the eldest of the Jablonka siblings. Burgundy marble. His motto, as an epitaph: "When I lose, I win, because my children are winning." Before his grave, standing alongside his daughter Celia, I recall some highlights of his life: Parczew, Communism, sailing on the *Conte Verde* from Genoa, Buenos Aires, the wool-stuffed mattresses, the shoe shop, three children, seven grandchildren, a good father, a good grandfather. May you rest in peace, Simje, great-uncle of mine, 1904–1985. This is the best Kaddish I can manage.

But what about them, the other two? The Auschwitz museum replies that most of the archives were destroyed. The *Sterbebücher*, the death certificates filled out by the camp's political department, are woefully incomplete. Of this archival shipwreck, the lone survivor is the logbook for convoy no. 49, with its 1,000 names carefully typed out. The International Tracing Service at Bad Arolsen, created after the war to help locate "displaced persons," has nothing in its 50 million records. Nor is there anything at the Holocaust Museum in Washington, D.C. They have to be somewhere, since they are neither on earth nor in the heavens. They are printed out in Klarsfeld's *Mémorial*, in gilded letters on the wall of names at the Shoah Memorial, in digital form inside the Yad Vashem databases. Tamara, Henya's daughter, has been kind enough to engrave their names on her mother's tombstone, as if they were also there, among the cactuses of the Hadera cemetery, under the searing Israeli sun. And they are in this book that I am growing, as I stand here before this grassy meadow while the minute of silence slowly ticks by.

In the camps, in the ghettos and in the West, the very first historians of the genocide were its victims. In Birkenau, the Sonderkommando men wrote in secret. Reluctant accomplices to the crime, they resisted, up to the armed revolt of 7 October 1944, by telling the story of destruction from its very epicenter. Rather than simply giving up, overcome by despair and shame, their souls deadened by grief, these living shadows among the dead managed to snatch a few minutes of freedom, between two batches of human remains, to reach within themselves and report what they were seeing, what they were doing, to construct a narrative. Such was the clear-sightedness of Lewental, former yeshiva student who, risking everything, decided to "write down systematically a historical chronicle for the world to read; from this day forward, we will bury it underground for safekeeping" (it would be found in 1962, hidden in a glass jar near Krematorium II).[19] Such was the piety of Leib Langfus, a rabbinical judge from Maków, to whom is attributed the anonymous text about the 3,000 dead women that a vehicle dumped onto the Krematorium II grounds like a truckload of gravel.[20] Such was the prayer of Zalmen Gradowski, one of the leaders of the revolt, so that others might weep tears that his eyes could no longer shed, since "the ongoing and systematic process of annihilation of our people that I am experiencing each and every day has stifled my sense of individual misfortune, and suppressed all feeling." Before he was murdered on the day of the Sonderkommando revolt, at the age of thrity-three, Gradowski hid his manuscript near Krematorium III, whose gas chamber had served to exterminate tens of thousands of Hungarian Jews that spring. Recovered a few months after the liberation of Auschwitz, his text was not published until 1970, under the title *In Harz fun Gehenem* (*In the Heart of Hell*).[21] These manuscripts overcome three deaths—that of their authors, of the Jewish people and of Yiddish as a language—to arrive in our hands today bearing witness to the truth and removing any possibility of complacency. They represent the moral high ground, based in intelligence, selflessness and dignity that shine all the brighter in that their authors' own deaths were imminent at the time of writing. A torch cast into the abyss, they shed light into the darkest depths of the twentieth century, inextinguishable.

By 5 March 1943, it would thus appear that Matès was working as an "undertaker" in the Sonderkommando. There were "undertakers" in other Kommando units as well, working inside the camp. This was the job of Moshe Garbarz, deported to Auschwitz in July 1942: "We pick up the corpses in front of the barracks, but instead of transporting them on boards, we, the newly arrived, are supposed to carry them on our backs: their backs against ours, their heads dangling down, their knees bent over our shoulders, their calves against our chests. We hold their feet somewhat like the straps of a backpack."[22] The more senior workers, like Mayer Szyndelman, deported in the first Drancy convoy, were given a *veyguele*, a kind of stretcher on wheels, where they could pile up the bodies. Every evening, each team would bring in three dozen or so, which the trucks would then send over to the crematoriums at night.[23] The *Begrabungskommando* (or burial commando) was in charge of the digging and filling of burial pits in the wooded zones. André Balbin, a Polish Jew born in 1909, a tailor in Nancy, deported to Pithiviers in 1942, was working a variety of hard labor jobs before he was assigned to this "undertaker Kommando." The eighty detainees of his team were in charge of burying the corpses delivered on the carts, laying them "head to foot, like sardines." They would also dig pits and leave them empty, to be filled with gassing victims overnight. In this sense, the *Begrabungskommando* could be seen as an auxiliary to the Sonderkommando.[24]

Like Chaim Herman and the men selected from convoy no. 49, Matès worked in "the notorious Sonderkommando," the one that operated directly in the gas chambers. But in March 1943, there were still two kinds of gas chambers: the bunkers still in operation, and the Krematoriums then under construction. The deportees assigned to the bunkers had to first separate the intertwined bodies, children clinging to their mothers, then remove any valuables, load the still warm corpses onto carts, and unload them at the other end before incinerating them. Straight off convoy no. 49, the painter David Olère worked digging burial pits for bunker 2 before being transferred to Krematorium III. We can easily imagine that Matès got handed the same assignments, starting with one or the other bunker. In this case, he may have been the one to throw his wife's body onto the pyre.

But the large crematoriums were nearly ready by that point. In Krematorium II, after the trial run for the Nazi experts, further tests were conducted starting on 10 March 1943: heating and deaeration of the gas chamber, piping in the Zyklon B, venting, etc. By 13 March, the ventilation system was ready. August Brück, a furnace operations specialist for Topf, had just arrived from Buchenwald, to be named *Kapo* of Krematorium II. The engineers had barely finished their final trials when the array was put to the test on the night of 13 to 14 March, on a convoy of 1,492 women, children and elderly men coming from the Krakow ghetto.[25] From the roof, four SS soldiers wearing gas masks poured Zyklon B crystals down the mesh-covered chute into the chamber; in the heated atmosphere, the crystals became gas and killed the people inside. As soon as the cries had ceased, the ventilators started up. Within fifteen to twenty minutes, the Sonderkommando men entered the chamber and began their work. Unless he had been assigned to the bunkers, Matès had to have been one of them.

In *Shoah*, Filip Müller tells of his initiation into the old crematorium of Auschwitz I, in May 1942, after a gassing: "Nothing made sense anymore. It was like a blow to the head, as if I had been struck by lightning. I didn't even know where I was! How was it possible to kill that many people at once?" He set about undressing the corpses (the SS had not yet invented the ruse about undressing for showers), but a guard rushed up and ordered him to go "poke the bodies" with a long iron rod. "I was in a state of shock at that point, as if hypnotized, ready to execute any and all orders. I had gone literally mad, I was so horrified."[26] Work in the large crematoriums of Birkenau, however rationalized, was not fundamentally different. At the exit to the chamber, the bodies were relieved of their hair, rings and other jewelry and gold dental work, and sent to the ground floor on a freight elevator and dragged over to the ovens. To make the Sonderkommando's job go more smoothly, the crematorium engineers set up a kind of slide filled with water along one wall, which one can clearly see in one of David Olère's drawings. One of his other pictures shows a *shleper* (a "dragger") hauling a woman using a cane or a belt: the detainee—Matès or another— is frighteningly thin, bent over like an old man, while the woman's body looks young and healthy. In his manuscript, Gradowski describes a similar scene: "We will drag her, this lovely young blossom here, along this cold, filthy cement floor. And her body will mop up all the mire in its path."[27] Other members of the team, equipped with metallic stretchers, would in- sert the bodies into the oven opening, poking them into the furnace. The incineration of 1,492 bodies took two days.

The profanation and destruction of bodies are part of the genocide. "Now," writes Chaim Herman in a letter, "they have told us that we were brought in to work as undertakers, or as *Chevra Kadisha.*" *Chevra Kadisha*? What are these words doing here, which in Aramaic mean "the brother- hood of the final duty"? In traditional Jewish society, the *Chevra Kadisha* handles mortuary rites: combing the deceased's hair, cutting his nails, wrapping him in his fringed prayer shawl, making sure he is safe from flies or rats, reciting psalms at his bedside, placing him whole in his shroud (without, for example, removing any prostheses). And finally comes the burial itself, since cremation is strictly forbidden by Jewish law. The carts sent along the road into Parczew in 1940 to collect Jewish soldiers killed by the Germans attest to the consideration owed them in death. For the soul of the *bar-menan* (he who is no longer among us) is not dead, only the body is gone. The tragic irony of the expression *Chevra Kadisha* as used by the men of the Sonderkommando expresses their despair at having to contribute to this ultimate negation: destroying hundreds of thousands of their fellow Jews while violating Judaism's most sacred rites. Ever the

Communist, Matès probably cared little about heeding ancient funeral laws, but this son of a Kabbalist, raised in a traditional milieu, must surely have realized that these counter-rituals of humiliation and profanation were sounding the death knell of European Judaism.

And the deadly routine began. Krematorium II sat idle until 20 March 1943, the date on which 2,191 Jews from Salonica were gassed. The super-heated ovens, working straight through from the 20th through the 22nd, caused a fire to break out. After minor repairs, the crematorium came onstream officially on the 31st. As regards the men of convoy no. 49, we know that Joseph Dorembus, Yankel Handelsman and David Lahana were assigned to Krematorium II, and that Chaim Herman and David Olère worked at III. By spring 1943, there were 400 men in the Sonderkom-mando. Isolated from the other detainees of Birkenau, they were housed in sector BIb, in the vicinity of Krematorium II, and then, starting in July 1943, in block 13 of sector BIId, which meant they were practically living on site, at the workplace. Living conditions were appalling. Chaim Her-man writes: "At first, I suffered a lot from our famine-like conditions, and would dream of a scrap of bread even more than hot coffee; every week, several fellow workers die of illness or are killed." Block 13, surrounded by a wall with a watchtower, was divided into boxes occupied by bunks where men slept five to a level. The barrack was heated by two stoves fac-ing each other at the entrance; many detainees went without covers and slept right on the wooden planks. Despite all that, Matès and his fellow crew members lived better than the other Birkenau detainees, not least because they could recover food and clothing left behind in the gas cham-ber undressing room. The sick got sent to a quarantine area where they were treated by a doctor from Paris, who made use of the medications left behind by the victims (he himself would be murdered in November 1943).[28] Perhaps my grandfather died during this period, an anonymous death among all those who "die of illness or are killed" every week.

In the spring of 1944, with convoys arriving from Hungary in rapid succession, the Sonderkommando men noticed an improvement in their living conditions. Chaim Herman: "We have lots of everything (except our freedom), I'm well-clothed and fed, in good health, trim and athletic, no paunch, and were it not for my white hair, you'd say I was thirty."

Yakov Gabbay, deported from Athens, arrived at the camp on 11 April 1944 and was assigned to Krematorium II with other Greek Jews; he described there being cakes, meat, sausage and even alcohol, with a whole range of warm clothing, lined trousers, wool undershirts, jackets, caps, overcoats. They worked twelve-hour shifts, day and night. At 06:00, roll call was taken for the morning crew that was starting its day and the night crew that was finishing (each made up of roughly eighty-five men). In the evening, they ate, drank and sang, the German guards sometimes joining in. Lights out between 22:00 and 23:00.[29] Gradowski, also assigned to Krematorium II, declares that all his needs were met, but a full stomach, a warm stove and one's own bunk could not erase the monstrosity of their daily existence. The two went hand in hand: it was because they were expected to be sturdy and energetic in their servitude that the Sonderkommando men were privileged compared to the other detainees.

Here were some of their chores:

—Extracting the dead from the gas chambers. Filip Müller, assigned to Krematorium V, survivor of the five mass killings of Sonderkommando crews: "The most awful moment was the opening of the gas chamber, the unbearable sight: people, pressed like basalt, like compact blocks of stone, and how they would come apart once outside the chambers!"[30] Since the bodies were slippery, they had to use rags, ropes or canes to pry them apart.

—Incinerating the corpses. Henryk Tauber, assigned to Krematorium II and then IV, describes the modus operandi: two of the crew would place a corpse on the stretcher, then another, head to toe, then as many child corpses as would fit, usually five or six. Two other crew members would stand on the side by the oven, near the bar underneath the stretcher; they would open the oven door and position the wheels. A fifth crew member, at the other end of the stretcher, would tilt it with the help of the first two and slip it into the oven. Once the corpses were inside, a sixth person would hold them back with a pitchfork while the fifth withdrew the stretcher, which was then sprinkled with soapy water, so that the bodies would slide more easily. Body fat fed the combustion, but when *"Musulmann"* bodies—emaciated, lacking fat—were being incinerated, the fires had to be stoked.[31]

—Removing the pelvic bones that were only partially burned, and grinding them; collecting the ashes spit out of the ovens (less than two pounds per body) in a wheelbarrow; taking them out to the courtyard; loading them onto a truck that came regularly to pick up this "fish food," as the SS called it.[32]

—Sometimes, earlier in the process, the Sonderkommando crew would accompany victims along the way or calm them down in the undressing room. Shlomo Venezia, who arrived at Auschwitz on 11 April 1944, stood in front of a mother with her two daughters so that they could undress in relative privacy.[33] In October 1944, Yakov Gabbay sat and chatted with cousins of his before they entered the gas chamber.[34]

Tragically dehumanized, brainwashed and exhausted, these men: you got used to it, as survivors subsequently report to historians, you acted like a robot. Chaim Herman never got used to it, though: "Dante's inferno is a colossal joke compared to the real thing here." Dante, Bosch and Michelangelo depicted refined tortures, giant bats devouring sinners, demons clinging to the heels of the damned. A failing of human imagination, which can conceive of nothing but "colossal jokes." Hell was here at Birkenau: a factory assembly line where men who were themselves on death row destroyed hundreds of thousands of lives. Any refusal to comply meant immediate execution. André Balbin, a member of the *Begrabungskommando*: "There was a lot of 'turnover.' It seems they had the privilege of being burned alive in the ovens or being gassed ahead of time. It was up to them."[35] By the summer of 1944, for the extermination of Hungarian Jews, the numbers of the Sonderkommando had risen to 900 men, the largest it got.

Distant cousins of mine in Ramat Yohanan are troubled when I refer to Yoyne Jablonka's role in the Parczew *Judenrat*. Some are ashamed to admit that even some vague uncle would have had dealings with the Germans, or that their grandfather had been close to a Vichy minister. My own grandfather burned Jews. Not because he chose to, that much is certain; he would meet his end in the same inferno. In this moral terra incognita, the mind is staggered, but I keep moving forward, obsessed by one question: did Matès take part in this evil? Does he have a share of responsibility, however tiny, for the century's madness? Primo Levi writes that the invention of the Sonderkommando is the Nazis' "most demonic crime":

they transferred onto the victims the burden of their own infamy, and succeeded in damning the souls of innocents before annihilating them. But Levi, a survivor who went only to Auschwitz III Buna-Monowitz, comes down rather hard on the Sonderkommando men, whom he describes as the most pathetic creatures of the "grey zone": alcoholic brutes devoid of so much as a glimmer of human dignity, shunned in disgust by the other deportees.[36] Georges Wellers has a different response: "The author of these lines, who experienced the hell of Auschwitz, says in all sincerity that these wretches deserve nothing but our pity."[37]

As for me, I'm wavering. Contemplating this nadir of the human condition makes my head spin: I have to wonder what a leftist militant whose dream was to build a better world, to bring about a society free from oppression, and who was willing to spend several years in prison defending this ideal, could feel as he watched unsuspecting mothers and children entering a gas chamber, people whose bones he would soon be pounding into dust. With Idesa, with his brothers and sisters, his KPP comrades, he had imagined the world to come; and now it had come, this was it. In the "rope regiments" of the Foreign Legion, he had risked his life to save future generations; and this is what had become of the future generations. And again, I wonder what happens to the liberating energy, the lust for life of a thirty-four-year-old man, when he is forced to channel all that drive into a criminal act. Was it possible for him to refuse, when it meant instant death? Weren't these *Totenjuden*, the "Jews of death," as they were called in Treblinka, the ultimate victims, the pawns of cynicism and cruelty, innocents in the midst of a crime perpetrated by those who would go on to murder them once they had been thoroughly exploited? Isn't the struggle to survive, even in the midst of genocide, a form of resistance? "You hated death," writes Lanzmann, "and in its kingdom, you have sanctified life absolutely."[38] Chaim Herman's letter, a summary of twenty months spent in the Sonderkommando, suggests that one could do this work while keeping faith, and remaining human: "If you are living, you will read quite a bit about this sonder commando, but I ask only that you do not think ill of me, for if there were both good and bad among us, I was certainly not one of the latter." Matès did not take part in evil; he was destroyed by it.

At night, I sketch out a typology of the possible fates that might have befallen Matès, between the moment the boxcars were opened at the *Judenrampe*, in the twilight of 4 March 1943, and his death, seen by an eye-witness and reported after the war to Maria or Annette. For he did die there, in the end. There were countless ways it could have happened: a typhus epidemic was raging at the camp at the time of their arrival; on 9 March 1943, two Sonderkommando fugitives were executed after being hunted down in a forest near the Vistula; on 24 February 1944, 200 Sonderkommando men were sent to Majdanek to be killed (among them, David Lahana); two fresh waves of executions took place in late September 1944; during an uprising, hundreds of detainees were slaughtered.[39] I am tempted to think that Matès was already dead when Maria and Sarah got to the camp, in June 1944; otherwise, they would have heard from him. And Niremberg the butcher on Rue des Maronites, "the man who saw your father in the camp," did he witness his death? At the camp, Niremberg worked in the kitchens; the Poles would bully him and prevent him from eating, so that he ended up in the block 12 infirmary, where he became a "*Musulmann*," but he got his strength back and survived, in the end.[40] Perhaps he witnessed Matès's final hours in block 12. Or conversely, Matès may well have been sent to the kitchens to fetch the Sonderkommando's meals, like the Dragon brothers.

All of these scenarios would make sense, whether murder, typhus, exhaustion, suicide or botched escape, but the truth is that his life and my narrative have no end: Matès ceased to be, his life unraveled like the scraps of flesh that mixed with the earth in the burial pits; he is no longer of this world. In truth, there is no truth, no place, no deed, only a no-man's-land between life and nonlife, a sudden absence, a vanishing that no one realized until the war was over: Matès Jablonka was no longer there. 1909–1943, or 1909–1944, no one knows which. But that's an unimportant detail, since there is no marble in which to engrave those dates anyway, and the only document we have is a pathetic death certificate that has him dying "in Drancy (Seine)."[41] Was he killed for some random reason? Did he believe that fascist capitalism was bent on destroying him for being a Communist, or was it Hitler's anti-Semitism that wanted to be rid of him as a Jew or was it simply human self-destructiveness? Did he go into death with his eyes wide open?

I imagine Matès sliding into despair. The man of iron finally gives up. His legendary cheerfulness—"he sings, and everywhere he goes, folks sing along"—dying away like candlelight at dawn. The *Kapo* beating him mercilessly, but he hardly feels it anymore. In his manuscript, Gradowski pleads with his virtual readers to shed a few tears over his family: my mother, my two sisters, my wife, my brother-in-law, "this is my family, incinerated here on Tuesday 8 December 1942, at nine in the morning."[42] David Lahana, the merchant from Toulouse deported on convoy no. 49, talks about nothing but his family, repeating as he goes: "Lord, Lord, why do you make me suffer like this, have mercy, mercy . . ."[43] Like them, Matès must be seeing in his mind's eye his mother baking bread, his father reciting the Canticle of Canticles on the eve of the Sabbath, majestic and luminous in his satin caftan, Simje and Reizl making a new life across the Atlantic, little Henya imprisoned at only seventeen, Hershl, Gitla, the half-brothers. In the empty corridor of the crematorium, inside its cement walls, he speaks a name aloud: Idesa. He sees the kerosene shop where she timidly enters with her plate of herring and potato pancakes. He unbraids her heavy hair, he listens to the baby moving in her belly, and when he wakes, it takes a moment to realize it was only a dream, all of that is over now. "We are leaving with no provisions or effects, but this is hardly our concern. All our thoughts go out to the children," writes Matès on his postcard from Drancy. Where are they today, who is looking after them? Have they been killed, like the thousands of other children, blond or dark-haired, once full of life, whose crushed bodies we drag out of the gas chamber and deliver to the ovens, piled atop their mothers? Like Gradowski, perhaps stretched out on the opposite bunk, Matès is watching the opalescent moon: it is hideously beautiful, russet, indifferent to these restless insects doomed to disappear. Matès feels his mind is coming apart, cracked with visions. There are no more free men on this earth.

Matès works mechanically now, pupils dilated, hair sticky with soot. His fingers grip the bodies of Jews, flaccid and heavy. Head down, he avoids their fixed gaze that once looked to a future. He is trembling despite the incandescent furnace, he drinks brandy stolen from the dead. In his chronicle hidden away in a glass jar, Lewental writes: "More than one of them reached such a low point that we felt shame for them."[44] Matès's broken spirit is likewise adrift. Revolution in Poland, a classless society, the end to oppression, what a joke! His illusions burst one by one, like so many bubbles. His life is a failure, start to finish, a grotesque fiasco, a pathetic laugh. It's the story of a Jew who stopped being a Jew, a saddler who wanted to save the world, a *schlimazel* unable to find his place in the sun. Destroyed by fascism, but first cast out like rubbish by the bourgeois states of Europe, Pilsudski's penal code, National Security and the laws of the French Republic. Small-time legionnaire, weaponless, crouching in trenches as panzers rumbled through the forests of Villers-Cotterêts . . . Stand up! This is your place, at *Chevra Kadisha*: a Jew incinerating other Jews.

"We continued to hope that at least Matès would return, since his health was good and morale high," writes Annette in 1946 in her letter to the Argentinians. After our walk through the ruins of Caesarea, with its toppled stones still glowing red despite the centuries, Tamara evokes her mother's sadness in Kowel after the war. Henya doesn't understand why her brother never returned after the war. For her, it was worse than a mutilation. That dimwit Hershl somehow managed to survive, didn't he? Wasn't Matès the *mamzer*, the smart guy, the clever one who wasn't afraid of anything? He defended his father when they wanted to close his bathhouse, he hung banners in the middle of the night while the policemen's backs were turned. Even in prison, he sang to the glory of the great Soviet Union, he chided the Jews who would sway in prayer, he wrote to high-level Polish authorities to complain that their prison gruel was inedible and their bread full of sand.

But he did not return.

His death haunted Henya. She spoke about it relentlessly to whomever would listen. She strained to understand. Why didn't he come back? Why didn't he come back? At last, after years of self-torture, she finally found an explanation, or at least, one that would ease her pain: Matès could easily have escaped from the train, or from the camp, but he stayed for Idesa's sake. He could just as easily have resisted the cold and hunger, sickness and beatings, the selections. But once she was incinerated, he had no more reason to live, so he just gave up. That's the only way you can defeat a *mamzer*, a KPP fighter, a hero of our times. Simje and Reizl also spoke often of their brother, always with great respect. In the 1970s, the siblings, bereft of their best, their bravest and cheeriest, came briefly together in Buenos Aires. No sooner had he got off the plane than Hershl started complaining: he wasn't happy in Baku, there was no money, and the shops were all empty. His brother quickly put him in his place: "Matès had a hard life, not you!" In letters confiscated by the police in 1934, believing it was for Matès's own good, Simje suggested that maybe it was time for his brother to settle down, "do you understand what I mean?" Forty years later, did he regret those words? Or was he actually right? "Why am I still alive?"

Matès works in silence, bravely. Don't think, don't see, just tell yourself that another day's end is another day gained. He is going to save his skin, he won't leave two orphans behind. Only the strong survive, that's the way of the world. Dradowski: "The survival instinct brewing in each of us became our opium."[45] Soviet cannon thunder in the distance. Victory is nigh.

Matès resists. Good health, high morale. He encourages his fellow detainees. During work, he focusses on the memory of good times in Parczew, his craftsmanship, his sharp tools, the red banners of May Day, the smell of earthen weights in a kiln, the feel of handcuffs against his wrists, the dizzy light-headedness after three days of hunger strike, all of that comes back to him with incredible force. Before falling asleep each night, he tries to picture the scenes of his life in the greatest possible detail: Broad Street, Church Street, the leatherworkers union, the Parczew prison, and all the other jail cells he knew—Lublin, Wronki and Sieradz— then on to Paris, Ménilmontant, Rue des Couronnes, Rue du Pressoir, the Santé and Fresnes prisons, the Père-Lachaise, Rue Désirée, the Clignancourt barracks, La Valbonne, the Barcarès camp, Missy-aux-Bois, Pont-sur-Yonne, Châteaumeillant, the Septfonds camp, Passage d'Eupatoria, the Belleville police station, Drancy, no matter where he was, he struggled on, blessing these places with his undying faith in his cause, his will to change the world. His mind swims upstream all the way to the source: revolt!

Matès becomes good friends with the other Polish Jews in the Sonderkommando. And there are a lot of them, several dozen from his convoy alone. Yakov Gabbay, assigned to Krematorium II in April 1944, recalls Greek, Russian and Polish Jews, and adds: "At the ovens with me, there were also Polish Jews who had immigrated to France. They spoke French, and had been arrested by the Germans back in France."[46] Who will ever know their names? Matès spots his Party comrades among them, and they help one another. Even in the depths of hell, the brave never submit. Jean Améry, a deportee at Auschwitz III Buna-Monowitz, speaks with a blend of admiration and disgust when "Marxists unswervingly characterized the SS as the police force of the bourgeoisie and the camp as the natural product of capitalism." These diehards "held Marxist discussions on the future of Europe or they simply persevered in saying: the Soviet Union must and will win." Catholics, orthodox Jews, and Communists, all in the same boat: each group harnessing its own fanaticism to escape the camp's suffering and terror.[47] By 1944, the Red Army's success was rekindling hope among the de-tainees; and perhaps Matès was even alongside Gradowski when the Czech women marched down to the gas chamber singing "The Internationale."

By the summer of 1943, a core of resistance had formed in the Sonderkommando, prompted by the *Kapo* Kaminski, in tandem with Gradowski, Langfus, Lewental, Dorembus and Handelsman. This latter group, all Polish Jews who had immigrated to France, were experienced in the art of underground struggle. Born at the turn of the century into a working-class family, Joseph Dorembus was a leatherworker. In Warsaw, he was a militant in trade unions close to the Party. A refugee in Paris, he worked under the pseudonym Warszawski in the Jewish interunion com-mittee and took part in founding the Jewish Popular Movement in 1935. After fighting in the Legion in 1940, he returned to occupied Paris and or-ganized acts of sabotage in factories that worked for the Germans. Yankel Handelsman, his friend, had a job at the *Naye Presse*. In 1941, he led the strike by Parisian glovers.[48]

Joseph Dorembus and Yankel Handelsman were deported with their wives on convoy no. 49 on 2 March 1943, the same time as my grand-parents. A portrait of Dorembus by Lewental: "A very intelligent man, blessed with an excellent character and a cool head, but what a fiery, com-bative spirit he had!"[49] It wasn't long before Dorembus and Handelsman had joined the core of resistance inside the Sonderkommando; after *Kapo* Kaminski's murder in August 1944, they took it over. The group supplied food and medication to camp detainees, financed the Auschwitz resistance with the victims' money, networked with Polish resistance outside the camp, managed to leak photographs of the gassing of some women in Krematorium V and stored explosives that young women working in a munitions factory had smuggled out at huge risk to their own lives. But the uprising was forever delayed. In June 1944, the Nazis got wind of the plot and kept the Sonderkommando locked in the crematorium compounds day and night. The movement also lost momentum when the members failed to stick together over how to proceed, with the non-Jewish resisters advocating that they hold out as long as possible, while the Sonderkommando Jews knew they could be killed at any moment. Other obstacles impeded preparations: the general climate of violence and terror; the constant shifting of personnel; the language barrier (Dorembus and Handelsman had the advantage of speaking Yiddish, Polish, German and French); and finally, the sheer fatigue, dehumanization and moral degradation of their daily existence. Against that background, concludes former deportee Georges Wellers, and in light of the utter abandonment of the Jews by the outside world, the fact that any revolt was able to break out among Sonderkommandos in Treblinka, Sobibor, Chelmno and Birkenau was nothing short of a miracle.[50]

On 7 October 1944, a month and a half after the liberation of Paris, the men of Krematoriums II and IV rose up. While hundreds of detainees fled into the woods, Langfus and Handelsman stayed behind to blow up Krematorium IV. "Who can even begin to appreciate the generous hearts of these comrades, the heroism of their acts?" writes Lewental three days later. "It is our finest who perished, our dearest, and with dignity in both life and death." Dorembus, Langfus and Gradowski were executed along with 450 other members of the Sonderkommando.[51] In my parents' living room, eyes straight ahead, voice steady, Sarah relives this day for us: early October, she was working with her mother in a satellite camp, a mile or so from Birkenau. Throughout the day, gunfire could be heard. On the way back from work, around 17:00, they saw corpses strewn on either side of the road: both Germans and striped pajamas. Back at the camp, everyone knew that the Sonderkommando men had staged a revolt. Some fugitives took refuge in a barn near where Maria and Sarah worked, and were later dragged out like rabbits from their warrens.

Events then took place in rapid succession:

—10 October, Lewental wrote his chronicle and buried it in a glass jar.

—Late October, there were only 200 detainees remaining in the Sonderkommando.

—6 November, Chaim Herman wrote and buried his "ultimate fare-well" letter; out of the 100 men selected from convoy no. 49, only two were still alive. "I am now in the last crew of 204 persons, they are cur-rently destroying Krematorium II, where I am at present, with great inten-sity of purpose, and we have heard them talking about our own execution sometime this week. Forgive my jumbled text, and my French; if you only knew the circumstances of its writing."

—Late November, Himmler gave the orders to dismantle the Birkenau crematoriums.

—Late November, Chaim Herman and Zalmen Lewental were executed.

I have no evidence that my grandfather took part in this slave revolt, nor can I say for sure that he did not. I may well be the grandson of one of the twentieth century's great heroes, since Matès Jablonka bears an uncanny resemblance to the uprising's leaders, particularly to Joseph Dorembus, Polish leatherworker, Communist in his thirties, deported on convoy no. 49 after living as a refugee in Paris. But the frontier between plausibility and fantasy is easily blurred.

Final hypothesis. Clinging to life, dazed and feral, deeply depressed, linked to the network of resistors, Matès is all of that. But he dies of ty-phus before the moment to act arrives; or he is murdered; or who knows what else.

That's all. My research has come to an end. I sit at the breakfast table this morning, my eyes stinging, haggard. My investigation has brought me no peace. I can now look their life and death squarely in the face, but I will always remain that little boy lying in his tomb, his devoted gods watch-ing over him. Their death flows in my veins, not like a poison but like life itself. For my daughters, I dream something different: to proclaim the dignity of a man and a woman whose death was a milestone, not a destiny. For me, it's too late.

Living in the past, this past in particular, can drive one around the bend. But the real cause of my sleepless nights is my own failure. In the course of this research, which had me digging through some twenty different archives, meeting all sorts of witnesses, which took me to Poland, Israel, Argentina and the United States, reading texts in Yiddish, Hebrew, Polish, Spanish, English and German, I gave my very best, as a grandson and a historian, drawn to the flame of truth whose power we hope in vain will cauterize our wounded hearts. I did not strive for objectivity—the word means little, for we are stuck in the present, enclosed within ourselves—but rather for a radical honesty, and this kind of transparency with regard to the self implies both rigorous distancing and total investment. This twofold need to say "I" and to avoid the overwrought, lachrymose tone that the circumstances might well justify, the duty to make known both my certainties and my doubts, my hunches and my dead ends, make my work come across as intransigent, not unlike the way I imagine my grandfather to have been. There is no point setting up dichotomies between scientific rigor and personal engagement, between observable facts and the passion of those who record them, between history and the art of storytelling. Emotion derives not from pathos or from amassing superlatives, but from our striving for truth. This is the touchstone of a literature that fulfills the requirements of the historian's method.

And yet, I am left empty-handed. I know nothing of their deaths, and precious little about their lives. They were saddler and seamstress, revolutionaries in Yiddishland, persecuted for what they were and what they did, right to the bitter end of their time on earth. I am a Parisian researcher, a social democrat, borderline bourgeois. My assimilated Franco-Jewishness versus their conspicuous Judeo-Bolshevism. We have no language in common. But this is not the only reason I am banished to the fringe of their lives. One need only take one's self as an example to sense the inadequacy of what I was hoping to achieve: the sum of all our acts does not reveal who we are, and a few randomly collected ones reveal nothing at all. After all my gathering, shuffling, comparing and stitching together, I still know nothing. My only consolation is that I did my very best.

I was a historian when, at the age of seven or eight, I gazed in terror at an astronomy book that predicted the destruction of the earth by the sun a million years from now. You mean, nothing of ours will be left, our house, our street, our books and even our graves?

I am a historian, like Aeneas fleeing Troy in flames, carrying his father on his shoulders.

I am a historian to repair the world.

Repairing the world, *tikkun olam* in Hebrew. Am I also one of those "non-Jewish Jews," as radical as their forefathers in their all-consuming search for truth? This book expresses my loyalty to Judaism, I who speak no Yiddish and honestly couldn't care less about celebrating Passover. This is the only Judaism that has meaning for me, along with that of memory and study. None of us, neither my grandparents, nor my father nor myself, was "born Jewish," and the commemorative plaque at the entrance of my daughters' elementary school ought not to support that sort of identification: "Murdered because they were born Jewish." Obviously, my family and I are the ones who get shoved into the gas chambers, but it is also you and your children, you and your mother, your brother, your grandchildren. Why you? I don't know, but it is you, too. And you suffer for no reason, and you die before your time, leaving nothing behind but a medical or military record, some unimportant correspondence and a handful of photographs in an album or on a Facebook account. My personal history says nothing about Jews, much less about "Jews who suffered so much." No one in my family goes to synagogue. What possible connection did Matès and Idesa share with Parczew's venerable Jewish elders who wanted them thrown in prison for their impiety, or with the upstanding middle-class Parisian Jews, so appalled by the lumpen masses arriving from the East, other than that all of them, without distinction, were locked into the same boxcars and sent away to their deaths? But if we consider only their demise, we are adopting the executioner's point of view.

I focus on my family because they symbolize a whole generation. Because they were greater than themselves. With reference to what, exactly? Their march from the shtetl to the West? Their tragedy of being caught between Stalin and Hitler? A love story shattered by the Shoah? The life and death of a Sonderkommando slave? A biography of my grandparents? Such descriptors are at best reductive, at bottom untruthful, denying each person's multiplicity and personal agency. When I say "Jews," I am locking my grandparents into the identity bind that they spent their lives trying to escape in order to embrace universal values. When I say "my grand-mother," everyone thinks of a white-haired, bespectacled granny who sits me on her knee to read fairytales; but Idesa died at twenty-eight, and I am already older than she ever was. The longer I live, the more I will have to protect her, to keep watch over the eternal flame of her youth. Because of the splash of color they add, we can't help noticing poppies that dot our otherwise uniform wheat fields, but we rarely bother smelling or gathering them; as it happens, they have no fragrance, and their uneven petals scatter at the first breath of wind. When it comes to my field of knowledge, I haven't gathered much.

I'll never know if they would have been as proud of me as I am of them. Their lives were a string of unfulfilled dreams, but they never gave in, never gave up. Their drive toward emancipation carried them well beyond themselves. My own revolt, a timid one indeed, rises up against silence and oblivion, against the way of the world, indifference and triviality. My research has reached an end, as did their lives. But this ending is also a deliverance, for they can now return to what they were always destined to be, two beings meant, irreducibly and beyond all measure, to live. At this juncture, as we part ways, I want to tell them how much I love them, how often I think of them, how I admire the lives they led, their banner of freedom held so high, and how indebted I am to them, for if I can live in a peaceful and prosperous France today, it is thanks to them—even if they might have seen things differently. I want them to know how much I would have liked to know them, with their odd accents and strangely old-fashioned gifts, their wondrous stories. I would like them to learn the next chapter, that their children were naturalized French after the war, and that their grandchildren—my cousin, my brother and I—all have postgraduate degrees, proving that the Republic has shown a face different from the one they knew. I am getting on a plane tonight for Buenos Aires.

In June 1943, Kurt Gerstein, the SS officer in charge of delivering gas to the camps, expressed his concern to the manufacturer, the director of Degesch, the German pest control company, about "the cruelty of such a procedure": "The sufferings [of the victims] which he observed were due to the irritant contained in Zyklon as it is generally sold."[52] But Marion Samuel, old Anna Schwartz and the little Kagans are no longer here. They were killed not in the way a human being is killed—shot, strangled or beheaded—but in the way lice are crushed or dirty bedding is disinfected. In Vasily Grossman's *Life and Fate*, the doctor Sofiya Osipovna, barefoot on slick, cold concrete, dies wrapped around a little boy. The air they are breathing is not life-giving, but life-taking, and the child's head grows limp—thrown back like the head of a rag doll.[53] In *The Last of the Just*, Ernie Levy has just enough time to shout to the terrorized children: "Breathe deeply, my lambs, and quickly!"[54] But one wonders whether these fictional scenes are much help to us today.

On the other hand, from Kurt Gerstein's letter, we learn that death by Zyklon B causes horrible suffering. A number of testimonies suggest that the victims struggled at the end to breathe one last gasp of oxygen: when the chambers were opened after a gassing, says Shlomo Venezia, "you could find people whose eyes hung out of their sockets because of the struggles the organism had undergone. Others were bleeding from everywhere, or were soiled by their own excrement, or that of other people."[55] In the Krematorium II gas chamber that Henryk Tauber and his fellow workers entered one day in March 1943, the heat inside was stifling. The bodies had all turned a pink color, with greenish patches, blood flowing, mouths foaming. Some died crushed, before the gas had even taken effect. Others looked like statues, eyes wide open.[56]

At the time convoy no. 49 was arriving at Birkenau, corpses were no longer being dumped into pits (the so-called "swimming pools") but burned on open-air bonfires. Human fat would flow into a second trench, where it would be recovered to pour onto the fire to accelerate combustion. If my grandmother was not gassed on arrival, she died of illness or exhaustion in the camp, or had become a "*Musulmann*" and was sent to her death in a gas chamber, which means that her body was incinerated either in a pit or in an oven.

I'm taking one last look at the group portrait of their younger years in Parczew. At seventeen or eighteen, she is at the peak of her beauty. There is mystery in her gentle gaze, in her entire being; her hair falls onto her shoulders in dark swirls, her velvety complexion radiant even in the shade.

1922, she goes to Polish school in Parczew

1935, she is sentenced to five years in prison

1940, she sings my father to sleep, a real *yiddishe mame*

1943, she hurries back up to her room in Passage d'Eupatoria

1981, she comes to pick me up after school

Only the dead can have the last word on their own death. Even Gradowski, assigned to Krematorium II, who headed the Sonderkommando revolt and authored the harrowing "manuscript beneath the ashes," could not accompany them to the very end. He could only tell what happened next:

> Hair catches fire first. The skin blisters and explodes within seconds. Legs and arms contort, veins and nerves cause the extremities to move about. Then, the whole body goes up in flames, skin cracking open, fat flowing, and you can hear the crackling sound of a blaze. Bodies disappear into a hellish furnace that consumes its contents. The stomach bursts. The viscera emerge, and within minutes, not a trace remains. The head takes longer to burn. Two little blue flames flicker in the sockets, the eyes melt away along with the brain up inside, and in the mouth cavity, the tongue finally chars. The entire process lasts twenty minutes—a body, a world, is reduced to ashes.[57]

Suzanne and Marcel left the village of Luitré in late November 1944. The social worker simply came to get them, offering the foster family no explanation. They had little time for good-byes to Pyrame the dog and the pet pig. Mr. and Mrs. Courtoux accompanied the children to the stop at La Brebittière, on the Vitré–Fougères train line. Mrs. Courtoux, weeping uncontrollably, slipped a piece of paper with her address written in capitals into the children's pockets; Mr. Courtoux lifted them onto the train that had just pulled in, and handed over their pack to the social worker. And the train pulled away.

They spent the night in a hotel in Fougères. At dawn, the sudden clanging of a big, round alarm clock with hands broke the morning silence, and Marcel was awake, terrified.

They took another train at the Fougères station. Once in Paris, they were treated in a hospital for scabies. Constant and Annette took them in for a while, at Rue Saint-Maur. At Christmas, Marcel was given a new hobbyhorse. The Central Childhood Commission, an offshoot of the UJRE, started opening group homes: in early 1945, Suzanne and Marcel were sent with other Jewish orphans to Raincy-Coteaux, in the Paris suburbs. It was a medium-size house with a garden, not far from a sloping street. You could ski down it in winter.

On 9 January 1945, three weeks before the liberation of Auschwitz, they were enrolled in kindergarten.

ACKNOWLEDGMENTS

I would like to thank the *Fondation pour la mémoire de la Shoah* (Foundation for the Memory of the Shoah) for its generous support. I am especially indebted to Dominique Trimbur.

Audrey Kichelewski, Ewa Maczka and Dariusz Magier aided me in my search for archives in Poland; Pascal Carreau, Claude Charlot, Françoise Gicquel, Hélène Guillot and Karen Taïeb gave me assistance in France.

This work would not have been possible without the help of my highly discerning and accurate translators: for Yiddish, Bernard Vaisbrot; for Polish, Wojtek Kalinowski, Audrey Kichelewski and Ewa Maczka; and for Hebrew, Keren Gitaï, Erez Levy and Gil Mihaely.

Many witnesses graciously agreed to talk with me about their parents, about Poland, about emigration and about the war: Mireille Abramovici, Ida Apeloig, Liliane Balbin, Mrs. Chevry, Leslie Cokin, Richard Coren, Sheila Duerden, Robert Erpst, Serge Gardebled, Phyllis Goldberg, Marek Golecki, Liliane Gottheff, Renée Hardy, Ginette Kawka, Sarah Montard-Lichtsztejn, Mireille Negrinotti, Charles Raduszinski, Nathalie Rafal, David Rencus, Dominique Rzeszkowski, Cécile Servais, Sam Silverman, Paulette Sliwka, Phyllis Sonnenschein, Claude Szejnman, Jose Torres, Robert Vazghir, Georges Wajs, Colette Weibel and Sylvain Zylberstein. To all of them, I extend my heartfelt thanks.

Many colleagues and friends shared their knowledge and expertise: Jean-Marc Berlière, Sarah Gensburger, Raphaële Kipen, Nicolas Mariot, Pauline Peretz, Jean-Yves Potel, Paul-André Rosental, Tania Sachs, Pierre Savy and, most especially, Claire Zalc. Tal Bruttmann, Christophe Charle, Liza Méry and Benjamin Spector gave my manuscript a rigorous read, for which I am exceedingly grateful.

I am much obliged to Maurice Olender for his unfailing encouragement throughout my work, and for granting my original French edition a place in his series. It is a great honor to publish with Stanford University Press, and I am very grateful to Eric Brandt,

David Biale and Sarah Stein. I would also like to thank Marie-Pierre Ulloa for her key support. It has been a pleasure to work with my translator, Jane Kuntz.

It takes a family to put together a family biography. For their warm welcome, their kindness and their testimony, my deepest thanks go to Benito, Pocho, Celia, Mauricio, Susanna, Mark, Tamara, Ahuva, Zohar and their spouses, and in my generation, Gabriela, Sabrina, Sheila, Lili, Maya, Reut, Shir and Noam; as well as to the Jablonkas of France: my wife, Aline; my mother, Sylvie; my brother, Simon; my cousin, Pascale; and Marcel, my father, one of the protagonists of this story, without whose essential help I could not have undertaken this work. My Aunt Suzanne rests in peace; I believe she would have enjoyed pursuing this adventure with us.

This book is dedicated to Matès and Idesa's great-grandchildren, Raphaëlle, Héloïse, Maïa, Arthur, Clémence and Louise—light of our lives.

ABBREVIATIONS

AD	*Archives départementales* [Archives of individual French departments]
ANA	Archives of New Acts
APP	*Archives de la Préfecture de Police* (Paris) [Paris police prefecture archives]
AVP	*Archives de la Ville de Paris* [Archives of the City of Paris]
BDIC	*Bibliothèque de documentation internationale contemporaine (Nanterre)* [Library for Contemporary International Documentation at Nanterre, France]
CAC	*Centre des archives contemporaines (Fontainebleau)* [Center for Contemporary Archives at Fontainbleau, France]
CARAN	*Centre d'accueil et de recherché des Archives nationales (Paris)* [Reception and Research Center of the National Archives, in Paris]
CDJC	*Centre de documentation juive contemporaine (Paris)* [Center for Contemporary Jewish Documentation, Paris]
EMA	*État-major des armées* [Military Staff Chiefs]
EVDG	*Engagé volontaire pour la durée de la guerre* [Volunteer enlistee for the duration of the war]
FCP	French Communist Party
FFDJF	*Fils et filles des déportés juifs de France* [Sons and Daughters of Jewish Deportees of France]
JMO	*Journal de marche et opérations* [War Diary]
KPP	*Komunistyczna Partia Polski* [Polish Communist Party]

KZMP	*Komunistyczny Związk Młodzieży Polski* [Association of Polish Communist Youth]
LHR	League of Human Rights
MOE/MOI	*Main-d'œuvre étrangère / Main-d'œuvre immigrée* [Foreign Labor / Immigrant Labor]
MOPR	*Międzynarodowa Organizacja Pomocy Rewolucjonistom* [International Organization of Assistance for Revolutionaries, or International *Secours Rouge*, Red Aid]
NKVD	Russian acronym for the People's Commissariat for Internal Affairs, a Soviet state security organization known for its massive political repression
OSE	*Organisation de secours à l'enfance* [Organization of Aid for Children]
OZN	*Obóz Zjednoczenia Narodowego* [Camp of National Unity]
PJ	*Police judiciaire* [Judicial Police]
REI	*Régiment étranger d'infanterie* [Foreign infantry regiment]
RG	*Renseignements généraux* [Domestic Intelligence]
RMVE	*Régiment de marche des volontaires étrangers* [Foreign volunteer foot regiment]
SA	State Archives (of Lublin)
SHD	*Service historique de la défense, Vincennes* [Historical Department of the Ministry of Defense, Vincennes]
UGIF	*Union générale des Israélites de France* [General Union of French Jews]
UJRE	*Union des Juifs pour la résistance et l'entraide* [Jewish Union for Resistance and Solidarity]
UWL-WSP	*Urząd wojewódzki lubelski, wydział społeczno-polityczny* [The Sociopolitical Office of the Lublin Voivodeship]
YKUF	*Yidishèr kultur-farband* [Union for Yiddish Culture]

NOTES

CHAPTER 1

1. The word *shtetl*, or "village" in Yiddish, the diminutive of *shtot*, or city, designates an agglomeration of between 2,000 and 10,000 inhabitants. It implies a closeness, or even tenderness: for Jews, "it is not only a place inhabited by fellow Jews, but also a very particular economic and social structure, a network of relationships, whether individual or collective, a way of being in the world, a specific way of life, a Jewish space." Rachel Ertel, *Le Shtetl: La bourgade juive de Pologne* (Paris: Payot, 1982), 16.

2. There are photographs of the old synagogue and the study house in Wojciech Wilczyk's *Niewinne oko nie istnieje* [*There's No Such Thing as an Innocent Eye*] (Lodz: Atlas Sztuki, Krakow, Korporacja Ha! Art, 2009), 433–435.

3. According to Jan Gross, not only do the Poles perfectly remember the massacre of the Jews, but they were often actively involved in it. This would explain why the Righteous feared telling their neighbors that they had hidden Jews. Jan Gross, *Neighbors: The Destruction of the Jewish Community of Jedwabne* (Princeton: Princeton University Press, 2001), 238. Furthermore, "it was assumed that people who sheltered Jews had enriched themselves handsomely (which was often the case). . . . If found out, in addition to being stigmatized as 'Jew lovers,' they risked being identified as potential targets for robbery." Jan Gross, *Fear: Anti-Semitism in Poland after Auschwitz: An Essay in Historical Interpretation* (New York: Random House, 2007), 45.

4. Parczew Town Hall, Public Registry Department, Rabbinical Registry, marriage record of Matès and Idesa Jablonka (26 June 1937).

5. Ibid., birth certificates of Reizl Jablonka (7 January 1907, no. 41), Matès Jablonka (10 February 1909, no. 42), Hershl Jablonka (16 June 1915, no. 104), Henya Jablonka (3 April 1917, no. 408).

6. Isaac-Leyb Peretz, "Tableaux d'un voyage en province [1890]," in *Les oubliés du shtetl: Yiddishland* (Paris: Plon, 2007), 92.

7. Shlomo Zonenshayn, Elkana Niska and Rachel Gottesdiner-Rabinovitch (eds.), *Remembrances of Parczew* (Haifa, 1977) (in Hebrew and Yiddish). The expression *Yizkor Bukh* is a neologism coined after World War II, from the German *Buch* and the Hebrew *yizkor* (the title and 1st word of the prayer for the dead). It is a literary genre all its own that mixes reminiscences, emigrant narratives, short stories, poems, archival facsimiles, individual or group iconography, lists of victims of Nazism and so on. See Annette Wieviorka and Itzhok Niborski, *Les livres du souvenir. Mémoriaux juifs de Pologne* (Paris: Gallimard-Julliard, 1983).

8. Rachel Gottesdiner-Rabinovitch, "The Transition of Regimes" (in Hebrew), in *Remembrances of Parczew*, 52–55.

9. Pawel Korzec, *Juifs en Pologne. La question juive pendant l'entre-deux-guerres* (Paris: Presses de la Fondation nationale des sciences politiques, 1980), 51–52.

10. Rachel Gottesdiner-Rabinovitch, "The Transition of Regimes."

11. Ibid., "My Dear Little Town That I Will Never Forget" (in Hebrew), in *Remembrances of Parczew*, 29–38.

12. The *Endeks* (or "National Democrats"), led by Roman Dmowski, represented the clerical far right, the enemies of Jews, Socialists and Communists.

13. Sabina Seroka, "Les Juifs de Parczew," typed manuscript, undated (late 1980s).

14. Stanislaw Jadczak, *Parczew i powiat parczewski, 1401–2001* [historical brochure published by the Parczew Mayor's Office] (Lublin: Express Press, 2001), 9–72.

15. *Annual Directory of Polish Commerce, Industry, Crafts and Agriculture* (*Księega Adrsoza Polski*), 1929, available on the web at http://www.jewishgen.org/jri-pl/bizdir/start.htm.

16. Avrom Efrat-Hetman, "This Was Żabia Street" (in Hebrew), in *Remembrances of Parczew*, 106–108. One can see pictures of the old wooden synagogue of Parczew and of the Jewish fire brigade at this site: http://yivo1000towns.cjh.org.

17. The date of 9 Av 1942 (23 July 1942) is given by several contributors to the *Yizkor Bukh*. The 9th of Av, which corresponds to a different date in the Gregorian calendar from year to year, commemorates the destruction of the two temples of Jerusalem in 586 BCE and in 70 CE. The Nazis undoubtedly chose this date knowingly, to break the morale of their victims by using a key date in the Jewish faith. Another date is given (16 August 1942) for the entry "Parczew" in Shmuel Spector (ed.), *The Encyclopedia of Jewish Life Before and During the Holocaust*, vol. 2 (New York: New York University Press, 2001), 969.

18. Sabina Seroka, "Les Juifs de Parczew."

19. "Parczew," in Shmuel Spector (ed.), *The Encyclopedia of Jewish Life*, 969.

20. We have the account of one of the pogrom leaders, a member of WiN ("Freedom and Independence"), a group of nationalist resistance fighters. On 5 February 1946, the militias turned up in Parczew, disarmed and executed 3 Jews, then commandeered vans into which they proceeded to load their pillaged merchandise. Next, they headed for the homes of local Jewish notables. "These Jews surrendered their arms and went into hiding, without

demanding what was theirs. When the [Catholic] population realized what was happening, they came out into the street, with no fear of gunfire, happily greeting 'the backwoods boys.' The young people of Parczew, especially high school-aged boys, helped us out by searching for Jews and loading the vans. Four or five hours later, when the signal was sounded, everybody cleared out." Cited by Alina Cała and Helena Datner-Śpiewak, *Dzieje Żydów w Polsce, 1944–1968. Teksty źródłowe* (Warsaw: ZIH, 1997), 37–39.

21. Yehuda Leybl Beytl, "Parczew, Our Town" (in Hebrew), in *Remembrances of Parczew*, 89–91.

22. Shlomo Zonenshayn, "The Rabbi's Court: The Rabbi, His Servants and the Parczew Oratory" (in Hebrew), in *Remembrances of Parczew*, 17–28.

23. Yehuda Leybl Beytl, "Parczew, Our Town."

24. See in particular Gershom Scholem, *On the Kabbalah and Its Symbolism* (New York: Schocken Books, 1969).

25. Shlomo Zonenshayn, "In Remembrance of the Martyred Jewish Community of Parczew" (in Yiddish), in *Remembrances of Parczew*, 176.

26. Benjamin Mandelkern, *Escape from the Nazis* (Toronto: James Lorimer and Co., 1998), 13–16. Three articles in the *Yizkor Bukh* also refer to this episode.

27. Hocher Antchel Engelman, "The Portrait of Our Village" (in Yiddish), in *Remembrances of Parczew*, 109–112.

28. The photo of the elder Zalmen Zysman smoking on the Sabbath can be viewed at the site http://yivo1000towns.cjh.org/.

29. Sabina Seroka, "Les Juifs de Parczew."

30. Isaac-Leyb Peretz, "Tableaux d'un voyage en province," 114–115.

31. In *Dos Shtetl* (1904), Sholem Asch, born in Kutno in 1880, portrays an ideal shtetl, eternally preserved, by means of a few scenes: the family gathered on the Sabbath, a traditional wedding, holidays, signs of solidarity, the easy joy of the tradesmen, the beauty of nature, and so on. Itzhok Niborski, "Sholem Asch: L'écrivain de la cohésion et de l'éclatement," preface to Sholem Asch, *La Sanctification du nom* (Lausanne: L'Age d'homme, 1985), 9–20.

32. Isaac-Leyb Peretz, "Enchaînés devant le temple," in *Théâtre yiddish* (Paris: L'Arche, 1989).

33. Isaac-Leyb Peretz, "Die frumè katz" ["The Pious Cat"], in Cécile Cerf, *Regards sur la littérature yidich* (Paris: Académie d'histoire, 1974), 51–54.

34. This scene is recounted by Feygue Chtchoupak, untitled chapter (in Yiddish), in *Remembrances of Parczew*, 293–300.

35. Pierre Leurot, *Le livret du bourrelier-sellier-harnacheur: Manuel pratique* (Paris: Maison des métiers, 1984 [1924]), 4.

36. Rachel Ertel, *Le shtetl*, 187–189.

37. Baruch Niski, "A Visit to Parczew in 1968" (in Yiddish), in *Remembrances of Parczew*, 265.

38. State Archives of Lublin, Radzyń Podlaski branch, *Akta miasta parczewa* [town archives of Parczew], 68, census of men born between 1887 and 1937; and 74, tenants who replaced Jewish tenants, by street (1944).

39. Adam Kopciowski, "Anti-Jewish Incidents in the Lublin Region in the Early Years after World War II," in *Holocaust: Journal of the Polish Center for Holocaust Research* (2008): 177–205.

40. Marian Marzynski, *Shtetl*, 3 vol. (Boston: Marz Associates, WGBH, 1996); and Eva Hoffman, *Shtetl: The Life and Death of a Small Town and the World of Polish Jews* (New York: Public Affairs, 2007 [1997]), in particular, 48.

41. State Archives (Radzyń Podlaski), town archives of Parczew, 75, request for restitution of property on behalf of the Jews.

42. For eastern Galicia and Bukovina, Omer Bartov provides several examples, backed by photographs. Thus, the old Jewish cemetery of Kuty is an overgrown weed patch where goats graze; Omer Bartov, *Erased: Vanishing Traces of Jewish Galicia in Present-Day Ukraine* (Princeton: Princeton University Press, 2007), 97 and 110. After the war, the Polish government approved the transformation of Jewish places of worship, but "provided that the building not be used for purposes incompatible with its former religious character (e.g., movie theater, dance hall, performance space)." Likewise, in the region of Włodawa, the government is at odds with a local district official who wants to turn a synagogue into a movie theater; Jan Gross, *Fear*, 51. This was also the case in Parczew.

43. See Shana Penn, Konstanty Gevert and Anna Goldstein (eds.), *The Fall of the Wall and the Rebirth of Jewish Life in Poland, 1989–2009* (The Taube Foundation for Jewish Life and Culture, 2009); and Jean-Yves Potel, *La fin de l'innocence: La Pologne face à son passé juif* (Paris: Autrement, 2009).

CHAPTER 2

1. Motel Polusetski, "How the First Jewish Library in Parczew Was Created" (in Yiddish), in *Remembrances of Parczew*, 82–86.

2. Rachel Gottesdiner-Rabinovitch, "My Beloved Little Town That I Will Never Forget," in *Remembrances of Parczew.*

3. Motel Polusetski, "How the First Jewish Library in Parczew Was Created."

4. On the "irruption of ideologies," see Rachel Ertel, *Le Shtetl*, 146ff.

5. Emil Horoch, Albin Koprukowniak and Ryszard Szczygieł, *Dzieje Parczewa, 1401–2001* [History of Parczew] (Parczew: Urząd Miasta i Gminy, 2001), 218.

6. Faiwel Schrager, *Un militant juif* (Paris: Les Éditions Polyglottes, 1979), 19.

7. State Archives (SA) of Lublin, *Urząd wojewódzki lubelski, wydział społeczno-polityczny* [office of the Lublin voivodeship, political department], 1918–1939, serial 403, henceforward *UWL-WSP* 403.

8. The Komintern, or Third International, a group of Communist parties under the aegis of Moscow. On the KPP (formerly the KPRP) in the interwar years, see M. K. Dzie-

wanowski, *The Communist Party of Poland: An Outline of History* (Cambridge: Harvard University Press, 1959), ch. VIII; and Norman Davies, *God's Playground, A History of Poland,* vol. 2, *1795 to the Present* (Oxford: Clarendon Press Oxford, 1981), ch. XXII.

9. Myriam Tendlarz-Shatzki, "The Influence of the Russian Revolution on the Youth of Parczew" (in Hebrew), in *Remembrances of Parczew,* 285–287.

10. Rachel Gottesdiner-Rabinovitch, "The Transition of Regimes." The episode is also reported in Emil Horoch et al., *Dzieje Parczewa,* 212.

11. Daniel Beauvois, *Histoire de la Pologne* (Paris: Hatier, 1995), 296ff.; and Jerzy Lukowski and Hubert Zawadzki, *A Concise History of Poland* (Cambridge: Cambridge University Press, 2006). The conflict ended with the Treaty of Riga of 18 March 1921. With the annexation of the eastern territories, Poland numbered 14% Ukrainians, 10% Jews, 3% Belarusians and 2% Germans.

12. Emil Horoch et al., *Dzieje Parczewa,* 213–214.

13. Cited by Pawel Korzec, *Juifs en Pologne,* 213.

14. SA (Lublin), *UWL-WSP* 403, article 2012, 17.

15. Jaff Schatz, *The Generation: The Rise and Fall of the Jewish Communists of Poland* (Berkeley: University of California Press, 1991), 83; and Emil Horoch et al., *Dzieje Parczewa,* 213–214.

16. Archives of New Acts (ANA) of Warsaw, Lublin regional court, 198, ruling of the first criminal court (3 December 1934).

17. Jaff Schatz, *The Generation,* 53 and 108. (Schatz interviewed 43 former Communist Jews.)

18. ANA, Lublin regional court, 198; and 424/XVIII-228, record of detainee Matès Jablonka.

19. ANA, Lublin regional court, 198, expert appraisal protocol and translation of the accused's writings in the Jewish language (12 December 1933).

20. Guido Miglioli, *La Collectivisation des campagnes soviétiques* (Paris: Rieder, 1934), 277.

21. SA (Lublin), *UWL-WSP* 403, article 2022, report of 3 March 1933, 4–5.

22. Cited by Jaff Schatz, *The Generation,* 94.

23. Ibid., 106–107.

24. SA (Lublin), *UWL-WSP* 403, article 2022, report of 2 June 1933, 20–23.

25. Moshe and Élie Garbarz, *A Survivor,* trans. Jean-Jacques Garbarz (Detroit: Wayne State University Press, 1984), 37.

26. Max Wolfshaut Dinkes, *Échec et mat: Récit d'un survivant de Pchemychl en Galicie* (Paris: FFDJF, 1983), 21.

27. See Moshe Mishkinsky, "The Communist Party of Poland and the Jews," in Yisrael Gutman et al., *The Jews of Poland Between Two World Wars* (Hanover, London: University Press of New England, 1989), 56–74; Pawel Korzec, *Juifs en Pologne,* 112; and Jan Gross, *Fear,* ch. VII.

28. Mordkhè Rubinstein, "Three Biographies" (in Yiddish), in *Remembrances of Parczew*, 97–101.

29. Isaac Bashevis Singer, *Scum* (New York: Farrar, Straus & Giroux, 1991).

30. Joseph Minc, *L'Extraordinaire Histoire de ma vie ordinaire* (Paris: Seuil, 2006), 29ff.

31. Yanina Sochaczewska, cited by Annette Wieviorka, *Ils étaient juifs, résistants, communistes* (Paris: Denoël, 1986), 23–24.

32. Myriam Tendlarz-Shatzki, "The Influence of the Russian Revolution on the Youth of Parczew."

33. Isaac Deutscher, *The Non-Jewish Jew and Other Essays* (London: Oxford University Press, 1968), 26ff.

34. ANA, Lublin regional court, 198, report by the Włodawa *powiat* commander (21 January 1932); and report of the Parczew police station brigadier to his commander (30 May 1932).

35. SA (Lublin), *UWL-WSP* 403, article 2022, report of 2 June 1933 (p. 23); report of 2 November 1933, pp. 50 and 75.

36. Jerzy Lukowski and Hubert Zawadzki, *A Concise History of Poland*; Daniel Beauvois, *Histoire de la Pologne*, 308ff.

37. SA (Lublin), *UWL-WSP* 403, article 2021, report of 3 August 1932, 30–32. See also Emil Horoch, *Komunistyczna Partia Polski w województwie lubelskim, 1918–1938* [*The KPP in the Voivodeship of Lublin, 1918–1938*] (Lublin: Lublin University Press, 1993), 121–122.

38. SA (Lublin), *UWL-WSP* 403, article 2270, 34.

39. SA (Radzyń Podlaski), *Sąd Grodzki w Parczewie*, 1933–1934 (Parczew Justice of the Peace), 606.

40. *Code pénal polonais du 11 juillet 1932 et loi sur les contraventions du 11 juillet 1932* (Paris: Godde, Librairie des Juris-Classeurs, 1933).

41. ANA, Lublin regional court, 198, protocol including expert appraisal and translation of the accused's writings "in the Jewish language" (12 December 1933).

42. Rachel Gottesdiner-Rabinovitch, "My Beloved Little Town That I Will Never Forget"; and Even Zahav (formerly Itzhak Goldstein), "The Events of Our Town of Parczew in 1930" (in Yiddish), in *Remembrances of Parczew*, 112.

43. SA (Radzyń Podlaski), Parczew Justice of the Peace, 606, case 561, hearings of 6 October and 13 December 1933, 59; and case 582, hearing of 11 October 1933, 61.

44. SA (Lublin), *UWL-WSP* 403, article 2022, report of 2 December 1933, 65–66.

45. Enzo Traverso, *The Marxists and the Jewish Question: The History of a Debate, 1843–1943*, trans. Bernard Gibbons (Atlantic Highland: Humanities, 1994), 97–99; and Moshe Mishkinsky, "The Communist Party of Poland and the Jews."

46. Nathan Weinstock, *Le Pain de misère: Histoire du mouvement ouvrier juif en Europe. L'Europe centrale et occidentale, 1914–1945*, vol. 3 (Paris: La Découverte, 1986), 105–110.

47. SA (Lublin), *UWL-WSP* 403, article 2022, report of 2 December 1933, 65–66.

48. Louis Gronowski-Brunot, *Le Dernier Grand Soir: Un Juif de Pologne* (Paris: Seuil, 1980), 43.

49. Moshé Zalcman, *Histoire véridique de Moshé, ouvrier juif et communiste au temps de Staline* (Paris: Recherches, 1977), 28–29.

50. ANA, Lublin regional court, 198, protocol for inspection of material evidence (5 January 1934).

51. Ibid., note on the hanging of Communist banners on 16 and 19 December 1933; hearing protocol of witness Tauba Polusetska regarding the purchase of wire (20 March 1934).

52. Ibid., sentencing of the accused, 3 December 1934.

53. SA (Radzyń Podlaski), Parczew Justice of the Peace, 606, case III, Matès Jablonka and seven other accused, hearing of 9 April 1934, 100.

54. SA (Lublin), *UWL-WSP* 403, article 2023, report of 5 May 1934, 23–24.

55. ANA, Lublin regional court, 198; 424/XVIII-228, record of Matès Jablonka, detainee visitor permit (Reizl, 13 August 1934; Gitla, 17 September 1934; Karol Winawer, 18 October 1934).

56. Herman Marjan Winawer (ed.), *The Winawer Saga* (London: Winawer, 1994), 158ff.

57. Hersh Mendel, *Memoirs of a Jewish Revolutionary* (London: Pluto Press, 1989), 105–106.

58. ANA, Lublin regional court, 198, ruling of the first criminal court (3 December 1934, case I.3.K.333/ 34); and SA (Lublin), *UWL-WSP* 403, article 2023, 114.

59. Indictment against Idesa Feder, drawn up in Lublin on 28 February 1935, and the ruling of 18 June 1935 (case I.3.K 133/35) located at the *Bibliothèque de documentation internationale contemporaine* (BDIC) in Nanterre, France, LDH collection [League of Human Rights], F delta rés. 798/375, record of Idesa Feder (n° 9716). I will explain the reasons for it being located there later.

60. The new policy, which brought to a close the ultra-leftist strategy adopted in 1928, was introduced by Bukharin at the 17th Party Congress (January 1934) and definitively endorsed at the 7th and final Komintern Congress (summer 1935). See Nicolas Werth, *Histoire de l'Union soviétique*, 6th ed. (Paris: PUF, 2008), 311ff.; and M. K. Dziewanowski, *The Communist Party of Poland*, 141–142.

61. BDIC, LDH, F delta rés. 798/375, record of Idesa Feder, ruling of the Lublin regional court, presiding judge Zakrzewski (18 June 1935).

62. ANA, 424/XVIII-228, record of Matès Jablonka, detainee petition for the attention of the head prosecutor of the Poznan Appeals Court (18 August 1936).

63. Hersh Mendel, *Memoirs of a Jewish Revolutionary*, 232.

64. Private archive, autobiography of Gitla Leszcz (Gisèle Gardebled), undated, no location, in the 1950s. I am grateful to her son Serge for granting me access to this archive.

65. ANA, Lublin regional court, 198; and 424/XVIII228, record of Matès Jablonka; ruling of the Lublin regional court (3 December 1934).

66. Ibid., list of disciplinary punishments meted out to the detainee (1934); notice of information about the detainee released from the Sieradz prison on 8 December 1936.

67. Hersh Mendel, *Memoirs of a Jewish Revolutionary*, 238–239.

68. National Archives, Center for Contemporary Archives (CCA) at Fontainebleau, interior ministry, National Security file 19940454 (1), record of Matès Jablonka, certificate of release from Sieradz prison (8 December 1936). I will explain later why these records are in a French archive.

69. BDIC, LDH, F delta rés. 798/375, record of Idesa Feder, visit of 27 May 1938.

70. Jaff Schatz, *The Generation*, 218.

71. See Teresa Toranska, *Oni: Stalin's Polish puppets*, trans. Agnieszka Kolakowska (London: Collins Harvill, 1987), 203–204.

72. Adam Rayski, *Nos illusions perdues* (Paris: Balland, 1985), 198–199. La Main-d'œuvre immigrée (MOI) [Immigrant Labor] was a branch of the PCF [French Communist Party], linked to the Central Committee, which grouped immigrants according to their native language. There was a Yiddish-language branch in the MOI.

73. Hannah Arendt, *The Origins of Totalitarianism, Part Three, Totalitarianism* (New York: Harcourt, Brace and Co., 1951).

CHAPTER 3

1. *Erster Altveltlecher Yidisher Kultur-Kongres, Paris 17–21 Sept. 1937: Stenagrafisher Bericht* (Paris, New York, Warsaw, Tsentral-Garveltung fun Alveltlechen Yidishn Kultur-Farband, undated [1937]).

2. Cited by Louis Gronowski-Brunot, *Le Dernier Grand Soir*, 83.

3. Pawel Korzec, *Juifs en Pologne*, 72

4. See Ezra Mendelsohn, "Poland (after partition)," *Encyclopaedia Judaica*, vol. 16, 2nd ed. (Macmillan Reference USA, Thomson Gale, 2007), 300–306; see also the lively 1988 debate that appeared in the journal *Polin*, notably Jacek Majchrowski, "Some Observations on the Situation of the Jewish Minority in Poland During the Years 1918–1939," *Polin: A Journal of Polish-Jewish Studies*, vol. 3 (1988): 302–308; followed by Ezra Mendelsohn, "Response to Majchrowski."

5. Daniel Beauvois, *Histoire de la Pologne*, 320ff.; and Pawel Korzec, *Juifs en Pologne*, ch. VI.

6. Paul Zawadzki, "Quatre hypothèses comparatives France-Pologne sur la violence antisémite au XXe siècle," *Cultures & Conflits*, n° 9–10 (1993): 113–123.

7. Vicki Caron, *Uneasy Asylum: France and the Jewish Refugee Crisis, 1933–1942* (Stanford: Stanford University Press, 1999), 148–149.

8. Edward Wynot, "'A Necessary Cruelty': The Emergence of Official Anti-Semitism in Poland, 1936–1939," *The American Historical Review*, vol. 76, n° 4 (October 1971): 1035–1058.

9. Roman Vishniac, *A Vanished World* (New York: Farrar, Straus, and Giroux, 1983), photos 19, 20 and 34, and captions.

10. SA (Lublin), *UWL-WSP 403*, article 2016, report of 4 February 1935, 1–3; report of 3 October 1935, 54–55; and article 2017, report of 4 June 1936, 27–28.

11. Ibid., article 2017, report of 4 June 1936, 27–28.

12. Ibid., article 2017, report of 2 July 1936, 34–35.

13. Emil Horoch et al., *Dzieje Parczewa*, 215.

14. Elkana Niska, "Three Episodes in My Community of Parczew" (in Yiddish), in *Remembrances of Parczew*, 274–276.

15. Celia Heller, *On the Edge of Destruction: Jews of Poland between the Two World Wars* (New York: Columbia University Press, 1971).

16. SA (Lublin), *UWL-WSP 403*, article 2018, report of 5 June 1937, 30; and report of November 1937, 51.

17. Pawel Korzec, *Juifs en Pologne*, 207–208.

18. BDIC, LDH, F delta rés. 798/379, record of Matès Jablonka (no. 10815), visit of 4 November 1938.

19. Moshe and Élie Garbarz, *A Survivor*, 35–38.

20. Isaac Deutscher, "La tragédie du communisme polonais entre les deux guerres," *Les Temps modernes*, 145 (March 1958): 1632–1677.

21. Aleksander Wat, *My Century: The Odyssey of a Polish Intellectual*, trans. Richard Lourie (Berkeley: University of California Press, 1988).

22. Moshé Zalcman, *Histoire véridique de Moshé*, 171–184.

23. Norman Davies, *God's Playground*, 261 and ch. XI.

24. Rachel Gottesdiner-Rabinovitch, "My Beloved Little Town That I Will Never Forget."

25. The database of the Centro de Estudios Migratorios Latinoamericanos can be accessed at: http://www.cemla.com/buscador (Simje is inaccurately indexed under the name "Jabtonka Symeha"). See Haim Avni, *Argentina and the Jews: A History of Jewish Immigration* (Tuscaloosa: University of Alabama Press, 1991).

26. Reference site http://www.theshipslist.com; and Guy Mercier, "Histoire," *French Lines: Association pour la mise en valeur du patrimoine des compagnies maritimes françaises*, Bulletin 54 (September 2007): 2.

27. ANA, Lublin regional court, 198, translation of personal letters received by the accused.

28. See Jaff Schatz, *The Generation*, 158–160; Aleksander Smolar, "Les Juifs dans la mémoire polonaise," *Esprit*, 127 (June 1987): 1–31; and Pawel Korzec and Jean-Charles Szurek, "Juifs et Polonais sous l'occupation soviétique, 1939–1941," *Pardès*, 8 (1988): 8–28.

29. Cited by Nicole Lapierre, *Le Silence de la mémoire: Á la recherche des Juifs de Płock* (Paris: Plon, 1989), 139.

30. Trepper, born in Galicia at the turn of the century, a militant Zionist and then a Communist, arrived in Paris in 1930: "France! It would be difficult to imagine the emotional impact this name had on the young expatriate I was then." Leopold Trepper, *The Great*

Game: Memoirs of the Spy Hitler Couldn't Silence (New York: McGraw-Hill, 1977), 25. On this devotion, see also Pierre Birnbaum, *The Jews of the Republic: A Political History of State Jews in France from Gambetta to Vichy*, trans. Jane Marie Todd (Stanford: Stanford University Press, 1996); the documentary film by Yves Jeuland, *Comme un Juif en France* (KUIV Michel Rotman, 2 vol., 2007), 73 min. and 112 min.; and, outside continental France, Élizabeth Antébi, *Les Missionnaires juifs de la France, 1860–1939* (Paris: Calmann-Lévy, 1999).

31. Joseph Goebbels, *Journal, 1933–1939* (Paris: Tallandier, 2007), 437.

32. Parczew Town Hall, Division of Records, Rabbinical Records, marriage of Matès Jablonka and Idesa Feder (26 June 1937, at 22:00).

33. Ilex Beller, *De mon shtetl à Paris* (Paris: Éditions du Scribe, 1991), 59ff.

34. Faiwel Schrager, *Un militant juif*, 29.

35. Ilex Beller, *De mon shtetl à Paris*, 59–64.

36. Jean Améry, *At the Mind's Limits: Contemplations by a Survivor on Auschwitz and its Realities*, trans. Sidney Rosenfeld and Stella P. Rosenfeld (Bloomington: Indiana University Press, 1980), 41.

37. Family archives, letter from Shloyme, Tauba and Idesa to Simje and Reizl (undated, circa February 1938).

38. Family archives, passport of Idesa Jablonka, number 949697, 1065/38.

39. CAC, interior ministry, National Security file 19940445 (57), record of Idesa Feder.

CHAPTER 4

1. Vicki Caron, *Uneasy Asylum*, 206; Anne Grynberg, "L'accueil des réfugiés d'Europe centrale en France (1933–1939)," *Les Cahiers de la Shoah*, no. 1 (1994): 131–148.

2. Gérard Noiriel, *The French Melting Pot: Immigration, Citizenship, and National Identity*, trans. Geoffroy de Laforcade (Minneapolis: University of Minnesota Press, 1996), 62, 220; and Rahma Harouni, "Le débat autour du statut des étrangers dans les années 1930," *Le Mouvement social*, no. 188 (July–September, 1999): 61–75.

3. Cited by Philippe Rygiel, "Refoulements et renouvellement des cartes de 'travailleur étranger' dans le Cher durant les années 1930," in Philippe Rygiel (ed.), *Le Bon Grain et l'Ivraie: L'État-nation et les populations immigrées, fin XIXᵉ–début XXᵉ siècle* (Paris: Presses de l'ENS, 2004), 201.

4. CAC, interior ministry, National Security file 19940454 (1), record of Matès Jablonka.

5. Georges Ferrier, "Pour nos réfugiés politiques," *La Défense*, 10 September 1937. See Jacques Omnès, "L'accueil des émigrés politiques (1933–1938). L'exemple du Secours rouge, de la Ligue des droits de l'homme et du Parti socialiste," in Gilbert Badia et al., *Les Bannis de Hitler. Accueil et luttes des exilés allemands en France, 1933–1939* (Saint-Denis: Presses universitaires de Vincennes, 1984), 65–101.

6. See Nathan Weinstock, *Le Pain de misère*, 139ff.; Simon Cukier et al., *Juifs révolutionnaires: Une page d'histoire du Yidichland en France* (Paris: Messidor, Éditions sociales, 1987), 72ff.

7. CAC, interior ministry, National Security file 19940454 (1), record of Matès Jablonka, note for Mr. Bouvier, head of 6th Bureau (dealing with issues of territory and non-nationals).

8. William Irvine, *Between Justice and Politics: The Ligue des droits de l'homme, 1898–1945* (Stanford: Stanford University Press, 2007), ch. VII.

9. Maurice Milhaud, "La question des réfugiés politiques," *Les Cahiers des droits de l'homme*, no. 17 (15 August 1938): 510–516.

10. BDIC, LDH, F delta rés. 798/379, record of Matès Jablonka, record of visit (undated).

11. Ibid., F delta rés. 798/375, record of Idesa Feder, visits from 24 and 27 May 1938; and F delta rés. 798/374, record of Hersz Stol (no. 8953).

12. CAC, interior ministry, National Security file 19940445 (57), record of Idesa Feder, LDH certificate (30 May 1938).

13. On French police files in the 1930s, see Gérard Noiriel, *Les Origines républicaines de Vichy* (Paris: Hachette Littératures, 1999), ch. IV; and Jean-Pierre Deschodt, "Tous fichés!" *Historia* (September 2009).

14. Émile Kahn, "La police et les étrangers: Le décret-loi du 2 mai," *Les Cahiers des droits de l'homme*, no. 10 (15 May 1938): 295–299.

15. Claude Vernier (Werner Prasuhn), *Tendre Exil: Souvenirs d'un réfugié antinazi en France* (Paris: La Découverte/Maspero, 1983), 103–104. See also Clifford Rosenberg, *Policing Paris: The Origins of Modern Immigration Control between the Wars* (Ithaca: Cornell University Press, 2006) ch. II.

16. Claude Olievenstein, *Il n'y a pas de drogués heureux* (Paris: Robert Laffont, 1977), 18.

17. CAC, interior ministry, National Security file 19940454 (1), record of Matès Jablonka, ID notice for undocumented alien discovered on French soil (4 June 1938).

18. Ibid., National Security file 19940445 (57), record of Idesa Feder, ID notice for undocumented alien discovered on French soil (4 June 1938). See Ilsen About and Vincent Denis, *Histoire de l'identification des personnes* (Paris: La Découverte, "Repères" coll. 2010).

19. Vicki Caron, *Uneasy Asylum*, 174, 186.

20. CAC, interior ministry, National Security file 19940454 (1), record of Matès Jablonka, letter from the interior ministry to the police prefect, department of foreigners and passports (10 October 1938); police prefecture denial of residence (28 October 1938).

21. Ibid., National Security file 19940454 (1), record of Matès Jablonka, letters from Matès to the interior minister (16 November 1938 and 3 December 1938).

22. BDIC, LDH, F delta rés. 798/379, record of Matès Jablonka, letter from Matès to the general secretary of the LDH (17 December 1938).

23. CAC, interior ministry, National Security file 19940454 (1), record of Matès Jablonka.

24. Ibid., National Security file 19940445 (57), record of Idesa Feder, "request for residency permit," handwritten (13 March 1939); and police prefecture denial of residency (6 April 1939).

25. Cited by David Weinberg, *A Community on Trial: The Jews of Paris in the 1930s* (Chicago: University of Chicago Press, 1977), 193.

26. Xavier Barthelemy, "Des infractions aux arrêtés d'expulsion et d'interdiction de séjour" (Law dissertation, University of Paris School of Law, 1936), 262–264.

27. Ilex Beller, *De mon shtetl à Paris*, 77.

28. Benjamin Schlevin, *Les Juifs de Belleville* (Paris: Nouvelles Éditions latines, 1956 [1948]), 104, 120.

29. CAC, interior ministry, National Security file 19940474 (337), record of Abram Solarz.

30. Claude Vernier (Werner Prasuhn), *Tendre Exil*, 105.

31. I base my calculation on figures provided by Maurice Halbwachs, "Genre de vie," *Revue d'économie politique* (January–February 1939): 439–455.

32. *La Défense*, 13 May 1938, report on the *Congrès national du Secours populaire de France* (23–26 June 1938).

33. Charlotte Roland, *Du ghetto à l'Occident: Deux générations yiddiches en France* (Paris: Minuit, 1962), 136–137.

34. Michel Roblin, *Les Juifs de Paris: Démographie, économie, culture* (Paris: Picard, 1952), 102; Claire Zalc, *Melting Shops: Une histoire des commerçants étrangers en France* (Paris: Perrin, 2010), ch. IV.

35. Archives of the City of Paris (AVP), census figures, 1936, 20th arrondissement, Belleville quarter, Rue des Couronnes, D2M8 695 (185); and Rue du Pressoir, D2M8 697 (139–140, 150). See Claire Zalc, *Melting Shops*, ch. VII.

36. Clément Lépidis, "Belleville, mon village," in *Belleville* (Paris: Éditions Henri Veyrier, 1975), 61.

37. Michel Bloit, *Moi, Maurice, bottier à Belleville: Histoire d'une vie* (Paris: L'Harmattan, 1993), 72.

38. Moshe and Élie Garbarz, *A Survivor*, 41.

39. This passage is inspired by David Weinberg, *A Community on Trial*, 14–15. See also Nancy Green, *The Pletzl of Paris: Jewish Immigrant Workers in the "Belle Epoque"* (Holmes and Meier, 1985), ch. IV.

40. CAC, interior ministry, National Security file 19940474 (447), record of Hersz Stol, letter from the police prefect to the interior minister (8 January 1938).

41. Family archives, letter from Idesa to Simje and Reizl (9 May 1940).

42. Family archives, Korenbaum family tree and information kindly transmitted by Richard Coren. See Vanessa Jones, "Revealing Hidden Roots." Local DNA research has global implications," *Boston Globe*, 23 September 2008.

43. See Vicki Caron, *Uneasy Asylum*, 103 and 349ff.; and Pierre Birnbaum, *The Jews of the Republic*, 360–373.

44. CAC, interior ministry, National Security file 19940474 (447), record of Hersz Stol, letter from the police prefect to the interior minister (8 January 1938).

45. Moshé Zalcman, *Histoire véridique de Moshé*, 52.

46. Ralph Schor, *L'Opinion française et les étrangers en France, 1919–1939* (Paris: Publications de la Sorbonne, 1985), 661–662.

47. Nicole Lapierre, *Le Silence de la mémoire*, 68 and 133–135.

48. CAC, interior ministry, National Security file 19940464 (85), record of Jankiel (Yankel) Niski, letter from "a group of French workers" (2 September 1934).

49. Faiwel Schrager, *Un militant juif*, 46–47. See also Audrey Kichelewski, "La Nayè Presse, quotidien juif et communiste, 1934–1939" (Master's Thesis, University of Paris-I, 2000).

50. Louis Gronowski-Brunot, *Le Dernier Grand Soir*, 64–65.

51. Faiwel Schrager, *Un militant juif*, 35ff.

52. Moshe and Élie Garbarz, *A Survivor*, 34.

53. Joseph Minc, *L'Extraordinaire histoire de ma vie ordinaire*, 61ff. The phrase is cited by Philippe Lazar in his obituary of Minc (www.diasporiques.org/In%20memoriam%20Minc.pdf).

54. Roger Ikor, "La Greffe de printemps," in *Les Eaux mêlées* (Paris: Albin Michel, 1955), 107.

55. Benjamin Schlevin, *Les Juifs de Belleville*, 70.

56. Wolf Wieviorka, "Entre deux mondes," in *Est et Ouest: Déracinés* (Paris: Bibliothèque Medem, 2004 [1936–1937]), 14.

57. Léon Groc, "Il y a un problème des étrangers," *Le Petit Parisien*, 25 March 1939.

58. Arthur Koestler, *Scum of the Earth* (London: Eland, 2006 [1941]), 31.

59. CAC, interior ministry, National Security file 19940445 (146), record of Abram Fiszman.

60. Ibid., National Security file 19940459 (227), record of Gitla Leszcz.

61. Ibid., National Security file 19940474 (501), record of Rywka Szerman.

62. Ibid., National Security file 19940474 (509), record of Icek Sznajder, letter from the French consul in Warsaw to the minister of foreign affairs (25 November 1938).

63. Archives of the Paris police prefecture (APP), blotter of the police prefecture, "Street Traffic: Foreigners," entries by Domestic Intelligence (from 21 October 1938 to 18 September 1939).

64. AVP, D2 Y 14 (554), consignment register of the Santé prison.

65. AVP, D1 U6 (3552), criminal court rulings of 17 to 19 May 1939, 16th chamber of the criminal court of the Seine region (ruling of 17 May 1939).

66. Claude Vernier (Werner Prasuhn), *Tendre Exil*, 108.

67. Departmental archives of the Val-de-Marne, 2Y5/ 322, consignment register of the Fresnes prison; and 2Y/5DEV 71, record of Matès Jablonka at Fresnes.

68. Maurice Milhaud, "La question des réfugiés politiques," 511.

69. APP, BA 2428, letters from the police prefect to the cabinet of the interior minister (17 August 1939 and 6 September 1939).

70. Arthur Koestler, *Scum of the Earth*, 94. See Anne Grynberg, *Les Camps de la honte: Les internés juifs des camps français, 1939–1944* (Paris: La Découverte, 1991); and Denis Peschanski, *La France des camps: L'internement, 1938–1946* (Paris: Gallimard, 2002).

71. BDIC, LDH, F delta rés. 798/375, record of Nathan Tropauer (n° 9468).

72. Alexis Spire, *Étrangers à la carte: L'administration de l'immigration en France, 1945–1975* (Paris: Grasset, 2005), 146–147.

CHAPTER 5

1. Family archives, letter from Matès to Simje and Reizl (18 October 1939).

2. Communiqué from the Polish embassy, cited in "La révision des Polonais en France," *Le Populaire*, 18 October 1939.

3. Jean-Louis Crémieux-Brilhac, *Les Français de l'an 40*, vol. 1, *La guerre oui ou non?* (Paris: Gallimard, 1990), 491ff.

4. Philippe Landau, "France, nous voilà! Les engagés volontaires juifs d'origine étrangère pendant la 'drôle de guerre'" in André Kaspi, Annie Kriegel and Annette Wieviorka (eds.), *Les Juifs de France dans la Seconde Guerre mondiale* (Paris: Le Cerf, 1992); *Pardès*, no. 16, 20–38.

5. Stanislaw Jadczak, *Parczew i powiat parczewski*, 69–72.

6. Defense Ministry, Army, Foreign Legion Command, Veterans Bureau, record of legionnaire Matès Jablonka, certificate of good conduct issued by the police commissioner of the Père-Lachaise quarter (8 October 1939).

7. Jorge Luis Borges, *Book of Sand*, trans. Norman Thomas Di Giovanni (New York: Dutton, 1977), 41.

8. Defense Ministry, Army, Foreign Legion Command, Veterans Bureau, fitness certificate for Matès Jablonka (8 November 1939); affidavit of enlistment in the Foreign Legion as an EVDG, or volunteer enlistee for the duration of the war (8 November 1939).

9. Center for Contemporary Jewish Documentation (CDJC), collection of the Union of Volunteer Enlistees, Jewish War Veterans of 1939–1945 (UEVACJ), list of volunteer enlistees, 1st military region.

10. Cited by Jean-Louis Crémieux-Brilhac, *Les Français de l'an 40*, vol. 1, 179.

11. Arthur Koestler, *Scum of the Earth*, 53–54.

12. "Les 52 députés ex-communistes . . . convoqués par la justice militaire," *Paris soir*, 7 October 1939. See Stéphane Courtois and Marc Lazar, *Histoire du Parti communiste français* (Paris: PUF, 1995), 171ff.

13. Arnold Mandel, *Les Temps incertains* (Paris: Calmann-Lévy, 1950), 209–211.

14. Defense Historical Department (SHD), 7N 2475, EMA 1, foreigners, military training, letter from the council executive to the justice minister (2 November 1939); letter from the council executive to various generals (20 December 1939).

15. AVP, D1 U6 (3552), criminal court rulings of 17 to 19 May 1939, 16th chamber of the criminal court of the Seine region (ruling of 17 May 1939).

16. This is why the letter is in Idesa's record: CAC, interior ministry, National Security file 19940445 (57), record of Idesa Feder, letter from Matès to the interior minister (10 May 1940).

17. Léon Aréga, *Comme si c'était fini* (Paris: Gallimard, 1946), 4–7.

18. Zosa Szajkowski, *Jews and the French Foreign Legion* (New York: Ktav, 1975), 64. Szajkowski himself enlisted on 2 September 1939.

19. Family archives, letter from Matès to Simje and Reizl (18 October 1939).

20. SHD, 7N 2475 (3), EMA 1, foreigners, military training, note no. 5 on the enlistment of foreign volunteers (undated, early 1940).

21. Douglas Porch, *The French Foreign Legion: A Complete History of the Legendary Fighting Force* (New York: HarperCollins, 1991), 459.

22. Benjamin Schlevin, *Les Juifs de Belleville*, 174–175.

23. ANA, 424/XVIII-228, record of detainee Matès Jablonka.

24. Jean-Louis Crémieux-Brilhac, *Les Français de l'an 40*, vol. 2, *Ouvriers et soldats* (Paris: Gallimard, 1990), 429.

25. Manès Sperber, *All Our Yesterdays*, vol. 3, *Until My Eyes Are Closed with Shards*, trans. Harry Zohn (New York: Holmes and Meir, 1994), 165–166.

26. SHD, 7N 4198 (3), EMA (9th bureau), Foreign Legion, Legion Department of Registration and Mental Preparedness, foreign enlistment up to 6 November 1939 and various tables and figures.

27. Zosa Szajkowski, *Jews and the French Foreign Legion*, 61.

28. SHD, 7N 2475 (3), EMA 1, foreigners, military training, report of master sergeant Mazzoni, chief of the Barcarès annex (25 January 1940, confidential).

29. Claude Vernier (Werner Prasuhn), *Tendre Exil*, 122.

30. SHD, 7N 4198 (3), EMA (9th bureau), Foreign Legion, Legion Department of Registration and Mental Preparedness, translation of two coded telegrams from Algiers to *Guerre-Paris* (27 February 1940, secret).

31. Cited by Jean-Louis Crémieux-Brilhac, *Les Français de l'an 40*, vol. 1, 495.

32. SHD, 7N 4198 (3), EMA (9th bureau), Foreign Legion, Legion Department of Registration and Mental Preparedness, letter from legionnaire Fenykovy to a relative in Beirut (13 March 1940, secret).

33. Family archives, letter from Idesa to Simje and Reizl (9 May 1940).

34. Archives of *l'Assistance publique* [welfare bureau], inpatient registry at the Rothschild Hospital, 23 January 1939 (birth of Suzanne Feder) and 29 April 1940 (birth of Marcel Jablonka).

35. City Hall, 12th arrondissement of Paris, civil records, birth certificate of Marcel Jablonka (29 April 1940).

36. Family archives, letter from Idesa to Simje and Reizl (9 May 1940).

37. CAC, interior ministry, National Security file 19940445 (57), record of Idesa Feder, letter from legionnaire Jablonka to interior minister (10 May 1940).

38. Jean-Pierre Azéma, *1940, l'année terrible* (Paris: Seuil, 1990), 71ff.; Jean-Louis Crémieux-Brilhac, *Les Français de l'an 40*, vol. 2, 374ff. and 429ff.; and Karl-Heinz Frieser, *The Blitzkrieg Legend: the 1940 Campaign in the West* (Annapolis: Naval Institute Press, 2005).

39. According to the account of General Beaufre, *Le Drame de 1940* (Paris: Plon, 1965), 228ff.

40. *Képi blanc. La vie de la Légion étrangère*, no. 490, special issue "Volontaires étrangers, 1939" (May 1989): particularly 40–45.

41. SHD, 34 N 319, 23rd RMVE, logbook (JMO) of the foreign volunteer foot regiment.

42. SHD, 34 N 319, 23rd RMVE, report by Captain Digoine du Palais, undated.

43. Ilex Beller, *De mon shtetl à Paris*, 161ff.

44. SHD, 7N 4198 (4), EMA (9th bureau), Mental Preparedness of the Foreign Volunteer Foot Regiment, report by Lieutenant Colonel Aumoitte (31 May 1940, confidential).

45. Defense Ministry, Army, Foreign Legion Command, Veterans Bureau, service affidavit for Matès Jablonka (17 May 1940).

46. Jean-Louis Crémieux-Brilhac, *Les Français de l'an 40*, vol. 1, 586ff., and vol. 2, 644; see also Jean-Pierre Azéma, *1940, l'année terrible*, 100ff. and 130ff.

47. SHD, 7N 4198 (4), EMA (9th bureau), Mental Preparedness of the Foreign Volunteer Foot Regiment, letter from the general commander of the Barcarès camp to the general commander of the 16th military region (31 May 1940, secret).

48. S. Danowski, "Quelques souvenirs d'un toubib," in *Le Combattant volontaire juif, 1939–1945* (Paris: UEVACJ, 1971), 19–21.

49. Ibid.

50. I mainly used the collection SHD, 34 N 319, 23rd RMVE, JMO, Lieutenant Colonel Aumoitte's report (31 January 1943), the report by Captain Digoine du Palais (undated) and the report of Captain Talec (22 September 1946); and SHD, 34 N 317, 12th REI ("12th Foreign"), JMO, orders of Lieutenant Colonel Besson, report of battalion chief André (undated, late 1941) and report of Sergeant François (23 March 1942); to which I have added the memoir of Colonel Malézieux and Reserve Captain Jean Prim, *Mémorial du 93e Régiment d'infanterie pendant la campagne 1939–1940* (Le Mans: Amicale du 93e RI, undated).

51. SHD, 34 N 317, 12th REI, JMO, orders of Lieutenant Colonel Besson nos. 35 and following.

52. Samuel Maier, "Au front," in *Le Combattant volontaire juif*, 30.

53. SHD, individual record of Lieutenant André Recht (no. 83769).

54. SHD, 7N 2475 (3), EMA 1, foreigners, military training, affidavits of information files drawn up after the 1940 armistice by Commander Jacquot, no. 15 (undated).

55. Colonel Georges Masselot, "La guerre d'un officier de liaison," and Commander Louis Primaux, "La défense de Soissons," *Képi blanc* (May 1989), respectively 37–39 and 39–40.

56. SHD, 34 N 319, 23rd RMVE, JMO and report by Captain Digoine du Palais (undated).

57. S. Danowski, "Quelques souvenirs d'un toubib."

58. Henri Ribera, "'Je n'ai pas donné mon fusil': Un volontaire étranger en 1940," *Farac Info*, no. 349 (June 2000).

59. SHD, 34 N 319, 23rd RMVE, report by Second Lieutenant Bertholay (30 October 1940).

60. SHD, 34 N 319, 23rd RMVE, report by Captain Appolinaire-Esteux, undated.

61. SHD, individual record of Battalion Chief Raymond Digoine du Palais (no. 77756).

62. SHD, 7N 2475 (3), EMA 1, foreigners, military training, affidavits of information files drawn up after the 1940 armistice by Commander Jacquot, no. 15 (undated).

63. SHD, 34 N 319, 23rd RMVE, report by Captain Talec (22 September 1946).

64. Douglas Porch, *The French Foreign Legion*, 462; and "Le 22e RMVE," *Képi blanc* (May 1989): 44–45.

65. Hans Habe, *A Thousand Shall Fall* (1941), cited by Vicki Caron, *Uneasy Asylum*, 263.

66. Léon Aréga, *Comme si c'était fini*, 76–77.

67. Cited by Jean-Pierre Richardot, *100 000 morts oubliés: Les 47 jours et 47 nuits de la bataille de France, 10 mai–25 juin 1940* (Paris: Le Cherche Midi, 2009), 386.

68. SHD, 34 N 317, 12th REI, JMO and the orders of Lieutenant Colonel Besson.

69. Ibid., 12th REI, memo from Lieutenant Colonel Besson to the general commanding the 8th infantry division (12 June 1940).

70. Zosa Szajkowski, *Jews and the French Foreign Legion*, 74.

71. Georges Perec, *W, or a Childhood Memory*, trans. David Bellos (Boston: D.R. Godine, 1988), 37–38.

72. Éric Alary, *L'Exode: Un drame oublié* (Paris, Perrin, 2010), 159ff.

73. SHD, 34 N 319, 23rd RMVE, JMO.

74. Ibid., 23rd RMVE, report by Captain Talec (22 September 1946). See also SHD, individual record of Captain Désiré Talec (no. 12518).

75. Defense Ministry, Army, Foreign Legion Command, Veterans Bureau, demobilization affidavit of Matès Jablonka (28 September 1940).

76. Private archives, correspondence of legionnaire Abramovici (1940). I am grateful to his daughter Mireille for granting me access. See also Mireille Abramovici, *Dor de Tine. Une histoire de 1944*, Les Films d'Ici, La Sept Arte, TV 10 Angers, 60 min., 2001.

77. *Le Matin*, 4 August 1940; cited by Jérôme Gautheret and Thomas Wieder, "Histoire(s) de l'été 1940: De la haine dans l'air," *Le Monde*, 27 July 2010.

78. See Sylvain Zorzin, "Le camp de Septfonds (Tarn-et-Garonne): soixante ans d'histoire et de mémoires (1939–1999)," research paper, IEP Bordeaux, 2000; and Monique-Lise Cohen and Éric Malo (eds.), *Les Camps du Sud-Ouest de la France, 1939–1944: Exclusion, internement et déportation* (Toulouse: Privat, 1994), 35–41.

79. Joseph Ratz, *La France que je cherchais: Les impressions d'un Russe engagé volontaire en France*, 11th ed. (Limoges: Bontemps, 1945), 87.

80. Conrad Flavian, *Ils furent des hommes* (Paris, Nouvelles éditions latines, 1948), 20.

81. Joseph Ratz, *La France que je cherchais*, 95–96.

82. Conrad Flavian, *Ils furent des hommes*, 21.

83. "Le scandale de Sept-Fonds [sic]," *Unzer Wort*, no. 21 (29 September 1940); cited in Stéphane Courtois and Adam Rayski (eds.), *Qui savait quoi? L'extermination des Juifs, 1941–1945* (Paris: La Découverte, 1987), 123.

84. SHD, individual record of Lieutenant Colonel Edgard Puaud (no. 42225).

85. CDJC, Amelot Committee, microfilm 46-4, list of combatants from 1939–1940 interned at the Pithiviers camp; microfilm 72-6, list of combatants from 1939–1940 interned at the Beaune-la-Rolande camp.

86. Letter from Kalme Chimisz to the Septfonds demobilization center commander, undated (available at the website of convoy no. 73: http://www.convoi73.org/temoignages/026_kalme_chimisz/doc01.html).

CHAPTER 6

1. CAC, interior ministry, National Security file 19940448 (85), record of Raymond Gardebled.

2. Private archives, autobiography of Gitla Leszcz (Gisèle Gardebled).

3. CAC, interior ministry, National Security file 19940437 (395), record of Constant Couanault; and "Constant Couanault," in Jean Maitron (ed.), *Dictionnaire biographique du mouvement ouvrier français. Quatrième partie, 1914–1939*, vol. 23 (Paris: Éditions ouvrières, 1984), 247.

4. Constant Couanault, "Ce que nous avons vu en Espagne," *Le Combat syndicaliste*, nos. 190 and following: 8 January, 15 January, 22 January, 29 January, 5 February and 5 March 1937. See Jérémie Berthuin, *La CGT-SR et la Révolution espagnole, juillet 1936–décembre 1937. De l'espoir à la désillusion* (Paris: CNT-Région parisienne, 2000), notably 104–107.

5. I had already completed my research when Sarah published her autobiography: Sarah Lichtsztejn-Montard, *Chassez les papillons noirs* (Paris: Éditions Le Manuscrit-FMS, 2011). I have opted to make use of the interviews she granted me between 2007 and 2011, without systematically referring to the corresponding passages in her memoir.

6. CAC, interior ministry, National Security file 19940459 (270), record of Moises Lichtsztejn.

7. Ibid., National Security file 19940457 (192), record of Jascha Korenbaum.

8. AVP, population census, 1946, 20th arrondissement, Père-Lachaise quarter, Rue Désirée, D2M8 941 (2nd vol., 190).

9. See in particular Tal Bruttmann, *Au bureau des affaires juives. L'administration française et l'application de la législation antisémite, 1940–1944* (Paris: La Découverte, 2006).

10. Nicolas Mariot and Claire Zalc, *Face à la persécution: 991 Juifs dans la guerre* (Paris: Odile Jacob, 2010), 116.

11. *Le "Fichier juif." Rapport de la commission présidée par René Rémond au Premier ministre* (Paris: Plon, 1996); and Renée Poznanski, *Les Juifs en France pendant la Seconde Guerre mondiale* (Paris: Hachette Littératures, 1994), 56–58. By 21 October 1940, 150,000 Jews had been tallied in the Paris census, 65,000 of whom were foreigners.

12. Centre d'accueil et de recherches des Archives nationales (CARAN) [Reception and Research Center of the French National Archives], "family files" of the Paris police prefecture, record of Matès Jablonka. Matès is also listed in the police prefecture's "individual files" (F9 5646/2); his record, marked with a capital *J*, lists him as "head of household."

13. AVP, 2Mi3/304, business directory, by street (1938).

14. Family archives, letter from Tauba to Simje and Reizl (26 November 1940).

15. Feygue Chtchoupak, untitled chapter; Shlomo Zonenshayn, "In Memory of the Martyred Jewish Community of Parczew"; and Avrom Levenbaum, "A Warlike Environment" (in Hebrew), in Shlomo Zonenshayn et al. (eds.), *Remembrances of Parczew*, 139.

16. Family archives, reply coupon of the International Committee of the Red Cross (no. 65662), arrived in Geneva on 18 December 1940 and bearing Matès's reply on 8 February 1941.

17. Family archives, letter from Constant to a German commission (28 April 1957).

18. André Kaspi, *Les Juifs pendant l'Occupation* (Paris, Seuil: 1991), 212ff.

19. Odette Bagno, "Une rafle mal connue, le 20 août 1941: un arrondissement de Paris en état de siège," *GenAmi*, no. 29 (September 2004), available at the site: http://www.gen ami.org/culture/rafle-paris-20-aout-1941.php.

20. The neologism "Aryanization" refers euphemistically to the expropriation and pillaging of Jews. I found nothing in the CARAN archives, 42Mi38, AJ38 (police in charge of Jewish issues, inquest and control section, Aryanization), in AJ40 (German authorities) or in F1C3 (Prefect reports).

21. Michael Marrus and Robert Paxton, *Vichy France and the Jews* (New York: Basic Books 1981), ch. VI; and Renée Poznanski, *Les Juifs en France*, 290–295.

22. "Account by Sarah Lichtsztejn, student at the Lycée Cours de Vincennes, of her escape from Vél' d'Hiv on 16 July 1942," in Serge Klarsfeld, *Lettres de Louise Jacobson, 1er septembre 1942–13 février 1943* (Paris: FFDJF, Centre de documentation sur la déportation des enfants juifs, 1989), 55–57.

23. Clément Lépidis, "Belleville, mon village," 66.

24. Testimony of Michel Gavériaux (alumnus of the Rue Sorbier school), available at the site of the "École de la rue Tlemcen" committee: http://www.comit etlemcen.com/ Michel.html.

25. Serge Klarsfeld, *Le Mémorial de la déportation des Juifs de France* (Paris, 1978), 92 and 246. On the roundup, see in particular Claude Lévy and Paul Tillard, *Betrayal at the Vel d'Hiv*, trans. Inea Bushnaq (New York: Hill and Wang, 1969).

26. Anne Wellers, "En attendant son retour," in Georges Wellers, *Un Juif sous Vichy* (Paris: Éditions Tiresias, 1991), 289.

322 NOTES TO CHAPTER 6

27. Cited by Serge Klarsfeld, *Le Calendrier de la persécution des Juifs en France, 1940–1944* (Paris: FFDJF, 1993), 316.

28. Family archives, letter from Constant to a German commission (28 April 1957).

29. AVP, population census, 1946, 20th arrondissement, Père-Lachaise quarter, Rue Désirée, D2M8 941 (2nd vol., 190).

30. CAC, interior ministry, National Security file 19940455 (19), record of Calel Jagodowicz.

31. AVP, 2Mi3/304, business directory, by street (1938). Garnier and Co. ("Affordable Kitchen Stoves") located at 21–25 Rue d'Eupatoria.

32. Serge Klarsfeld, *French Children of the Holocaust*, trans. Glorianne Depondt and Howard M. Epstein (New York: New York University Press, 1996).

33. AVP, D9P2, 2696, business tax, 20th arrondissement, Belleville, no. 2690, 1935; and AVP, D9P2, 2900, business tax, 20th arrondissement, Père-Lachaise-Belleville, no. 2893, 1938.

34. AVP, population census, 1936, 20th arrondissement, Belleville quarter, Passage d'Eupatoria, D2M8 696, 47–49; and 1946, 20th arrondissement, Belleville quarter, Passage d'Eupatoria, D2M8 938, 17–18.

35. APP, police prefecture, Domestic Intelligence files, GA S4, record of Calel Sommer (no. 174673).

36. CAC, interior ministry, National Security file 19940474 (346), record of Calel Sommer. [Rough approximation of the writer's semi-literate prose, from the French.]

37. APP, police prefecture, Domestic Intelligence files, GA S4, record of Calel Sommer (no. 174673); AD Val-de-Marne, 2742 W 26, Fresnes prison register, and 2652 W 22, individual record of Calel Sommer at Fresnes Prison.

38. CDJC, CDLXXI 134, photograph of Mr. and Mrs. Georges, concierges of 15-17-19 Passage d'Eupatoria.

39. CDJC, Amelot Committee, microfilm 151-18, record of Sara Erpst, no. 872; record of Robert and Théodore Erpst, microfilm 182-30.

40. Sarah Lichtsztejn-Montard, *Chassez les papillons noirs*, 170.

41. Saul Friedlander, *Quand vient le souvenir* (Paris: Seuil, 1978).

42. Jules Jacoubovitch, "Rue Amelot" (1948), *Le Monde juif: Revue d'histoire de la Shoah*, no. 155 (September–December 1995): 169–246.

43. In her autobiography, Sarah writes that Matès and Idesa worked on the second floor (in a room rented under Constant's name), but lived and slept on the third floor (in a room rented under the name of the Pole, who lived opposite). Sarah Lichtsztejn-Montard, *Chassez les papillons noirs*, 92–93.

44. On the strike, see David Knout, *Contribution à l'histoire de la Résistance juive en France, 1940–1944* (Paris: Éditions du Centre, 1947), 92; and Jacques Adler, *Face à la persécution. Les organisations juives à Paris de 1940 à 1944* (Paris: Calmann-Lévy, 1985), 179–180.

45. CAC, interior ministry, National Security file 19940466 (12), record of Jankiel (Yankel) Odryzinski.

46. CAC, interior ministry, National Security file 19940459 (270), record of Moises Lichtsztejn.

47. AVP, population census, 1946, 20th arrondissement, Belleville quarter, Passage d'Eupatoria, D2M8 938, 17–18.

48. CAC, interior ministry, National Security file 19940434 (632), record of Hannah Brochsztejn.

CHAPTER 7

1. APP, police prefecture, biweekly report, "The situation in Paris to date, 8 March 1943," 8.

2. APP, Seine prefecture, cabinet report, monthly information bulletin covering 1 to 28 February 1943 (5 March 1943).

3. APP, police prefecture, biweekly report, "The situation in Paris to date, 8 March 1943," 178–179.

4. Departmental Archives, Seine-Saint-Denis, Diamant collection, 335J 31, communiqué of the second detachment.

5. Charles de Gaulle, *Discours et messages, 1940–1946* (Paris: Berger-Levrault, 1946), 291.

6. Pierre Panen, *Edmond Michelet* (Paris: Desclée de Brouwer, 1991), 31ff. and 133ff.

7. APP, BA 2433, administrative measures taken against Jews (January 1942 to December 1943), memorandum from Röthke ordering the "arrest of Jews" (9 February 1943, confidential).

8. Serge Klarsfeld, *Le Mémorial*, 190ff.; Klarsfeld, *Le Calendrier de la persécution*, 758–760; and Klarsfeld, *Vichy-Auschwitz. Le rôle de Vichy dans la solution finale de la question juive en France*, vol. 2 (Paris: Fayard, 1985), 31–33 and 225.

9. APP, BA 2436, transfer of Jews, telegrams and instructions, internal memorandum of the police prefecture (general management of the municipal police) to the branch commissioners in Paris and the suburbs (20 February 1943, classified).

10. APP, register of temporary consignments at the police prefecture jail (from 29 November 1942 to 15 March 1943): 25 February 1943 for Idesa and Krepch; 26 February 1943 for Matès.

11. APP, police prefecture, biweekly report, "The situation in Paris to date, 8 March 1943," 42.

12. APP, BA 2439, available figures concerning Domestic Intelligence Section 3 with regard to Jews (January 1941 to June 1943); APP, BA 2440, 3rd section of Domestic Intelligence, arrests from January to July 1943.

13. APP, KB 7, purge record of Albert Berger, police officer; and KB 15, purge record of Henri Bourniquey, police officer; both assigned to the police force of the 20th arrondissement.

14. APP, KB 84, purge record of Émile Petitguillaume, deputy inspector, assigned to the police force of the 20th arrondissement.

15. Nicolas Mariot and Claire Zalc, *Face à la persécution*, 185.

16. Joseph Minc, *L'Extraordinaire Histoire de ma vie ordinaire*.

17. David Diamant, *Héros juifs de la Résistance française* (Paris: Éditions du Renouveau, 1962), 227–228.

18. Annette Wieviorka, *Ils étaient juifs, résistants, communistes*, 158. See also Stéphane Courtois, Denis Peschanski and Adam Rayski, *Le Sang de l'étranger. Les immigrés de la MOI dans la Résistance* (Paris: Fayard, 1989); and Adam Rayski, *L'Affiche rouge* (Paris, Mairie de Paris, 2003).

19. APP, BA 2440, Domestic Intelligence Section 3, arrests from January to July 1943.

20. APP, police prefecture, Domestic Intelligence files, GA S4, record of Calel Sommer (no. 174673); and departmental archives of Val-de-Marne, 2652 W 22, individual record of Calel Sommer at Fresnes prison.

21. APP, BA 2440, Domestic Intelligence Section 3, arrests from January to July 1943, weekly report of 27 February 1943.

22. Jean-Marc Berlière, *Les Policiers français sous l'Occupation, d'après les archives inédites de l'épuration* (Paris: Perrin, 2001), 294ff.

23. See Louis Sadosky, *Berlin, 1942: Chronique d'une détention par la Gestapo*, intro. Laurent Joly (Paris: CNRS editions, 2009), 205–206.

24. CARAN, F9 5702/3, Drancy files, Matès Jablonka and Idesa Jablonka née Feder.

25. APP, register of persons consigned to jail by Domestic Intelligence (DI items added from 18 February to 3 May 1943), 26 February 1943, 44–45 (Matès is registered under number 5212).

26. *Unzer Wort*, 15 January 1943; in the departmental archives of Seine-Saint-Denis, Diamant collection, 335J 37.

27. Ilex Beller, "Deux parmi d'autres," in *Le Combattant volontaire juif*, 31–34.

28. Arthur Koestler, *Scum of the Earth*, 67.

29. APP, register of temporary consignments at the police prefecture jail (26 February 1943).

30. This dialogue is reproduced in APP, KB 84, purge record of André Philippe, special inspector at Domestic Intelligence.

31. CARAN, F9 5702/3, Drancy files, Matès Jablonka.

32. Cited by Serge Klarsfeld, *Le Calendrier de la persécution*, 762.

33. Georges Wellers, *De Drancy à Auschwitz* (Paris: Éditions du Centre, 1946), 16ff.

34. APP, GB2, 511A 599, deposits, record no. 5838.

35. Julie Crémieux-Dunand, *La Vie à Drancy (Récit documentaire)* (Paris: Gedalge, 1945), 81–82; and Serge Klarsfeld, *Le Mémorial*, 179ff. and 190.

36. CARAN, F9 5780, Drancy camp transfer log.

37. Saul Friedlander, *Les Années d'extermination: L'Allemagne nazie et les Juifs, 1939–1945*, trans. Pierre-Emmanuel Dauzat (Paris: Seuil, coll. "L'Univers historique," 2008), 569–574. Originally published as *Nazi Germany and the Jews, 1939–1945: The Years of Extermination* (New York: HarperCollins, 2007).

38. Cited in Claude Lanzmann, *Shoah* (Paris: Gallimard, coll. "Folio," 2001), 270.

39. See Jan Gross, *Neighbors*; Gross, *Fear*, ch. II.

40. Saul Friedlander, *Les Années d'extermination*, 283ff.

41. Götz Aly, *Into the Tunnel: The Brief Life of Marion Samuel, 1931–1943* (New York: Metropolitan Books, 2007 [2004]), 49–74. See also Götz Aly, *Hitler's Beneficiaries: Plunder, Racial War, and the Nazi Welfare State* (New York: Metropolitan, 2007).

42. Georges Wellers, *De Drancy à Auschwitz*, 31.

43. François Montel and Georges Kohn, *Journal de Compiègne et de Drancy* (Paris: FFDJF, 1999), 169.

44. Hélène Berr, *Journal, 1942–1944* (Paris: Tallandier, 2008), 209, 259.

45. *Unzer Wort*, no. 1, 1 February 1943 (Seine-Saint-Denis departmental archive, Diamant collection, 335J 37).

46. Georges Wellers, *Un Juif sous Vichy*, 195–196.

47. Family archives, postcard letters from Matès and Idesa, mailed from Drancy (2 March 1943).

48. Maurice Rajsfus, *Drancy, un camp de concentration très ordinaire, 1941–1944* (Paris: Manya, 1991), 131ff.

49. APP, GB/8, Drancy, file no. 4, search of personal effects on 1 March 1943, sheets no. 46 and 80.

50. Georges Wellers, *De Drancy à Auschwitz*, 53ff.

51. François Montel and Georges Kohn, *Journal de Compiègne et de Drancy*, 196 (entry of 2 March 1943).

52. Georges Wellers, *De Drancy à Auschwitz*, 51–52.

53. Serge Klarsfeld, *Le Mémorial*, 190ff.

54. Serge Klarsfeld, *Le Calendrier de la persécution*, 765. Most of the Jews arrested in "retaliation" for the Pont des Arts attack were deported in convoys 50 and 51 on, respectively, 4 and 6 March 1943.

CHAPTER 8

1. Saul Friedlander, *Quand vient le souvenir*, 91.

2. Jules Jacoubovitch, "Rue Amelot" (1948); and Jacqueline Baldran and Claude Bochurberg, *David Rapoport. "La Mère et l'enfant" 36 rue Amelot* (Paris: Mémorial de la Shoah, 1994), notably 81ff. and 157–178. More generally, see Jacques Adler, *Face à la persécution*; and Lucien Lazare, *La Résistance juive en France* (Paris: Stock, 1987).

3. CDJC, Amelot Committee, microfilm 150-17, record of Annette Couanault, no. 589.

4. Jules Jacoubovitch, "Rue Amelot" (1948), 214–216.

5. CDJC, Amelot Committee, microfilm 150-17, record of Annette Couanault, no. 589; microfilm 182-30, record of Suzanne and Marcel Jablonka, no. 0042; record 318/0042.

6. Ibid., microfilm 182-30, record of Suzanne and Marcel Jablonka, no. 0042.

7. Ibid., microfilm 190-31, number of children placed, no. 1; list of children placed by

13 December 1943, no. 4; lists of childminders, Paris, nos. 42, 91 and 96; list of children placed, no. 77; microfilm 201-32, list of children returning home, no. 2, and handwritten list of children placed (undated).

8. See in particular Claude Cailly, "L'industrie nourricière dans le Perche aux XVIIIe et XIXe siècles," *Cahiers percherons* no. 4 (1998): 1–26; and Ivan Jablonka, *Ni père ni mère. Histoire des enfants de l'Assistance publique 1874–1939* (Paris: Seuil, 2006). It goes without saying that Jewish children were hidden and saved all over France.

9. Jules Jacoubovitch, "Rue Amelot" (1948), ch. VII. See also Jacqueline Baldran and Claude Bochurberg, *David Rapoport*, 190ff.

10. Jacqueline Sainclivier, *La Bretagne dans la guerre, 1939–1945* (Rennes: Éditions Ouest-France, 1994), 108ff.

11. CDJC, Amelot Committee, microfilm 187-31, total assets (November 1944).

12. Cited by Jacqueline Baldran and Claude Bochurberg, *David Rapoport*, 207.

13. Jacqueline Sainclivier, *La Bretagne dans la guerre*, 122–123.

14. See Catherine Poujol, *Les Enfants cachés: L'affaire Finaly, 1945–1953* (Paris: Berg international, 2006).

15. Jacqueline Sainclivier, *La Bretagne dans la guerre*, 153ff. and 197ff.; and Christian Bougeard, *Histoire de la Résistance en Bretagne* (Paris: Gisserot, 1992).

16. Ille-et-Vilaine departmental archives, 213 W 27, Court of law, dossier 34, trial of son F., Rennes judicial police report (20 October 1944) and final arraignment (2 March 1945).

17. Ibid., judiciary police proceedings, hearing of militiaman B. (19 October 1944); and police investigation of the accused (30 October 1944).

18. Ibid., report of Mrs. Le Donné (15 August 1944).

19. "La libération de la ville quand j'avais 16 ans," *Ouest-France* (Fougères edition), 22 July 2009.

20. Feygue Chtchoupak, untitled chapter, in *Remembrances of Parczew*, 293–300.

CHAPTER 9

1. Primo Levi, *If This Is a Man*, trans. Stuart Woolf (London: Bodley Head, 1966), 8–10.

2. Cited in Claude Lanzmann, *Shoah*, 67–69.

3. Rudolf Hoess, *Commandant of Auschwitz: The Autobiography of Rudolf Hoess*, trans. Constantine FitzGibbon (Cleveland: World Pub. Co. 1959), 166–171.

4. Family archives, letter from the Auschwitz-Birkenau State Museum to my father, Marcel (23 September 1970), and to my Aunt Suzanne (19 July 1979); also, Danuta Czech, *Auschwitz Chronicle, 1939–1945: From the Archives of the Auschwitz Memorial and the German Federal Archives* (New York: Holt, 1990), 344ff.

5. Letter from Chaim Herman to his family, written at Birkenau on 6 November 1944, found in 1945 in a bottle buried near Krematorium II; reproduced in Ber Mark, *Des*

voix dans la nuit: La résistance juive à Auschwitz (Paris: Plon, 1982 [1977]), 325–330. I have respected the syntax of the original.

6. See Eric Friedler, Barbara Siebert and Andreas Kilian, *Zeugen aus der Todeszone: Das jüdische Sonderkommando in Auschwitz* (Munich: Deutscher Taschenbuch Verlag, 2005), particularly 129–135 (Matès's name is included in the long list of men in the Sonderkommando at the end of the book); and Gideon Greif, *We Wept without Tears: Testimonies of the Jewish Sonderkommando from Auschwitz* (New Haven: Yale University Press, 2005).

7. David Olère and Alexandre Oler, *Un génocide en héritage* (Paris: Wern, 1998), particularly 31–33; and Serge Klarsfeld, "Preface" in *L'Œil du témoin: David Olère, a Painter in the Sonderkommando at Auschwitz* (Paris: The Beate Klarsfeld Foundation, 1989).

8. Jean-Claude Grumberg, *L'Atelier* (Paris, Stock, 1979); and Jean-Claude Grumberg, *Mon père, inventaire* followed by *Une leçon de savoir-vivre* (Paris: Seuil, coll. "Librairie du XXIe siècle," 2003).

9. Family archives, letter from Annette to Simje and Reizl (18 May 1946).

10. Family archives, letters from the Auschwitz-Birkenau State Museum; and Danuta Czech, *Auschwitz Chronicle*, 344ff.

11. "Récit par la mère de Sarah Lichtsztejn (Sourèlè) de leur arrestation et de leur déportation le 30 mai 1944," in Serge Klarsfeld, *Lettres de Louise Jacobson*, 61–68.

12. AVP, population census, 1936, 20th arrondissement, Belleville quarter, digitized version D2M8 697, 3.

13. On the reverse side of Matès's record: "Cert. sent on 28 September 1945 to his sister [*sic*], Mrs. Lichtszten [*sic*], 106 rue Saint-Maur Paris. Deported with his wife née Feder Idessa [*sic*]" (CARAN, F9 5702/3, record of Matès Jablonka). The record, which bears a capital D, for "deceased," probably comes from the Ministry of Veterans' Affairs.

14. Götz Aly, *Into the Tunnel*, 77–80.

15. Rudolf Hoess, *Commandant of Auschwitz*, 164.

16. Testimony of Shlomo Dragon at the Krakow trial (1946), in *Des voix sous la cendre: Manuscrits des Sonderkommandos d'Auschwitz-Birkenau* (Paris: Mémorial de la Shoah, Calmann-Lévy, 2005), 184–185. In 1942, the corpses were buried in large pits, the so-called "swimming pools" that were excavated in wooded areas, but in September, the order was handed down to disinter the bodies and dispose of them on enormous, open-air bonfires. From that point on, until the crematoriums went into service in the spring of 1943, the bodies of persons just gassed were burnt immediately in the pits. During the extermination of the Hungarian Jews in 1944, however, the crematoriums could not handle the volume, and thousands of bodies were once again burnt out in the open.

17. These two paragraphs are based on Jean-Claude Pressac, *Auschwitz: Technique and Operation of the Gas Chambers*, trans. Peter Moss (New York: Beate Klarsfeld Foundation, 1989), Part II, ch. 5.

18. Testimony of Henryk Tauber before the commission of inquiry into the Nazi crimes at Auschwitz (1945), in *Des voix sous la cendre*, 206–207; and Jean-Claude Pressac,

Auschwitz: Technique and Operation of the Gas Chambers, 482–502. Danuta Czech situates the scene the following day, 5 March.

19. Lewental's "Chronicle" is reproduced in Ber Mark, *Des voix dans la nuit*, 265ff.; and in *Des voix sous la cendre*, 91ff.

20. The text "3,000 nues" [3,000 naked female bodies], attributed to Leib Langfus, is reproduced in Ber Mark, *Des voix dans la nuit*, 259ff.

21. Zalmen Gradowski, *Au cœur de l'enfer: Témoignage d'un Sonderkommando d'Auschwitz, 1944* (Paris: Tallandier, 2009), 52.

22. Moshe and Élie Garbarz, *A Survivor*, 65.

23. Pierre Oscar Lévy, *Premier convoi* (Paris: Paradiso Productions, 1992) 102 min.

24. André Balbin, *De Lodz à Auschwitz en passant par la Lorraine* (Nancy: Presses universitaires de Nancy, 1989), 74–76.

25. Jean-Claude Pressac, *Auschwitz: Technique and Operation of the Gas Chambers*, 227.

26. Cited by Claude Lanzmann, *Shoah*, 90–91. See also Filip Müller, *Eyewitness Auschwitz: Three Years in the Gas Chambers*, trans. Susanne Flatauer (New York: Stein and Day, 1979).

27. Zalmen Gradowski, *Au cœur de l'enfer*, 154.

28. Eric Friedler et al., *Zeugen aus der Todeszone*, 129–135.

29. This interview with Yakov Gabbay is found in *Des voix sous la cendre*, 290ff.

30. Cited in Claude Lanzmann, *Shoah*, 180–181.

31. This description comes from the testimony of Henryk Tauber before the commission of inquiry into the Nazi crimes at Auschwitz (*Des voix sous la cendre*, 212–213).

32. The expression is cited by Yakov Gabbay in *Des voix sous la cendre*, 289.

33. Shlomo Venezia, *Inside the Gas Chambers. Eight Months in the Sonderkommando at Auschwitz*, trans. Andrew Brown (Cambridge, UK: Polity, 2009), 74.

34. *Des voix sous la cendre*, 283.

35. André Balbin, *De Lodz à Auschwitz*, 73.

36. Primo Levi, "The Grey Zone," in *The Drowned and the Saved*, trans. Raymond Rosenthal (New York: Summit Books, 1988), 53–54.

37. Georges Wellers, *Un Juif sous Vichy*, 278.

38. Claude Lanzmann, *The Patagonian Hare: A Memoir* (New York: Fararr Straus and Giroux, 2012), 29

39. *Des voix sous la cendre*, 402ff.

40. Moshe and Élie Garbarz, *A Survivor*, 98.

41. Town hall, 20th arrondissement of Paris, public records department, death certificate of Matès Jablonka, "who died on 2 March 1943 in Drancy (Seine)," 5 October 1951; ibid., death certificate of Idesa Feder, "who died on 2 March 1943 in Drancy (Seine)," 12 June 1951.

42. Zalmen Gradowski, *Au cœur de l'enfer*, 35.

43. Cited by Chaim Herman in his letter, in Ber Mark, *Des voix dans la nuit*.

44. Cited by Ber Mark, *Des voix dans la nuit*, 276.

45. Zalmen Gradowski, *Au cœur de l'enfer*, 57.

46. Cited in *Des voix sous la cendre*, 295.

47. Jean Améry, *At the Mind's Limits*, 13–15.

48. David Diamant, *Héros juifs de la Résistance française*, 227–228; and Ber Mark, *Des voix dans la nuit*, 152.

49. Zalmen Lewental, "Notes," in *Des voix sous la cendre*, 104.

50. Georges Wellers, *Un Juif sous Vichy*, 275–277. The revolts took place at Treblinka on 2 August 1943, at Sobibor on 14 October 1943, at Chelmno on 18 January 1944, at Ponar on 15 April 1944 and at Auschwitz on 7 October 1944.

51. On the revolt, see Ber Mark, *Des voix dans la nuit*, 159ff. (Lewental quote, 297); Eric Friedler et al., *Zeugen aus der Todeszone*, 223–224ff.; and *Des voix sous la cendre*, 400ff.

52. Cited by Saul Friedländer, *Kurt Gerstein: The Ambiguity of Good*, trans. Charles Fullman (New York: Knopf, 1969), 191.

53. Vasily Grossman, *Life and Fate*, trans. Robert Chandler (New York: NYRB Classics, 2006), 554.

54. André Schwarz-Bart, *The Last of the Just*, trans. Stephen Becker (New York: Atheneum House, 1960), 242.

55. Shlomo Venezia, *Inside the Gas Chambers*, 64.

56. According to the testimony of Henryk Tauber in *Des voix sous la cendre*, 208–209.

57. Zalmen Gradowski, *Au cœur de l'enfer*, 195–196.

GLOSSARY OF FOREIGN WORDS

I have chosen not to standardize the spelling of words and proper names in Yiddish. Rather than make use of the YIVO phonetic system, I have used the form that seems most familiar in current French usage [and for the translation, English usage]: goys instead of *goyim*, shtetls instead of *shtetlekh*, Israel instead of *Yisroel*, *Poale Zion* and not *Poaley Tsiyon*, etc.

For the sound *kh* (pronounced like the German *ch* in Bach, for example), I write *kh*eyder and Yizkor Bu*kh*, but also Alei*ch*em, *Ch*aim and *Ch*evra Kadisha, as well as *H*aifa.

For names, I have used whatever form the person in question has chosen. Thus, you will find both Shloyme (Yiddish) and Shlomo (Hebrew); Moyshe (Yiddish) and Moshe (Hebrew); Simje, the Spanish form of Simkhe (Yiddish) and Symcha (Polish); Raquel (Spanish), Rachel (Hebrew) and Rushla or Rushele (Yiddish).

Polish lettering and spelling has only been kept for a very few place names, such as Włodawa and Radzyń-Podlaski. All other such names have been anglicized.

Aktion (German): in Nazi terminology, a pillaging or assassination "operation"

aliyah (Hebrew): immigration of Jews from the diaspora to Israel

barbe (Italian Piedmont dialect): (plural of *barba*) any elderly male relatives, even distant ones

beder (Yiddish): person in charge of the *bod*, or public baths

bitul zman (Hebrew): waste of time

bod (Yiddish): public baths, steam baths, often run by the city

Bund (Yiddish): Jewish socialist movement, autonomous and pro-Yiddish. Its militants are "Bundists."

cartoneros (Spanish): waste pickers in Buenos Aires who collect and recycle discarded paper and cardboard for a small profit

Chevra Kadisha (Aramaic): Jewish holy society of men and women in charge of preparing bodies for burial, protecting them from desecration

Endeks (Polish): "National Democrats," far-right militants

ganef (Yiddish): thief

geriatrico (Spanish): retirement home

gleyzele (Yiddish): a little glass, often of tea or an alcoholic beverage

grine (Yiddish): newcomer

groszy (Polish): a subdivision of the zloty, Poland's basic unit of currency

Judenrampe (German): in the extermination camps, the "Jews' ramp" was the platform where deportees disembarked from trains

Judenrat (German): "Jewish council," set up by the Nazis with the purpose of better administering the ghettos

judenrein (German): in Nazi vocabulary, purged of all Jews

Kapo (German): a prisoner in the Nazi camps, often a common criminal, assigned to supervise work gangs in exchange for privileges

khen (Hebrew): grace or favor

kheyder (Yiddish): religious school for children

kippah (Hebrew): brimless cap worn by orthodox Jews in fulfillment of the requirement to cover one's head at all times

komuna (Polish): a group of political prisoners, a "commune"

Krematorium (German): at Auschwitz II Birkenau, an integrated death factory consisting of gas chambers for killing people and crematoria for disposing of their corpses

Lag Ba-Omer (Hebrew): Jewish holiday commemorating the revolt of the Jews against the Romans in the year 135 CE

landsmanshaft, plural *landsmanshaftn* (Yiddish): charitable society created on the basis of the shtetl or town of origin

leykekh (Yiddish): traditional cake

makher (Yiddish): a dynamic person who can cut deals and get things done

mamzer (Yiddish): bastard, but figuratively, clever, cunning, sly

melamed, plural *melamdim* (Hebrew): a teacher in a *kheyder*

mezuzah (Hebrew): a decorative oblong case containing verses from the Torah, affixed to the doorframes of Jewish homes

mikvah (Hebrew): Jewish ritual bath

Musulmann (German): in Nazi camps, a starving, exhausted captive resigned to death

patronatn (Yiddish): support groups organized within *landsmanshaftn* to help political prisoners back in the Polish homeland

powiat (Polish): administrative unit equivalent to a county or district, subdivision of a voivodeship

Reb (Yiddish): honorific title equivalent to "Sir" or "Master"

Revkom (Russian): Bolshevik revolutionary committee

rynek; *Rynek* (Polish): a city square, piazza; Parczew's Grand Square

saba (Hebrew): grandfather

schlimazel (Yiddish): a loser, an unfortunate person

Shabbat (Hebrew): day of rest (Saturday) during which all work is prohibited

Shema Yisrael (Hebrew): "Hear [O] Israel," first two words of a section of the Torah and of a basic prayer in Jewish services

shtetl, plural *shtetlekh* (Yiddish): traditional little Jewish village or town

Sonderkommando (German): At Auschwitz-Birkenau, Jewish death camp prisoners assigned to empty the gas chambers and burn the corpses

technik (Polish): Communist party militant in charge of producing and distributing propaganda materials

tefillin (Hebrew): small black leather boxes containing scrolls of parchment inscribed with verses from the Torah, to be attached to the left arm and head with thin leather straps prior to prayer

tía, tío; Tía Reizl (Spanish): aunt, uncle; Aunt Reizl

Vél' d'Hiv: Vélodrome d'Hiver, the winter velodrome, an indoor sports stadium in Paris, where the Jews rounded up on 16 and 17 July 1942 were temporarily confined

Tsukunft (Yiddish): the youth organization founded in 1910 within the general Jewish Labor Organization, or *Bund*

voivodeship (anglicized Polish): administrative division in Poland, similar to a province, or in early times, duchy

yeshiva (Hebrew): a religious educational institution where young Jews study the Torah and the Talmud under the direction of a rabbi

yiddishe mame (Yiddish): "Jewish mother," loving and tender toward her children; title of a famous song

yiddishkeyt (Yiddish): way of life linked to Yiddish culture

Yizkor Bukh (Yiddish): "book of remembrance," of a shtetl or town, published by the survivors of World War II

żydo-komuna (Polish): anti-Semitic stereotype that associates Jews with Communism (the "Judeo-Communist Plot")